GRAMSCI AND ITALY'S PASSIVE REVOLUTION

EDITED BY JOHN A. DAVIS

CROOM HELM LONDON

BARNES & NOBLE BOOKS · NEW YORK
(a division of Harper & Row Publishers, Inc.)

© 1979 John A. Davis
Croom Helm Ltd, 2-10 St John's Road, London SW11

British Library Cataloguing in Publication Data

Gramsci and Italy's passive revolution.
   1. Italy – History – 19th century
   2. Italy – History – 20th century
   I. Davis, John A
   945.09   DG848.58
   ISBN 0-85664-704-7

Published in the USA 1979 by
Harper & Row Publishers, Inc.
Barnes & Noble Import Division

ISBN 0-06-491609-X

LC 79·53440

Printed and bound in Great Britain

CONTENTS

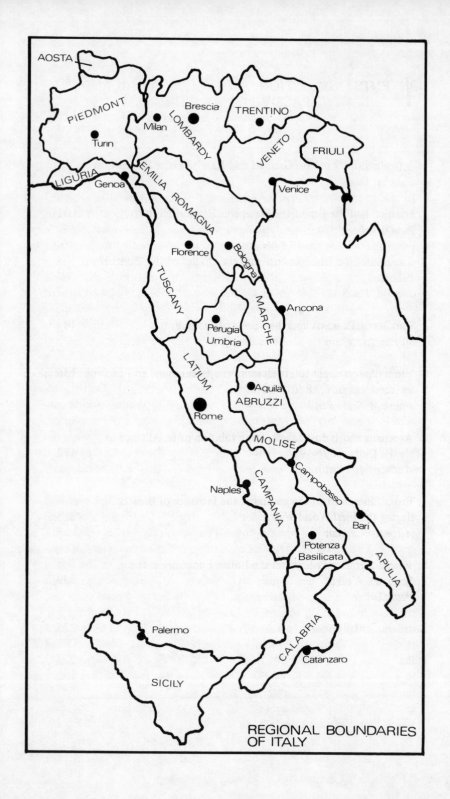

REGIONAL BOUNDARIES
OF ITALY

1 INTRODUCTION: ANTONIO GRAMSCI AND ITALY'S PASSIVE REVOLUTION

John A. Davis

In the thirty years since the publication of the *Prison Notebooks* the interest and importance of Antonio Gramsci's contribution to Marxist thought and political analysis has become widely recognised. It is in particular on the basis of his analysis of the structure of the capitalist state and his insistence on the essentially political nature of power exercised through what Hegel had termed the 'institutions of civil society' that this reputation has been established. Deeply influenced both by Lenin's appeal for a more revolutionary interpretation of Marx's writings and by his own aversion to the sterile gradualism of the reformist socialism of the Second International, Gramsci sought to rehabilitate that area of social activity which had been relegated to a subservient and almost irrelevant 'superstructure', and to demonstrate the essentially political function and class orientation of culture, ideology and social institutions. It was from this that the now familiar concept of 'hegemony' emerged, together with the call for the revolutionary movement to extend the front of its struggle in order to combat the capitalist classes at the level of ideology and civil institutions, as well as in the more traditional and restricted sphere of the so-called 'state apparatus'.[1]

The concern to explore and identify the structures of the capitalist state is not only the principal characteristic of Gramsci's theoretical and political writings, but also the inspiration for his writings on Italian history. The problem of the nature and structure of the capitalist state in Western Europe is the central theme of those sections of the *Prison Notebooks* which are devoted to the century of Italian history which witnessed national unification, the formation of the liberal state and the establishment of Mussolini's fascist dictatorship. Gramsci the historian cannot be separated from, or contrasted to, Gramsci the political theorist or Gramsci the revolutionary. His historical writings were not the product of a retirement from active politics enforced by seclusion in a fascist prison. One of the principal motives for analysing Italy's immediate past was to reveal to his colleagues the inadequacy of their awareness of the fundamental structures and organisation of the state which they had unsuccessfully attempted to replace.[2] In his address to

the Lyons Congress of the Communist Party in 1926, Gramsci had
already pointed uncompromisingly to the 'political, organizational,
tactical and strategic weaknesses of the workers' party' as a cause of the
success of the fascist movement in Italy.[3] It was from this insistence on
the need for unsparing and unsentimental self-criticism and reflection
that much of the originality of Gramsci's thought was to derive. And it
was along this *via crucis* that Gramsci embarked on a *post mortem* not
only of Italian socialism, but also of the corpse of the liberal state. Only
through careful analysis of the political structures and organisation of
that state could a basis be laid for constructing a more effective and
realistic revolutionary strategy. This could be achieved only by looking
first at the origins and evolution of that state, and then by attempting
to assess the relationship between Mussolini's fascist dictatorship and
the earlier liberal state.

At first sight the essentially political emphasis of Gramsci's historical
writings might seem to make them an inappropriate focus for a collection of essays concerned predominantly with economic and social
aspects of Italy's history in this period. One recent Italian commenta-
tor, who could not be considered hostile to Gramsci, has indeed
claimed that the *Prison Notebooks* contribute nothing new to an understanding of Italy's economic development in this period, because this
was not Gramsci's primary concern.[4] But it is, perhaps, precisely for
this reason that so many of the questions and problems which Gramsci
raised have shown the need for wider investigation of the economic and
social structures around which the political systems of the liberal state
were organised. It was certainly no accident that the debate on Italian
industrialisation in the late nineteenth century – one of the few aspects
of modern Italian history, other than fascism of course, to attract wide
attention outside Italy – began with the criticisms which Rosario
Romeo levelled against Gramsci's assessment of the shortcomings of
national unification.[5]

It would be wrong to suggest, however, that Gramsci's analysis is of
interest to the economic or social historian for purely negative reasons,
or that the problems it poses are simply a matter of filling in gaps or
demonstrating incongruencies. Few historical writers have been more
impressed than Gramsci by the need to reveal the nature of the relations and inter-relations which united the disparate material, social and
political aspects of the historical process both in, and over, time. If
Gramsci had little that was new to say about the economic structure
and development of the modern Italian state, this structure remained
his fundamental point of reference. The alliance between the progres-

sive manufacturing and industrial bourgeoisie of the North and the traditional landowners of the South, the 'historical alliance', was the central reality of the Italian state, and the point from which his analysis of its political systems begins. And if much of the originality of Gramsci's analysis is to be found in the exploration of the ideological aspects of political relations, and in particular the relationship between social forces and forms of political representation, the material basis of those relationships is never called into doubt. Not only, then, are economic structures and relationships an integral part of Gramsci's historical analysis, but they are also the stuff on which that analysis is founded.

Gramsci was not, of course, the first to have identified the alliance between northern industry and southern landlords as the central and determining feature of the liberal state. Since the adoption of industrial and agrarian protectionism in the 1880s this had been one of the dominant themes in both socialist and free-trade liberal political writing. But Gramsci was the first to argue that the origins and consequences of this alliance constituted the fundamental feature of continuity running through Italy's political development from unification to fascism. This was the material reality which he set against Benedetto Croce's claim that the inspiration of the modern Italian state lay in the spirit and ethos of liberalism. Putting Croce through the same undignified exercise to which Marx had earlier subjected Hegel, Gramsci argued that the politics and ideology of Italian liberalism could only be understood in relation to the material and social structure within which they had taken form. Written in the same decade as the publication of Croce's *History of Italy* and *History of Europe in the Nineteenth Century*, Gramsci's *Prison Notebooks* at times read almost as a dialogue with Croce. But from this dialogue emerged an interpretation of the continuities running through Italy's history from the Risorgimento to fascism which drew together in a single comprehensive analysis a wide range of earlier socialist and anti-Crocean ideas and writing. And whereas for Croce fascism had represented an irrational and therefore temporary aberration from the guiding tendencies in Italy's development, for Gramsci it was an explicable, although not inevitable, continuation of the economic and political structure which had been present from the birth of the unified state. It is this alternative interpretation of the fundamental features and tendencies in modern Italian history that has become one of the principal bases for historical debate and discussion in Italy since the publication of the *Prison Notebooks*.

As Perry Anderson has recently pointed out, few Marxist writers are more difficult to read accurately or systematically than Gramsci.[6]

There are many reasons for this: the appalling circumstances and restrictions under which he was writing; the peculiar economy and terseness of his style, and the rapid juxtaposition of assertion and suggestion; the sheer breadth and complexity of his imagination. At any one moment his analysis develops at a series of levels: the problem of the state in general, that in Italy in particular, the role of ideology and intellectuals in general terms, and in the Italian state in particular; the relations between city and countryside in general, and in the particular circumstances of Italy. The list of problems that are confronted is long, and the relationship between the general and the particular is something that Gramsci rarely loses sight of; in his search for the unity of the historical process, each individual piece of the historical jigsaw is carefully related to a final overall pattern.

Not only does this mean that any descriptive account of necessity loses the richness of Gramsci's own writing, but it also makes it difficult, and potentially misleading, to single out any one theme of interpretation. There is, however, one theme which recurs time and time again in his analysis of the modern Italian state, and around which his interpretation of the fundamental tendencies in this period is based. This is the 'passive revolution'. Although the term is used in a number of ways, it is in essence both a description of the nature of the liberal state and an assessment of the shortcomings of that state.

The way in which 'passive revolution' was defined by Gramsci shows clearly the inseparability of his political and historical method. The central problem was always the state, and the variety of forms which political power might take within the state. But if the state — and Gramsci was concerned primarily, of course, with the capitalist state, and in particular the Western versions of that state — could in practice take a variety of forms which would differ in important ways from one country to another, so too would the political processes which created the state. Just as there were different types of capitalist state, so there were different forms of bourgeois revolutions. In Italy the form taken by both was 'passive revolution'.

In theoretical terms Gramsci explained this concept by reference to Marx's well-known assertion in the *Preface to the Critique of Political Economy* that 'no social formation disappears as long as the productive forces which have developed within it still find room for further movement, a society does not set itself tasks for whose solutions the necessary conditions have not already been incubated'.[7] On one hand, this might seem to provide a good explanation of the type of state which had resulted from unification in Italy. The Italian bourgeoisie of the early nineteenth century had been, in economic terms at least, relatively weak and heterogenous. It would therefore be entirely consonant with Marx's statement to find 'pre-capitalist' groups – in other words, the traditional aristocratic and landowning interests – represented strongly in the new political structure.

But such a definition also presented serious problems for Gramsci, because to define the basis of the Italian bourgeois state in such terms came close to an open invitation to the kind of political gradualism adopted by the Second International. It implied that the bourgeois revolution in Italy had been incomplete, hence introducing endless possibilities of procrastination for the revolutionary parties while they comfortably and inactively awaited the Second Coming. What Gramsci was concerned above all to stress was that such a form of revolution was still revolution. National unification had not simply provided a first step towards the capitalist state in Italy, but had created that state. It had permitted industrialisation, the establishment of bourgeois democracy, and Italy's elevation to the status of a Great Power (formally recognised in the Versailles Peace Treaty). At the same time, the circumstances in which that state had been created, and the nature of the social forces on which it was based, gave Italian capitalism both its particular, unique form and also determined limits beyond which it could not progress.

The argument becomes clearer if we look at the passage in which Gramsci contrasted the different forms taken by the state in Russia and in the West:

> In Russia the state was everything and civil society was primordial and gelatinous: in the West there was a proper relation between the state and civil society, and when the state trembled the sturdy section of civil society was at once revealed. The state was only an outer ditch, behind which was a powerful system of fortresses and earthworks.[8]

It was the presence, for historical and cultural reasons, of these 'fortresses and earthworks' in European societies that made 'passive revolution' possible. The material weaknesses of the nineteenth-century Italian bourgeoisie, for example, could be compensated by political action directed, consciously or unconsciously, to achieve domination through the institutions of civil society – through culture and literature, through professional institutions and ethos, through education. By achieving 'hegemonic' power in this fashion, even a numerically small advanced bourgeois elite could give a decisively 'capitalist' imprint to a political revolution which necessitated support from more traditional social forces. This, in Gramsci's view, was what had occurred in Italy in the nineteenth century, and the alliance between the advanced bourgeoisie of the North and the traditional landowners of the South was both cause and effect of the 'passive revolution'.

This provides at least one reason for Gramsci's very detailed analysis of the factors which contributed to the success of the Moderate 'Party' (the term is clearly anachronistic), which after 1848 became increasingly identified with the policies of Cavour, in providing the leadership for the national revolution.[9] They were confronted by 'very powerful and united forces which looked for leadership to the Vatican and were hostile to unification'.[10] The Moderates had little economic strength and even fewer physical resources. They had, therefore, to seek allies. First they looked to Piedmont and its army to carry through their revolution, and hence the national question became predominant. Secondly they had to choose between alliance either with the more traditional social groups on the peninsula or with the people. For the Moderates, any alliance with the people was out of the question, partly as a result of the terror which French Jacobinism had implanted amongst the European bourgeoisie, and they opted for alliance with the traditional groups. The result was, in Gramsci's phrase, '"revolution" without "revolution"'.[11]

But revolution none the less, and it is here that the issue of 'hegemony' becomes relevant. Although the resources for establishing leadership on the basis of coercion were, in Gramsci's view, limited, the Moderates succeeded in compensating this by eliciting voluntary support and consensus. The ideology of Moderate liberalism, at once progressive in material terms and conservative in social terms, dominated Italian culture, and won over the professional and bureaucratic classes. Hence the Moderates became 'hegemonic', and it was this which constituted the dynamic element of the 'passive revolution'.

The process of passive revolution had other important features, which Gramsci developed in contrasting the success of the Moderates with the failure of the Radicals — that is, Mazzini, Garibaldi, Pisacane, Ferrari and their followers. At every point they were outmanoeuvred by the Moderates. The Moderate programme had a broad eclectic appeal; the Moderates learned from their mistakes; they used the national question and the external enemy, Austria, to unite a heterogenous following; they were prepared to adopt radical measures such as the expropriation of Church land. The Radicals, on the other hand, were unsure of their radicalism. They did not attempt to counter the 'spontaneous' support won by the Moderates with an alternative 'organised' political force; they had no unified programme, no understanding of the political forces opposing them. Above all they failed to play the card of agrarian reform, and hence failed to recruit to their platform the vast potential of peasant unrest. Hence the notion of 'the failed revolution'.

The debate which developed around the 'failed revolution'[12] has perhaps served to draw attention away from what was undoubtedly Gramsci's principal concern in examining the relationship between the Moderates and the Radicals. Because, in the Moderates' ability to dominate and even absorb the Radicals, Gramsci saw one of the central features of the type of political system which would emerge from the passive revolution. Particularly important was the conclusion that the 'Action Party (i.e. the Radicals) were in fact led "indirectly" by Cavour and the King'.[13] This was a demonstration of the 'hegemonic' power of the Moderates, but it also foreshadowed a political system which was to become a fundamental feature of the liberal state – *trasformismo*. In *trasformismo* the lines of distinction between the different historical political parties and interests were gradually eroded in a single undifferentiated ruling alliance. 'One might say – Gramsci noted – that the entire state life of Italy from 1848 onwards has been characterised by trasformismo.'[14]

An even more fundamental feature of the 'passive revolution' than the absorption of the Radicals, however, was the alliance with the South. In Gramsci's view this alliance not only lay at the heart of the 'passive revolution', but its continuation after 1870 was the principal reason why 'passive revolution' remained the framework for political action within, and after, the liberal state.

The origins and development of the North-South alliance are analysed by Gramsci at two levels – one economic and the other ideological.[15] To explain the economic origins of the unification of these two very distinct sections of the peninsula, Gramsci drew heavily on Marx's discussion of the relationship between city and countryside.[16] This was a relationship, or series of relationships, which had a particular fascination for Gramsci. While on one hand the problems could be posed in purely economic terms – the ways in which the city, the nucleus of capitalist development, transmitted the germs of capitalist modes of production and social relations to the surrounding rural areas, and hence dominated the countryside – on the other, these relationships demonstrated precisely that inter-penetration of economic and cultural influences which constituted so important a feature of Gramsci's own thought.

Applying the concept to the South, Gramsci argued that the region as a whole stood in relation to the North as countryside stands to city. The South was predominantly rural and semi-feudal. The great Southern cities (Palermo and Naples were the largest cities not only on the peninsula but also in the Mediterranean for most of the nineteenth century) were essentially 'silent', pre-capitalist cities.[17] They were centres of consumption but not of production, in which the absentee Southern landlords spent their rent-rolls. They were, then, dependent on revenues from the agrarian economy, and their inhabitants simply provided the services required by the urbanised landowners. For this reason, this predominantly agrarian economy of the South was irresistably drawn into the more advanced urban economy of the North. The South came to constitute a classical *Nebenland*, an area of colonial dependence which the Northern economy could exploit at will and from which, in particular, it could draw off capital through taxation and through the internal imbalance of trade, in order to further the development of the Northern economy.[18] The alliance between North and South embodied in national unification was not merely an unequal partnership, but a partnership which ensured the continuing, and even worsening, backwardness of the South.

Equally important, however, was the political partnership which accompanied this economic symbiosis. What made the South an essential feature of the 'passive revolution' was the fact that it provided extensive possibilities for the exercise of that type of political influence which Gramsci described as 'hegemony'. The economic structure of the South meant that the Southern bourgeoisie, other than the great landowners, was predominantly professional, bureaucratic and intellectual. It was the sons of the Southern gentry who filled the law courts, the schools, the universities and the political institutions of the liberal state, and it was they who provided the most effective evangelists of the ideology of that state. The social basis of the Southern bourgeoisie had made them particularly susceptible to the attraction of the Cavourian programme, and as a result the Southern bourgeoisie provided one of the most important bases for the continued exercise of Northern hegemonic power. It was for this reason that Gramsci singled out two of the great Southern intellectuals, Benedetto Croce and Giustino Fortunato, as the bastions of Italian capitalism.[19]

Both the theory of economic exploitation and the political contribution of the Southern bourgeoisie had been widely discussed by earlier Italian writers. Gaetano Salvemini, for one, had described the block of Southern deputies who obediently gave their votes to any government prepared to offer them in return political patronage and privilege as 'Giolitti's askaris'. But the originality of Gramsci's argument lies not only in the way in which the economic and political features of the alliance become reciprocally self-sustaining, but also in the claim that the backwardness of the South was a necessary condition for the development of Italian capitalism. The 'Southern Problem', that open wound in Italian society, was not accidental or even, given the structure of the state, open to remedy. It could not, therefore, be argued that the South simply represented a 'feudal residue' which would wither away as the Italian economy progressed. In fact, the contrary was true. For this reason, not only was the alliance between North and South an essential feature of the 'passive revolution', but was to remain the main limitation to the subsequent development of the Italian state thereafter.

North and South, *trasformismo* and passive revolution, all then became part of a single process which determined the essential character of the liberal state. But the process did not end with national unification. For Gramsci, Italy's political development between 1870 and 1914 was dominated by the attempt to maintain and extend both the structure and the strategy of the 'passive revolution'. Crispi's attempt to speed up the rate of development and establish Italy among the Great Powers failed because he stepped outside the confines of the passive revolution. Trade war with France alienated both export-orientated industrialists and many landowners, so threatening the base of the system of political and economic alliances. But in Giolitti, Gramsci recognised the master of the strategy of 'passive revolution'. Giolitti's parliamentary alliance with the Socialists in the face of mounting opposition to the exclusive political power of the traditional ruling class constituted, for Gramsci, the high point of *trasformismo*, the incorporation of the workers' representatives, but not the workers, in the political system.[20]

Yet if the strategy of passive revolution reached its culmination in the pre-war decade, it was shortly to be thrown into serious crisis for the first time. When Mussolini and the Intransigents wrested control of the Socialist Party from the reformists, the trasformist alliance broke down. War with Libya in 1911 made reconciliation impossible, and in 1913 Giolitti 'changed his rifle to the other shoulder' and set out to woo the Catholic peasantry of Northern Italy by means of the Gentiloni Pact. But the concessions made on the way made it difficult to keep the system together. The crisis which followed the outbreak of war in Europe and the fierce debate over whether and how Italy should intervene served to polarise attitudes further, making the politics of 'passive revolution' unworkable. The introduction of universal suffrage in the South also made electoral manageering more difficult, further weakening the traditional system, and Giolitti for once was unable to find a formula to bridge the growing diversity of interests and political ambitions.

Although the war brought crucial changes to Italy's economic and social structure, the crisis which followed the peace was, in Gramsci's view, essentially a continuation of the pre-war problem. The rapid expansion of certain sectors of heavy industry in particular and the parallel mobilisation and politicisation of large strata of the working class and the peasantry which had resulted from the war, meant that the circumstances had changed radically. But underlying the crisis and underlying the emergence of the 'fascist solution', Gramsci saw the attempts of the traditional capitalist classes to restore the structure of passive revolution.

Gramsci did not provide any comprehensive analysis of the rise of Italian fascism, and clearly in the case of his prison writings it was a difficult subject for him to approach directly.[21] However, his earlier writings and his address to the Lyons Party Congress in 1926 make it clear that he saw fascism as the consequence not of any single cause, but rather as the product of a convergence of developments and problems, not least of which was the strategy of the left in these years. But if he avoided any single explanation, and so implicitly denied that the fascist solution was in any sense predetermined or inevitable, he did insist on the continuities which linked fascism to the liberal state.

Other socialists, like Bordiga, had argued that the fascist experiment was no more than a temporary expedient adopted by the capitalist classes in response to the panic aroused by the show of proletarian strength in the post-war crisis. But it was an expedient which could not outlive that sense of panic, because it was only in a system of bourgeois democracy that Italian capitalism could continue to develop. The fascist counter-revolution was useful only in the short term, but would thereafter begin to damage the interests of the bourgeoisie. But for Gramsci such an interpretation risked perpetuating the unjustified optimism which had encouraged the left to under-estimate the strength of the capitalist state throughout the post-war crisis. Fascism was something more than a capitalist 'White Guard', and it bore a more permanent relationship to the structure of the liberal state. Only if the nature of that relationship was made clear would it be possible to construct an effective strategy of opposition.[22]

Gramsci's writings on fascism from the time of the first appearance of the blackshirt squads to the corporatist regime which became established by the early 1930s are filled with this search for continuities and links. He was amongst the first to point to the significance of the *petit bourgeois* following which the fascist movement had developed from its earliest appearance. Comparing this urban and rural *petit bourgeoisie* to Kipling's Bandar Log people[23] — mindless apes ready to follow any leader prepared to flatter their vanities and aspirations — Gramsci drew two conclusions. First, the presence of this *petit bourgeois* following suggested that fascism was something more than an anti-socialist strike-breaking force at the service of Italian capitalism, and that it had a firm base in certain aspects of the social structure. Secondly, the means by which this following had been achieved suggested a parallel with the liberal state. In order to win the support of these groups the fascists had created a programme and an ideology which appealed directly to their aspirations. And in this Gramsci saw a successful attempt to create a new form of hegemonic power which, in the changed circumstances of post-war Italy, was able to replace the earlier forms of hegemony exercised by the traditional ruling classes within the liberal state.[24] The form, together with the circumstances, had changed, but the structure of political domination remained the same.

If fascism as a new form of hegemonic power suggested one continuity with the liberal state, another lay in the city-countryside relations which underlay the emergent fascist movement. It was the rapid expansion of agrarian fascism in the Po Valley and in Tuscany in particular, in the years between 1920 and 1922, which had transformed Mussolini's early urban fascism into a mass movement. For Gramsci, the adoption of the fascist solution by the Northern agrarians was of the utmost significance. After the factory occupations he had written: 'By striking at the peasant class, the agrarians are attempting to bring about the subjugation of the urban workers as well.'[25] In other words, agrarian fascism was not a separate phenomenon, but was closely related to the struggle in the cities to dominate the organised working classes. In fact, what this amounted to was a revival and continuation, in the new circumstances created by the war, of the traditional industrial-agrarian axis of the Italian political structure. And because the counter-offensive directed against the peasantry struck at the weakest sector of the proletarian front, it made the question of the formation of an effective worker-peasant alliance all the more immediate.

On the nature of this new city-countryside partnership Gramsci seemed less certain. Northern agriculture was certainly very different from that of the South, as was the agrarian structure. But the objectives of the new alliance seemed unchanged. The agrarians had come to the rescue of the Northern industrialists who had been abandoned by the state in their struggle with the workers. In so doing, the agrarians seemed to be attempting to restore the political influence of which they had in important ways been deprived by the war. The result was to restore and reconstruct the 'passive revolution'.

Despite the anti-capitalist rhetoric of early fascism, Gramsci had little doubt that the movement which emerged from the post-war crisis represented an attempt to reconstruct and reconsolidate bourgeois power in the new circumstances resulting from the war. This continuity was strengthened and confirmed, in Gramsci's view, by the behaviour of the regime once it had established power. In the introduction of corporatist institutions, particularly those in the economic and financial fields in the early 1930s, Gramsci saw evidence of a direct connection between the fascist experiment and the problems posed for Italy by developments in the international economy since the war. In the essay on *Americanism and Fordism* he suggested that fascism was in some senses a response to the problems created for the European economies as a whole, and that of Italy in particular, by the advent of mass production, rationalised planning and scientific management in America. The changes associated with Henry Ford and Frederick Taylor posed a terrible threat to the antiquated 'liberal' structures of the Western economies, which they could not afford to neglect. The question that Gramsci asked was whether fascism could be seen as an attempt to introduce such forms of economic organisation in Italy:

> The ideological hypothesis could be posed in the following terms: that there is a passive revolution involved in the fact that through the legislative intervention of the state and by means of the corporate organisations, far reaching modifications are being introduced into the country's economic structure in order to accentuate the 'plan of production' element; in other words, that socialisation and co-operation in the sphere of production are being increased without, however, touching (or at least not going beyond the regulation and control of) individual and group appropriation and profit.[26]

As Paul Corner points out in the last essay in this book, this is a question on which there is both little agreement and little research. But although Gramsci believed that the fascist economic system could in some senses be seen as an attempt to modernise and develop the Italian economic structure within the context of passive revolution — that is, without permitting any parallel political and social development — his own conclusion was that this intention could not be realised. The crucial difference between America and the Western European countries lay in their social structures.[27] Like Lenin, Gramsci argued that the distinctive feature of American society lay in the absence of a pre-capitalist structure. The American bourgeois revolution had been born *ex nuovo*. In

Europe, on the other hand, the capitalist revolutions had been established in the context of the struggle against pre-capitalist social classes which had never entirely disappeared. In Italy, in particular, the legacy of this pre-capitalist structure weighed heavily. The 'passive revolution' had meant that Italian society remained trapped in a framework in which capitalist and pre-capitalist groups co-existed side by side in mutual inter-dependence. Unlike America, Italian society contained large parasitic and non-productive groups, superfluous bureaucrats and professionals, whom Gramsci described with a characteristic flourish as 'pensioners of economic history'. The presence of such groups, he argued, made impossible the type of reorganisation and rationalisation of production which was taking place in America. Rather than reduce their numbers, in fact, the experiments embodied in the corporate institutions of the fascist state simply served to increase the opportunities for bureaucratic and non-productive employment. Fascism was not a new departure, but a continuation of the traditional structure of the passive revolution, and for that very reason was incapable of advancing the structure of Italian society beyond the limits dictated by the 'passive revolution'.

It is then 'passive revolution' which both defines and explains the continuity of Italian history from unification to fascism. At every stage there were alternatives: the Radicals might have taken up the peasant cause, Giolitti might have gone further towards effectively incorporating the working classes into the political system; in the post-war crisis other alternatives were available and might have been adopted. But in each case, Gramsci argued, to have accepted such alternatives would have implied moving outside the framework of 'passive revolution'. It would have forced the Italian capitalist classes to accept some broader degree of social and political change as the concommitant of economic development. This they were not prepared to do because it would have jeopardised the alliance between industry and agriculture, of which 'passive revolution' was the direct political expression.

It is against this interpretation that the essays which follow can be set. While they do not provide a comprehensive discussion of Gramsci's analysis, they do attempt to explore further certain of the problems and relationships identified by Gramsci. Although the range of topics with which they deal is too narrow to provide the basis for any thorough revision of Gramsci's arguments, the conclusions of each of the contributions would tend to confirm that the predominant relations in, and between, industry and agriculture, constituted one of the principal obstacles both to development and stability in the liberal state. On the other hand, the conclusions reached are less easily reconcilable with the more general interpretative concepts which Gramsci uses, and in particular they raise a number of questions concerning the 'passive revolution' and the implications of immobility and continuity which surround it.

It is not, I think, very helpful to pose the question in terms of whether Gramsci's reading of Italian history was right or wrong, at least in part because such a question is unanswerable. The question that would appear to be more relevant and useful is to what extent the concept of 'passive revolution' adequately serves to identify the aspects of the relationship between social forces and political organisation which were particular to Italy, and hence would explain the particular development of the Italian state. Following on from this one can also ask how adequate was Gramsci's analysis of the social and, in particular, economic bases of those social forces — the agrarian and industrial classes in particular — and to what extent does more detailed study of these relationships confirm or modify his own analysis.

First, to what extent was the 'passive revolution' a specific characteristic of the bourgeois state in Italy? Certainly the alliance between industrial and agrarian sectors of the national bourgeoisie was not in itself unique. Paul Ginsborg, in the first of the essays which follow, argues that the relationship between these two sectors of the middle classes played a major role in determining the timing of the delays between political and economic change throughout Europe. Both the partnership of manufacturing and agrarian interests and also the role played by the agrarian question — in other words, the satisfactory absorption of the countryside in capitalist relations of production — were not problems unique to Italy, but rather general features of the European bourgeois revolutions. In which case the social and economic base of the political system in Italy might be compared with that of Louis Philippe's France or Bismarck's Germany, and the transition from the liberal state to fascism with Louis Napoleon's Caesarism or German National Socialism. Such comparisons are of course frequently made, but they have not, it must be said, proved particularly fruitful. Highly specific political, cultural and economic realities tend to inhibit comparison of any but the most general and superficial features of these developments. Does the concept of 'passive revolution' identify any qualitative feature, then, of this reasonably typical political system?

Gramsci uses the term 'passive revolution' in both a comparative and a particular sense. He applies it at times to Europe as a whole, for the period between 1815 and 1870, and then again for the years after the First World War. He also uses it at other times as a synonym for 'war of position', in contrast to 'war of manoeuvre'. At the same time, it was only in Italy that 'passive revolution' became the permanent form of political organisation and strategy. There were also particular characteristics of the Italian state and society which made this form of 'passive revolution' possible. As we have described above, it was the hegemonic power of the advanced sectors of the national bourgeoisie which, in Gramsci's view, enabled them to establish and maintain control over the direction and programme of the revolution. But this resulted from two features which were peculiar to Italy — the material weakness of the bourgeoisie and the opportunities for hegemonic action provided by the peculiar social and economic situation of the South. Hegemony is used not only to designate forms of political power dependent on consensus rather than coercion, but also to provide the qualitative distinction of the 'passive revolution'. But it is precisely in the evaluation of this qualitative feature that Gramsci's argument seems least certain.

The general remarks which Gramsci makes on the importance of the formation of hegemonic power before achieving control of the state suggest that he saw certain parallels between the situation of the nineteenth-century Moderates and that of the Communist Party after the fascist victory. Like the earlier Moderates, the Communist Party lacked the resources and organisation to mount a frontal assault on the fascist state. Did Gramsci then see in the Moderate strategy of 'passive revolution' a possible model for the Communist Party to adopt? The suggestion has been vehemently denied,[28] and even if such a model is not entirely foreign to the policies of the present-day Communist Party in Italy, there would not seem to be any grounds for believing that Gramsci was recommending such a strategy. Certainly he did advocate that the revolutionary struggle should also be waged through the institutions of 'civil society', but this was something far short of advocating the adoption of 'passive revolution'.

It is not so much Gramsci's revolutionary philosophy which becomes unclear as a result of this parallel, but rather his interpretation of the national revolution. On one hand, he stressed the strength of the opposition which the nineteenth-century Liberals overcame, their willingness to adopt certain policies which were more 'radical' than those of the Radicals, and he even described the 'passive revolution' on one occasion as a 'brilliant solution' to the problems facing the Liberals.[29] On the other hand, there can be no doubt as to the negative character of his overall evaluation. Echoing Mazzini, he wrote: 'They [the Moderates] were aiming at the creation of a modern state, and they created a bastard.'[30] Such a 'failed revolution' would hardly provide a healthy model for the Communist Party to adopt in the 1930s. But this also places a major question mark against the concept of hegemony. How effective was the much discussed hegemonic role of the Italian bourgeoisie? Did it, in particular, provide an outcome which in any way went qualitatively beyond the material interests of the dominant social forces? The answer is clearly, no. In which case the prop on which the distinctive feature of the 'passive revolution' rested collapses. If hegemony ceases to be the distinctive feature of the bourgeois political ascendancy in Italy, then we are forced back on to the industrial-agrarian alliance — and in particular the specific features and content of that alliance — in order to discover the peculiarities of the 'Italian case'.

If 'passive revolution' presents problems in terms of the specificity of the political system which resulted from unification, the continuities implied in it also raise certain questions. In the first place, the argument that passive revolution was both cause and effect involves a degree of *a posteriori* rationalisation. As Paul Ginsborg argues, in the case of the Risorgimento this results in an undue subordination of the 'moment' of revolution to the more general 'process', and causes Gramsci to under-estimate the real alternatives open to the Italian Liberals in 1848 and 1860. My own essay also suggests that neither 'passive revolution' nor the industrial-agrarian alliance can be seen as causes, rather than results, of the unification of North and South. Similarly, Paul Corner's argument that it was the South that lost most heavily under fascism would also question one of the most fundamental aspects of the continuity of the 'passive revolution'.

What these problems suggest, I think, is a certain tension between the different levels of Gramsci's analysis. At one level, he was always extremely alert to specific social and economic relations, and to specific circumstances of time and place. At a more general and comparative level, however, such distinctions tend to become lost in a series of broader and more abstract categories which perhaps owe much to the Idealist tradition in Italian historiography. The search for the unity and the integral relations binding the different elements of the historical process together is not reconciled wholly satisfactorily with Gramsci's own awareness of distinctions of time and place, and of the peculiar diversities of social and economic conditions in Italy. As a result these broad comparative concepts do not really help to identify the particular features of the economic and social structure around which the Italian state evolved. As Gramsci himself argued 'the state is only conceivable as the concrete form of a specific economic world, a specific system of production',[31] and it is therefore the nature of the relations embodied in the highly diversified texture of the Italian economic system which requires closer examination.

It is with one such set of relations, those between landlord and peasant, that Adrian Lyttleton's essay is concerned. Arguing that the failure to resolve the agrarian question constituted a fundamental weakness of Italian liberalism, he shows that relations between landlords and peasants developed in a variety of forms which differed not only between North and South, but also at a more localised level. Although in certain areas – in particular the Po Valley and Tuscany – the links between agrarian instability and fascism might seem direct, he warns against any simple equation of the two. Even in cases where agrarian conflict assumed the character of open class antagonism, the political consequences were far from uniform. Rather than determining any one political outcome, Adrian Lyttelton concludes, the failure to solve the agrarian question both undermined the liberal state and also served to obstruct any gradual process of social or political development at either local or national level.

Frank Snowden takes up a similar argument in his detailed study of one of the forms of agrarian contract discussed in Adrian Lyttelton's essay, the Tuscan *mezzadria*. Describing the gradual collapse of the traditional *mezzadria* system under the impact of commercialisation from the 1880s to the early 1920s, he shows how the contractual situation of the peasants deteriorated rapidly in the face of unbending landlord conservatism. The growing insecurity of the landlords on the one hand, and the growing but still disorganised resentment of the peasants on the other, combined to produce a peculiarly volatile situation in the province by the close of the First World War, making the region very vulnerable to the influence of the early fascist movement. This particular case lends further support to Adrian Lyttelton's more general conclusions, and shows the importance of studying both specific economic relations and also the specific regional circumstances within which they evolved.

The element of regional diversity is again stressed in the essays by Alice Kelikian and Anthony Cardoza, which examine the relations between and within industry and agriculture in two different regional contexts in the early twentieth century. Anthony Cardoza traces the growing inter-penetration between industrial and agricultural capital in the Po Delta, a region which was to play a vital part in the development of agrarian fascism. He argues that this economic inter-penetration should not be seen as an attempt to put the clock back, but marked the advance of industrial capitalism into the countryside. At the same time, the political consequences of this partnership by the time of the outbreak of the European war were far from clear. The uncertainty and insecurity which accompanied the partnership, together with the difficulty of expressing these new economic interests within the framework of existing political parties helps to explain the particular susceptibility of the Po Valley agrarians to the blandishments of the fascists. But while Anthony Cardoza's argument confirms the importance of the relationship between industry and agriculture in this region, which Gramsci had pointed to, it also demonstrates that it was of a very different nature from the earlier North-South alliance of industry and agriculture, and was not therefore simply a continuation of the 'historical alliance'.

Similar political uncertainty and confusion resulted from the economic changes caused by the war in the province of Brescia which Alice Kelikian has studied. The war broke down the earlier equilibrium between agriculture and industry in the province, brought about qualitative changes in industrial organisation and reduced the region's economic isolation. However, these changes were far from completed by the end of the war. The Brescian workers were little better organised than they had been before, and the traditional Brescian entrepreneurs were far from reconciled to the new forms of industrial corporatism which the war had encouraged. This again serves not only to indicate the regional diversity of economic structures and relations, but also shows the complexity of the divisions and distinctions within specific economic groups.

In the final essay, Paul Corner takes up the question which Gramsci had posed on the economic significance of the fascist regime. He argues the highly unconventional case that the fascist period, far from being a phase of economic stagnation which masked a tendency to protect agriculture at the expense of industry, in fact brought about a major shift in the structure of the Italian economy. The 'Battle for Wheat' and the 'Quota 90', he argues, did not, as has generally been assumed, protect the more backward sectors of Italian industry and agriculture, but rather subordinated them to the interests of heavy industry and capitalist farming in the North. As a result these two key sectors were able to develop and consolidate despite the international economic circumstances of the 1930s, and laid the basis for the post-war 'economic miracle'.

Paul Corner's argument is highly original and will certainly be contested, but if he is right it would seem to cast doubt on the economic continuities between fascism and pre-fascism. It would also question the continuity of the 'historical alliance' of North and South in the fascist period. And this touches on what is perhaps the least tidy part of Gramsci's analysis. Because he does not define the role played by the South in the transition to fascism, the relationship between the new agrarian-industrial partnerships which had emerged in the North and the traditional 'historical alliance' remains unclear. Those, like Sereni,[32] who have examined this relationship more fully have tended to emphasise the continuity. One of the problems, of course, lies in the essentially passive role played by the South in the transition to fascism. Adrian Lyttelton's conclusions on the continuing fragmentation and isolation of the Southern peasantry — which reflect Gramsci's own analysis — provide one explanation of this relative passivity. The absence of effective or organised peasant opposition in the South meant that the type of counter-offensive adopted by the Tuscan and Emilian landlords was simply not needed. But if, as Paul Corner argues, the Southern landlords as well as the Southern economy were losers under the fascist regime, this passivity may well reflect a shift in the political structure which deprived the Southern landowners of their former privileged political position. And the fact that, of all the traditional groups in Italy, it was the Southern landowners who emerged weakest from the Second World War, would seem to support such an argument.

The specific characteristics of the economic relations and structures on which the political system of the liberal state were based would then confirm Gramsci's arguments on the weaknesses and limitations of Italian capitalism. But they also indicate that industry and agriculture encompassed a variety of relationships which make it difficult to talk of any single agrarian or industrial interest, or any fixed relationship between the two. The arguments raised in these essays would also suggest that the fundamental continuity of the economic structure on which the political systems from Risorgimento to fascism were based is a problem which still remains very much open to debate.

Notes

(For reasons of space the bibliographical references to this introduction have been kept to a minimum. More detailed bibliographies on specific issues will be found accompanying the essays which follow. The most recent and useful general survey of Italian economic historiography for the period covered by this volume is: V. Castronovo, 'Dall'Unità à oggi — storia economica' in the new *Storia d'Italia*, vol.4 (Turin, 1974).)

1. Wherever possible reference will be made to Gramsci's writings in English in the excellent edition of the *Prison Notebooks*, edited by Q. Hoare and G. Nowell Smith (London, 1971: hereafter *PN*) and A. Gramsci, *Selections from Political Writings (1921-6)*, ed. Q. Hoare (London, 1978). In addition to the Introduction to the Q. Hoare and G. Nowell Smith edition of the *Prison Notebooks*, more general guides are provided by: J. Joll, *Gramsci* (London, 1977); J. Cammet, *Antonio Gramsci and the Origins of Italian Communism* (Stanford, 1967);

M. Clark, *Antonio Gramsci and the Revolution that Failed* (New Haven, 1977);
A. Davidson, *Antonio Gramsci: Towards an Intellectual Biography* (London,
1976). There is a useful bibliographical guide to works in English on Gramsci:
P. Cozens, *Twenty Years of Antonio Gramsci* (London, 1977).

2. The 'revolutionary' nature of Gramsci's history is particularly stressed by
A. Macciocchi, *Pour Gramsci* (Paris, 1971).

3. P. Spriano, *Storia del Partito Comunista Italiano*, vol.I (Turin, 1967),
p.492.

4. A. Pizzorno, 'A propos de la méthode de Gramsci, de l'historiographie, des
sciences sociales', *L'Homme et la Société* (April-June 1968) p.163.

5. See P. Ginsborg and A. Lyttelton below. Romeo's essay is included in
Risorgimento e Capitalismo (Bari, 1970) but has never been translated. A. Gershen-
kron's first interventions are in *Economic Backwardness in Historical Perspective*
(Cambridge, Mass., 1962), chapters 2, 4, 5 and Appendix 1. There is also an
interesting summary of the debate in the postscript to J. Cammet, *Antonio
Gramsci and the Origins of Italian Communism*.

6. P. Anderson, 'The Antinomies of Antonio Gramsci', *New Left Review*, 100
(Nov. 1976-June 1977) p.5.

7. *PN*, p.106.

8. *PN*, p.138.

9. *PN*, pp.58-62.

10. A. Gramsci, *Il Risorgimento* (Turin, 1966), p.54.

11. *PN*, p.59.

12. See note 5 above.

13. *PN*, p.57.

14. *PN*, p.58.

15. *PN*, pp.90-102: also the important essay on 'The Southern Question' in *The
Modern Prince & Other Writings*, ed. L. Marks (New York, 1957).

16. See in particular *The German Ideology*.

17. *PN*, p.91.

18. E. Sereni, *Il Capitalismo nelle Campagne (1860-1900)* (Turin, 1968), pp.36-
40.

19. A Gramsci, 'The Southern Question', p.42.

20. *PN*, p.94.

21. There is a useful introduction to Gramsci's writings on fascism in A. Gramsci,
Sul Fascismo, ed. E. Santarelli (Rome, 1969), pp.15-30.

22. P. Spriano, *Storia del Partito Comunista Italiano*, pp.480-93.

23. V. Guerratura, 'Il popolo delle scimmie tra reazione e rivoluzione', *Rinascita*
(27.10.72) pp.31-3.

24. Ibid.

25. Ordine Nuovo 1922, cited in L. Paggi, *Gramsci e il Moderno Principe* (Turin,
1970), p.408.

26. *PN*, pp. 117-18.

27. *PN*, pp.278-318 ('Americanism and Fordism'); F. De Felice, 'Una chiave
per la letteratura in Americanismo e Fordismo', *Rinascita* (27.10.72) pp.33-5.

28. V. Guerratura, 'Il popolo delle scimmie', p.32.

29. *PN*, p.59.

30. *PN*, p.90.

31. *PN*, p.116.

32. E. Sereni, *La Questione Agraria nella Rinascita Nazionale Italiano* (Turin,
1946, 1st edn).

2 GRAMSCI AND THE ERA OF BOURGEOIS REVOLUTION IN ITALY*

Paul Ginsborg

The concept of bourgeois revolution has been under attack for some time now. The terrain chosen for the offensive is, hardly surprisingly, that of the so-called 'classic' bourgeois revolution which took place in France between 1789 and 1794. Ever since Alfred Cobban in the mid-1960s launched his swingeing onslaught on the Marxist interpretation of the French Revolution, the term 'bourgeois revolution' has fallen into considerable disrepute amongst Anglo-Saxon historians. What, asked Cobban, does the bourgeois revolution mean? His answer for France in the 1790s was typically belittling and polemical: 'A class of officials and professional men moved up from the minor to the major posts in government and dispossessed the minions of an effete court.'[1] Not every one agreed with all that Cobban had to say, but few had doubts about the bankruptcy of Marxist terminology. G.V. Taylor, at the end of a widely-acclaimed article published in 1967, officially declared the Marxist interpretation obsolete: 'The phrases "bourgeois revolution" and "revolutionary bourgeoisie" with their inherent deceptions, will have to go, and others must be found that convey with precision and veracity the realities of social history.'[2]

More recently, and more surprisingly, the attack has come from another quarter. Roberto Zapperi, a scholar of the school of the Italian Communist Mario Tronti, has reached a point of view startlingly similar to that of Taylor. In his book, misleadingly entitled *For a Critique of the Concept of Bourgeois Revolution*, Zapperi analyses the writings of the Abbe Sieyès. He produces indisputable evidence to show that Sieyès was in no way the theoretician of a flourishing French capitalist bourgeoisie. Galvanised by this discovery, Zapperi feels free to leap to the most iconoclastic of conclusions: 'The concepts of bourgeoisie and of bourgeois revolution ... melt under the pressure of their own aporias and reveal, beneath their definitive appearance, a substantially mystifying nature.' Marx, decides Zapperi, has got it all wrong. Before the rise

*I am grateful to Norman Hampson, Gwyn Williams and Alberto Tovaglieri, all of whom have made me think about this subject. None of them, naturally, bears any responsibility for what follows.

31

of the proletariat there were 'no classes', and the concept of bourgeois revolution was Marx's 'unwarranted projection into the past of the prospect of proletarian revolution'.[3]

Traditional Marxist historiography has left itself sadly exposed to such cross-fire. Confusion reigns paramount, even in the most distinguished of minds. Albert Soboul is just one example among many. After a lifetime of study of the French Revolution, he seems quite unable to decide whether the Revolution marked the beginning, the middle or the end of the development of capitalism in France. In his 1973 Foreword to the English edition of his *Précis d'Histoire de la Révolution française*, Soboul contradicts himself three times in fifteen pages. On p. 3 he proudly announces that 'the Revolution of 1789-94 marked the *arrival* of modern bourgeois capitalist society in the history of France'. But by p. 8 the Revolution has become only a *'decisive stage* in the development of capitalism'. By the end of the Foreword the French Revolution, while still 'a classic bourgeois revolution' is relegated to being 'the *starting-point* for capitalist society'.[4] [All italics are mine.] Soboul's Foreword reminds the present author of nothing so much as being on another great bourgeois institution, the inter-city train between London and Newcastle. The tape-recorded announcement of the various stations *en route* had been inserted the wrong way round, so that as the train pulled into London a recorded voice solemnly intoned 'this is Newcastle, this is Newcastle'. But it wasn't.

At the heart of the problem lies the absence of any adequate definition of the concept of bourgeois revolution. Marx himself never elaborated systematically on the concept, and much of the subsequent confusion has derived from what he did write. In a famous passage from the *Manifesto* he and Engels described the way in which the bourgeoisie achieved economic and political power:

> At a certain stage . . . the feudal relations of property became no longer compatible with the already developed productive forces; they became so many fetters. They had to be burst asunder; they were burst asunder. Into their place stepped free competition, accompanied by a social and political constitution adapted to it, and by the economical and political sway of the bourgeois class.[5]

This passage seems to have been widely interpreted as being a blueprint for bourgeois revolution. The task of Marxist historians became that of demonstrating how, in any given bourgeois revolution, the revolutionary bourgeoisie *at a certain moment* broke the bonds of feudal society, seized political power and established a new economic and political order. From Jean Jaurès onwards, all the great Marxist historians of the French Revolution have worked within this framework. For Jaurès, the frenzied activity of the eighteenth-century French bourgeoisie lead to 'the deforestation of entire regions, sacrificed to the needs of industrial furnaces'. He continues: 'All this was a huge flaming fire of bourgeois power, which sweeping through the ancient mediaeval forest, lit up the furthest corners with its purple glow. A furnace of wealth and work; a furnace also of Revolution.'[6]

Wonderful stuff, but non-Marxist historians had every right to question if this was what really happened. The more historical evidence that was accumulated, often by Marxists themselves, the more it became obvious that the facts would not fit the straitjacket. The actual development of the eighteenth-century French bourgeoisie could not in all honesty be said to resemble 'a huge flaming fire'; many of the bourgeois representatives in Paris were positively reluctant to abolish feudal dues on the night of 4 August 1789; the immediate economic consequences of the Revolution damaged more than stimulated the development of French capitalism; and so on and so forth. Cobban and Taylor triumphantly concluded that the concept of bourgeois revolution made no historical sense, and that the Marxist interpretation was therefore disproved. In the world of Anglo-Saxon *academia* every one could sleep a little more easily at night.

The purpose of this chapter is to argue the need for a more rigorous and accurate elaboration of the Marxist concept of bourgeois revolution. The suggestions that follow are, as will become obvious, more tentative than definitive, cover only some aspects of the question, use only a European frame of reference, and are intended to stimulate and provoke those more able and knowledgeable than myself. The first part of the chapter deals with general problems of definition. The remainder attempts to assess Antonio Gramsci's contribution to our understanding of bourgeois revolution in a single country, Italy.

What is Bourgeois Revolution?

Process

It is impossible to examine a single bourgeois revolution, like that in France between 1789-94, without first having some conception of the *era* of bourgeois revolution in any particular country. The passage quoted above from the *Communist Manifesto* would seem to make historical sense only if applied to an historical process, not to a specific moment in history.[6a]

The epoch of bourgeois revolution can perhaps be best characterised in terms of a twofold process, both economic and political. In economic terms, the period witnesses the definitive triumph of capitalism as the dominant mode of production. In the political sphere, the absolutist state comes to be replaced by one founded on the principles of bourgeois democracy. It is as well to begin by examining separately these two processes.

The economic transition from feudalism to capitalism is the only aspect of bourgeois revolution that has received the detailed attention it deserves. Ever since Maurice Dobb wrote his famous book *Studies in the Development of Capitalism*, debate has raged fast and furious as to where the transition begins, how it develops and what are its decisive stages. Space does not permit an adequate summary of this debate. But if French history remains our principal field of enquiry for the moment, it can be seen that whatever the disagreements over the exact pattern of development of French capitalism, there is some measure of accord on an end date for the transition. By 1880, on the admission of both bourgeois and Marxist historians, France had developed a fully-fledged capitalist economy.[7] Obviously backward sectors remained, especially in the countryside and in some areas of manufacturing like the Parisian luxury crafts. But the vital point is that after the great industrial boom of 1840-80, capitalism had become the *dominant* mode of production in France.

The political process of the establishment of bourgeois democracy has been the subject of less attention, though a very recent comparative article by Goran Therborn may well serve to revive debate.[8] Therborn's definition of bourgeois democracy is worth repeating here as a basis for future discussion. He uses the term to denote a state with a representative government elected by the entire adult population whose votes carry equal weight and who are allowed to vote for any opinion without state intimidation. 'Such a state', continues Therborn, 'is a *bourgeois* democracy in so far as the state apparatus has a bourgeois class composition and the state power operates in such a way as to maintain and promote capitalist relations of production and the class character of the state apparatus.'

It requires little historical common sense to realise that nowhere in Europe did such a state come into being at one fell swoop. In France, despite the singular achievements of 1789-94, a whole century elapsed before bourgeois democracy was firmly established. Gramsci, in a perceptive passage from the *Prison Notebooks*, describes the nature of this process in French society:

In fact, it was only in 1870-71, with the attempt of the Commune, that all the germs of 1789 were finally exhausted. It was then that the new bourgeois class struggling for power defeated not only the representatives of the old society unwilling to admit that it had been definitively superseded, but also the still newer groups who maintained that the new structure created by the 1789 revolution was itself already outdated; by this victory the bourgeoisie demonstrated its vitality *vis-à-vis* both the old and the very new.[9]

However, if Therborn's definition is to be followed, the process would have to be significantly elongated. Gramsci maintained that the *substance* of bourgeois power had been achieved by 1871, but universal suffrage did not come into being in France until 1946.

During the epoch of bourgeois revolution, therefore, it is an essential preliminary task for the historian to trace the dual process which led to the dominance of the capitalist mode of production and the creation of a modern bourgeois-democratic state. An immediate and thorny problem presents itself. What is the connection between the two processes, the one economic, the other political?

Marx wrote in the *Communist Manifesto*: 'Each step in the development of the bourgeoisie was accompanied by a corresponding political advance of that class.'[10] In practice, it is difficult to demonstrate any such direct co-relation. The French bourgeoisie, it is true, achieved economic and political supremacy at approximately the same time — the 1870s and 1880s. However, they seem far more the exception than the rule. In the same period, their German neighbours, to take one example among many, enjoyed immense economic power but more limited political power. Of course, it could be argued that the bourgeoisie of Wilhelmine Germany exercised *effective* control even if *formally* deprived of full political rights. But Marx was quite categorical that the bourgeois-democratic state was the highest expression of the bourgeois political order. The German bourgeoisie, then, was politically out of step in the second half of the nineteenth century. They had yet to make their 'corresponding political advance'.

In general, as has often been noted, it seems difficult to sustain any mechanistic relationship between economic 'base' and political 'superstructure'. The degree of capitalist development would seem to be a dominant but not exclusive factor in explaining the political rise of the bourgeoisie. Capitalism and democracy are not yoked inseparably together. The complex connection between the two can only be located satisfactorily in the specific historical experience of each national

bourgeoisie. One of the most important ways of identifying this connection is to turn from the general processes at work in the epoch of
bourgeois revolution to an examination of the particular moments of
conflict in that era.

Moment

It is tempting, in view of the very real difficulties of comprehension and
coherence, to describe bourgeois revolution *solely* in terms of a process.
Many modern Marxist historians seem to take this point of view. Giorgio
Candeloro, for instance, at the beginning of his magnificent multi-volume
history of Italy, describes the whole of the Risorgimento as 'a national
and bourgeois revolution'.[11]

However, every major Marxist thinker has so far used the term prim=
arily to denote *not* the period of transformation to a bourgeois economy
and state, but to describe a specific upheaval such as the French revolution of 1789-94 or the English revolution of the 1640s. It is a moment
of conflict, not a process of change, that has habitually borne the Marxist
label 'bourgeois revolution'. For Lenin, who came as close as anyone
to distinguishing between process and moment, the Russian peasant
'emancipation' of 1861 marked the beginning of 'bourgeois Russia' or
'the era of bourgeois revolutions'. Within this era, however, the revolution
of 1905 was the first 'bourgeois revolution'.[12]

This being so, it is incumbent on Marxist historians to try to define
what they mean by the moment of bourgeois revolution. As far as I am
aware any such attempt at definition has been notably absent from
Marxist historiography on the French revolution. The vagueness with
which the term has been habitually used goes a long way to explain the
ease and joy with which the Cobbanite vultures have been able to
swoop upon their prey.

As a first approximation, a successful bourgeois revolution is perhaps
best defined both by its course and by its achievements. Its course, like
that of all revolutions, is marked by a violent social upheaval which
overthrows the existing political order. Its achievements, specific to
bourgeois revolution alone, lie in the creation of a state power and
institutional framework consonant with the flourishing of bourgeois
property relations, and with the development of bourgeois society as a
whole.

The two parts of this definition are perhaps worth a few words of
elaboration. The course of bourgeois revolution has been described in
this way precisely to distinguish process from moment, gradual transition
from violent upheaval. Its achievements are given empirical content in a

characteristically vigorous passage written by Marx in 1851. No single bourgeois revolution ever carried through all the items that Marx lists, but taken together they represent most of the foundations of bourgeois society. Marx, examining the cumulative effects of two bourgeois revolutions — the English of 1640 and the French of 1789 — states that they meant

> the proclamation of the political order for the new European society
> ... the victory of bourgeois property over feudal property, of nation-
> ality over provincialism, of competition over the guild, of the partition
> of estates over primogeniture, of the owner's mastery of the land over
> the land's mastery of its owner, of enlightenment over superstition,
> of the family over the family name, of industry over heroic laziness,
> of civil law over privileges of mediaeval origin.[13]

Immediately a number of caveats must be issued and confusions dealt with. In the first place, obvious though it sounds, no two bourgeois revolutions are the same. The 'classic' bourgeois revolution would seem to be a contradiction in terms. The historian, in trying to trace the pattern of events and eventual achievements of any particular bourgeois revolution, has to pay great attention to a wide number of variants: the particular pattern of capitalist development in the country in question; the specific structure of the state; the peculiar tensions created by differ-ing relations between the social classes. Nearly always there is a dominant question, a specific unresolvable contradiction that lies at the heart of a revolution and decisively influences its trajectory.

Secondly, many anti-Marxist historians (and some Marxists as well) have made the mistake of assuming that in all circumstances it must be the bourgeoisie who make the bourgeois revolution. In other words, the leading role of the bourgeoisie (and sometimes just the commercial and manufacturing bourgeoisie) has been taken as a *definitive* feature of bourgeois revolution. This common confusion has led to a highly popular historical game: hunt the bourgeoisie, often to be played on a board of eighteenth-century France. One side tries to show that a revolutionary bourgeoisie did not exist and hopes to win a certificate bearing the words: 'Marxist history is bunkum'. The other strives to demonstrate exactly the opposite, aiming to gain the coveted title of 'hero of the Revolution'. Both pursue a false model of bourgeois revolution.

The specificity of bourgeois revolution, as has been outlined above, does not depend on its leading actors but on its contribution to the general development of bourgeois society.[14] Quite often classes other

than the bourgeoisie objectively further the bourgeois revolution while
pursuing their own aims. Sometimes they do this in opposition to sections
of the bourgeoisie itself. This paradox is perhaps best explained by an
historical example already mentioned *en passant*. In the summer of 1789
the revolt of the French peasantry constrained the National Assembly to
decree the partial abolition of feudal dues and obligations. The decision,
as Cobban showed ('advance to go' in the board game), was taken against
the wishes of many bourgeois landowners and in the face of opposition
from representatives of the Third Estate. The decree of 4 August 1789,
however, was quite clearly a critical step in the establishment of bourgeois
property relations in the countryside. The driving force behind it had
been the peasantry, not the bourgeoisie.

This mode of reasoning about bourgeois revolution is patently present
in the writings and political activity of both Marx and Lenin. In the
German revolution of 1848, in the face of the hesitations of the German
liberal bourgeoisie, Marx urged the German workers and artisans to fight
for a programme of advanced bourgeois democracy. In the most extreme
of cases, that of Russia in 1905-7, Lenin continuously stressed that the
bourgeois revolution was going to have to be made by the peasantry and
workers in open opposition to a weak and terrified bourgeoisie.[15] In this
last case, however, Lenin's insistence on a bourgeois revolution *against*
the bourgeoisie cannot help but raise serious terminological doubts.
While one can remain quite clear about the meaning of the term 'bourgeois revolution', the term itself here seems profoundly unsatisfactory.

Finally, another common misapprehension must be dealt with.
Bourgeois and *bourgeois-democratic* revolutions are often casually
regarded as being synonymous. In fact, as we have seen earlier, the magic
hyphen between 'bourgeois' and 'democratic' masks a very complex
question. The political freedoms associated with bourgeois democracy
are sometimes a corollary of successful bourgeois revolution, but cannot,
any more than bourgeois leadership, be regarded as an essential part of
a general definition. None of the great bourgeois revolutions, as Therborn
has pointed out, actually established bourgeois democracy.[16] The
Jacobin constitution of 1793 remained a model for the democrats of
nineteenth-century Europe, but was never operative during the French
Revolution itself. Only in the latter half of the European epoch of
bourgeois revolution do we find the stable establishment of bourgeois
democracy, and then very often not as a result of revolution.[17]

For a Typology of Bourgeois Revolution

Any brief attempt at defining bourgeois revolution, such as the one above, is bound to raise, intentionally and unintentionally, as many problems as it solves. Yet a number of yardsticks have emerged which may be of use in the future work of historical analysis: the distinction between process and moment, a definition of bourgeois revolution in terms of its course and its achievements, an insistence on avoiding the twin pitfalls of necessarily identifying bourgeois revolution in terms of bourgeois leadership and democracy. These instruments need to be refined or discarded before any systematic categorisation of bourgeois revolution can be attempted.

A typology of this kind would be a major historical undertaking of the sort which Perry Anderson has promised us and which we eagerly await. Here it is possible only to make a few preliminary observations before turning to examine Gramsci's writing and the Italian experience.

Up till now, comparative analysis of bourgeois revolutions has hardly reached exalted levels. In his *Prison Notebooks* Gramsci refers the reader to Engels's considerations of the German, French and English revolutions.[18] If, as Anderson has justly exhorted, 'there is no place for fideism in rational knowledge, which is necessarily cumulative',[19] then Engels's attempt at comparison can hardly be called enlightening. According to Engels, 'the long fight of the bourgeoisie against feudalism culminated in three great decisive battles' — the Protestant Reformation in Germany, the English revolution of the 1640s and the French of 1789. Implicit in this schema is the idea of defining the *moment* of bourgeois revolution primarily by its causation — the need of a revolutionary bourgeoisie at a certain moment to break decisively the bonds of feudalism. This, as I have already tried to argue, would seem to present serious historical problems. While the *era* of bourgeois revolution undoubtedly has its foundations in the contradiction between relations of property and productive forces, the specific moments of conflict within that era can rarely, if ever, be described as 'decisive battles' which resolve this contradiction.

Even if we abandon the schema and merely consider the examples, it is hard to see how the Protestant Reformation was a successful bourgeois revolution. During its course the existing German political order was not overthrown, in spite of the Peasants' Revolt. Its most significant result, according to Engels, was the triumph of Calvinism, a creed 'fit for the boldest bourgeoisie of his time'. However, the partial victory of a specific ideology is by itself scant justification for such a prominent position in the bourgeois hall of fame.

On England and France, Engels is more judicious, and the events themselves are obviously more worthy of the terminology employed.

Yet with regard to the French Revolution it is worth noting that Engels repeats the famous and sweeping historical judgement of the Marx of the *Eighteenth Brumaire*. For both of them the Revolution signified 'the complete triumph of the bourgeoisie', 'the smashing of the feudal base to pieces', 'the destruction of the aristocracy', etc.[20] Modern Marxist historians would tend to be more cautious. No one but the most diehard Cobbanite could deny the decisive contribution of the *moment* of the French Revolution to the general *development* of the French bourgeois state and society. Yet that development was in no way complete even by 1815, and the residues of a pre-revolutionary past (and of some aspects of the Revolution itself) weighed heavily on the France of the nineteenth century. Marx himself recognised this clearly in other passages of his work. Yet his frequent over-estimation of the *actual* historical achievements of the French Revolution began a historical school which, as we shall see when we turn to Gramsci's writings, has taken a long time to die.

Later attempts at comparison have been, as far as I know, no more than half-hearted. In 1904 Jaurès made a passing reference, later taken up by Soboul, to the English Revolution as being 'strictly bourgeois and conservative' when compared to 'its mainly bourgeois and democratic French counterpart'.[21] The bases for these judgements are not easy to discover. Taken at face value, the idea of the English Revolution being 'strictly bourgeois' seems a very strange one.

Anderson, at the end of his *Lineages of the Absolutist State*, makes the distinction between bourgeois revolutions from below (Spain, England and France), and those from above (Italy and Germany).[22] Until this distinction is fully developed in a future work, it would be unfair to pass definitive judgement upon it. At first sight it looks unpromising. The formative *process* of the bourgeois national state in Italy and Germany was, it is true, carried through from above (though Garibaldi's exploits in southern Italy are hardly to be forgotten in this respect). But to describe this process as a 'bourgeois revolution from above' is to risk lumping together process and moment indiscriminately. It also implies the abandonment of any idea of defining bourgeois revolution in terms of its course, i.e. as a moment of violent social upheaval which overthrows the existing political order.[22a]

At present, no satisfactory methodology for the comparative analysis of bourgeois revolutions exists. It has yet to be created. A few schematic considerations on this subject may not be entirely useless. Without becoming date fetishists, the duration of the dual process which characterises the era of bourgeois revolution would have to be identified for any given country. Once this time span has been established (no easy task), an analysis of process could give way to that of moment. Here both quantative and qualitative factors come into play: not only the number of revolutions, but also their precise nature, the degree of their success, their partial or all-embracing character.

The critical question then arises of the connection between process and moment. Here it is not possible to make more than one or two initial comments. In the absence of any single successful bourgeois revolution (as in Germany), the process by which the bourgeois-democratic state comes into being is of necessity unusually protracted and heavily influenced by the residues of a feudal past. The opposite also appears historically valid. In France, the decisive nature of the revolution of 1789-94 meant that even under the Restoration there could be no going back on the centralised and essentially modern state structure created by the Jacobins and Napoleon. For the great majority of European countries it is worth reiterating an historical commonplace: namely that the clamorous failure of the bourgeois-democratic revolutions of 1848-9 retarded by many decades the process by which bourgeois democracy was established on the Continent. Finally, it would seem that the connection between bourgeois revolution and the development of capitalism as the dominant mode of production is by no means a linear one. While successful revolutions, like the French, provided the institutional framework for capitalism, there is no immediate chronological link between bourgeois revolution and industrial growth.

In any typology of bourgeois revolution, certain key historical variants have to figure centrally. Periodisation is of prime importance. The difference between early and late revolutions is in general very marked, because in the latter (as is well known) the 'threat from below', the growth of an industrial working class, conditioned and constrained the bourgeoisie, forcing it to seek compromise rather than confrontation with the forces of the *ancien régime*. The degree of international intervention seems no less important. The nature of bourgeois revolutions in the more backward European countries was often heavily determined both by direct foreign intervention (Napoleon's *Grande Armée*), and by the historical examples provided by the English and French experience.

Lastly (though the list would be enormously extended in any systematic study), the agrarian question merits particular attention. The epoch of bourgeois revolution in the different nation states has been marked by extremely diverse solutions to the problem of the land. This diversity has been much commented upon, from Lenin's notorious distinction between the 'American' and the 'Prussian' roads, to Barrington

Moore's comparative study of the political importance of differing peasant/landlord relationships.[23] The agrarian question, in fact, is much more than a partial aspect of a general economic transition. It lies at the heart of any comparative history of bourgeois revolution.

The Italian Case

It is as well to start by trying to establish the broad outlines of the epoch of bourgeois revolution in Italy. Immediately we run into controversy. Are the beginnings of the definitive transition to a bourgeois state and economy to be sought in the eighteenth century or at a much earlier date, at the time of the highly prosperous city states of the late Middle Ages and the Renaissance? The present author is in no way qualified to answer this question, which itself requires the elaboration of a sophisticated set of criteria and many pages of accurate historical analysis. Here a methodological suggestion will have to take the place of detailed discussion. Maurice Dobb has written:[24]

> the process of historical change is for the most part gradual and continuous. In the sense that there is no event which cannot be connected with some immediately antecedent event in a rational chain it can be described as continuous throughout. But what seems necessarily to be implied in any conception of development as divided into periods or epochs, each characterised by its distinctive economic system, is that there are crucial points in economic development at which the tempo is abnormally accelerated and at which continuity is broken.

Dobb's observation can be applied to the Italian case in a negative way. Continuity was broken, but in the sense of a dramatic interruption in the process of bourgeois development, both economic and political. This interruption was so profound as to last nearly two hundred years, until the mid-eighteenth century. Such a protracted regression (with very few exceptions) makes it almost meaningless to talk of any continuity of transition from the fourteenth to the nineteenth century.[25] In general, the *irreversibility* of the twofold process of change, understood not in the sense of temporary setbacks but of long-term trends, would seem to be one essential criterion for identifying the beginnings of a definitive transition to bourgeois society. In Italy the decisive acceleration of tempo is perhaps best located, both in economic and political terms, in the second half of the eighteenth century.

The same difficulty surrounds what is often confusingly called 'the completion of the bourgeois revolution'. In economic terms (though here too the criterion of judgement needs to be much refined), it is possible to argue that, in spite of the grave and continuing backwardness of the South, capitalism had become the dominant mode of production in Italy by the beginning of the twentieth century.[26]

As for the triumph of bourgeois democracy, a case can be made for 1913, when for the first time elections were held on the basis of adult male suffrage. Supporters of this thesis would maintain that the *substance* of the modern bourgeois state existed as much in Giolitti's Italy as, say, in Gambetta's France. But a more purist argument, along Therborn's lines, would be that bourgeois democracy triumphed only in 1947 with the creation of universal suffrage, the abolition of the monarchy and the setting up of the first Italian Republic.

The question of course is an exquisitely political one, for it relates directly to the strategy of the working-class movement in Italy. If the epoch of bourgeois revolution had not come to a close by 1943 then it could be argued that the task of the left-wing forces during the Resistance and afterwards was to fight for its completion. This was the position substantially adopted by Togliatti and the Italian Communist Party. In a speech of June 1945 Togliatti claimed that the 'democratic revolution in our country has never been either brought to an end nor seriously developed'.[27] Togliatti, of course, always spoke of the need for 'progressive democracy', but this somewhat vague formula came to mean in reality, as Quazza has shown, the acceptance of a standard bourgeois parliamentary regime.[28] Indeed Togliatti himself stressed the *essential continuity* between the political struggles of the democratic wing of the bourgeoisie in the Risorgimento and the PCI (Partito Comunista Italiana) in the Resistance: 'In demanding a national Constituent Assembly, we find ourselves in the company of the best men of our Risorgimento, in the company of Carlo Cattaneo, of Giuseppe Mazzini, of Giuseppe Garibaldi, and we are proud to be in such company.'[29] If, on the other hand, the epoch of bourgeois revolution had come to a close some decades before the Resistance, then the theoretical framework for the Italian working-class movement from 1943 onwards had perforce to be a very different one.

Let us assume, for the sake of argument, that the era of bourgeois revolution in Italy extends from the middle of the eighteenth century to the second decade of the twentieth century. In that period it is not difficult to distinguish five moments of bourgeois revolution: the years 1796-9, a profound revolutionary upheaval carried throughout the peninsula on the bayonets of the French army, a revolution interrupted in

1799 but many of whose achievements were consolidated and developed in Napoleonic Italy; the revolutionary waves of 1820-1 and 1830-2, both partial in geographical extent and unqualified failures; the extraordinary nationwide sequence of revolutions in 1848-9, promising so much in their early stages but destined to ultimate defeat; and finally the events of 1859-60, a mixture of dynastic war in the North, nationalist revolution in the Centre and volunteer-led insurrection in the South, all of which combined to produce the unification of the majority of the peninsula.

Examining these revolutions and the process which connects them, certain broad characteristics of the Italian case are immediately identifiable. These are in no way novel or controversial, but are worth noting here before proceeding further. Many of them derive directly from Gramsci's observations. In the first place, even a cursory glance is sufficient to reveal that the *dominant* question in all of the Italian revolutions of the nineteenth century was the national one. The need for national independence and unification rapidly over-rode every other problem – whether economic, social or political. Manin was not alone when he told Nassau Senior in 1857: 'I would take Murat, the Pope, Napoleon Bonaparte, the devil himself for king, if I could therefore drive out the foreigners and unite Italy under a single sceptre. Give us unity and we will get all the rest.'[30]

Secondly, there was an extraordinarily high degree of foreign participation in the Italian bourgeois revolutions. The only two revolutions which can be categorised as successful (in differing measures) – those of 1796-9 and 1859-60 – were both heavily dependent on French intervention. Those in between, purely autochthonous affairs, were catastrophic failures. In fact the Italian bourgeoisie, unlike the French or the English, never made its own revolution at any stage. Even if, in polemical fashion, the Resistance of 1943-5 is to be included here as the 'last bourgeois revolution', the major contribution of Allied troops in liberating the peninsula can hardly be forgotten.

The historic weakness of the Italian bourgeoisie is also revealed by the predominant role played by a single dynastic state, Piedmont, during the critical years of the era under examination. The reliance upon a monarchist army and subservience to a monarchist constitution, this *substitution* of a state for a class, was heavily reflected in the political ordering of the new nation state. The basic elements of bourgeois democracy which are to be found in Mazzini's Rome and Manin's Venice in 1848-9 are not present in the Italy of Cavour and Victor Emmanuel II. In 1859-60 plebiscites took the place of parliaments. The supreme moment of bourgeois revolution in Italy was therefore a deeply flawed one. While the creation of a national market and state were considerable achievements, the exclusion of the mass of the population from the right to vote and the continuing powers of the monarchy retarded the creation of bourgeois democracy in Italy for many decades.

Above all, the Italian revolutions failed to resolve the agrarian question. If the English liquidated the peasantry and the French maintained a significant stratum of rural small-holders, the Italians did neither, leaving the southern peasantry in particular in a state of abject misery and permanent revolt. Soboul is right when he traces this failure back to the revolutions of 1796-9 and to Napoleonic Italy.[31] The reforms of this period tended more to unite bourgeois and aristocratic landowners than to confront the peasant problem. But the question remained an open one, to reappear in dramatic form in the revolutions of 1848-9 and again during Garibaldi's expedition of 1860. The final solution, if such it can be called, was the civil war in the South between 1860-70, when a Piedmontese army of occupation slowly annihilated the subversion in the southern countryside. This tribute of blood was the material basis for the formation of the new Italian ruling class — the 'historic bloc' of southern landowners and northern bourgeoisie.

Gramsci's 'Prison Notebooks'

Gramsci's notes on the Risorgimento abound with insights and stimuli with regard to those distinctive characteristics of the Italian case which have been briefly outlined above. However, our task here is not to provide an exegesis of his work (though most of his principal themes will of necessity emerge in due course).[32] It is rather to attempt a critical analysis of the *categories* he uses. In other words, we need to try to assess how much he contributes to those theoretical and historiographical problems outlined in the first part of this essay.

Immediately a somewhat surprising and saddening fact emerges. Since the war no less than three major congresses have been organised by the Italian Communist Party to examine Gramsci's writings.[33] In spite of the interventions of a number of extremely able and accomplished historians, it is impossible to say that any substantial *Marxist* critique of Gramsci's historical writing has emerged. Part of the reason for this lies with an initial, justifiable concern to defend Gramsci's notes on the Risorgimento against the summary liquidation of them by Croce, Chabod and others. Later there was the task of replying to the much more substantial criticism launched by Rosario Romeo.[34] But much of the reason also lies with the persistence of the sort of fideism towards Gramsci which Anderson has warned against when dealing with the historical writings of Marx and Engels. This excess of deference is nothing but a disservice to Gramsci himself.[35] His own exhortations and the very nature of his notebooks — their unfinished, convoluted and often contradictory character — would strongly suggest a quite different approach.

Of the categories that Gramsci uses when writing on the Risorgimento, only those of 'passive revolution' and 'war of position/war of manoeuvre' relate directly to the *overall* problem of defining bourgeois revolution. It is as well to start with these, before turning to other terms such as 'hegemony' and 'Jacobinism' which are more categories *within* bourgeois revolution than descriptions of bourgeois revolution itself.

Passive Revolution

When writing of bourgeois revolution Gramsci employs the concept 'passive revolution' in two closely related ways.[36] The term is used *first* to describe the transformation of society in a bourgeois direction without an upheaval like the French Revolution and without the active participation of the popular masses. In *Quaderno 4* he writes:[37]

Vincenzo Cuoco has called 'passive revolution' that which happened in Italy as a reaction to the Napoleonic wars. The concept of passive revolution seems to me exact not only for Italy, but for other countries which modernised the State by a series of reforms or national wars, without undergoing a political revolution of the radical Jacobin variety.

Similarly, when reviewing Croce's *History of Europe*, Gramsci uses 'passive revolution' (and also Quinet's expression 'restoration-revolution') to describe the period 1815-70. In those years, writes Gramsci,[38]

the demands which in France found a Jacobin-Napoleonic expression were satisfied in small doses, legally, in a reformist manner — in such a way that it was possible to preserve the political and economic position of the old feudal classes, to avoid agrarian reform, and, especially, to avoid the popular masses going through a period of political experience such as occurred in France in the years of Jacobinism, in 1831, and in 1848.

In the *second* place the term is used to signify a process of 'molecular' change by which *either* the bourgeoisie as a whole slowly exerts its supremacy with regard to the forces of the *ancien régime*, or a *section* of the bourgeoisie succeeds in grouping the whole of the rest of the class around it. Thus, in *Quaderno 15*, Gramsci describes how[39]

> under a fixed political canopy, social relations are necessarily modified and new effective political forces arise and develop. These indirectly exert their influence, by means of slow but inexorable pressure, on the official political forces which are themselves modified almost without being aware of it.

And again, this time with explicit reference to changes within the nationalist bourgeoisie:[40]

> One may also apply to the concept of passive revolution (documenting it from the Italian Risorgimento) the interpretative criterion of molecular changes which in fact progressively modify the pre-existing composition of forces, and hence become the matrix of new changes. Thus, in the Italian Risorgimento, it has been seen how the composition of the moderate forces was progressively modified by the passing over to Cavourism (after 1848) of ever new elements of the Action Party, so that on the one hand neo-Guelphism was liquidated, and on the other the Mazzinian movement was impoverished.

This second use of the term (to paraphrase drastically, passive revolution as molecular transformation) seems a particularly appropriate description of certain historical processes. It conveys well that gradual but remorseless fusion of aristocracy and bourgeoisie, with the eventual triumph of the latter, which is so frequent and fascinating a pattern in the era of bourgeois revolution.

Passive revolution would also seem an accurate description of certain dynamics of change within the bourgeoisie itself. Gramsci's subtle analysis of the way in which the Italian liberal Moderates absorbed the major elements of the radical Action Party (and were themselves changed in the process), is probably his greatest contribution to the history of the Risorgimento. In this context, as we shall see in a moment, the Gramscian concept of hegemony is also of fundamental importance.

However, to revert to the central problem, it is Gramsci's first, slightly different use of passive revolution (the transformation of

society in a bourgeois direction without violent upheaval and without
mass participation), that is relevant to the larger task of defining
bourgeois revolution. Here Gramsci's contribution seems a more dubious
one. In the *Prison Notebooks* Gramsci rarely employs the term 'bourgeois revolution'. In *Quaderno 19* he writes of 'the bourgeois revolution
in England which took place before that in France', clearly referring to
the moments of the English revolution of 1640 and the French Revolution of 1789.[41] But in general he seems to avoid the term, perhaps
because he found it unsatisfactory. However, his own adoption of
'passive revolution' to describe a broad period of history such as the
Risorgimento, does not help to dispel the confusion. Implicit in its
usage is the idea of bourgeois revolution taking place over a long period
of time, and of its being defined primarily as a *process*. Any attempt to
distinguish between process and moment tends to disappear, as does
any analysis of the relationship between the two.

On an historical level it is difficult to accept this vision of the era of
bourgeois revolution in Italy. The course of the Risorgimento (to
concentrate only on the central years of this era) was by no means as
'passive' as Gramsci implies. Certainly, no section of the Italian lower
classes went through a political experience comparable to that of the
Parisian *sans-culottes*. But the Risorgimento is rich in moments which
witnessed the intense participation of the artisans and urban poor of
the major Italian cities. In 1848, for instance, the urban lower classes
were the driving force behind the revolutions in Palermo, Milan and
Venice. As for the peasantry, the whole history of the South in the first
half of the nineteenth century is marked by their involvement in
recurring moments of revolution.[42]

Perhaps the term 'passive revolution' can be used to stress the failures of the Risorgimento, in the sense that the masses were excluded
from the political life of the new nation state and from any of the benefits deriving from its creation. But as a description of the *course* of the
Risorgimento it is inaccurate. Too many of the moments of revolution,
and of their actual class composition, come to be obscured.

In fact, Gramsci himself levels a somewhat similar criticism against
Croce, reproving him for beginning his *History of Europe* from the date
1815 and his *History of Italy* from 1871. In this way, argues Gramsci,
Croce tendentiously excludes 'the moment of struggle; the moment in
which the conflicting forces are formed, are assembled and take up
their positions; the moment in which one ethical-political system dis-
solves and another is formed by fire and steel'.[43] Here Gramsci reveals
unequivocally his awareness of the need to distinguish between process

and moment, and the impossibility of reducing bourgeois revolution simply to a process. However, nowhere in his work is there a systematic or coherent development of this problem. Had there been, Gramsci would perhaps have been forced to look again at his use of 'passive revolution'.

War of Position, War of Manoeuvre

At first sight, it may appear that Gramsci's use of the categories 'war of position' and 'war of manoeuvre' go some way to cover the lacunae outlined above. Quintin Hoare has briefly summarised the meaning of the two terms: '[war of position] is the form of political struggle which alone is possible in periods of relatively stable equilibrium between the fundamental classes, i.e., when frontal attack, or war of manoeuvre is impossible'.[44] And he goes on to quote the important passage from the *Prison Notebooks* where Gramsci asks the question:

> does there exist an absolute identity between war of position and passive revolution? Or at least does there exist, or can there be conceived, an entire historical period in which the two concepts must be considered identical — until the point at which the war of position once again becomes war of manoeuvre?[45]

Though Gramsci himself does not attempt a systematic application of this schema, it could be used to analyse the era of bourgeois revolution in Italy. The period 1815-48, for instance, could be termed a war of position, to be followed on a national scale by the war of manoeuvre of 1848-9. The disasters of the revolutionary biennium then led to a new war of position (perhaps also aptly termed passive revolution in Gramsci's second meaning of the term). In 1859 the cycle repeats itself, though this time the war of manoeuvre — laborious in the North, breathtaking in the South — is crowned with success.

However, while appropriate in some situations, a consistent use of these military analogies leaves more than a vague sense of dissatisfaction. The terms war of position/war of manoeuvre strongly imply the existence of armies and hierarchies of command. There is the danger of a quite false picture of bourgeois revolution emerging, with a bourgeois 'army' under the leadership of its most advanced sectors passing through alternate phases of war in its quest for final victory. A systematic use of this terminology could give the impression (quite historically mistaken) of a constantly class-conscious bourgeoisie planning its strategy for the seizure of power, and choosing its moment to move onto the offensive. The heroic figure of the 'revolutionary bourgeoisie', principal actor in a long-running historical drama on bourgeois revolution, here stages a comeback, disguised under a First World War greatcoat.

Hegemony

Of all the categories that Gramsci uses in the *Prison Notebooks* that of hegemony is undoubtedly the one that has most profoundly influenced Marxist historians. What he means by the term is clearly revealed in a passage from *Quaderno 19*, where he deals with the leadership question in the Risorgimento:

> the supremacy of a social group manifests itself in two ways, as 'domination' and as 'intellectual and moral leadership'. A social group dominates antagonistic groups, which it tends to 'liquidate', or to subjugate perhaps even by armed force; it leads kindred and allied groups. A social group can, and indeed must, already exercise 'leadership' before winning governmental power (this indeed is one of the principal conditions for the winning of such power); it subsequently becomes dominant when it exercises power, but even if it holds it firmly in its grasp, it must continue to 'lead' as well. The Moderates continued to lead the Action Party even after 1870 and 1876, and so-called 'transformism' was only the parliamentary expression of this action of intellectual, moral and political hegemony.[46]

In this extract Gramsci applies the term 'hegemony' to relations *within* the newly emergent Italian ruling class, to the function of control, absorption and leadership exercised by the liberal monarchists over the democrats of the Action Party. When 'hegemony' is linked with 'passive revolution' (understood as molecular transformation), then we are provided by Gramsci with an extremely valuable framework for analysing the formation of the Italian bourgeoisie. The constituent elements upon which the Moderates built their hegemony can be examined one by one: their solid class base in northern and central Italy, the shared interests of progressive aristocracy and bourgeoisie, the example of Cavour's Piedmont, the Moderates' profound ideological harmony with the dominant European values and attitudes of the time, the way in which they 'were a real, organic vanguard of the upper classes, to which economically they belonged'.[47]

The Action Party had no answers when faced with so coherent and cohesive an opponent. Gramsci concentrates most of his attention on the period after 1848, in which 'the Moderates formed a national bloc under their own hegemony — influencing the two supreme leaders of the Action Party, Mazzini and Garibaldi, in different ways and to a different extent'.[48] Certainly, the way in which Garibaldi 'fitted the boot of Italy' onto Victor Emmanuel's leg is the most striking example of the Moderates' devastating 'leadership' of the Action Party. But it is interesting to note that this hegemony existed strongly even at an earlier stage of the Risorgimento. In 1848 both Cattaneo in Milan and La Masa in Palermo led popular insurrections which gave them the possibility of undisputed power in the two cities. Neither of them felt able to proceed without invoking the aid of the Moderates, who rapidly reassumed control of the situation. La Masa gave way to Ruggero Settimo, Cattaneo to Casati.[49] In the spring of 1848 the democrats gained power through revolution, but it was the Moderates who exercised the real leadership.

Hegemony thus appears a key concept for analysing the leadership struggles *within* the Italian bourgeoisie. However, this is not Gramsci's only use of the term. Hegemony is also employed to denote the leadership (in the widest sense) by the bourgeoisie of other classes that lie below it. This is quite a different kettle of fish. Here what is implied is not just that one section of the ruling class exerts its hegemony over another, but that the dominant class *as a whole* 'leads' those classes which are by their very nature antagonistic to it. In the section 'Relations of force' Gramsci writes:

> It is true that the State is seen as the organ of one particular group, destined to create favourable conditions for the latter's maximum expansion. But the development and expansion of the particular group are conceived of, and presented, as being the motor force of a universal expansion, of a development of all the 'national energies'.[50]

The Italian Moderates in the nineteenth century were as unsuccessful in this task as they were successful in establishing their hegemony over the Action Party. Gramsci, with every justification, is quite explicit in this respect. The Moderates, based on the Piedmontese monarchist state and deriving their force from it, were one of those groups which 'have the function of "domination" without that of "leadership": dictatorship without hegemony'.[51]

The consequences of this failure were clear for all to see: the civil

war in the South between 1860-70, the narrow and corrupt nature of
Italian political life, the forced emigration of hundreds of thousands of
the peasantry, from both North and South; this was the tragic balance-
sheet of the Moderates' ill-contrived bourgeois revolution. Gramsci's
condemnation of the solution of 1860 rings out unambivalently: 'They
said that they were aiming at the creation of a modern State in Italy
and they in fact produced a bastard.'[52]

Could all this have been prevented or at least mitigated? Could the
bourgeoisie have established its hegemony instead of an outright and
uncompromising dominion? At the heart of any answer to these questions lies the agrarian problem. With nine-tenths of the population in
1860 living on the land, for the most part in abject poverty, any hegemonic aspirations on the part of the bourgeoisie had to come to terms
first and foremost with the rural masses. Gramsci had few doubts that
it was quite historically impossible for the Moderates to have acted in
any other way, to have established any relationship other than that
based on repression, on exploitation, on forced enrolment in the army.
Their attitudes were governed by the system of alliances they had
created, by an historic bloc whose material bases were in direct opposition to those of the peasantry: 'their [the Moderates] approach to
the national question required a bloc of all the right-wing forces —
including the classes of the great landowners — around Piedmont as a
State and as an army'.[53] And this bloc included not just the great
latifondisti but 'a special "rural bourgeoisie", embodiment of a para-
sitism bequeathed to modern times by the dissolution as a class of the
bourgeoisie of the Era of the Communes (the hundred cities, the cities
of silence)'.[54]

But if these considerations ruled out the Moderates, there remained
the other wing of the bourgeoisie, the Action Party. Their class base did
not tie them indissolubly to the landowners. Their strength lay in the
northern and central cities, where they succeeded at various stages in
the Risorgimento in establishing a real leadership over the artisans and
urban poor (the bases of which Gramsci does not examine and which,
as far as I know, have never been seriously studied by any historian).
Could the Action Party have established some sort of link with the
peasantry as well?

It is this question which runs like a tormented refrain right through
Gramsci's writing on the Risorgimento. At times he was quite categorical, stating that the interests of a section of the urban bourgeoisie
'should have been tied to those of the peasantry'; at times he was less
sure, writing that 'agrarian reform "could have" taken place because the

peasantry were nearly all the people and it was a strongly felt need'. At other moments he was still more cautious, maintaining only that 'an action on the peasantry was always possible'.[55] Behind all these remarks, and others like them, lay Gramsci's attempted analysis of the failure of the Action Party to construct a different bourgeois hegemony, a hegemony based on the popular masses and in contraposition to that of the Moderates, a hegemony which would have led to a less repressive, backward and undemocratic construction of the modern Italian nation state. And behind this lay a precise historical experience which Gramsci did not tire of citing; a bourgeois revolution in which, according to Gramsci, a section of the bourgeoisie had done exactly what the Action Party did not do. The wheel has come full circle, for Gramsci's model was the Jacobins in the French Revolution.

Jacobinism

Gramsci uses 'Jacobinism' in two senses. The first is a general one, as a method of describing those parties or individuals who display 'extreme energy, decisiveness and resolution'.[56] The second, which directly concerns us here, is historical and finds it most concise summary in his note on the problem of leadership in the Risorgimento:[57]

Without the agrarian policy of the Jacobins, Paris would have had the Vendée at its very doors ... Rural France accepted the hegemony of Paris; in other words, it understood that in order definitively to destroy the old regime it had to make a bloc with the most advanced elements of the Third Estate, and not with the Girondin moderates. If it is true that the Jacobins 'forced' its hand, it is also true that this always occurred in the direction of a real historical development. For not only did they organise a bourgeois government, i.e. make the bourgeoisie the dominant class – they did more. They created the bourgeois State, made the bourgeoisie into the leading, hegemonic class of the nation, in other words gave the new State a permanent basis and created the compact French nation.

These judgements are repeated incessantly. For Gramsci Jacobinism represented 'the union of city and countryside'; the Jacobins 'succeeded in crushing all the right-wing parties up to and including the Girondins on the terrain of the agrarian question'; they were successful 'not merely in preventing a rural coalition against Paris but in multiplying their supporters in the Provinces'; they were convinced of 'the absolute truth of their slogans about equality, fraternity and liberty,

and what is more important, the great popular masses whom the
Jacobins stirred up and drew into the struggle were also convinced of
their truth'.[58]

Gramsci's exaltation of the Jacobin experience must itself be considered on two levels — the first purely historical, the second more
general, concerned with the overall problem of alliances in a bourgeois
revolution.

On an historical level, Gramsci continues that long-lasting Marxist
tradition to which we referred earlier in this article. The tendency to
exaggerate the actual achievements of the French Revolution and
render mythical its principal heroes is not one he manages to avoid. In
this Gramsci follows Marx (the French Revolution 'destroyed large
landed property by dividing it up into smallholdings'[59]), but more
specifically Mathiez, whose three volumes on the Revolution were
amongst the books which he was allowed in prison.

Mathiez, whose academic love affair with Robespierre was never a
closely guarded secret, presents a riveting but idealised picture of the
brief period of Jacobin supremacy. With regard to the relationship
between the Jacobins and the peasantry, Mathiez writes that the
Montagnards 'understood especially the need to enlist the support of
the masses, giving them positive satisfaction in accordance with the plan
laid down by Robespierre'.[60] Mathiez then lists the first, decisive measures taken by the Jacobins: the law of 3 June 1793, establishing the
sale of emigré land in small plots; that of 10 June, regulating the division of village common land 'in accordance with a scrupulously lawful
method'; and the famous law of 17 July which abolished without
obligation all remaining feudal dues and rights in the French countryside. As a result, concludes Mathiez, 'the fall of the Girondins appeared
to the peasantry as the definitive liberation of the land'.

However, the picture of peasant consent constructed by Mathiez
and adopted by Gramsci seems no more than half the truth. The
Jacobin decrees favourably influenced the peasantry in some areas of
France, but their importance should not be exaggerated. Certain parts
of the countryside, particularly those near the borders, responded
enthusiastically to the demands of the *levée en masse* but others were
lukewarm if not overtly hostile. Nor can the peasant community, even
in a single area, be treated as a whole. If the *labourers* and the middle
peasantry stood to gain from the survival of the Republic, the landless
labourers, as Lefebvre has pointed out, were those who benefited least
from the legislation of the Revolution.[61]

Above all, the element of *coercion* (and not just 'decisiveness' or 'resolution') explicit in the Jacobin experience needs to be given its rightful place. The Jacobins succeeded in putting more than 700,000 men into the field in the space of a few months, they overcame the threat to the survival of the Republic, they ensured the bases of the modern French nation state. But all this was at a price. In the country-side they did not hesitate to use the instruments of the Terror if faced with opposition of any sort. Desertion and resistance to conscription were more frequent than Mathiez would have us believe. The need to feed the towns meant the forced requisitioning of entire rural areas; the *armées revolutionnaires*, composed in great part from the towns, sowed panic and despair among the rural communities on which they descended. Without wishing to simplify grossly a very complex situation, one fact seems quite clear. The Jacobins, to use Bouloiseau's expression, did all they could to 'seduce' rural France, but if rejected they did not hesitate to impose their will by force.[62] Thus the alliance between the Jacobins and the peasantry, presented by Gramsci primarily in hege-monic terms, as the 'union of city and countryside', was in reality a bond based as much on force as on consent.

This brings us on to the more general question of the nature of alliances in the epoch of bourgeois revolution. Perry Anderson's obser-vations in his recent article on Gramsci, though referring principally to bourgeois/proletarian relations in the contemporary Western state, seem relevant here as well. Anderson is at pains to stress the *combination* of 'leadership' and 'domination' which lies at the heart of bourgeois politi-cal power.[63] Bourgeois power cannot be based purely on hegemony because of the necessary antagonism between the bourgeoisie and the classes below it, necessary because it derives directly from different and conflicting positions in the capitalist mode of production.

Much the same applies to the bourgeois/peasant relationship in the period under discussion. This relationship can be one of pure domi-nance, as exercised by the Italian Moderates in the nineteenth century. But if the question is one of *alliance* rather than domination, then the admixture of coercion and consent typical of the Jacobin experience would seem a more accurate characterisation of the relationship than any consensual model based primarily on 'intellectual, moral and political leadership'.

We need to go further. There have been very few attempts to study the nature of alliances in bourgeois revolution. A number of elemen-tary questions come immediately to mind. It is imperative to establish not only which fractions of the bourgeoisie are or could be involved (and how far they were represented by political divisions like Girondins and Jacobins, Moderates and Action Party), but also *which fractions of the peasantry*. In his notes on the Risorgimento Gramsci devotes a few lines to the distinctions (or lack of them) between landless labourers and smallholders in the Italian peasantry.[64] But these insights are never developed with reference to the problem of alliances, in either the French or Italian cases.

Secondly, we need to try and establish *on what terms* any such alliance is made. Gramsci tackles this problem on a general level in his notes on Machiavelli:

> The fact of hegemony undoubtedly presupposes that the interests and tendencies of the groups over which hegemony is exercised will be taken into account. A certain equilibrium of compromise must be formed; in other words the leading group has to make sacrifices of an economic/corporative nature. But it is also beyond dispute that such compromise and such sacrifices cannot touch the essential. For if hegemony is ethico-political it cannot help but be economic as well, it cannot help but have its foundation in the decisive function that the leading group exercises in the decisive nucleus of economic activity.[65]

The question therefore arises of what 'sacrifices' the bourgeoisie (or a section of it) are willing or able to make in any given historical situation, while preserving their own supremacy in the economic field. Any alliance between bourgeois and peasant is thus bound to be unequal. The bourgeoisie may grant certain concessions or reforms, but any peasant demand which threatens its long-term economic dominance must be ruled out of court. The terrain for historic compromise exists, but within carefully stipulated limits.

Thirdly, we need to examine the *temporal* aspect of any alliance. Gramsci again offers a valuable guideline in his prison writing, where he notes that 'the peasant policy adopted by the French Jacobins was no more than an immediate political intuition'.[66] An alliance may be only short-term but of decisive importance if it coincides with, or is created during the *moment* of revolution. Indeed the connection between a successful if temporary bourgeois/peasant alliance and the survival of any given bourgeois revolution would seem a very strong one. It was not by chance that Gramsci concentrated so much of his attention on this question. As Walter Maturi has observed, the intervention of the peasant masses was for Gramsci what Hannibal's elephants were for the German High Command before the First World War.[67] Both seemed, in different ways, to be decisive instruments employed at the critical moment on the great battlefields of history.

The Agrarian Question in Italy

It is now possible, by way of a conclusion, to turn back to Gramsci's recurring question: in the Italian situation could the Action Party have made some sort of alliance with the peasantry? In trying to provide an answer, both the partial falseness of his Jacobin model and the elementary categories of alliance outlined above (with which section of the peasantry, on what terms, at what moment?) need to be borne in mind.

The debate surrounding this aspect of Gramsci's writing has been very considerable. It is dominated by Rosario Romeo's intervention and the reactions to it. The relevant section of Romeo's argument is that in which he attributes to Gramsci the thesis of the 'failed agrarian revolution' in Italy during the Risorgimento. Romeo, in the early pages of his critique of Gramsci, expresses profound scepticism as to 'a real possibility of an agrarian revolution'. A little later he writes that 'a peasant revolution, aimed at the conquest of the land' would have attacked inevitably the most advanced sectors of the agrarian economy 'especially in the north and centre of the peninsula' and would have imposed on Italian democracy 'a physiognomy of rural democracy'. In this way 'an agrarian revolution' would have 'protected the peasants from exploitation' and have prevented or retarded the original accumulation of capital in Italy.[68]

Apart from the fact that Romeo's account of the mechanics of accumulation has been very strongly contested by Gerschenkron,[69] the disturbing factor in his critique is his totally false insistence on 'agrarian revolution'. Gramsci insistently and consistently writes of agrarian *reform* not *revolution*, and always in the wider context of the 'decisive economic function' exercised by the bourgeoisie. Many Marxist historians have remarked on this point, none more clearly than Renato Zangheri:

I cannot find in Gramsci any prediction that this process (of capitalist transformation in the countryside) would have developed in the direction of a rural democracy as Romeo suggests. Romeo confuses agrarian reform with the creation of peasant property, which is only one particular form of it; while it is by no means certain that the laws of capitalism, as they became more widely operative in the countryside, would have refrained from subjugating new peasant property to the normal capitalist process of differentiation and 'selection'.[70]

Romeo's references to the likely destruction of the most advanced sectors of the agrarian economy in the north and centre seem equally wide of the mark. The idea that Gramsci was suggesting the break-up of the large landed estates of the Po valley seems about as likely as his advocacy of the re-introduction of the guilds. The problem for Gramsci was not one of trying to turn back the capitalist clock. It was rather to examine the possible historical alternatives to the Moderates' immobile and in many ways catastrophic solution to the peasant question.

To deal satisfactorily with this problem would demand a full-scale study quite beyond the scope of this article. It would be necessary not only to examine in detail agrarian conditions throughout the peninsula (on which much valuable work has been done), but also to relate these conditions to specific political situations (and this has been much less frequently attempted).[71] Here it is only possible to give one or two tentative indications.

Gramsci, towards the end of his section on the city-countryside relationship during the Risorgimento, sketched the beginnings of an answer to the question he had posed. He realised the importance of looking at different sectors of the peninsula and divided them up as follows: the northern urban force, followed by the rural forces of the southern mainland, the North and centre, Sicily and finally Sardinia. Then, in one of his most provocative analogies, he suggested a way to examine the connection between them: 'the first of these forces (the northern urban force) retains its function of "locomotive" in any case; what is needed, therefore, is an examination of the various "most advantageous" combinations for building a "train" to move forward through history as fast as possible.'[72]

Gramsci's own analysis of these possible 'combinations' did not, for obvious reasons, get very far. Nor did he deal with the very real problem of the internal class divisions *within* the various sectors that he had outlined. However, it is possible to identify at least two moments of bourgeois revolution when the 'locomotive' of the northern urban force (or at least a section of it) was presented with a real opportunity of combining with the countryside in a decisive fashion. The account that follows is of necessity simplified but not, I hope, entirely distorted.

The first occasion was in the spring of 1848. The temporary weakness of Austria, the successful insurrections in Milan and Venice, and the sympathy with which the revolution was initially viewed in the Lombardo-Venetian countryside, all created the conditions for a successful 'national-popular' alliance at a turning point in the history of the Risorgimento. Two factors deserve particular attention. The international situation, determined by the revolutions of Paris, Vienna and Budapest, was uniquely favourable to such a development. And, for the only time in nineteenth-century Italy, the strongest ideological influence in the countryside — the network of parish priests — was sympathetic to the national cause. Gramsci himself, so attentive to the cultural elements in any successful alliance, did not let this point slip by. Indeed, in his section on the origins of the Risorgimento he goes as far as to say that Pius IX's espousal of Catholic liberalism (for however short a period) can be considered 'the political masterpiece of the Risorgimento'.[73] At the time, this masterpiece was not valued at its true worth.

It is important to stress that the *sort* of alliance feasible in the North in 1848 was not one which could have called into question (let alone reversed) the basic lines of development of northern agriculture. If agrarian reform meant anything in the North, it was an amelioration of agrarian contracts for at least part of the peasantry, and measures to combat the chronic pauperism of the *braccianti* of the Po Valley. Thus of Gramsci's multiple formulations of the Action Party/peasant relationship, that which refers to an action 'on' the peasantry is probably the most appropriate in this context. In the Veneto, Manin's abolition of the personal tax and reduction of the salt tax were steps in the right direction, but insufficient by themselves. The democrats of Milan and Venice failed to evolve a strategy, based on limited material concessions, to utilise peasant enthusiasm at this critical moment. They would have had the great advantage of building on the basis of a belief in a Holy War against the Austrians. But in the rural areas they never acted in any planned, let alone 'Jacobin' manner. As a result, the myth of Radetzky soon replaced that of Pio Nono.[74]

A second moment of possible convergence was in the South in 1860. Gramsci himself noted the need to study the 'political conduct of the Garibaldini in Sicily'.[75] Here too the 'northern urban force' can be called the locomotive because Garibaldi's Thousand were for the most part radicals and democrats, artisans and students from the northern Italian cities. The agrarian situation in Sicily and on the southern mainland was in striking contrast to that of the North. The hidebound and parasitic class of *latifondisti*, replenished in the nineteenth century by a new wave of bourgeois landowners, had taken every opportunity of usurping the common land of the villages and reducing the peasantry of the inland areas to a state of absolute deprivation and almost permanent revolt. In 1841 the Bourbon Ferdinand II had passed a law promising the peasantry at least one-fifth of any land where they could establish a custom of ancestral usage, in return for their abandonment of 'promiscuous rights', such as grazing, the collecting of wood, etc. The peasantry were forcibly excluded from exercising these rights, but very little land came their way.[76]

Agrarian reform in the South therefore meant something quite different from that in the North. It meant, as Candeloro has argued, an effective splitting up of the demesne land promised to the peasantry from the time of Zurlo onwards, and an equitable division of the vast ecclesiastical estates that came onto the agrarian market in the wake of Garibaldi's successful expedition. Only in this way could the savage divide between landlord and destitute sharecropper have been overcome by the formation of a stratum of peasant proprietors. Certainly the idea of a 'rural democracy' in the South seems entirely improbable. Not all the peasantry could have gained land and many of those who might have received holdings would soon have sold them again in the face of mounting debt and the absence of capital. But the peasant community none the less could have become more stratified, as landholding extended further down the rural social ladder. Such a solution, to quote Candeloro again, was one 'which would have generated new contrasts and social differentiations, but which would undoubtedly have been more dynamic and progressive in terms of the general development of the country than that which in fact established itself in 1860'.[77]

Garibaldi at first seemed intent on carrying out a reform of this sort. His proclamation of 2 June 1860 promised the peasants 'an equitable division of the land, as well as the abolition of the food excise and the grist tax'.[78] At the same time spontaneous peasant insurrection had resulted in the breakdown of Bourbon local government and contributed significantly to the early successes of the Garibaldini. Yet an alliance was never forged between the two sides. Garibaldi and his officers put the national war effort before all else, and decided that the support of the local landowners was a more effective weapon for conscription than a programme of social reform. Outright coercion rapidly took the place of initial peasant consent and enthusiasm. At Bronte, to the west of Mount Etna, an exasperated peasantry, having waited in vain for the implementation of reform, rose up and slaughtered the local notables. Nino Bixio, despatched by Garibaldi to put down the rising, executed five of the villagers, including the radical lawyer Lombardo who had tried to enforce the just division of the demesne land. The events at Bronte signalled the end of all hopes of a different solution to the agrarian question in the South.[79]

Thus on at least two occasions of great importance the Action Party failed to link with the peasantry and effectively challenge the Moderates' strategy of bourgeois revolution. Many of the reasons for this failure have already become apparent. Others appear with regularity in Gramsci's writing: Mazzini's notions of religious reform and his lack of attention to social problems; the Action Party's fears, shared with the Moderates, of stirring up class warfare (and in this respect the Jacobin experience and 1848 in Paris were for them negative models); Austrian threats to use the peasantry, as at Cracow in 1846, against liberal and nationalist landowners; an international climate that was unfavourable, especially after 1848, to any other than a moderate solution to the Italian question. To these must be added the Action Party leaders' profound ignorance of the problems of the peasantry. Coming from urban backgrounds, living a great part of their active political life in exile, the historic figures of the democratic wing of the Italian bourgeoisie were quite unprepared for those dramatic moments in the history of the Risorgimento in which they were called upon to formulate agrarian policy.

The importance of their failures cannot be under-estimated. Here the connection between process and moment, a connection founded centrally on the agrarian question, reappears with great clarity. The shortcomings of Cattaneo, Mazzini and Manin in northern Italy in the spring of 1848 were the starting point for that decomposition of the democrats which Gramsci describes so well. Bourgeois democratic principles were henceforth always to be subordinate to the somewhat different political programme of Camillo Cavour. As for the South in 1860, the limited horizons of the Garibaldini meant that the strident problems of the *Mezzogiorno* received a purely repressive solution at the supreme moment of bourgeois revolution in Italy. The historic backwardness of the South became a permanent feature of the new nation state, decisively influencing the whole process of Italian economic and political development.

Notes

1. A. Cobban, 'The myth of the French Revolution', in Cobban (ed.), *Aspects of the French Revolution* (London, 1968), p. 106.
2. G.V. Taylor, 'Non-capitalist wealth and the origins of the French Revolution', *American Historical Review*, vol. 72 (1967) p. 496.

3. R. Zapperi, *Per la critica del concetto della rivoluzione borghese* (Bari, 1974), pp. 13, 83, 91.

4. A. Soboul, *The French Revolution, 1787-1799* (London, 1974). For a summary of recent Marxist writing on the French Revolution, centring on the figure of Soboul, see G. Ellis, 'The "Marxist interpretation" of the French Revolution', *The English Historical Review*, vol. 93 (1978) pp. 353-76.

5. *Manifesto of the Communist Party*, in K. Marx, *The Revolution of 1848*, ed. D. Fernbach (London, 1973), p. 72.

6. J. Jaurès, *Histoire socialiste de la Révolution française*, vol. 1 (Paris, 1901), p. 70.

6a. In a later formulation of the problem, Marx himself writes of 'a period [or 'epoch' in some translations] of social revolution', engendered by the conflict between the material forces of production on the one hand, and the existing relations of production on the other; see Marx's 'Preface' to *A Contribution to the Critique of Political Economy* (Chicago, 1904), p. 12.

7. See R. Price, *The Economic Modernisation of France* (London, 1975), Introduction and p. 225; and, more guardedly, T. Kemp, *Economic Forces in French History* (London, 1971), pp. 200-4 and 217-18. D. Richet places the decisive transformation 'in the second half of the XIXth century'; 'Autour des origines idéologiques lointaines de la Révolution française', *Annales, économies, sociétés, civilisations*, vol. 24 (1969) p. 22. But see also R. Robin's criticisms of Richet's account of the transition to capitalism, and a suggested periodisation, in 'La natura dello stato alla fine dell'Ancien Regime: formazione sociale, Stato e transizione', *Studi Storici*, yr. 14 (1973) pp. 645-6 and 653-4.

8. G. Therborn, 'The rule of Capital and the rise of Democracy', *New Left Review*, no. 103 (1977) p. 4.

9. A. Gramsci, *Selections from the Prison Notebooks*, eds. Q. Hoare and D. Nowell-Smith (London, 1971), p. 179. Reference is made wherever possible to this English selection (hereafter *PN*). Where no English translation exists, the reader is referred either to the complete critical edition of the *Quaderni del carcere*, ed. V. Gerratana (Torino, 1975: hereafter *Ec*); or to C. Vivanti's amply annotated edition of one of these notebooks, *Quaderno 19, Risorgimento italiano* (Torino, 1977: hereafter *Q 19*).

10. Marx, *Manifesto*, p. 69.

11. G. Candeloro, *Storia dell'Italia moderna*, vol. 1 (Milano, 1956), p. 16. See also S. Soldani, 'Risorgimento', in *Il Mondo contemporaneo. Storia d'Italia*, eds. F. Levi, U. Levra, N. Tranfaglia, vol. 3 (Firenze, 1978), p. 1159, where the Risorgimento is described as 'a decisive stage in the development and affirmation of the bourgeois revolution in the peninsula'. I too plead guilty to using the term bourgeois revolution in this way in my *Daniele Manin e la rivoluzione veneziana del 1848-49* (Milano, 1978).

12. V.I. Lenin, ' "Riforma contadina" e rivoluzione proletaria-contadina' (19 Marzo 1911), in *Opere complete*, vol. 17 (Roma, 1966), pp. 107 and 112.

13. K. Marx, 'The bourgeoisie and the counter-revolution' (*Neue Rheinische Zeitung*, 15 December 1848), in *The Revolutions of 1848*, pp. 192-3.

14. Isaac Deutscher makes this point clearly in his *The Unfinished Revolution, Russia 1917-67* (London, 1967), p. 22.

15. 'Does the concept of bourgeois revolution not imply perhaps that only the bourgeoisie can accomplish it? The Mensheviks often err towards this point of view. But such an opinion is a caricature of Marxism. Bourgeois in its economic and social content, the liberation movement need not be so with regard to its driving forces. These can be not the bourgeoisie, but the proletariat and the peasantry'; V.I. Lenin, 'La questione agraria e le forze della rivoluzione' (1 April 1907), *Opere complete*, vol. 12 (Roma, 1965), pp. 304-5.

16. Therborn, 'The rule of Capital and the rise of Democracy', p. 17.

17. It is perhaps worth adding that Therborn's definition of bourgeois democracy seems deficient with respect to the question of civil liberties. The right of assembly and the freedom of the press would appear as intrinsic a part of bourgeois democracy as the right to vote. The struggle for their implementation forms a central and recurrent theme in the bourgeois revolutions of the nineteenth century. Indeed, for the Russian Marxist dissident Leonid Pliusc, civil liberties *are* the bourgeois revolution. Intentionally standing Marxism on its head, Pliusc declared in December 1977 that in order to establish civil liberties, Russia, 'having made the socialist revolution, has now to make the bourgeois one'; *Il Manifesto*, 12 Nov. 1977. More polemic than serious attempt at definition, Pliusc's remark nevertheless provides food for thought.

18. F. Engels, introduction to *Socialism, Utopian and Scientific* (London, 1892), pp. xxi-xxx.

19. P. Anderson, *Passages from Antiquity to Feudalism* (London, 1974), p. 9: 'Marx and Engels themselves can never be taken simply at their word: the errors of their writings on the past should not be evaded or ignored, but identified and criticized. To do so is not to depart from historical materialism, but to rejoin it.'

20. Engels, introduction to *Socialism, Utopian and Scientific*, p. xxviii; Marx, *The Eighteenth Brumaire of Louis Bonaparte*, in *Surveys from Exile*, ed. D. Fernbach (London, 1973), p. 147. For a useful introduction to Marx's writing on the French Revolution, see J. Bruhat, 'La Révolution française et la formation de la pensée de Marx', *Annales historiques de la Révolution française*, yr. 38 (1966) pp. 125-70.

21. Soboul, *The French Revolution, 1787-1799*, p. 5.

22. P. Anderson, *Lineages of the Absolutist State* (London, 1974), p. 431.

22a. Unfortunately, the brief but provocative remarks of N. Poulantzas in the chapter 'Sur les modèles de la révolution bourgeoise' in his *Pouvoir politique et classes sociales*, Paris, 1971, vol. 1, pp. 178-95, were brought to my attention too late to incorporate in this article. Poulantzas tries to compare the British, French and German experiences.

23. Barrington Moore Jr., *The Social Origins of Dictatorship and Democracy* (Boston, 1966); V.I. Lenin, 'Il programma agrario della socialdemocrazia' (Nov.-Dec. 1907), *Opere complete*, vol. 13 (Roma, 1965), pp. 400-1. Some very general remarks on what the author calls the 'revolutions of the liberal-bourgeois period' are to be found in E.J. Hobsbawm, 'La Rivoluzione', *Studi Storici*, yr. 17 (1976) pp. 32-3.

24. M. Dobb, *Studies in the Development of Capitalism* (London, 1963), pp. 11-12.

25. See G. Candeloro, *Storia dell'Italia moderna*, vol. 1, pp. 48-63.

26. Central to this question is the work of S. Merli, *Proletariato di fabbrica e capitalismo industriale. Il caso italiano: 1880-1900*, 2 vols. (Firenze 1972-3). Merli argues against those Marxist and bourgeois historians who have placed Italy's industrial revolution *after* 1896. According to Merli, such a periodisation ignores the fact that by the end of the nineteenth century 'the working class has already discovered the political party, trade union and sectional organisation is already at a high level of development, the Italian proletariat has already undergone a social, political and human experience that has made it emerge from prehistory and has formed it as an alternative class' (vol. 1, p. 33).

27. Speech to the Prima Conferenza femminile del PCI, Rome, 2-5 June 1945, quoted in G. Quazza, *Resistenza e Storia d'Italia* (Milano, 1976), p. 170.

28. Ibid., p. 181.

29. From his 'Rapporto ai quadri dell'organizzazione comunista napoletana, 11 aprile 1944', now in G. Manacorda (ed.), *Il Socialismo nelia storia d'Italia* (Bari, 1966), p. 747. It is interesting (and sad) to,note Togliatti's rather different judgement of these figures during the 'social-fascist' period of world Communism.

In an article of 1931 he wrote: 'Its [the Risorgimento's] heroes are mediocre figures of provincial politicians, court intriguers, intellectuals behind their times, oleographic men of arms . . . it is absurd to think that there is a "Risorgimento" to take up again, to finish, to carry through afresh, and that this is the task of democratic anti-fascism'; P. Togliatti, 'Sul movimento di Giustizia e Libertà', in *Opere*, vol. 3, pt. 1 (Roma, 1973), p. 418. This contrast was brought to my attention by the outstanding article of C. Pavone, 'Le idee della Resistenza: antifascisti e fascisti di fronte alle tradizione del Risorgimento', *Passato e Presente*, no. 7 (1959) pp. 850-918.

30. Nassau Senior, *Conversations with M. Thiers, M. Guizot, and Other Distinguished Persons during the Second Empire*, vol. 2 (London, 1878), p. 127.

31. A. Soboul, 'Risorgimento e rivoluzione borghese: schema di una direttiva di ricerca', in Istituto A. Gramsci, *Problemi dell'Unità d'Italia. Atti del II Convegno di studi gramsciani tenuto a Roma, 19-21 marzo 1960* (Roma, 1962), p. 814.

32. In order not to clash with John Davis's essay, I have intentionally avoided as far as possible a discussion of the city-countryside relationship in Gramsci's writing.

33. Istituto A. Gramsci, *Studi Gramsciani. Atti del Convegno tenuto a Roma 11-12 gennaio 1958* (Roma, 1958); Istituto A. Gramsci, *Problemi dell'Unità d'Italia*; Istituto A. Gramsci, *Politica e storia in Gramsci. Atti del Convegno internazionale di studi Gramsciani, Firenze 9-11 dicembre 1977*, vol. 1, *Relazioni a stampa* (Roma, 1977).

34. Romeo's two essays are published in his *Risorgimento e Capitalismo* (Bari, 1959). See also F. Chabod, 'Croce storico', *Rivista Storica Italiana*, vol. 64 (1952) p. 521; and the remarks of Croce in *Quaderni della Critica*, vol. 15 (1949) p. 112.

35. The latest example of this attitude is C. Vivanti's introduction and notes to *Quaderno 19*. Although informative his comments are intentionally acritical.

36. See Quintin Hoare's useful summary in *PN*, p. 46.

37. *Ec*, p. 504.

38. *PN*, p. 119.

39. *Ec*, pp. 1818-19.

40. *PN*, p. 109.

41. Ibid., p. 83.

42. For the most important of these moments, that of 1860, see below.

43. *PN*, p. 119.

44. Ibid., p. 206. Gramsci's other use of the terms, to differentiate between the strategy of the working-class movement in the West and the East, does not concern us here.

45. *PN*, p. 108.

46. Ibid., pp. 57-8.

47. Ibid., p. 60.

48. Ibid., p. 76.

49. G. La Masa, *Documenti della rivoluzione siciliana del 1847-9*, vol. 1 (Torino, 1850), p. 75; C. Cattaneo, *Dell'insurrezione di Milano e della successiva guerra* (Lugano, 1849), chap. 5.

50. *PN*, p. 182.

51. Ibid., p. 106.

52. Ibid., p. 90.

53. Ibid., p. 100.

54. *Ec*, p. 2045.

55. For the first of these formulations, *Ec*, p. 1930, but note the square brackets around the words *avrebbero dovuto essere legati* indicating that they are a later addition by Gramsci; for the second, *Q 19*, pp. 44-5; for the third, *PN*, p. 82, where Gramsci's *'azione sui contadini'* is translated as 'action directed at the peasantry'.

56. *PN*, p. 66.

57. Ibid., p. 79.

58. The four quotations cited are respectively from *Ec*, p. 961; *PN*, p. 102; ibid.; and *PN*, p. 78.

59. 'Review of M. Guizot's book on the English Revolution', in K. Marx, *Surveys from Exile*, p. 254.

60. A. Mathiez, *La Rivoluzione francese* vol. 3 (Milano, 1933), p. 17. This is the edition which Gramsci used in prison. For the Jacobin laws of 1793, see pp. 17-18.

61. See G. Lefebvre, 'La Révolution française et les paysans' in *Etudes sur la Révolution française* (Paris, 1954), p. 268.

62. M. Bouloiseau, *La Francia rivoluzionaria. La Repubblica Giacobina, 1792-1794* (Bari, 1975), p. 203. (Original French title, *La République jacobine, 10 août 1792-9 thermidor an II* (Paris, 1972).

63. P. Anderson, 'The antinomies of Antonio Gramsci', *New Left Review*, no. 100 (1976) pp. 42-4.

64. *PN*, pp. 75-6.

65. *Ec*, p. 1591.

66. Ibid., p. 962.

67. W. Maturi, *Interpretazioni del Risorgimento* (Torino, 1962), p. 624.

68. R. Romeo, *Risorgimento e capitalismo* (Bari, 1974: 1st edn. 1959), pp. 23-9. I realise that my piecemeal quotation of Romeo is an unsatisfactory procedure, but there is no single extract from these pages that summarises his position adequately. I have tried my best not to distort his argument in any way.

69. A. Gerschenkron, 'Rosario Romeo and the original accumulation of capital' in Gerschenkron (ed.), *Economic Backwardness in Historical Perspective* (Cambridge, Mass., 1962), pp. 90-118. See also their debate and attempted reconciliation at Rome in July 1960, now published as 'Consensi, dissensi, ipotesi in un dibattito Gerschenkron-Romeo', in *La formazione dell'Italia industriale*, ed. A. Caracciolo (Bari, 1969), pp. 53-81. Gerschenkron (p. 65) shows as little understanding as Romeo of what Gramsci was saying.

70. R. Zangheri, 'La mancata rivoluzione agraria nel Risorgimento e i problemi economici dell'Unità, in Istituto A. Gramsci, *Studi Gramsciani*, p. 375. See also the acute critiques of G. Candeloro, 'Intervento', in Istituto A. Gramsci, *Studi Gramsciani*, pp. 515-23 and L. Cafagna, 'Intorno al "revisionismo risorgimentale" ', *Società*, yr. 12 (1956) pp. 1015-35.

71. Amongst the fundamental recent works on Italian agrarian conditions are: M. Romani, *L'Agricoltura in Lombardia dal periodo delle riforme al 1859. Struttura, organizzazione sociale e tecnica* (Milano, 1957); R. Villari, *Mezzogiorno e contadini nell'età moderna* (Bari, 1961); P. Villani, *Mezzogiorno tra riforme e rivoluzione* (Bari, 1962); M. Berengo, *L'Agricoltura veneta dalla caduta della Repubblica all'Unità*, (Milano, 1963); C. Poni, *Gli aratri e l'economia agraria nel Bolognese dal XVII al XIX secolo* (Bologna, 1963); C. Pazzagli, *L'Agricoltura toscana nella prima metà dell'800. Tecniche produttive e rapporti mezzadrili* (Firenze, 1973); G. Giogetti, *Contadini e proprietari nell'Italia moderna. Rapporti di produzione e contratti agrari dal secolo XVI a oggi* (Torino, 1974).

72. *PN*, p. 98.

73. *Q 19*, p. 19. Note also Gramsci's observation, taken from Momigliano, that Italian national consciousness could be formed only by overcoming two other 'cultural forms': municipal particularism and Catholic cosmopolitanism; *Ec*, p. 1801.

74. F. Della Peruta, 'I contadini nella rivoluzione lombarda del 1848', in Della Peruta, *Democrazia e socialismo nel Risorgimento* (Roma, 1965), pp. 59-108. Ginsborg, *Daniele Manin e la rivoluzione veneziana*, chaps. 3-6.

75. *PN*, p. 101.

76. D. Mack Smith, 'The Latifundia in modern Sicilian history', *Proceedings of the British Academy*, vol. 51 (1965) pp. 95-7. On p. 96, n. 1 he writes: 'It was roughly calculated by A. Battaglia in 1907 that if only this "fifth part" had been in fact distributed as the law of 1841 prescribed, there would have been land to settle 700,000 peasants'. See also the excellent chapter entitled 'Linee di sviluppo dei contratti nelle regioni del latifondo' in G. Giogetti, *Contadini e proprietari nell'Italia moderna*, pp. 200-77.

77. G. Candeloro, *Storia dell'Italia moderna*, vol. 5 (Milano, 1968), p. 50.

78. D. Mack Smith, 'The peasants' revolt in Sicily, 1860', in *Victor Emanuel, Cavour and the Risorgimento* (London, 1971), pp. 198-9. The demesne lands due to the peasantry were to be split up by lottery, and plots to be reserved for those fighting in the war of liberation. See also the detailed study by S.F. Romano, *Momenti del Risorgimento in Sicilia* (Messina, 1952), pt. 3, pp. 111-268.

79. D. Mack Smith, 'The peasants' revolt', pp. 212-14.

3 THE SOUTH, THE RISORGIMENTO AND THE ORIGINS OF THE 'SOUTHERN PROBLEM'

John A. Davis

Gramsci's most comprehensive analysis of the significance of the South in Italy's economic and political development since unification is to be found in the *Prison Notebooks*, and yet it was a problem which had attracted his attention long before this. At the Socialist Party Congress of 1921, which saw the birth of the Italian Communist Party, Gramsci had declared that the South constituted 'the central problem of our national life'.[1] In the highly concentrated essay on 'The Southern Problem', which was unfinished at the time of his arrest, Gramsci made his first systematic attempt to set the problem of the South in the context of Italy's political development, and to analyse in particular the social basis of the southern agrarian 'bloc'. In the *Prison Notebooks* the South becomes not only the central feature of national life after unification, but also a central feature in the making of the national revolution.

As a Sardinian, Gramsci's concern for the South is easily explicable. But behind this concern also lay over half a century of debate, investigation and polemic on the conditions of the South in the national state and their causes — a debate which had been accompanied by some of the finest examples of economic and sociological investigation of the period. It was on this vast, and often impressive, body of literature and research that Gramsci was able to draw as he developed his own analysis of the origins and development of the Southern Problem. Like Gaetano Salvemini and others before him, he saw in the alliance between the industrialists of the North and the reactionary landowning classes of the South the fulcrum of the Italian political system. But while it was the industrial and agricultural protective tariffs of the 1880s which had given fullest expression to this alliance, Gramsci saw its origins in the earlier absorption of the southern liberals into the hegemonic programme of the Cavourian moderates. The dominant political structure of the unified state was therefore 'organically' related to the relationship between the dominant social forces which had brought about the national revolution. The Southern Problem was not a casual consequence of unification, but was rather inherent in the 'passive revolution' from which unification resulted.[2]

In many respects Gramsci's analysis of the origins of the Southern Problem is very persuasive. The emphasis, for example, on the weaker position of the South with respect to the North, and hence on its relative backwardness, even before unification, is an important corrective to the simplistic notion that the poverty of the South resulted solely from unification. Also, the emphasis on the passivity of the political contribution of the southern liberals during the Risorgimento would seem apt, even if one might wish to give this an interpretation which differs slightly from Gramsci's. Similarly, Gramsci's observations on the peculiarities of the Southern social structure provide the essential starting point for any further research.

But Gramsci's analysis of the origins of the Southern Problem and of the relations between North and South during the Risorgimento also raises certain important problems. It was, of course, primarily with the forces of political and ideological attraction that he was concerned. But underlying these he also saw a parallel and necessary process of economic attraction and subordination. There was, he claimed, '[d]uring the Risorgimento . . . embryonically the historical relationship between North and South similar to that between a great city and a great rural area', and there was 'ever since 1815 . . . a relatively homogenous politico-economic structure' between the two parts of the peninsula.[3] The political and economic forces of attraction combined to form, in Gramsci's analogy, a locomotive and its wagons, so that the collapse of the Bourbon dynasty in the South in the face of Garibaldi and his volunteers in 1860 was an almost mechanical sequel to Cavour's victories of the previous year.

It is precisely this economic parallelism which we wish to question in the following pages. Not only does the interpretation of the economic relations between North and South in terms of the relationship between city and countryside give rise to a number of empirical difficulties, but the implication that the two parts of the peninsula formed a complementary economic system even before unification would seem to beg important questions on the origins of the Southern Problem. We shall argue, in fact, that Gramsci's search for the origins of the national political elite led him to project backwards a unity of political purpose and economic logic which may distort and even over-simplify the economic and political forces which drew the South into the national state. His emphasis on the spontaneous and complementary attraction between the two regions, in particular, might lead one to overlook the widespread economic and social crisis which was evident in the South both before and after unification. And what was hinted at by the flight of the ruler whom Garibaldi contemptuously described as 'that poor little devil Francis' was soon to be demonstrated more fully by the chaos and confusion which followed unification, and by the four long years of tortured civil war in the southern provinces. The involvement of the South in national unification and the origins of the Southern Problem cannot be seen apart from this evidence of widespread crisis and collapse.

It is in the origins and nature of this crisis in southern society that an explanation of the forces which drew the Mezzogiorno and Sicily into the national movement can be found. The complex and contradictory pressures which accompanied this crisis reveal not only the undoubtedly 'passive' nature of the political revolution in the South, but also that the economic experiences of the two parts of the Italian peninsula in the century before unification were very different and distinct. The origins of the 'Southern Problem' were, then, perhaps more complex than Gramsci's interpretation allows.

Like Gramsci, most recent historians of the social and economic development of the South have tended to concentrate on the problem of the southern agrarian bourgeoisie. The emergence of a new rural bourgeoisie has been traced from the first opportunities for the introduction of more commercially orientated and emancipated forms of agricultural organisation in the eighteenth century. Increasing demand for foodstuffs and raw materials generated by population growth and economic expansion in Northern Europe brought about a steady upswing in prices, exports and production in the Italian South in the first two-thirds of the century. This buoyant market fell away in the last decades of the century, but, it is argued, had been sufficient to create a new social force whose voice can be heard behind the growing clamour for reform, culminating in the premature Jacobin Republic of 1799. The great step forward came with the occupation of the mainland in 1805 and its inclusion in the Napoleonic Empire. In 1805 Joseph Bonaparte declared feudalism abolished, and the consolidation of the new rural bourgeoisie went ahead apace. Estate bailiffs, small provincial merchants, wealthier peasants and others were able to take advantage of the emancipation of the land market to become landowners. Those parts of the former feudal estates which had been subject to common rights of pasture, wood-gathering and so forth, were expropriated and destined for division amongst the destitute landless peasantry. In practice, the new capitalist farmers were more often the beneficiaries of such divisions, hence the growing tension in social relations in the countryside. Under the Restoration this new class continued to expand, it is argued, although increasingly coming into conflict with the archaic and immobile structure of the Bourbon state, its restrictions on free trade, its obscurantism, clericalism and opposition to the circulation of ideas and political democracy.[4]

What this implies is that the South, before unification, was experiencing a process similar, albeit more limited and chronologically unsynchronised, to that which was occurring in the North. The gap between the two should not be under-estimated, for the southern bourgeoisie was only just and more tentatively beginning to set out on the path that the Jacinis, the Cavours, the Ricasolis and so many others in the North had been following for over a century. But despite the distance of achievement which separated the two, they were moving in the same direction and were pioneering and establishing the same process – the introduction of an agriculture organised on capitalist lines.

The relative weakness of the southern bourgeoisie and the limitations of its development in the period has also been emphasised. In his study of Sicily, Romeo concludes that despite the gradual process of land redistribution which took place on the perimeters of the latifundia economy, the changes in the early nineteenth century 'did not substantially change the character of Sicilian society, which remained much as it had been in the 18th Century'.[5] Villani has also stressed the weaknesses and limitations of the mainland bourgeoisie:

> . . . the fact that it was created and grew up in the shadow of the feudal system, the fact that it received its inheritance from the feudal class without any dramatic struggles, tended to limit its drive and prevented it becoming a fully 'hegemonic' class capable of providing or even imposing a programme of rapid and soundly based economic growth.[6]

Despite these weaknesses and limitations, however, the new bourgeoisie remains the focus of attention. Its establishment upsets traditional social relations, and in particular leads to the disappearance of the lands on which the common rights which played such a fundamental role in the subsistence peasant economy were located. The growing violence and disorder in the countryside which followed served to increase the timidity and conservatism of the new capitalist farmers. Although arguing from different positions, both Romeo and Villani place the responsibility for the failings and limitations of the southern Risorgimento on the weaknesses and inadequacies of the new rural bourgeoisie. As another Italian economic historian has put it, the South suffered from both too much and too little capitalism.[7]

The emphasis on the weakness of the new social forces in the South would certainly seem right, and bears out Gramsci's own insistence on the relative weakness of the southern bourgeoisie. But the sense in which this bourgeoisie was in fact 'new' is less clear. Nor is it necessarily very helpful to couple the emphasis on the limitations of the agrarian bourgeoisie with the rather elusive notion that they formed a 'rising' social class. As in other 'rising gentry' debates, the room for semantic muddle and woolliness is ample, and it is essential to define the terms carefully. If, as would seem to be implicit, the term 'rural bourgeoisie' means a new and vital class which was engaged in introducing and establishing new methods and new relations of production in the feudal or semi-feudal agrarian structure of the South, then this would seem to bear very little relation to the economic realities of the southern countryside in the early nineteenth century. Had such a class been present, the subsequent failure of the South to develop along lines comparable with the North would be the more difficult to explain, as would the conservative and even reactionary contribution of the South to the national political structure after 1860. As an abstraction, it also encourages some rather circular explanations of southern backwardness; the continuation of archaic systems of social relations in the South, of backward economic and political organisation, are blamed on a weak agrarian bourgeoisie which held back from doing away with them. But if that was the case, then it is not clear in what sense this 'new' class was a capitalist class at all — and if it was not, as Gramsci would undoubtedly have pointed out, this would suggest that the traditional feudal landlord class had not yet exhausted its historical function. In other words, in making the southern bourgeoisie 'responsible' for the lack of development, there is the risk of blaming it for not being something different to what it in fact was. Tautology and contradiction spin out of control if we insist on seizing on such mastodontic 'ideal types' as feudalism and capitalism to describe the often subtle and complex changes occurring within a backward but still complex agrarian society.

If it is to be argued that the southern economy was growing, then it is not enough simply to demonstrate that land was changing hands, or that the ownership of property was becoming less concentrated. We must also show that new forms of technique and organisation were being introduced, that productivity, and not just volumes of production, increased (because so of course did the population — massively).[8] And throughout the century before unification there is indeed scant evidence that such was in fact the case.

The last decades of the eighteenth century saw the reversal of the relative prosperity which had accompanied the upswing in agricultural prices in the early part of the century. And just at the moment when commercial and political problems outside the Mediterranean were unsettling the basis of that short-lived prosperity, the demographic trend which had been rising steadily over the century began to catch up with and even bear down on the expansion in production.[9] As the demographic balance shifted and began to outstrip production, a situation began to emerge which was to become an almost permanent feature of southern society for the remainder of this period. The demographic trend and the growing commercial crisis combined to bear down brutally on precisely those groups who had benefited from the earlier prosperity to acquire some share of land. As the rural population grew relentlessly and the falling agricultural market drove small tenants off their holdings in increasing numbers, social relations in the country-side began to deteriorate rapidly. The distance and the tension between those who succeeded in clinging on to their property and the ever growing army of landless *braccianti* (agricultural labourers) which surrounded them widened and grew.

The process is clearly illustrated by the movements in the distribution of property in a region recently studied by Gérard Delille. In the period between 1754 and 1816, the percentage of those owning land covering an area of between 1 and 20 *moggia* (1 *moggia* = 1/3 hectare) in the region fell from 70 per cent to 40 per cent of the total, while in the same period the total of those holding tiny and in agricultural terms quite unviable parcels of less than 1 *moggia* increased threefold (from 18 per cent to 56 per cent of the total), whereas the percentage owning larger properties over 20 *moggia* fell from 7.4 per cent to 2.9 per cent.[10] What this suggests is a rapid decline and deterioration in the agrarian economy which may well have wiped out many of the gains made earlier in the century, and certainly engendered a similar and violent decline in social relations due to the insecurity of both the smaller landowner and the landless peasants. But within this context, the smaller landowner begins to appear not so much as the prototype of a new economic class, but rather as the survivor of a previous wave of upward social and economic mobility — an embattled survivor, many of whose colleagues had been, or were in the process of being, thrown back into the ranks of the landless *braccianti*. This demographic and economic reversal in the late eighteenth century was sufficiently exten-sive for Delille to speak of a return to the economic and demographic patterns of the seventeenth century.[11]

The economic fortunes of the southern mainland during the ten years of French rule between 1805 and 1815 are still far from clear. While on one hand the Continental System provided new and privileged markets for many southern agricultural products and even important openings for manufacturing enterprise, especially textiles, the war and the Allied blockade disastrously disrupted trade in the Mediterranean.[12] For Sicily, British occupation did bring trade and wealth, but this was similarly short-lived and dependent entirely on the conditions created by the war. But the most difficult problem remains that of the effect of the reforms introduced on the mainland by the French, and the degree of land redistribution which followed from them. It is still the case that the decrees by which Joseph Bonaparte abolished feudal system are widely seen as marking the end of the *ancien régime* and the establishment of the new bourgeois order.

There are a number of reasons for doubting the effectiveness of these measures, especially in view of the very short period in which to implement them. Giuseppe Zurlo's Feudal Commission, which was established to administer the new legislation, was faced by enormous difficulties, not least of which was the absence of any land register. The pressing military needs confronting Murat's government placed a premium on raising cash from the sales of ex-demesne and Church property as quickly as possible. This created great opportunities and fat pickings for those with capital and contacts with the government, and in the opinion of a later British consul in Naples it was the Neapolitan financiers and courtiers who benefited most from the sales.[13] But whereas the sense of urgency may have produced good bargains at knock-down prices for the wealthy of the capital, it did less to favour the small landowners and landless peasants who were intended to be the primary beneficiaries. In 1806, for example, the vast sheep-run similar to the Castilian *Mesta* which covered some 300,000 ha in Apulia and was known as the *Tavoliere di Puglia,* was emancipated by decree of the rights and restrictions which reserved the area for transhumance, provision being made for existing feudal tenants to convert their holdings into emphyteuts (annual quit-rents). In order to qualify, however, these tenants were obliged to apply for the conversion of their holdings within only 20 days of the publication of the law. In addition, the rents for the newly disencumbered properties were increased considerably, and the peasants also had to pay various other surcharges such as entry fees.[14]

More specific information on the degree of redistribution can be found in the only quantitative study of the land sales which has been attempted. Villani's study shows that with the exception of only the two most advanced agricultural regions (Apulia and Salernitano) the great bulk of the purchases were made by a small handful of purchasers – whose names included some of the oldest and most powerful feudal families in the Kingdom. Some 65 per cent of all the purchases were made by individuals representing less than 7 per cent of the total number of purchasers.[15]

Evidence on the way in which the process of dividing ex-feudal estates into small peasant properties developed does not add much support to the notion of a major or effective redistribution either. On the vast latifundum of Conigliano in Calabria the emancipation of those parts of the feudal estate subject to 'common rights' meant that the huge area of 5,000 ha was destined for division amongst about 900 small proprietors and tenants. The division was not made until 1817, and the rents for the allotments were then set at over 40 times higher than those for similar allotments ten years earlier.[16] Not surprisingly, within a year the peasants were surrendering their land because they could not pay the rent. By 1855 the man who had purchased the latifundum from the feudatories, the Duke of Conigliano, had himself taken over 134 of the allotments originally designed to establish a small peasant landowning class.[17]

Whether it was new men like Baron Compagna at Conigliano or former feudatories who were making the purchases, the main consequence of the land sales in this period seems to have been a process of concentration, and even reconcentration, of large property in the hands of a relatively small group, surrounded by a myriad of tiny properties always teetering on the limits of economic feasibility and chronically vulnerable to any change in the economic climate. While this was certainly true of the classic latifundia terrain of Calabria, it seems also to have been true of more advanced areas as well. In the case of Capitanata, for example, a recent study concludes that the main beneficiaries were 'the former leading feudatories' together with a number of merchants and others from Foggia and the Abruzzi.[18] A. Lepre has also used information from later census returns to examine the structure of property in the 1820s and 1830s and has drawn similar conclusions – a very small number of large properties and high rent rolls, surrounded by a mass of tiny fragmented parcels of land.[19] Although Sicily was unaffected by the French legislation, the attempt to reform the feudal estates on the island led, according to Romeo, to a similar result – the Socilian latifundum remained intact, but was surrounded by a proliferation of tiny peasant properties.[20]

There can be no doubt that the French reforms brought changes, and the acreage of land removed from the control of former feudal holders was considerable. But the changes were quantitative rather than qualitative. The lands that were lost were generally those of least value, as those parts of the feudal estates which were not subject to common rights were not touched by the legislation. There is scant evidence that the new owners adopted techniques of farming which differed from their predecessors. Again the Calabrian latifundia provide a good, if exaggerated, example. When the Jacini Enquiry into the State of Agriculture was conducted in the 1880s, the report on the Calabrias showed that Giuseppe Compagna still held the estates which he had originally acquired in 1806, and that these now covered some 10 million ha. Even this was dwarfed by his neighbour, Luigi Quinteri, who owned over 20 million ha. The investigator reported that both families had built up their estates through influence acquired as government officers, through the purchase of former feudal and demesne lands, and also from the renewed sales of Crown lands after 1860.[21]

What struck the investigator was the way in which these 'new men' had preserved the traditional structure of the latifundum without making any attempt to overcome its limitations. The latifundum was, after all, a system based on grassland, sheep grazing and minimal use of labour. The scattering of peasant properties around the perimeter served to keep wages low, and the integrity of the latifundum was carefully protected by the Calabrian custom which permitted only the youngest son in a family to marry. The estate was not seen as a source of production in itself, but rather as a base for exploiting the needs and poverty of the fragile peasant economy which surrounded it. The Jacini investigator, Branca, noted with some astonishment that virtually every landowner in Calabria was endebted to the latifundist Quinteri, who was the only source of credit and loans in a capital-starved, unproductive and precarious economy. In this he differed little from the former feudal Dukes of Conigliano.[22] But despite his wealth, Quinteri lived in spartan frugality in Cosenza: 'The fable of Midas who turned to gold everything he touched, that telling allusion both to the torments of avarice and the power of savings, is still a reality here in distant Calabria due to the absence of any awareness of the needs and costs of a more refined form of civilization.'[23]

Calabria was, of course, one of the most backward regions in the South, but the attitudes and behaviour of the latifundist Quinteri were still in many ways 'typical'. Even in areas such as the Terra di Lavoro which had a more advanced and diversified agriculture, men who built up estates through purchases of demesne lands showed little interest in the agricultural exploitation of that land, but were content to use it as a base for penetrating the local economy, providing credit for local landowners and peasants, and investing in remunerative government offices, to collect taxes, build roads and so forth.[24]

Changes in personnel did not, therefore, necessarily lead to the adoption of new methods, although the changes that were taking place did often lead to a deterioration in the state of agriculture. This was due to the fact that although the structure of the feudal estate had outlived its usefulness, it had often originally been designed to accommodate the realities of the natural agricultural environment.[25] This of course was also the weakness, in the sense that no attempt was made to overcome the obstacles created by the environment. But in those areas, especially the cereal and sheep-grazing regions, where large feudal properties had developed, they provided a degree of centralised organisation which was often vital for the preservation of workable farmland. This did not prevent problems like deafforestation and the destruction of the natural hydrographic systems on which most of the fertile land in the South was dependent, but it did serve to restrain further damage. One of the most apparent consequences of the removal of these traditional restraints without any new controls being put in their place, was the disastrous increase in the destruction of mountain woodland, the collapse of irrigation systems and the resulting rapid impoverishment of the soil.[26]

All this provides further evidence of the lack of any real structural change accompanying the land redistribution which resulted from the abolition of feudal rights over property. The negative consequences of the changes that did occur well illustrate the absence of new methods and techniques, and the failure to inject any new productivity into a traditional agriculture based on the defence of extremely poor levels of production. Features of renewal and revival are not readily apparent. It should also be remembered that the capital invested in the land sales between 1805-15, as in the sales after 1860, was almost entirely lost to agriculture in the South and was transferred to meet the financial obligations of the state.[27] The developments during the French period, in fact, seem in many ways similar to those of the mid-eighteenth century – a phase of short-lived prosperity, resulting in both the expansion of cultivation (through use of previously uncultivated land – and much of the ex-feudal property fell into this category) and the establishment of a band of precarious peasant properties. A very similar process would occur again in the years after 1860. But in each case, the consequences were similar. The new properties were vulnerable to the slightest shift in the economic climate, and when conditions deteriorated they were the first victims. Rather than evidence of progress they represent a relentless but a Sisyphean struggle to create tiny anchor-holds of security on the margins of the traditional agrarian structure.

The economic storm which revealed the instability and weakness of the changes which had occurred during the French occupation was quick to follow. One of the central issues in any explanation of the chronic instability and state of crisis in the South in the years immediately prior to unification must be the prolonged agricultural depression which set in within a few years of the close of the European war and, in the South, began to relent only in the 1850s.

The immediate cause of the slump was the fall in value of the Kingdom's staple exports. Wheat and olive oil accounted for over 50 per cent of the Kingdom's exports,[28] and these were precisely the products worst affected. With the ending of the Blockade and the Imperial System prices were bound to fall, and Neapolitan and Sicilian products were faced with new competitors – olive oil from Spain, vegetable oil from North Africa (especially Egypt), and cereals from the Black Sea which now began to appear on the European markets. At the same time, technological progress was also undermining traditional markets for oil (the introduction of gas lighting, for example), hence placing a premium on improved quality and diversification.[29]

Of the two, the fall in cereal prices was the more damaging. Average wheat prices in the Kingdom fell from 2 ducats per tomola during the Muratist period, and 2.6 ducats in the post-war boom, to no more than 1.50 ducats for the whole period 1820-34.[30] The consequences were to be felt by the agrarian economy as a whole due to the duration of the depression, but they were to be felt most particularly once again by the small and middling landowners. This was partly due to the fact that their economic margins were narrow, but the situation was aggravated by the fact that the high cereal prices of the French period had encouraged a massive extension of cereal production, and it was on this that the new properties had become dependent. Olive groves and vines had been ploughed up to make way for cereals, woodland had been pulled down and unsuitable hillsides sown with wheat and coarser cereals.[31] The capital costs of production were low, and most soil would provide a yield for a few years anyway. But this was a source of terrible vulnerability once the market fell, because the new owners were still weighed down with the mortgages and debts entered into when they acquired the land. Rents, too, had also been fixed against the higher prices of the earlier years, with the result that their true incidence gradually increased.

The new and precarious properties were not the only ones to suffer, however. The fall in prices began to affect agrarian rent-rolls more widely. The increased burden of rents for the tenant was matched by the increasing incidence of the land tax for the landowner. The new tax had been assessed in terms of notional yields at average prices in the period 1807-20. As prices fell so the true incidence of the tax rose, and by the 1830s was calculated to represent some 26 per cent of gross agricultural income.[32]

Contemporaries were in little doubt over the consequences. Reviewing the situation in the Apulian provinces in 1839 De Samuele Cagnazzi claimed that:

> these difficulties have damaged rural capital and have destroyed all the smaller landowners in spite of the distribution of the common lands amongst the landless, and now nearly all the land is in the hands of a few great landowners.[33]

Giuseppe della Valle saw a chain effect of consequences working its way up and down the agrarian hierarchy. Initially landowners tried to offset declining profits by increasing the exactions from their tenants, with the result that many of the latter defaulted on their leases and were reduced to the status of *braccianti*. But as the depression moved into its second decade this form of evasion was no longer possible for want of replacement tenants, and so the crisis began to work its way back up the hierarchy. As income from land fell, so the indebtedness of the landlords rose, and these debts:

> represented arithmetically not only the quantity of capital belonging to each landowner which has already been destroyed, but also that which will be eaten up within a short time due to the difference between farming income and the high interest rates on the loans incurred. Consequently this has been accompanied by a progressive decay of rural property, made worse by the obstacle to free trade in land as a result of those obligations which still encumber land, and the general discredit into which agriculture is fallen.[34]

With average returns on agriculture estimated at 3.5 per cent and less, and average loan interest over 20 per cent and often very much higher,[35] the trap of indebtedness was one from which escape was difficult for even the most substantial landowner.

To some extent the South was protected by its very backwardness. Lack of communications meant that only those areas with direct access to the sea could specialise in commercial production, and much of the Kingdom's agriculture was conducted in a landlocked circle of subsistence consumption. In the isolated mountain valleys, and even well down on to the malarial plains, fragmented economies existed in which the producers' main enemy was over-production, bringing inevitably lower returns: 'It was necessary to have lived in those days to remember how little farmers desired good harvests which simply cause them more work without providing them with any reward for their labours.'[36]

But this isolation from the market economy should not be exaggerated, because it was continuously being penetrated, not least by the development of a centralised administrative state which had been the real innovation of the French occupation. The encroachment of a single centralised land tax, however inefficiently assessed and administered, brought even the most distant sectors of agriculture into contact with a money economy.[37] The economic policies of the later Bourbon governments were also aimed at reducing regional disparities in agrarian markets.

The seriousness of this prolonged crisis affecting southern agriculture has been under-estimated, to some extent because of evidence that the volume of production was increasing and the volume of the Kingdom's trade continued to expand. But this of course was itself a product of the same crisis, and landowners attempted to increase production in order to offset lower unit prices. Again, the problem of the balance between demographic expansion and increased production must be taken into account. The depression produced a frontal collision, and behind the growing violence and disorder in the countryside can be seen the efforts of a threatened landowning class to defend falling incomes through the acquisition of further land, so coming directly into conflict with the ever more desperate land-hunger of a pauperised peasantry. The anger and frustration of the peasants was increasingly expressed in the demand for the restitution of those common rights which had existed under the feudal order, while the lands on which those rights were based were being drawn away to support the ailing landlord economy.

Increased production in this period cannot then be taken as an indication that the economy was improving.[38] There is no evidence that the balance between production and population improved, that there was any increase in productivity, or any move towards specialisation. In fact the reverse seems to have been the case. Increased production resulted from farming less suitable and so less productive land, and was concentrated almost entirely in the traditional crops. As a result, the *per capita* value of foreign trade in the Kingdom remained lower than in any other European state except Tsarist Russia,[39] and the trade balance remained in deficit.[40]

The same depression also affected the North of the peninsula, of course, and a comparison between the reactions and responses of the two regions well illustrates the fundamental differences between their economies. In the North the depression seems to have had damaging effects only in the less advanced regions. In Tuscany it was the same crisis which called into question the whole structure of the classical Tuscan *mezzadria*, the rigidity of which made it difficult to respond to changing market conditions. But even the debate on the *mezzadria* illustrates a difference, because it was a debate inspired by an awareness and knowledge of a more advanced and specialised form of agriculture than was possible within the structure of the subsistence orientated mixed-farming system of the *mezzadria*.[41] In the Po Valley, however, the fall in wheat and oil prices was to some extent, although not always, offset by the presence of more specialised crops, such as rice and silk. The agricultural depression certainly hit the North hard in the 1820s and 1830s, but the evidence of recovery in the 1850s suggests that a different process was at work.[42] The investments in production in Lombardy and the Po Valley which had been going on for at least a century gave the economic structures of these areas a resilience to the crisis which was quite lacking in the South. In some cases the depression may even have served to speed up the development of specialist production, although it is true that silk was one of the products worst affected in these years. In the South, however, the picture was very different, and, as we have seen, the main response was simply to produce more of the traditional devalued staples. Even if it would be exaggerated to claim that the depression in fact encouraged specialisation, experimentation and increased unit productivity in the North, the much stronger economic and organisational base of northern agriculture certainly helped mitigate the effects of the crisis. In the South, the depression accentuated and revealed the weaknesses and backwardness of agricultural organisation, and revived the elements of crisis and tension in southern society.

Although one should avoid exaggerating the degree of economic development in the North, and also remember that many regions of the

North, the Venetian mainland being one obvious case, were quite as backward as those of the South,[43] the comparison between the more advanced areas of the two regions shows a clear distinction. In one, the depression could be absorbed; in the other, it led to little short of disaster.

Taking the development of the southern economy as a whole in the century before unification, there would seem to be at least two tendencies which are difficult to reconcile with the implications of Gramsci's arguments. First, the analogy of city and countryside does not seem to fit the realities of economic development in the North and South. The pattern of economic development in the South was not only different, but even the reverse, of that in the North. Rather than a single, if chronologically unsynchronised, economic system, we would seem to be faced with two different and divergent economies. The second point follows from this; in the absence of evidence for a process of steady economic revival and growth in the South, it becomes difficult to identify in the agrarian bourgeoise the principal agent of economic and social change. Those changes which did occur were often aimless and inconclusive, and did little to alter the traditional structure of agrarian society. In fact, Romeo's conclusions on Sicily could well be applied to the Mezzogiorno as a whole. But if a new, capitalist, agrarian bourgeoisie cannot be held responsible for the widespread social tension and economic disruption in the South, what had brought about this crisis?

One result of the attention which has been devoted to the problem of the rising bourgeoisie is that the importance of what was clearly the principal agent of economic and political disruption in the South — and hence the real force behind the integration of the South into the new Italian state — has been under-estimated. What lay behind the growing economic, social and political crisis in the South was the often contradictory and destructive impact on this backward and peripheral society of the developing European commercial system. It was the inability of the southern economy to respond to the pressures and demands of the new markets dominated by the industrialising powers which undermined its traditional agrarian structure without putting anything new in its place, just as it was the political pressures exerted within the same system that ultimately undermined the political and economic independence of the southern state. The Bourbon regime's attempts to resist the political and economic encroachment of the northern powers, and in particular Great Britain, was not only to lead to the collapse of the dynasty, but was also to reveal the backwardness and immobilism of the economy and social structure of the South. The international economic context within which the southern crisis was played out in the first half of the nineteenth century was certainly as important as that international ideological system with which Gramsci was more concerned.

The political and economic strategy of the last Bourbon kings in the South after 1815 was developed against a permanent backdrop of foreign indebtedness. Penniless in 1815 because of the military costs of their deposition and restoration, the Bourbon governments were subsequently confronted by a permanent foreign trade deficit, frequent budget deficits and a massive foreign debt. This was particularly aggravated by the massive cost of the Austrian assistance in 1821 to suppress the Revolution, a situation which resulted in the purchase of the Kingdom's national debt by the Viennese Rothschilds.[44] Thereafter the largest single item on the Kingdom's expenditure was servicing a debt which was held predominantly by foreign investors.[45]

The economic strategy which was adopted to meet and overcome this situation was largely the work of one of the ablest financial administrators of his day, Luigi de' Medici. After the Revolution of 1820 had ruined his first attempts to restore the state's finances through careful economy, de' Medici was quite literally forced to adopt a more challenging policy. In order to service the massive foreign debt, it was essential to increase revenue. The depressed state of agriculture meant that any increase from that source was politically inadvisable, while the level of indirect taxation on the poor was already high.

As the opportunities for increasing revenue from traditional sources were limited, de' Medici came to the conclusion that a fresh source of production and wealth in the Kingdom must be created – a native manufacturing sector. The strategy was established with the tariffs which were introduced between 1823 and 1825, imposing an impenetrable barrier against the import of foreign manufactures and subjecting a range of domestic export goods to duty. The preamble to the 1823 measures clearly stated the objectives: the protective measures adopted by other governments had put the Kingdom at a trading disadvantage and caused her merchant fleet and industries to languish; Naples was therefore simply responding in kind to ensure the well being of its own economy.[46]

De' Medici's hope was that protectionism would recreate the conditions of the period of the French occupation, and thereby allow a new flowering of industrial and manufacturing activity in the Kingdom. The artificial shortages at that time resulting from the Imperial system and from the British blockade had created the opportunity for a number of industries to develop in the South. Swiss textile manufacturers, in particular, who were unable to keep their factories in production at home because of the lack of raw materials, were attracted to the Kingdom by the possibilities of producing cotton there. And they remained there because of the warm welcome they received from Murat's government.[47] Through protection, de' Medici was hoping to revive and build on these initiatives, and thereby not only create new sources of wealth and revenue within the Kingdom, but also improve the national trading account by reducing the need to purchase foreign manufactured goods. But protective tariffs could only partly restore the circumstances of the French period − they could protect native industries and keep foreign goods out of the home market. They could not create foreign markets − indeed the danger was that reprisals would reduce traditional markets for other goods, and this in fact occurred. Secondly, the industrial initiatives of the Muratist period had been accompanied by high agricultural prices, giving the domestic market a degree of vitality which in 1823 was certainly lacking.

The flaws in the analogy on which de' Medici's strategy was based were less immediately apparent than the dramatic deterioration in the Kingdom's relations with Great Britain which it brought about. Ostensibly the cause lay in yet another heavy debt of gratitude incurred by the Bourbons; this time for the gracious protection of His Britannic Majesty's Navy during their exile in Sicily while Murat occupied their capital. The debt was paid in the form of a concession of 10 per cent on Neapolitan tariffs for goods carried on British vessels. This concession was contained in the Treaty of 26 September 1816 between the two countries, and was not extended to native vessels.[48] In other words, not only British goods but also British shipping were given considerable advantage over their native competitors. But when in 1823 the level of the tariffs was increased, the 10 per cent concession was also extended to Neapolitan shipping as well. At this, the British government declared that the Treaty of 1816 had been violated, and in 1828 responded with penal discriminatory tariffs against one of the staple Neapolitan exports, olive oil. Increasing diplomatic pressure was put on the Bourbon government to see the error of its ways. In the mid-1830s negotiations were begun, in the face of the very damaging British retaliation, to establish some form of reciprocal trading agreement, but little progress was possible as the British could not be moved from their insistence on the restitution of their 10 per cent concession.[49] As Great Britain was the Kingdom's single most important trading partner in the period before unification, accounting for about a third of the Kingdom's total trade and, with the exception of a short period in the 1850s,[50] a net exporter, the importance and value of this concession was considerable. As a result, trading and diplomatic relations were poor.

In 1840 the conflict produced an open clash which provides a minor but instructive example of the 'imperialism of free trade', and gives a clear picture of the Bourbon Kingdom's position in the European trading system. The 'Affair of the Sicilian Brimstone', as the suitably gothic title went, arose from the fact that Sicily enjoyed a natural world monopoly over the production of sulphur in the early nineteenth century, although this was shortly to be undermined by the development of pyrites substitutes.[51] Expanding demand from British and French industries in the 1820s and 1830s led to a rapid increase in production in Sicily. The difficulties which beset the Sicilian industry, however, well illustrate the problems facing a backward economy attempting to take advantage of new opportunities and challenges.

The system of mining was extremely primitive ('A Sicilian sulphur mine is generally a labyrinth of confusion' reported a British consular agent),[52] and was largely dependent on a brutal exploitation of a labour force which the poverty of the island made abundant and cheap. The opening of new mines and the use of this large and expendable labour force had made it possible for production to expand to meet the increasing demand, but the wholly disorganised manner in which this happened led to over-production. Prices for best quality sulphur in Sicily fell between 1833 and 1838 by over 50 per cent (from 41.2 to 18.4 *carlini* per *cantaro*) and this was reflected by a similar drop in import prices in Britain.[53]

The situation caused great concern in Sicily and Naples, because sulphur was, after all, one of the Kingdom's very few natural assets. It also caused concern amongst the merchants, most of whom were British. Although the British colony in Sicily had an important interest in the mines, the trade was dominated by some 20 English houses operating from Messina, Syracuse and Palermo.[54] In return for advances of working capital, the Sicilian mine-owners 'were obliged to commit their produce in advance at very low prices and often for several years at a time'.[55] The buoyancy of the market in the 1820s and early 1830s encouraged many of these English factors to invest directly in production. In 1838, for example, one of the leading British merchants, George Wood, acting as agent for houses in Liverpool and Glasgow, leased the *Fiume del Riesi* mine from its owner, Don Giuseppe Fainici, who lacked the capital to work it. Wood invested heavily in drainage and pumping and brought in English engineers to work the mine. But

Wood and others quickly found that production costs were highly un-
economic, in particular because expansion in production meant using
mines that were distant from the ports and less easy to work. Even
before prices began to fall, it was estimated that the mines were running
at annual losses of 20 to 25 per cent on outlay.[56]

It seems very probable that the English merchants played a very
effective double game. Realising that his investments were at risk, Mr
Wood in April 1837 wrote to the Neapolitan government suggesting
that some control should be imposed on the production of sulphur, and
that in view of the desperate state of the industry this might be done
through the granting of a monopoly over the export of sulphur to a
licensed company.[57] In fact this was precisely the course which the
Bourbon government adopted, although clearly to Mr Wood's chagrin
they conferred the licence on a French company, Taix and Aycard. In
return for the guarantee of customs revenue and the purchase of fixed
quotas at fixed prices from the producers, Taix and Aycard were granted the exclusive right to export sulphur from the Kingdom.

The move threw the British merchants in Sicily into uproar, and
they began mobilising 'their Connections and Partners in London,
Liverpool, Manchester, Newcastle, Birmingham, Glasgow, Dundee and
Aberdeen'.[58] In the House of Commons their case was to be put by
Lord Landor and Mr William Gladstone.[59] But Palmerston's reaction
anticipated that of the British merchants. He had always found the
Neapolitan commercial policies particularly irritating, commenting on
an earlier occasion: 'The continuance however, of their High Duty on
our commodities . . . is not a matter of indifference because it tends, as
far as the Neapolitan and Sicilian markets are concerned, to cramp
important Branches of British Industry.'[60] His distemper had been
increased by a series of smaller wrangles over quarantine policies, steam
navigation licences and other matters,[61] so that the proposed concession to the French company provided an excellent focus for his anger.
On being informed in October 1837 of the possibility of such a concession, he wrote at once to inform the British consul in Naples, Temple,
that this would constitute a violation of the 1816 Treaty 'the fourth
Article of which expressly stipulates that British commerce in general
and the British subjects who carry the commerce on, shall be treated
throughout the dominions of the King of the Two Sicilies upon the
same footing as the commerce and subjects of the most favoured
nations, not only with respect to the persons and property of such
British subjects but also with regard to every species of article in which
they may traffic.'[62] The following February orders were given for

visits of British naval vessels to Sicily to be increased 'in order to support the representations which H.M. Consuls may make against the acts of vexation or injustice committed towards British subjects'.[63] As the Neapolitan government chose to proceed with 'this most objectionable project' the British representative in Naples was instructed in January 1840 to pass on the message: 'If the Sulphur Monopoly be not immediately abandoned, H.M. government will be compelled to resort to unfriendly measures.'[64]

The Neapolitan government could not revoke the licence without suffering complete humiliation, and accordingly Admiral Stopford was ordered to sail from Malta on the 13 March 1840 with a squadron to blockade the Neapolitan and Sicilian ports and seize Neapolitan vessels. The Neapolitan government had no means of resisting, but there was growing concern in Europe that the British action might spark off more serious trouble in Italy, which made it possible for the Bourbon government to escape the humiliation of open surrender behind the discreet veil of French mediation. Britain agreed to the mediation, although only on the 'condition' that it would concede nothing.[65] In fact, the settlement was concerned almost entirely with assessing the damages which the Neapolitan government should pay both the holders of the monopoly and the injured British merchants.

The episode is the more extraordinary because not only was Britain's case that the monopoly constituted a violation of the 1816 Treaty not recognised by any other European state, but it had also been deemed invalid by the Crown Attorney General in Britain as well.[66] Britain's action had no legality in international law, and Admiral Stopford's action verged on piracy on the high seas. To make matters even worse, the pretended injuries suffered by the British merchants turned out to be entirely fictitious. Sullivan, one of the Commissioners appointed to assess the damages, was Palmerston's nephew, and he wrote in some embarrassment to his uncle in 1841 to inform him that the original claims had been 'quite preposterous' and even when reduced were still highly dubious. 'The great difficulty will be to bring *proofs* forward that any *actual* losses have been incurred in consequence of the monopoly, whereas it might be proved that positive gains were made.'[67] To the surprise of the Commissioners one of the largest claims was from the same Mr Wood who had originally proposed the monopoly as a solution to the problem of over-production. Sullivan did not conceal his opinion that far from sustaining losses, the British merchants had benefited enormously from the whole affair because the disruption of the sulphur trade had resulted in the value of their sulphur stocks being greatly increased: 'if they obtain one half of what they actually claim, I think that they will have no just cause for complaint.'[68]

The dramatic confrontation over the sulphur monopoly was, in British eyes, simply another distasteful but unavoidable episode in the unfolding of the mission of free trade, but for the Neapolitan government it marked the end of their bid for economic and commercial independence. The real heresy of the Bourbons — and, in view of his earlier involvement with the sulphur lobby, this may have added some warmth to Gladstone's later charge that the Bourbon regime was 'the negation of God erected as a system of government'[69] — was that they resisted the new gospel. Macgregor, the British negotiator in the talks on reciprocal trade, had been one of the firmest advocates of the use of force over the sulphur issue and his motives were clear:

> I beg leave to assure your Lordship that my best judgement and abilities shall be exerted to assist in carrying through these measures which, considering the great natural Resources of the Two Sicilies hitherto by restrictions and other Administrative means paralysed as to their commercial development, will . . . be attended by the greatest practical advantage to British Trade and Navigation.[70]

Although it did not follow until 1845, the outcome of the sulphur confrontation was the reciprocal trade agreement signed in 1845 with Britain, followed by a further series of similar agreements with other nations.

It was because de' Medici's strategy for economic independence and industrial growth conflicted with British trading interests in the Mediterranean that it was destined to fail sooner or later. But the consequences were to prove fatal, because economic rivalry was also accompanied, as we have seen, by political hostility. With the failure of their economic strategy, the Bourbons began to look for diplomatic assistance, especially as the signs of Austria's growing weakness became more evident. There was little choice, but the ally they chose to woo — St Petersburg — could not have been better selected to exacerbate British fears. The diplomatic isolation of the dynasty was then formally concluded when the Powers at the Paris Peace Conference publicly censured the Neapolitan government and broke off diplomatic relations.[71]

In fact, the sulphur conflict was never more than a rearguard action. The structure of the Kingdom's trading balance over the period from 1820 to 1860 shows clearly the degree of economic dependence on the great industrial powers. The Kingdom's principal trading contacts were not with the other states on the peninsula, but with Britain, France and Austria. The Kingdom's imports were supplied mainly by Britain (roughly 35 per cent) and France (roughly 30 per cent), followed at some distance by Austria (8 per cent). The same three, this time in the order France, Austria and Britain, were the principal purchasers of the Kingdom's exports (accounting for between 65 per cent and 70 per cent).[72] While the Sardinian states also provided an outlet for exports, the Kingdom's main trading axes were with London, Marseilles and Trieste. And it was only for a short period in the 1850s, due to the particular demands created by the Crimean War, that the Kingdom's trade balance with her principal partner, Great Britain, was out of deficit.[73]

Bourbon political strategy was dictated then by an awareness of the realities of this economic subordination and a quite unrealistic, or simply desperate, under-estimation of the strength of the opposition. But the nature of this subordination shows that the concept of even an embryonic city-countryside relationship between North and South prior to 1860 is, in economic terms at least, misleading and premature. The peripheral and backward southern economies (since we have been glossing over the distinctions between and the relations between the mainland and Sicily) were firmly embedded in a trading relationship dominated by Britain and France, rather than in an incipient national economy. And this of course was to provide at least one of the factors in the post-unification Southern Problem. Not only was the economic unification of the two regions the product of a political rather than an economic process, but the economies of the two regions, although different in structure, were often parallel rather than complementary in what they produced.

There would then appear to be an element of anachronism in the economic and social parallelism between North and South implied in Gramsci's city-countryside analogy, evocative as it may be in other respects. But to emphasise the degree of disparity between the economic conditions and situations of the two parts of the peninsula is not necessarily to imply that their subsequent unification was purely fortuitous or accidental. The political and economic initiatives taken, however fitfully and inconsistently, by the last Bourbon rulers in the South led both to their diplomatic isolation, as we have seen, and also increasingly to their estrangement from the most powerful economic forces within their own state. This was the political consequence of the predicament of the South and this was what lay behind the collapse of the Bourbon state.

In many ways Gramsci's concept of 'passive revolution' provides an excellent description of the process of political dissolution in the South and also an explanation of the absence of any effective social change in the political revolution of 1860-1. But in focusing attention exclusively on the developing relationship between the conservative southern Liberals and the Cavourian Moderates, there is again a risk of seeing the origins of the crisis in the South too much through a later, post-unification perspective. This not only distorts the nature of the political crisis in the South before 1860, but also over-simplifies it. The principal factor in this political disintegration was the initiative taken by the Bourbon government in response to their Kingdom's international economic and political predicament and it is this which reflects the real 'passivity' of the political revolution in the South: the Bourbons' efforts to defend and protect the Kingdom's independence led to their diplomatic and domestic isolation; the Liberal opposition not only failed to exploit the collapse of the dynasty to effect any significant political, never mind social or economic change, but also showed itself incapable of comprehending the fundamental features of the southern predicament or envisaging any effective solutions to them. The 'failed', or absent radical revolution was matched at least by the political failure of the future southern ruling classes.

Just as the international consequences of the Bourbons' economic and political strategy earn them a footnote in the history of the imperialism of free trade, so the domestic implications provide an interesting example of an unsuccessful attempt at modernisation. Arguably the greatest legacy of the French occupation on the mainland was the model and example of a modern, centralised and rational bureaucracy. Nearly all the more perceptive contemporary observers and administrators were agreed that an effective, centralised bureaucracy was not only an essential practical prerequisite for the modernisation of the southern state, but that it held within it the possibility for creating the basis of a new type of political system.[74] Joachim Murat had himself well understood the way in which bureaucracy functioned as a reservoir of political patronage, and the extension and centralisation of the bureaucracy before 1815 was intended as much to strengthen the political base of the foreign regime as to effect the reforms which had been introduced. It was equally significant that the returning Bourbons swallowed their pride and refrained from any large-scale purge of the Muratist administration in order not to damage their political position.[75] On the other hand, the political purges after the Revolution of 1820-1 were to provide a large army of political opponents and perhaps one of the strongest breeding grounds for the Liberal opposition.

De' Medici was clearly well aware of the economic and political advantages of a modern bureaucratic structure, and perhaps did more than anyone else to create a new administrative 'ethos' in this period. An impressive line of administrators, including men like the economist Ludovico Bianchini and the civil engineer Carlo Afan de Rivera, were all part of the tradition which he established, and which drew heavily on the reform movement of the previous century. But just as de' Medici's industrial policy was frustrated by the reactions of the European powers, so his strategy of modernisation at home was to be undermined by the economic and financial realities of the Kingdom. In the reaction after 1820 the attempt to build on the French model floundered and collapsed. The purges of the administration and the liberal professions were the result as much of financial necessity as of political vindictiveness. The huge financial burden which the Bourbons incurred for the assistance provided by the Austrian army in restoring them to their throne was to remain as a recurrent charge until 1830, and meant economy to the bone.[76] But even more damaging than the loss of jobs was the fact that the same financial necessity brought about a return to the earlier practice of farming out principal sources of tax revenue. In 1823 the revenues on customs duties, on the salt, tobacco, playing cards and gun-powder monopolies were farmed out to private speculators, and the same was in effect true of the collection of the new land tax, as the office of tax collector was one that was freely bought, sold and inherited.[77] Despite the disclaimers by Bianchini and others, this clearly showed that the attempts to break away from the old hand-to-mouth expedients of the *ancien régime* had been unsuccessful. As happened so often in the South, the new modern institutions introduced by the French were quickly adapted to fit older corporate and decentralised realities. The economic vulnerability of the bureaucracy continued, so that it never became either an effective administrative tool or an effective political base. When Ferdinand II came to the throne, 'being unable to ask sacrifices from property or industry without causing them grievous harm, it was therefore necessary to turn to those who were paid by or received pensions from the State'.[78]

The failure to create an effective modern bureaucracy was largely determined, then, by the lack of means, but it was to have consequences which were typical of many other situations of 'under-development'. The scarcity of alternative forms of employment meant that the bureaucracy remained a primary focus of job hunger in the South.

Bianchini, normally an over-optimistic reporter, rightly pointed to the economic realities which lay behind this:

> From time immemorial the absence of industry, crafts, careers and professions amongst us has driven people to seek jobs from the government, so that for a long time it was generally believed that a portion of our public expenditure ought to be devoted to providing wages for the large number of citizens who lack jobs. Also, public office was highly honourable because it conferred privilege, and offices were often held virtually as part of a family's patrimony, with uncles being succeeded by nephews, fathers by sons . . .[79]

Precarious and unrewarding as they might appear, such jobs were havens of security in the circumstances of the surrounding economy. At times of political insecurity and change the permanent, relentless pressure for jobs burst into an avalanche, as was evident in both 1848 and 1860. Settembrini claimed, doubtless with a degree of exaggeration, that in 1848 the new constitutional ministers were unable to get into their offices because of the vast throng of place-seekers.[80] And of the flood of petitions which rained down on the new parliament, one can stand for all:

> Gaetano Borruto of Reggio in 1843 set out to teach the people the benefits of the constitutional regime. He called together the craft guilds and was the first to explain the message of regeneration. He begs for a pension for himself and his family, and also some positions for his two brothers . . .[81]

Such pleas were to accompany revolutions everywhere in Europe, but the degree of dependence on state employment was exceptional, if not unique, in the Italian South. And the existence of the problem prior to unification does show that later observers, such as Salvemini, were wrong to see the distortion of bureaucratic employment as a peculiar feature of the post-unification 'Southern Problem'.[82] As Bianchini understood, in the passage quoted above, the real significance of the problem was not that it constituted a novelty — on the contrary. The failure of the Bourbon state to build on the basis provided by Joseph Bonaparte and Joachim Murat meant that in place of a modern bureaucratic structure, the older uncontrolled and uncontrollable corporate structures of the *ancien régime* survived, in which the state was no more than a nominal head of the administrative structure and in which real power came to be exercised by private patronage and clientism. It was also the persistence of the institutional disorganisation of the *ancien régime* which was to provide one of the most important institutional bases for what Gramsci and others described as the phenomenon of social 'disintegration' in the South.[83]

Politically, the consequences were very dangerous for the regime. On one hand, it was committed to an economic strategy which required some degree of organisation and control, while lacking the necessary administrative resources to provide this. Secondly, economic and financial pressure meant that it proved impossible to use the bureaucracy to create a political base. As Luigi Blanch noted, the regime found itself in an uncomfortable half-way house, being neither a feudal nor yet a national monarchy.[84] The President of Ferdinand II's Consulta put the same point rather differently in a letter to the King in 1843:

> Cavalier de' Medici described the present state of our Monarchy well when he said that it was a Monarchy *à la Napoleon*. It lacks support from either the clergy or the aristocracy, so that its only physical strength lies in the Army and the Civil Employees — and the latter are for the most part quite happy to watch revolutions taking place from their windows, so long as someone goes on paying them . . . [85]

The political consequences of the Bourbons' failure to create a new political base in a modern, or modernising bureaucracy was the more damaging because the economic strategy to which they had committed themselves was to have the effect of isolating the dynasty from the dominant economic interests in the South. It was the landowning class in particular which became increasingly disaffected, and it was the loss of the loyalty of this group which sealed the fate of the dynasty.

But both the nature of the grievances of the agrarian lobby in the South and also the very uncertain and inadequate manner in which they were channeled into a political programme again shows clearly the weakness and backwardness of the social forces which after 1860 were to become the southern ruling class. In contrast to the North, for example, where increasingly the free trade platform came to provide a meeting point for agrarian and commercial liberalism, in the South the agrarian and the commercial interests remained deeply divided. In part this was a throw-back to an earlier mentality — the 'honest' farmer's suspicion of the 'speculations', 'games' and 'tricks' carried out at his expense by the merchant and entrepreneur which was a commonplace of the *ancien régime*. The rivalry was evident in 1820 when concerted attempts were made to restrict the franchise qualification in Naples to landed property alone. But unlike other parts of the peninsula, this division did not weaken, and was as evident not only in 1848 but also in 1860. While this reflected the backwardness of the southern agrarians, it was also to some extent a result of the government's economic strategy.

The agrarians' hostility to the commercial and industrial interests was greatly increased by the protective tariffs introduced by de' Medici. For the agrarians such a strategy could only be interpreted as indifference to their own interests, and worse. First, it laid the Kingdom open to reprisals, and it was the agrarian interests which had to bear the cost of Britain's retaliation against Neapolitan olive oil. Not only were markets for agricultural products reduced, but the landowners also were aware that as the principal consumer group — indeed the only significant consumer group — in the Kingdom, they would also be called on to subsidise the domestic manufactures which de' Medici was keen to establish through the prices they would pay for the products. When agriculture was in the depths of devastating depression, the industrial gamble seemed little more than lunacy to many landowners. The attack on the government's strategy in the 1830s and 1840s, although inevitably cautious, became increasingly vocal, and many of those who were to become leading spokesmen of the Liberals — De Augustinis, Dragonetti, Scialoja, Durini and others — became fierce critics of a policy which seemed to sacrifice agriculture to the fantasy of industrialisation. To some extent, then, Palmerston's efforts to break down the barriers of Bourbon protectionism were matched by a similar internal pressure from the agrarian lobby.

The government's industrial strategy was, however, only one limb of the agrarians' growing discontent with the Bourbon regime. An equally powerful irritant lay in the controls over the free movement of grain and staple foodstuffs in and out of the Kingdom. In their concern to preserve the popular loyalty to which the dynasty had owed its restoration in 1799, the Bourbons revived the spirit, although not the form, of the traditional *Annona*[86] regulations in 1815, in an attempt to ensure cheap food supplies. The export of cereals and certain other foodstuffs was prohibited until such time as the government's agents were able to report that the coming harvest would be adequate for domestic needs. At the first sign of possible shortage, on the other hand, the free import of cereals was permitted.[87] In fact, the logic of the Neapolitan Corn Laws was quite the reverse of those of England in the same period. Whereas the latter were designed to protect the producer and keep prices high, the Neapolitan restrictions were designed to protect the consumer and tended to guarantee the producer the lowest possible return. Prices would only rise when supplies were short, but this was precisely the condition that triggered the freeing of imports, which naturally resulted in prices falling. The restrictions also made it extremely difficult for Neapolitan producers to take advantage of opportunities on foreign markets in view of the unpredictability of the controls. And when in 1845 the principle of reciprocal trade was admitted in the trade agreement with Great Britain, while the restrictions on the export of cereals were retained, the frustration of those producing for the commercial sector became even greater.

The attractiveness of the free trade platform of the Cavourian Moderates for the southern landowners needs little explanation in such a context. But, as Gramsci was quick to note, there is need for some caution in talking of a platform in so far as the southern Liberals were concerned. The major southern contribution was to come after not before unification, and lay in that transformation of liberalism into a moral and ethical doctrine which reached its fullest expression in Croce. Even in terms of 'economic liberalism' it is difficult to identify any coherent platform in the South before or in 1860 which went beyond a crude and imitative mixture of economic *laissez-faire* and social conservatism.

On one hand, this does no more than reflect again the 'passivity' of the southern revolution and indicates that the southern agrarians were not in any sense the principal agents in the changes that did occur. But certain features of the developing fascination with the northern free trade philosophies were to have major consequences for the future development of the South in the new unified Italian State. The great weakness of southern liberalism was the failure to learn from the contradictions which had brought about the collapse of the Bourbon regime.

In the first place, the anti-industrial tendency in southern liberalism did not slacken, nor did the hostility between the agrarian and the industrial and commercial interests. To some extent this reflected the fact that the small group of Neapolitan financiers and industrialists were mainly foreigners, and tended to work hand-in-glove with the Crown. The very small handful of industrial manufacturers in the Kingdom — engaged mainly in textile production, together with the engineering industry which developed around the government's ship and railway building programme — were totally dependent on de' Medici's protective tariffs, and often more direct subsidies as well, so that they had little interest in the agrarian free trade platform. Even the merchants of the capital were lukewarm, because they were well aware of the very cramped opportunities for the Kingdom to participate in reciprocal trade due to the narrow range of its products. If they argued for free trade, it was generally through expediency, and in particular the desire to avoid British reprisals.[88]

On the few occasions when the mercantile and industrial interests were able to express their interests clearly, they showed themselves hostile to the Liberal movement and tied to the existing regime. Antonio Scialoja, who had been Minister of Trade in the Liberal government of 1848, was to write scathingly a decade later that the mercantile class in Naples was:

> partly in the hands of foreigners who, with only a few noble exceptions, are quite happy with any form of government so long as they are not asked to pay for it and will be quite content to praise it, and partly in the hands of a class of nationals who, to speak the truth, are totally indifferent to political liberty, but who might perhaps be woken from their slumbers if they were called on to pay . . .[89]

Scialoja was to prove no friend of the commercial interest, but his criticisms do not seem exaggerated. When the Liberal government set up a Finance Committee in July 1848 it did not include any of the leading financiers or merchants of Naples.[90] The same government's attempts to raise a portion of a 3 million ducat forced loan from industry and commerce (700,000 ducats) and liquid capital (500,000) gave rise to an outcry that was 'impossible to describe'. Within a week the levies on commerce and the professions had been abandoned.[91]

The difficult commercial situation resulting from the revolution might at first sight appear to explain this reluctance. However, when the King in October wished to raise funds he had little difficulty in selling rent of 600,000 ducats (i.e. 4,327,432 ducats capital) on the national debt, and the principal subscribers were the Rothschilds and a number of leading Neapolitan financiers.[92] Early in the following year the leading textile manufacturer in the Kingdom, Davide Wonwiller, was able to sell 200,000 ducats of Neapolitan government stock in his native Switzerland on behalf of the government.[93] The Neapolitan expeditionary force which suppressed the separatist revolution in Sicily was also financed by the Rothschild Bank. Again in Sicily, the leading financial interests seem to have behaved similarly to their Neapolitan counterparts, and refused to subscribe to the forced loan which the

Liberal leader Michele Amari attempted to raise in 1848.[94]

In the perennial rivalry between the mainland and Sicily, the Neapolitan commercial interests again showed themselves to be staunch defenders of privilege and the *status quo*. When the Palermo government in 1848 granted Messina the status of a free port, the Neapolitan merchants at once began to agitate for its abolition. The matter was put on the Chamber of Commerce agenda under the peremptory heading: 'Damages caused in Good Faith & Damages committed through Fraud and through Abuse of Free Trade.' The merchants reminded the constitutional government that: 'all citizens are equal, especially under the present representative regime, so that all privileges must be considered inadmissable.'[95] Rather than call for similar facilities, the merchants demanded that the free port at Messina be suppressed before it ruined trade and commerce on the mainland. They threatened that if the 'incalculable damages caused to those merchants involved in manufacture and trade' were not stopped forthwith, 'they would find themselves forced into the necessity of dismissing all their employees, who amount to hundreds of thousands of men'.[96] This was not a threat which the beleaguered Liberal regime could take lightly.

Such attitudes and political loyalties reflect the precariousness and dependence of the commercial and industrial groups in southern society. This is perhaps one of the clearest examples of the failure of de' Medici's strategy to take root. Like the government's initiative itself, the commercial and manufacturing structure of the Kingdom never progressed beyond that of the *ancien régime*. The manufacturers and merchants were not an independent, self-assured class with its own interests and programmes: they were still, like their eighteenth-century forebears, *gens du roi*, the King's men.[97] Their industries, and often their commerce too, could only survive if they had protection, and often more permanent assistance too, from the government. De' Medici and his successors had intervened personally in the case of virtually every manufacturing venture which was established in the Kingdom after 1820. Protection was afforded through the tariffs, and further assistance in the form of free accommodation, free convict labour and guaranteed markets through government contracts. The most important ventures were reliant on all these forms of aid. Even in commerce, the most lucrative opportunities were to be found in catering for and supplying the state's needs, especially those of the armed forces. Elsewhere limited opportunity encouraged monopoly and exclusion, with the result that the merchant often became identified as not only one of the staunchest defenders of the restrictions on which the backwardness of the economy was grounded, but even as the principal vested interest in backwardness and its continuity.

The failure of de' Medici's strategy to bring into being any independent or broad-based manufacturing and commercial interest meant in turn that support for the bid to establish an industrial sector was very limited. The close contacts between the administration and the few entrepreneurs made the Liberals suspicious and hostile. As a result they tended to under-estimate both the fragility of the industrial sector which had developed since 1805 and the problems facing its expansion. As a result, when Scialoja returned to Naples in 1860 he was one of the principal supporters of the immediate extension of the much lower Piedmontese tariff system to the South.[98] The inevitable consequences were pointed out by the Swiss textile manufacturer Wonwiller and others, but the Liberals were unmoved. As a result the Neapolitan industrial sector was almost destroyed within a few years.

What is at issue here is not so much whether unification destroyed those industries which had been able to develop in the South — it did, but they were already in very serious difficulty before 1860 and their existence had always been 'artificial'.[99] What is important is that the Piedmontese tariffs were introduced at the instigation of southern Liberals without any regard for the consequences. There was not any debate — as there has been in more recent times — as to whether or not the economic solution to the problems of the South lay in industrialisation. The action was supported because the southern Liberals had no clearer understanding of the nature of the economic problems of the South than had, for example, Macgregor in the letter quoted above. They shared the belief that free trade was the answer to everything, and that this would unlock the unexploited natural resources of the Kingdom. The myth that the South was an unexploited Eden was one that was as common in the South as in the North.

This was the real key to the 'failure' of the southern revolution. The Liberal programme was something adopted and external, which bore little relation to the realities of the southern predicament. In particular, it was largely untouched by the tradition of serious applied investigation which had begun in the Southern Enlightenment of the eighteenth century.[100] Curiously, it was not the Liberals, but rather the Bourbon administration which was the heir of this tradition, and this was partly why it was to be lost. What men like de' Medici, Bianchini, Afan de Rivera and others had in common, and what made them heirs of eighteenth-century reformism, was an understanding that the nature of the obstacles holding back the development of agriculture, commerce and manufacturing in the South required collective action. Collective action which could only be attempted and directed by an enlightened and modern state. Nowhere were the limitations of the free-trade solution more obvious than in the face of the ever growing problem of the physical destruction of the productive structure of the Kingdom — rampant deafforestation, with the consequent flooding of coastal agricultural land which malaria quickly rendered uninhabitable. This was precisely the problem which the effects of the cyclical patterns of economic development in the century before unification tended to aggravate. It is difficult to find a finer or more perceptive analysis of the state of the agrarian economy in the South and the obstacles to its improvement than that provided by Carlo Afan de Rivera in the 1840s, nor a clearer appeal for what we would now call rational planning.[101]

The dilemma of the South, even before unification, was that the Bourbon state was quite inadequate to provide the framework within which such a reformist programme might be effected. One of the heaviest penalties of unification was that this tradition was to be lost and neglected until the new forms of political and economic subordination to which the South was subjected had served to worsen and aggravate even further those same fundamental problems. The failure of those who in 1860 found themselves as the ruling classes in the South to learn from that tradition was to have the greatest consequences, and reflects their lack of any effective programme or alternative. Just as the traditional economy had been disrupted by the encroachment of the new international commercial economy without anything new emerging to replace lost traditional equilibria, so the passing of the old political order failed to lead to anything new — beyond a new sense of instability. As Raffaele de Cesare remarked 'Not so much new times, new faces, as new times, old faces'.[102]

The process which lay behind the collapse of the Bourbon state in the South and its absorption into the new unified Italy was, then, both more complex and less mechanical than is implied in Gramsci's interpretation. And this, in turn, adds to the complexity of the problem which was to become — and still remains — one of the central features of the Italian state: the economic and social backwardness of the South.

The forces which undermined the Bourbon regime and threw the traditional structures of agrarian society into crisis were almost entirely external. The impact of the contradictory and complex pressures exerted by the emerging international manufacturing economy offered incentives and opportunities for one part of the peninsula, dislocation and uncertainty for the other. The crisis in the South was induced from outside, and in this lies the explanation of the passive nature of the political revolution that followed. It was for the same reason that unification brought no signs of revival in the South, but was in turn to aggravate existing difficulties with new economic, fiscal and political burdens. The same forces which encouraged growth in the North and brought confusion to the South acted to mould the peninsula into a single political and economic unit, but in a way that was both less neat and less complementary than Gramsci suggested.

It is precisely the absence of a process of economic and social integration to parallel the growing political attraction between the Cavourian Moderates and the southern agrarians that reveals the emptiness of the southern revolution. The fact that the majority of the spokesmen of the southern Liberals were exiles as well as 'intellectuals' has often been noted. But this was a symptom and a reflection of the failure of the southern agrarians to develop a political or economic programme of their own which bore any relation to the realities and imperatives of southern society. The creed of Free Trade was alien and imitative. Within twenty years it was to be discarded with the same enthusiasm that it had been seized on in 1860. But the new protectionism of the Crispi tariffs, which christened the formal political alliance between industry and southern agriculture, was not in any sense a return to the earlier strategy which the Bourbons, with all their reluctance, uncertainty and inadequacy, had attempted. In de' Medici's strategy there lay an awareness that the problem of growth must be posed in the context of the entire economy of the South, together with a recognition that new sources of production could only be created with the support of the stronger sectors of the traditional economy. It would be wrong to exaggerate the coherence and clarity of this strategy, but the recognition of the need for solutions which were both collective and planned in order to overcome the fundamental economic disabilities of the South was the great achievement of the tradition which had begun with Genovesi and Galanti in the eighteenth century and was kept alive by the more enlightened Bourbon administrators of the early nineteenth century. But in the protectionism of the agrarian-industrial alliance of the 1880s this vision had disappeared, and was replaced by a cruder mechanism whereby the weaker and most vulnerable sectors of the southern economy were forced to support the most entrenched and the most traditional. Although agricultural protectionism was, in view of the international situation which provoked it, unavoidable, the political form which it took in Italy served to petrify and perpetuate the backwardness of the economic and social structure of the South.

There is, and was, no single, unchanging, 'Southern Problem', and the economic, social and political predicament of the South both pre-dated unification and changed with unification. To see the participation of the South in national unification as a pre-history of the later agrarian-industrial alliance is an over-simplification which distorts the nature and origins of the Southern Problem. The agrarian-industrial alliance was a political consequence of unification, but it was not already present as a dominant influence in the making of the national revolution. On the other hand, the economic and social malaise of the South was clearly evident and critical before 1860. What changed in 1860 was that the problems of the South were transposed into an economic and political context in which the need to find solutions was outweighed by the advantages of preserving and exploiting those very weaknesses. The predicament and contradictions of the last period of Bourbon rule in the South should warn against any facile diagnosis of the nature and origins of the problems of the Italian South. It also suggests that one of the great sacrifices in 1860 was the loss of a tradition of inquiry and analysis firmly rooted in the realities of the southern predicament. The Bourbon state did not and could not provide an effective framework to implement this tradition, but the new state was not even concerned to make the effort.

Notes

1. M. Salvadori, *Gramsci e il problema storico della democrazia* (Turin, 1970), p. 79.
2. For Gramsci's writings on the South in English see: 'The Southern Question' in *The Modern Prince & Other Writings*, ed. L. Marks (New York, 1972), pp. 28-51; and *Prison Notebooks*, eds. Q. Hoare and G. Nowell Smith (London, 1971: hereafter *PN*), pp. 90-102; J. Joll, *Gramsci* (London, 1977), chap. 6; A. Davidson, *Antonio Gramsci* (London, 1978): Introduction above.
3. *PN*, pp. 92-3
4. The most recent general survey is A. Caracciolo 'La Storia Economica', in *Storia d'Italia* (Einaudi) vol. 3. *Dal Primo Settecento all'Unità*, pp. 515-617. See also A. Lepre, *Storia del Mezzogiorno nel Risorgimento* (Rome, 1969); D. Demarco, *Il Crollo del Regno delle Due Sicilie* (Naples, 1960), pt. I; G. Galasso, *Il Mezzogiorno nella storia d'Italia* (Florence, 1979).
5. R. Romeo, *Il Risorgimento in Sicilia* (Bari, 1973), p. 253.
6. P. Villani, 'Il Capitalismo Agrario in Italia', *Studi Storici*, a. vii (1966) p. 494.
7. E. Sereni, quoted in P. Villani, ibid., p. 512.
8. G. Galasso, 'Lo sviluppo demografico del Mezzogiorno prima e dopo l'Unità' in *Mezzogiorno medievale e moderno* (Turin, 1964), pp. 303 ff.; A. Caracciolo 'La Storia Economica', p. 520.
9. On the late eighteenth century crisis see: G. Aliberti, 'Economia e società a Napoli da Carlo III ai Napoleonidi' in *Storia di Napoli*, vol. 8 (Naples, 1972);

G. Delille, *La Croissance d'une Société Rurale* (Naples, 1973), pp. 222-40; P. Macry, *Mercato e Società nel Regno di Napoli* (Naples, 1974), pp. 423-76.

10. G. Delille, ibid., p. 212.

11. Ibid., pp. 208 ff.

12. P. Villani, 'Le Royaume de Naples pendant la domination française (1806-1815)', *Annales Historiques de la Revolution Française*, a. xliv (1972); J. Rambaud, *Naples sous Joseph Bonaparte 1806-8* (Paris, 1911): A. Valente, *Gioachino Murat e L'Italia Meridionale* (Turin, 1941).

13. J. Goodwin, 'Progress of the Two Sicilies under the Spanish Bourbons', *Journal of the Royal Historical Society*, vol. 5 (London) 1842, p. 61.

14. L. Matucci, 'La riforma del Tavoliere e l'eversione della feudalità in Capitanata 1806-15', *Quaderni Storici*, n.18 (1972), p. 263.

15. P. Villani, *La Vendita dei Beni dello Stato* (Milano, 1964), pp. 156-7.

16. R. Merzario, *Signori e Contadini in Calabria* (Milan, 1975), p. 127.

17. Ibid., p. 129.

18. L. Matucci, 'La riforma del Tavoliere', p. 277.

19. A. Lepre, 'Classi, movimenti politici e lotta di classe nel mezzogiorno dalla fine del settecento al 1860', *Studi Storici*, a.xvi (1975) pp. 357-60.

20. R. Romeo, *Il Risorgimento*, pp. 189-90.

21. *Atti della Giunta per l'Inchiesta Agraria*, vol. IX (Rome, 1882), p. xxv.

22. R. Merzario, *Signori e Contadini*, p. 72: see also, G. Delille, *Agricoltura e demografia nel Regno di Napoli nei secoli XVIII e XIX* (Naples, 1977), esp. pp. 104-50.

23. *Atti della Giunta*, vol. IX, p. xxvii.

24. See for example J. Davis, 'The Case of the Vanishing Bourgeoisie', *Mélanges de l'Ecole Française de Rome*, t. 88 (1976) n.2, pp. 866-71.

25. R. Merzario, *Signori e Contadini*, p. 72.

26. On land reclamation in the period see: G. Arias, *La Questione Meridionale*, vol. I, pt. II, (Bologna, 1921) Chap. 2; R. Ciasca, *Storia delle Bonifiche del Regno di Napoli* (Bari, 1928).

27. L. De Rosa, 'Property rights and economic change – economic growth in the 18th & 19th centuries in Southern Italy' in *Proceedings of the VIIth International Economic History Conference* (Edinburgh, 1978).

28. A. Graziani, 'Il Commercio Estero del Regno delle Due Sicilie', *Archivio Economico dell'Unificazione Italiana*, ser. 1, vol. x (1960) p. 27.

29. *Naples Chamber of Commerce*, Register of Proceedings: 11 April 1843.

30. L. Bianchini, *Storia delle Finanze del Regno di Napoli*, vol. VII (Naples, 1859), p. 545.

31. G. Della Valle, *Della Miseria Pubblica, Sue Cause ed Indizzi* (Naples, 1833), pp. 26-7.

32. Ibid, pp. 29-30.

33. L. de Samuele Cagnazzi, *Saggio sullo Stato presente della populazione del Regno di Puglia ne' passati tempi e nel presente*, vol. II (Naples, 1839), 245.

34. G. Della Valle, *Della Miseria Pubblica*, p. 35.

35. L. Bianchini, 'Se la conversione delle rendite pubbliche del R. di Napoli sia giusta ed utile', *Il Progresso*, vol. XIV (Naples, 1836) p. 122.

36. *Atti della Giunta*, vol. VII, p. 155.

37. e.g. C. Afan de Rivera, *Considerazioni sui mezzi da restituire il Valore proprio a' doni che ha la natura largamente conceduto al Regno delle Due Sicilie* 2 vols (Naples, 1833).

38. For a contrary view see: D. Demarco, *op. cit.*

39. D. Demarco, *Il Crollo del Regno delle due Sicilie*, p. 173.

40. A. Graziani, 'Il Commercio Estero'; I. Glazier and V. Bandera, 'Terms of Trade between South Italy and the UK 1817-1869', *Journal of European Economic History*, vol. I (1972) pp. 14-15.

41. See E. Sereni, *Il Capitalismo nelle Campagne 1860-1900* (Turin, 1968), pp. 179 ff.

42. M. Romani, *Storia economica d'Italia nel secolo XIX* (Rome, 1970), who does however stress the damage caused by silk worm and vine disease in the North in the 1850s; A. Caracciolo, 'La Storia Economica', pp. 597-605.

43. See A. Lyttelton below, pp. 111-120.

44. G. Cingari, *Mezzogiorno e Risorgimento* (Bari, 1970), pp. 139-56.

45. Ibid.

46. The preamble to the tariff is in L. Bianchini *Dell'influenza della Pubblica Amministrazione sulle Industrie* (Naples, 1828), pp. 20 ff.

47. G. Wenner, *L'Industria Tessile Salernitana 1824-1918* (Salerno, 1953).

48. E. Pontieri, 'Sul Trattato di Commercio Anglo-Napoletano del 1815' in *Il Riformismo Borbonico nella Sicilia del Sette e del Ottocento* (Rome, 1945), p. 289.

49. Ibid.

50. I. Glazier and V. Bandera, 'Terms of Trade', pp. 15-17.

51. On the sulphur crisis see: D. Mack Smith, *Modern Sicily* (London, 1968), pp. 385-6; V. Giura, 'La Questione degli Zolfi Siciliani 1838-41', *Cahiers Internationaux de l'Histoire Economique et Sociale* (Droz-Geneva, 1973), n. 19.

52. *Public Record Office* FO vol. 185: report to Ld. Aberdeen from British agents Sullivan and Parish, 30 Dec. 1841.

53. Ibid.

54. Ibid: 'Exposé de la question des soufres de Sicile' (1840).

55. Ibid.

56. Ibid.

57. Ibid: Sullivan and Parish to Palmerston, 27 Aug. 1841.

58. *PRO*: Board of Trade 2/11; Macgregor to Palmerston, 3 Nov. 1839.

59. *PRO*: FO vol. 161; Kennedy to Palmerston, 18 May 1839.

60. Palmerston Letter-Books (Brit. Museum Add. 48522) Naples, Sardinia, Tuscany; 20 Oct. 1835.

61. Ibid., 6 Sept. 1836; 13 Dec. 1836.

62. Ibid., 10 Oct. 1837.

63. Ibid., 3 Feb. 1838.

64. Ibid., 15 Jan. 1840.

65. V. Giura, 'La Questione degli Zolfi Siciliani', p. 75-80.

66. Ibid., p. 83.

67. *PRO*; FO 60 vol. 185; Sullivan to Palmerston, 22 June 1841.

68. Ibid.

69. J. Morley, *Life of Gladstone* vol. 1, (London, 1903), p. 391.

70. *PRO*: B.T. 2/11; 492-3 – Macgregor to Palmerston, 20 Sept. 1839.

71. See R. Moscati, *La fine del Regno di Napoli* (Florence, 1960).

72. A. Graziani, 'Il Commercio Estero, p. 21.

73. I. Glazier and V. Bandera, 'Terms of Trade', p. 15.

74. e.g. L. Blanch, 'Memoria sullo Stato di Napoli' (1830) in *Scritti Storici*, ed. B. Croce (Bari, 1945), II, pp. 302-34.

75. R. Romeo, 'Momenti e problemi della restaurazione nel Regno delle Due Sicilie' in *Mezzogiorno e Sicilia nel Risorgimento* (Naples, 1963), pp. 51-115.

76. G. Cingari, *Mezzogiorno e Risorgimento*, ch. iv.

77. L. Bianchini, *Storia delle finanze*, p. 476.

78. Ibid., p. 465.

79. Ibid., p. 493.

80. L. Settembrini, *Ricordanze della mia vita* (Feltrinelli, 1961), p. 202.

81. *Le Assemblee del Risorgimento*, vol. X (Rome, 1910), p. 256.

82. e.g. 'La piccola borghesia intelletuale nel Mezzogiorno d'Italia' in G. Salvemini, *Opere*, vol. IV (Feltinelli, 1963), pp. 483-92.

83. *The Modern Prince*, p. 42.

84. L. Blanch, 'Memoria sullo Stato di Napoli'.

85. *Archivio di Stato, Naples*: Archivio Borbone; f.807, pt. II, inc. 823; C. Ceva Grimaldi to Ferdinand II, Aug. 1843.

86. *Annona* – the name given to the complex regulations in force in the eighteenth century and earlier to guarantee urban food supplies.

87. A. Graziani, 'Il Commercio Estero', p. 8.

88. See J.A. Davis 'Oligarchia capitalistica e immobilismo economico a Napoli (1815-60)' in *Studi Storici* a xvi, n. 2 (1975) pp. 384-414; *Società e Imprenditori nel Regno Borbonico (1815-60)* (Bari, 1979), chap. 3.

89. A. Scialoja, *I Bilanci del Regno di Napoli* (Turin, 1858), p. 15.

90. *Le Assemblee del Risorgimento*, vol. X, p. 166.

91. L. Bianchini, *Storia delle Finanze*, p. 475.

92. *ASN*: Archivio Borbone; f. 866.

93. Ibid.

94. D. Mack Smith, *Modern Sicily*, p. 424; S. Romano, *Momenti del Risorgimento in Sicilia* (Florence, 1952), p. 102.

95. Chamber of Commerce, Naples: 7 Nov. 1848.

96. Ibid.

97. Cf. J. Bouvier, *Finances et Financiers de l'Ancien Régime* (Paris, 1964).

98. A. Scirocco, *Governo e paese nel Mezzogiorno nella crisi dell'unificazione* (Milan, 1963), pp. 63 ff.

99. See: R. Villari, *Problemi dell'economia napoletana alla vigilia dell'Unificazione* (Naples, 1957).

100. There is a wide bibliography on the Southern Enlightenment but see: F. Venturi, *Italy and the Enlightenment* (London, 1972); R. Romeo, 'Illuministi meridionali' in *Mezzogiorno e Sicilia*, pp. 17-51; P. Villani, 'Il Dibattito sulla feudalita nel Regno di Napoli dal Genovesi a Canosa' in *Saggi e Ricerche sul Settecento* (Naples, 1969), pp. 252-331.

101. See especially: C. Afan de Rivera, *Considerazioni*.

102. Quoted in A. Scirocco, p. 138.

4 LANDLORDS, PEASANTS AND THE LIMITS OF LIBERALISM

Adrian Lyttelton

The relationship between liberalism and the rise of industrial capitalism is variable and can take on many different forms. The two leading new nations of the later nineteenth century, Germany and Italy, provide an interesting contrast in this respect. In Germany the genius of Bismarck helped to preserve illiberal political structures and values in an industrialising society. In Italy, on the other hand, under the leadership of Cavour a liberal elite took power in a predominantly agrarian society. In both cases, though in different ways, the lack of symmetry between political and economic structures ended by discrediting them and facilitating the flight into dictatorship.[1] In Italy, the part played by agrarian conflict in bringing about the final breakdown of liberal institutions was decisive. In the years after the First World War, in spite of such dramatic episodes as the occupation of the factories, the breakdown of the state's mediating function and the consequent crisis of confidence among the employers was not so complete or radical in industry as it was in agriculture. The political aims of the agrarians were more extreme than those of the urban fascists; nothing less than a total reconstruction of the state could consolidate their rural counter-revolution.[2] So if one looks for the long-term origins of fascism, the agrarian question must be held to be of primary importance.

This essay will attempt to investigate some of the ways in which the agrarian problem shaped and constrained Italian liberalism. My concern will not be with the story of organised class conflict, but with its prehistory. It is part of my argument that much of the initial thrust behind Italian liberalism came from the activities of an elite of enlightened, modernising landlords. Although little work has been done on the political attitudes of landlords during the nineteenth century, enough is known at least about their economic performance to make clear the extent of inertia and resistance to innovation even in the most progressive regions. Yet, because the old order did not offer satisfactory answers to the problems posed by the industrial revolution and the changing structure of markets in Europe, the progressive minority came to occupy a strategic position. It has been a commonplace in criticism of the Risorgimento to point out that the 'bourgeois revolution' in Italy was incomplete because of the continued influence of the traditional landed classes. While this criticism seems in essence valid, its formulation has often obscured the nature of the problem. Liberalism had never been the ideology of an autonomous bourgeois revolution (Mazzinian nationalism might perhaps make that claim); nor were agrarian capitalism and innovation exclusively the work of the new bourgeoisie. In short, the compromise was not so much one between social groups as between social principles. The same men who sincerely promoted the formation of a national market for commodities and a national public for information, tried to reconcile these liberal ideals with relations of production which did not meet the needs of capitalist rationality and with forms of patronage which prolonged the fragmentation of politics.

The most ambitious and influential recent theory that has attempted to link the course of political development with that of agrarian change is contained in the well-known book by Barrington Moore Jr., *The Social Origins of Dictatorship and Democracy*.[3] It is a book with very valuable insights, but some serious weaknesses. One of the major drawbacks is that his method of analysis leads him to write as if agricultural and political systems were co-extensive, i.e. as if nations had one dominant system of agriculture. This is a dubious assumption anywhere and it would be particularly inapplicable to Italy. Not only the variations of climate and relief but the absence of unifying political institutions have produced an extraordinary variety of different agricultural systems in Italy. Any adequate analysis of political development must take account of their plurality. One can, however, salvage the spirit rather than the letter of Barrington Moore's enterprise by maintaining that the major paths of development which he suggests led to dictatorship, democracy or revolution were all present within the complex and regionally fragmented reality of Italy. To put things differently, we can distinguish − as a rough guide − four or five different modes of relationship between landlord and peasant, each of which had different political consequences. The names I have given these are dependence, antagonism, communal rebellion, factionalism and co-operation. The last of these plays little part in the story. To simplify considerably, the North and Centre of Italy, and especially the regions where share-cropping was dominant, were distinguished by the breakdown of traditional relationships of dependence leading to antagonism and finally to overt and organised class conflict, whereas the South was distinguished by an alternation of communal rebellion and factionalism. The reader should be cautioned against one weakness inherent in this approach. It does not do justice to the importance of the linkages between local communities and the larger world, or to the role of the 'fringes' of rural society in maintaining these links.[4] Unfortunately, with a few exceptions, notably in the study of the Sicilian *mafia*, this is a field which has been little explored.

One of Barrington Moore's main ideas is of great relevance to the understanding of the Risorgimento. This is his argument that the character of the response made by the landed upper class to the opportunities of increased production for the market is crucial for political development. By focusing attention on the relationship between the landed upper classes, the state and the peasantry, he avoids many of the pitfalls contained in the concept of the 'bourgeois revolution'.[5]

The argument against attributing the main role in the Risorgimento to the commercial or industrial bourgeoisie had been stated, long before Barrington Moore, by the American historian K.R. Greenfield. In his study of Lombardy, the region where an aggressive capitalist class might most plausibly have been expected to develop, he showed that the antithesis between dynamic progressive entrepreneurs and reactionary noble landlords did not fit the facts. The merchant class of Milan was for the most part highly traditional in outlook; it was not interested in the development of distant markets but in monopolising the existing opportunities, particularly in the luxury trades. On the other hand, members of the landed aristocracy were prominent in the liberal movement.[6] However, Greenfield's arguments against a materialist interpretation of the Risorgimento seem dubious in one respect. In so far as the nobility and large landed proprietors were interested in commercial agriculture, increasing specialisation and raising crop yields, they also had an interest in the removal of obstacles to trade. Moreover, as Greenfield himself shows, a number of landowners were also industrialists, who built silk-reeling mills on their estates.

The origins of the liberal movement can be traced back to the reforms of the eighteenth century. In Lombardy particularly the continuity is evident. A small number of patrician families provided much of the leadership; in the eighteenth century the circle of the Caffè around Pietro Verri and Beccaria, in the Restoration period Confalonieri and his friends of the review *Il Conciliatore*.[7] It would be wrong to suggest that the reformers of the eighteenth century were moved primarily by material interest, or that most noble landowners found it easy to accept their ideas. Certainly the reforming programme would have had little success if it had not coincided with the action of the Austrian state. The governments of Maria Theresa and Joseph, acting in conjunction with the reformers among the nobility, ended the patricians' monopoly of office and expropriated their valuable rights of taxation.[8] At the same time as the nobles lost the old basis of their power as an office-holding and feudal order, the market offered them new economic opportunities. The rising prices of wheat and other agricultural produce in the later eighteenth century stimulated a search for ways in which marketable surpluses could be increased. Since feudal rents and revenues had at first risen together with prices, it is fairly clear that without state action the nobility would not have had much incentive to change its attitudes. But the combination of a new vulnerability and a new opportunity made the ideas of the reformers relevant to the situation in which the landed upper classes found themselves. Before the coming of Napoleon in 1796 they were only a minority of the patriciate, though a significant one.[9] However, the French occupation greatly accelerated change by abolishing altogether the formal privileges of the nobility, and put the reformers in a position of great strategic importance. One of their number, Francesco Melzi d'Eril, became vice president of the Republic of Italy under Napoleon.

What the moderate reformers of the eighteenth century wanted was to transform the mentality of the nobility and thereby put their power on a new basis. They sought to convert their fellow nobles from an order of feudal office-holders educated in jurisprudence into a class of enlightened landlords educated in economics. Active participation in agriculture and commerce was to compensate for the loss of income derived from exclusive privileges. Melzi advised the nobles to give up the illusory advantages of rank and concentrate on the real advantages of property.[10] The model was clearly something like the English aristocracy, a class whose power was founded on a solid economic base but which still enjoyed certain formal marks of deference. These last, however, had to be earned by the merits of the nobility as a ruling class. Verri's argument for the continuing preponderance of the nobility in the state did not rest on a defence of the existing structure of legal privileges, but on the sociological argument that only a class of hereditary landowners had both the experience and the leisure needed for the pursuit of the public interest.

A principal aim of both eighteenth-century reformers and nineteenth-century liberals was to establish the political and economic prerequisites for a developed system of commercial agriculture. These were: the establishment of unambiguous and clearly defined property rights in land, with the abolition of feudal tenure and the cutomary rights of tenants and peasant communities; the conversion into private property of communal, Church and public lands; the creation of an active and free land market by the abolition of trusts, entails and primogeniture; and the removal of both administrative and physical obstacles to free trade in agricultural produce. This was the economic side of the 'national programme', which was adopted by the progressive section of the nobility and won wide support among the middle classes.[11]

The place of economics in the reform movement cannot be dismissed as mere ideology. Class interest, rather, acted as a selective force, implementing those points in the programme which were acceptable to the landed classes. Economics to the reformers was 'the science of public good', and the 'public good' at which reformers like Beccaria aimed was not simply that of increased production; a just distribution of the product should also be among the aims of the economist. However, optimistic presuppositions veiled the possible conflict between the needs of production and those of distribution. Beccaria, it is true, recognised that the large capitalist farms of Lombardy, run by leaseholders, were more efficient than small peasant farms. In general, nevertheless, he believed that small property was more efficient than large, and that a better distribution from the point of view of social justice would also lead to an increase in production. The second crucial presupposition was that the establishment of a free market in land would automatically bring about this optimum distribution. Concentration of landholding was seen as an unnatural evil arising from entails and primogeniture.[12]

The first serious attempt by governments at agrarian reform showed that the task of reconciling optimum production with optimum distribution was not easy. The precarious viability of small peasant property was shown by the outcome both of Peter Leopold's reforms in Tuscany and of those of Caracciolo in Sicily. The hardly fortuitous coincidence between the freeing of the grain trade and the rise of prices produced violent reactions from peasants (and urban artisans) in several regions of Italy. In Tuscany, after the 1790 riots which led to the fall of the reforming minister Gianni, discontent erupted again in the 1799 movement of the *Viva Maria* bands against the French occupation. In Piedmont, peasant hatred of the new class of capitalist leaseholders found expression both in sporadic outbreaks of violence and in petitions to the King.[13] Centralisation and the attack on the privileges of the Church were also frequently resented by the peasants as a menace to the values of the local community. In Tuscany, the traditionalist clergy were able to guide peasant agitation into the channels of religious reaction against the reforms of the Jansenist clerics which had been temporarily backed by the state. These reformers aimed to reduce unproductive diversions such as processions and feast-days, and particularly objected to what seemed to them the grotesque proliferation of local cults of the saints. To the peasant, a religion which attacked familiar rituals and struck at the symbols of local community must have seemed cold and incomprehensible.

From these early failures, the later heirs of the reforming programme learnt a lesson of caution. The liberals of the nineteenth century were more limited and less optimistic in their social aims, and they had notable and well-grounded hesitations about disturbing the traditional order either in religion or in property relations. Yet if their broader aim, that of bringing Italy into the family of advanced nations, was to be achieved, they had to effect change both in modes of production and in values. Ultimately they had to choose; but men and societies can stand a lot of inconsistency, and it was a long time before the contradictions inherent in the liberalism of enlightened landlords showed themselves to be irreconcilable.

Under the *ancien régime* the prevalent form of tenure in most of North and Central Italy, except in the mountain areas, was the *mezzadria* or sharecropping system. In its classical form, peasant and landlord each had a half share in all produce, although there were many local variations and exceptions to equal division. Even in the regions of classical *mezzadria* there is an important distinction to be made between areas where the peasants were expected to provide most of the farm's working capital and those where the landlords did. Thus the relatively prosperous *mezzadri* of Bologna and the Po Valley were required to furnish the draught animals for the farm. In the hills of Tuscany and Umbria, however, where the *mezzadria* system was most solidly rooted, the landlord provided the cattle and the sharecropper usually owned only a few tools. Under the *mezzadria* system the landlord always had the obligation to provide a house — for which he could charge rent — and an integrated farm or *podere*. The *podere* had to be a workable unit of cultivation with proper drainage and was usually planted with vines, olives or fruit trees. *Appoderamento* or the creation of *poderi* required a quite considerable initial investment on the part of the landlord.[14] Once set up, however, the *mezzadria* system had the advantage from the landlord's point of view of minimising the outlay of working capital. The *mezzadria* system was associated with a pattern of highly dispersed settlement and with large, extended or multiple family units. The dominance of the towns over the country established in the communal period had exerted itself to the detriment of the cohesion of peasant communities. The scattered families of cultivators who delivered their produce to urban landlords were largely self-sufficient.

The relationship between landlord and tenant was in theory governed by a freely revocable contract. In law, the right of the landlord to dispossess the sharecropper at the end of the year was unrestricted, and it was frequently employed. The threat of eviction allowed the landlord to exercise a high degree of control over the lives of his tenants. The agent or *fattore* was expected to watch carefully for any signs of immorality or unreliability, such as frequent visits to the inn or extravagance in dress. The structure of the peasant family was highly patriarchal. The head of the family was responsible to the landlord for the work and good behaviour of all the household's members, even if they were married adults. He controlled all the regular agricultural earnings of the household.

The *mezzadria* contract usually contained supplementary obligations on the tenant to perform certain kinds of labour, such as carting and the maintenance of ditches. These, and the heavy overtones of personal allegiance surrounding the relationship, give some content to the Marxist term 'feudal residues'. In spite of the heavy burdens it imposed, the *mezzadria* system offered some advantages to the peasant family. It allowed the family to work together as a single productive unit, and in spite of the legal insecurity of the peasants' position, a high degree of actual stability often prevailed. The *mezzadria* contract was a partnership, although an unequal one. The landlord could prescribe what crops were grown and how they should be cultivated, e.g. how often land should be ploughed. The obligation to work fields by the spade, a method which required heavy labour from the peasants, was often included in contracts. But the landlord could not easily alter practices or methods without the agreement of the peasant. This was always seen by agricultural reformers as one of the major drawbacks of the system, since it made innovation very difficult. The first interest of the peasant was to secure subsistence for his family.[15] He tried as far as possible to achieve self-sufficiency and to restrict cash purchases, and in consequence opposed specialisation. I should add that this description does not apply to sharecroppers in the immediate vicinity of large cities, who were often more market-orientated. In general, however, the *mezzadria* system was bound up with the mode of agriculture known as *cultura promiscua* — promiscuous cultivation — in which fields of wheat or maize were interspersed by rows of vines, olives or fruit trees. This system of cultivation was often denounced as economically irrational because it achieved lower yields than specialised cultivation would have done. But it was not irrational from the peasant's point of view. As well as ensuring self-sufficiency, the *cultura promiscua* system allowed the peasant to spread his risks; a bad year was unlikely to affect all crops equally. Even the criticism which reformers and Marxist historians have levelled at *mezzadria*, namely that it rested on the premise that the labour of the peasant family would receive remuneration inferior to its real cost, while valid in the context of a modern economy, may be historically misleading. As theorists of the peasant economy like Chayanov and Kula have pointed out, such a criticism fails to take account of the following: (1) that in an economy largely dominated by self-sufficient producers, it does not make much sense to value their labour at the current market rate; and (2) that it is in the interest of the head of the peasant family to maximise its production, even if the rate of return is very low, as otherwise some of the family's labour power might not be utilised at all.[16]

The *mezzadria* system put a premium on the size and cohesion of the peasant household. In theory, at least, the landlords distributed the various farms among the *mezzadri* in relation to the amount of labour they could command. Consequently, a large family unit with several able-bodied men stood to obtain a large farm, and would enjoy economic advantages as well as social prestige. Carlo Cattaneo wrote: 'In order that such a sharecropping system may prove useful it is necessary that the peasant family should be numerous and fit for labour.'[17] A family whose labour did not meet requirements could hire wage labourers, but their higher cost meant that the family would usually be hard-pressed to maintain their obligations to the landlord. In addition, the multiple family system, in which peasants and married children or married brothers lived and worked together, again served to reduce risks. A complex household is less exposed to the normal fluctuations of birth and death than a simple one. The death of one adult wage-earner may be fatal to the labour capacity of a simple nuclear family: it will have proportionately less effect on the larger unit. So from both the peasant and the landlord's point of view the multiple family served to maintain continuity and ensure a supply of labour adequate to the needs of the farm.

During the 1820s and the 1830s the *mezzadria* system came under severe attack in its heartland, Tuscany. The dramatic fall in prices after the Napoleonic wars, which put an end to 50 years of profitable inflation, stimulated some landlords to make greater efforts to raise productivity. Some reformers argued that *mezzadria* should be substituted by direct farming with wage labour, which would yield a higher rate of return on capital. The defenders of the system often admitted the truth of the purely economic criticisms. However, they argued that the social and political benefits of the system outweighed its economic disadvantages. They described it as a 'fraternal society between capitalist and worker', in which the latter was 'not a machine but a man', not a slave but a companion.[18] Fifty years later the writer of the report on Tuscany in the great Jacini agrarian enquiry still uses the same arguments. In terms of social relationships, 'the system of *mezzadria* in Tuscany fully achieved the solution of the most difficult problem of our age and removes all antagonism between capital and labour. The Tuscan *mezzadro* feels he is a partner and not a slave of the landowner ... neither historical memories nor present facts awake the ideas of oppressor and oppressed; while instead the classes see each other as protector and protected.'[19] The intellectuals among the landlord class, like Gino Capponi were influenced by events outside Italy. The 1830 revolution in France and the rise of industrial class conflict in England alarmed them and increased their caution about provoking social change in the interests of economic efficiency. One should note here the use of the modern terms 'capitalist' and 'worker' to describe, somewhat paradoxically, a system in which the antagonism arising from an unequivocal cash nexus was avoided.

Behind these lofty motivations, however, other reasons for the maintenance of *mezzadria* may be discerned. Landlords too wished to minimise risk, and a lot of capital had been sunk in peasant housing, which could not easily be adapted to a system of wage labour. From the point of view of profit, the experiments of the reformers were not particularly successful.[20] Underlying the rhetoric of co-operation and 'affection' between landlord and peasant, we can easily discern the logic of dependence. The *mezzadria* system ensured peasant submissiveness. One of the secrets of landlord control lay in the system of accounting and debt. The landlord was expected by custom though not by law to 'carry' his tenant's debt from one year to another: the same was true if the peasants had a credit against the landlord. Either way, this made the ties hard to break. The isolation of the *mezzadri* was another strong guarantee of social order. The English economist Bowring noted: 'the universal isolation of the peasants, a necessary consequence of the *mezzadria* system. Where there is no association, there is necessarily extreme ignorance. Every family of peasants in Tuscany lives as if it were alone.' Social tranquillity was thus ensured, but, he added, only at 'the terrible cost of a stationary civilisation'. Gino Capponi, in his defence of *mezzadria* wrote that the peasant families associated with each other only at Church or at the market; and visits to market were rare 'because they buy and sell little. A good farmer goes to market seldom.'[21] The importance of this isolation comes out clearly if we read the correspondence of the future Prime Minister of Italy, Bettino Ricasoli, during the period of the 1848 revolution. During the rule of the democrats in 1849 Ricasoli's letters insist that it is both vital and possible to keep the peasants in complete ignorance of what was happening.[22]

Other aspects of the Ricasoli correspondence show the strains imposed on the *mezzadria* by an ambitious landlord whose urge for achievement as well as search for profit led him to apply intense effort and will-power to the rationalisation of agriculture. Tuscany produced few fine wines because the peasants valued quantity more than quality.[23] Ricasoli was one of the few landowners who succeeded in emulating French wine-growers in the consistency of his vintage. To achieve this he had to introduce a rigid discipline and conformity which went beyond the normal pressures of the system. Ricasoli's distinctive religious views, for his was a peculiarly Protestant kind of Catholicism, underpinned his adherence to a particularly rigorous form of the work ethic. He was particularly annoyed when he found out that his peasants had been making donations of oil to the friars before he received his share. On this issue, as on that of the right to gather wood, Ricasoli's interpretation of property rights came into collision with custom and with the peasants' sense of fairness. The religious issue had even wider significance. Here two different mentalities were involved. For the peasants, giving alms to the Church was not only a duty but a spiritual investment, designed to secure better harvests through the intercession of the friars.[24] The conflict between the liberal movement and the Church must be seen as the major influence which undermined the hegemony of the landed classes, though its political effects did not become evident until after the irreparable breach of unification.

North of the Appennines, the landlords' response to the new opportunities and necessities of production for the market was eventually more decisive. In Emilia and the Veneto, cultural and political innovation lagged behind Tuscany. But the flat land and heavy, rich soil of the Po Valley had far higher potential for the new agriculture than the light soils of the Tuscan hills. The incentive to destroy *mezzadria* tenure and to extend the area of specialised farming, particularly cattle-raising, was consequently greater. The irrigated Lombard plain had for centuries offered the example of the possibilities of capitalism and high farming. However, even in the Po Valley the elimination of *mezzadria* tenure was a slow and incomplete process. By 1848 population growth had already produced large agglomerations of landless labourers in the villages around Bologna. In the commune of Molinella, for example, which achieved legendary status in the twentieth century as a centre of peasant socialism and resistance to fascism, labourers formed 55 per cent of the agricultural population in 1847 compared to 40 per cent of sharecroppers. But in the Bolognese plain as a whole sharecroppers still outnumbered labourers by 52 per cent to 40 per cent, and in the hills they were almost three times as numerous.[25] Most other provinces would almost certainly have shown a lower percentage of labourers at this date. Even in the later nineteenth century *mezzadria* tenures remained prevalent in the hills and did not disappear altogether in the plains. Rather, with the reduction in their number, the *mezzadria* became a relatively privileged minority within the rural population as increased taxation and indebtedness forced many families down into the ranks of the agricultural proletariat. Falling infant mortality and the introduction of more intensive methods of cultivation both favoured the growth of the large multiple household; but at the same time the tensions always present within these large families were accentuated by the growing rebelliousness of the younger peasants. This was attributed by contemporaries both to the effects of military service and to the greater demand for labour especially on reclamation projects.[26]

Why did the landlords allow the *mezzadria* to survive even where the advantages of direct management were evident? In large part, I think, because the social and political dangers of a landless proletariat were evident even before the great agricultural strikes of the 1880s. The landless labourer might be economically necessary, but as a social type he was undesirable. His characteristics, as seen by the landlord, differed from those of the sharecropper as night from day. The uncertainty of employment — he was lucky if he could find work two days out of three — not only reduced him to desperate poverty but destroyed all incentives for regularity and sobriety. 'They live between a debauch and a fast.'[27] The *bracciantie* lived in large communities and rapidly acquired the habits of urban life. They were the first rural workers to acquire a taste for smoking, in spite of their poverty. Drink, disorder and unstable family ties were — with some exaggeration — believed to be as characteristic of them as of the urban proletariat. They took out their resentment in drunken abuse of their betters and they stole to keep alive. By the 1870s rural theft had become one of the main worries of landlords, second only to taxes. Policing was inadequate, and many local officials were afraid to take action. In some areas seasonal migration from the over-populated mountains aggravated the problem. A Venetian proprietor in the 1870s complained of the 'swarms' of 'nomads' who descended from the mountains with nothing but a stick and a handkerchief and slept out in haylofts. They lived, he said, not only by begging but by devastating the crops and fruit trees of the farms they passed.[28] Theft naturally hit the sharecropper or small tenant even harder than the landlord. Consequently it would not be an exaggeration to say that before the 1880s the major form of overt and endemic class hostility was that between peasant farmer and day labourer. This was another powerful influence in maintaining traditional patterns of dependence.

Ricasoli was only one of the liberal leaders who was also prominent as an agricultural reformer. Among the chief statemen of the Risorgimento, both Cavour and the Bolognese Minghetti played a leading role in their local agrarian associations. The ideology of liberalism was bound up with admiration for the English free trade system and received support from England for this reason. The economic and political strategy of Cavour depended on a vision of the complementary interests of Italian exporters of primary goods and English industry. It was only at a later stage that the incompatibility of free trade with the development of Italian industry was perceived. In any case, until the great agrarian crisis of the 1880s many landlords, though certainly not Cavour, were prepared to argue that large-scale industrialisation was undesirable because of its social consequences.

The mentality of Cavour was notably different from that of Ricasoli. The Cavours were altogether an odd family. Cavour's father was an extraordinary combination of place-seeker, large farmer and speculator. The absurdity of neat divisions between aristocratic and bourgeois mentality can be seen in the career of a man who continued to manipulate his family connections and his influence at court as zealously as any *ancien régime* noble, while at the same time investing in improved rice cultivation, merino sheep, steamers and, most striking of all, acting as agent to collect a Geneva banker's debts. This was unusual. The Piedmontese nobility preserved a far more prickly and exclusive consciousness of rank than the Lombards or the Tuscans right down to 1848.

The great Cavour was even less of a traditional aristocrat than his father. Court life was repugnant to him. He was an individualist, who regarded family traditions and controls with impatience. However in his vision of society he still assigned the landed upper classes a central role. Though his own estates in the rice-growing area of Vercelli were cultivated by wage-labour, like the Tuscan landlords he hesitated before the prospect of creating an agricultural proletariat on the English model. He was not, he said, 'the absolute partisan of the English agricultural system', which had transformed the land into 'a collection of vast workshops, where there is only a master and workers'. He praised the Lombard system of silkworm-raising for preserving 'the ties of sympathy and affection' between landlords and workers. Only a class of landowners who succeeded in retaining the loyalty of their tenants would be able 'to dominate the movement of society in such a way that it is progressive and ameliorative instead of destructive and revolutionary'.[29] The landed aristocracy should not promote change beyond the point where it would undermine their political influence.

It should be noted that Piedmont was the region in Italy where a property-owning peasantry developed most successfully. By the mid-nineteenth century some peasant proprietors had already made the transition from subsistence agriculture to specialised commodity production. This posed problems for the aristocracy since a more independent peasant class could turn to the alternative political leadership provided by the small-town notables from the professional classes. On the other hand, Piedmont was the one region in which liberalism could be said to have acquired a popular following in the countryside.[30] As has been pointed out by other critics of Barrington Moore, where the peasantry itself is capable of making the transition to commercial agriculture its survival, even alongside the landowning nobility, would seem to favour the development of democracy. The Piedmontese case would seem to confirm this. However, it is far more questionable whether the traditional deference of a subordinate class of tenants or sharecroppers to their landlords, such as existed in other regions of Italy, can successfully adapt to the pressures of change. The strategy of landlord control began to break down in some of the *mezzadria* areas soon after unification. In these areas, specialisation had already changed the nature of the *mezzadria* contract from within. Thus in Bologna province, the great expansion in hemp cultivation destroyed the traditional balance between crops on which the peasant economy had been based. Hemp was by far the most profitable crop for the landlord, but for the peasant it meant more intensive and more closely regulated work. The social character of the peasant's work changed and became more and more like day labour.[31]

The growing tensions between landlord and peasant arising directly out of the relations of production were accentuated by the wider social and political developments associated with unification. After 1860, the conflict with the Church weakened the liberal landlords' hegemony at the same time as the increased burden of state taxation sharpened the discontent of the peasants. The 1869 riots against the milling tax were the most serious outbreak of peasant discontent in north Italy since Napoleonic times. By the end of the next decade, the onset of the world agricultural depression destroyed the premises on which landlord liberalism had previously been ased. The majority of the

the landowning classes were converted to protectionism. Some groups, like the Tuscan landlords, whose best opportunities lay in developing wine and oil exports, remained relatively faithful to free trade. But the general European triumph of protectionism condemned this strategy to failure. In Tuscany particularly, the victory of protectionism destroyed the stimulus for innovation and with it the optimistic faith in progress.[32] It can be argued that the importance of the formation of the 'protectionist bloc' has been over-emphasised. In both agriculture and industry, interests which were favourable to free trade were later to lend enthusiastic support to fascism. What was vital was not so much the deliberate creation of a protectionist alliance as the failure of the previous strategy of development, made inevitable by the changing structure of world markets.

The 1880s also saw the first successes of the Socialists, unique in Europe, in organising agricultural labour in the lowland of Emilia and Lombardy. The prevailing response of the landlords was to demand repression. However, there were some who argued that the fault was in the system of wage labour, and that a reversal of the trend away from *mezzadria* would diminish militancy, while also cushioning the landlords against the effects of a rise in wages. At the same time, though, the improvement of communications and the spread of market relationships put the landlords under greater pressure to modernise. Productivity and social peace came more and more clearly into conflict. The advantage of *mezzadria* to the peasant also dwindled as wage labour became remunerative and as the consumption of urban goods increased. The landlords tried to lay the burden of modernisation on the peasant by making him pay all or a large part of the cost of fertilisers, protective crop sprays and threshing machinery.[33] Changes in methods of cultivation and type of crop were resisted by the peasant because they involved more risks, more expense and more work, while his security against eviction was not enough to allow him to put his faith in long-term improvements. Greater subordination was combined with greater uncertainty, and resentment at innovation sharpened the peasant's awareness of the traditional forms of exploitation.

Nevertheless, until the First World War the landlord continued to play an important role as patron, by mediating between the peasant and the foreign worlds of the law and state administration. Unification, by increasing the pressures of the latter, may even have made the landlord's protection more necessary than before. Perhaps only a major political crisis, such as the war provided, could have shaken this traditional pattern. Once confidence was broken, it could never be restored. Both landlords and peasants took an increasingly literal view of their contractual rights and obligations. The harsh outlines of the economic relationship were no longer obscured by the halo of social custom. As a 'strictly business contract'[34] the *mezzadria* did not work well. It did not guarantee to either party a sufficient certainty of profit and therefore discouraged innovation. Gains could only be made at the expense of the other party. Once landlord hegemony had broken down, coercion became necessary to the profitability of the system.

The *mezzadria* system in central Italy worked like a kind of dam. For a long time it effectively contained and limited peasant discontent and prevented it from finding an outlet. In the end, the dam broke, with dramatic results. Nowhere was the mobilisation of the peasantry so abrupt as in Tuscany and Umbria in 1919-20, and nowhere else was the counter-offensive of the landlords so brutal. The success of the system in delaying the emergence of peasant protest, and also of other forms of change, such as the break-up of large estates, contributed to this polarisation. The delay may help to explain why Tuscany became a 'red' region while the Veneto became a bastion of Christian democracy. In both regions, until the First World War, the strength of the right of the Liberal Party reflects the continued recognition of the landlord as patron by his tenants. But in the Veneto and Lombardy this went together with new forms of association sponsored by the Catholic movement. In these regions, the landlords' response had avoided a shift to wage labour. They kept their tenants on the land but compelled them to pay their rent either in money or in certain specified crops, rather than in a half share of all. The point of the latter arrangement was to increase the landlord's share of marketable cash crops, while leaving the tenants with those needed for subsistence. The most widely diffused contract of this sort was the *fitto a grano*, or wheat lease, in which the peasant paid a fixed rent in wheat; this contract was made possible by the spread in the cultivation of maize, which replaced wheat as the staple of peasant diet.[35] Since maize met the peasant's subsistence needs, wheat became a cash crop, which was handed over to the landlord for sale. As the yields of maize per acre were much higher than those of wheat the change made possible a great increase in the rural population. Maize did for Italy what the potato did for Ireland and Northern Europe. It lowered the threshold of survival. This is always an ambiguous benefit. Fewer peasants died of famine, but according to one observer the diffusion of the maize diet led to a 'sensible deterioration in bodily stature, colour, and strength'.[36] Reliance on an exclusive diet of maize could in fact cause the terrible deficiency disease of pellagra, leading to madness and death. Although by the mid-nineteenth century maize had spread almost everywhere it could possibly be cultivated, even in arid and mountainous areas of the South, where the crop was highly precarious, it was in the Veneto and Lombardy that it remained most important. The incidence of pellagra was highest in these areas, and the peasants' capacity to survive on maize explains why the wheat lease was most common in the Veneto.

The landlords also took steps to secure a larger take of other easily marketable crops such as wine, oil and silk. The growth in demand for silk on the markets of Lyons and London prompted the landlords to extend the planting of mulberry trees. In the late 1870s, according to Jacini, the hills of Lombardy were 'like one vast mulberry grove'. In order to secure the full co-operation of the peasants in protecting the trees and raising the silkworms, which were peculiarly vulnerable to neglect, it was necessary to concede them a share of the final product.[37] The landlords, however, controlled the disposal and marketing of the cocoons and paid the peasant in cash. So in the silk-raising areas a form of share-cropping survived and was actually strengthened by the advance of commercialisation. Incidentally, the landlords also took more care of rural housing and hygiene in these areas, but their real concern was for the health of the silkworm, rather than the peasants. The large role played by women both in raising the silkworms and in reeling the raw silk made it a family enterprise. Silk production was a highly profitable commercial enterprise which was none the less compatible with the preservation of the existing agrarian structure. It was this relatively tradition-bound form of commercialisation which gave the first real impulse to industrial development.[38] This did not take place according to the classical model by which the capitalist agricultural revolution simultaneously expels or 'liberates' labour from the land and ensures the surplus necessary for the subsistence of an urban working class: rather, for a long time industrial and agricultural work were 'intertwined'. Even after the introduction of the factory system much of the industrial workforce was provided by the women and children of peasant families who still worked the land. This part-time system allowed the industrialist to pay lower wages and provided the workers with some sort of cushion against unemployment. 'Getting rid of the peasants', as B. Moore puts it, does not necessarily turn them into industrial workers, and on the other hand in the first stage of industrialisation, labour in industry does not necessarily destroy the peasant family economy. The areas where this kind of industrialisation took place were likely to show a higher degree of participation by the peasants in organised political movements than elsewhere. Savings accumulated through industrial labour ultimately assisted peasant land purchase. Class tensions were less unmanageable in these areas and it is significant that fascism found it difficult to get a foothold.

At the same time, though, the effect of this pattern of industrialisation on the mentality of employers was unfavourable to liberal values. The peculiar nature of this type of industrialisation fostered the emergence of an anti-democratic paternalism which attempted to combine traditional values with modern techniques. The leading textile industrialist Alessandro Rossi, who was the architect of the protectionist bloc between industrialists and agrarians, was also an apologist for rural industry, the worker-peasant and for Catholicism and 'social imperialism' against liberalism.[39] The peculiar nature of industrialisation in parts of the Lombardo-Veneto area may help to explain the surprising success of the Catholic Church in maintaining its influence not only in rural areas but in partially industrialised communities.

The South presents a very different picture. The agrarian conditions of southern Italy and Sicily had more in common with Andalusia, or even Hungary, than with the Lombard plains. In the South, moreover, feudalism was still a political as well as an economic reality at the end of the eighteenth century. In spite of the reforms, feudal jurisdiction had resisted the inroads of royal absolutism much more successfully than in France or northern Italy. Outside Naples, about 70 per cent of the population still lived in communes subject to feudal control. Within the nobility, there was an enormous concentration of land and power in the hands of a small number of families. Eighty-four families controlled 2 million vassals out of a total population of 5 million; there were 18 families with more than 30,000 vassals each, headed by Prince Pignatelli with 70,000.[40] Yet this vast extension of feudal control was a source of weakness as well as of strength. The peasant communities of the South, living for the most part in highly concentrated settlements, had a tradition of active resistance to feudal claims, with the leadership usually coming from a small number of bourgeois rural notables. The barons could less easily obtain compensation for the loss of feudal revenues; the abysmal state of communications and of techniques in most areas precluded any resort to specialised commercial agriculture. Absenteeism undoubtedly often prevented the nobility from seizing what opportunities there were. Probably about one quarter of all noble families, and a much larger number of the higher nobility, lived in Naples, at a much greater distance from their estates than even the town-dwelling aristocracy of the north. Thus, while the political power of the nobility remained greater in Naples than in the North, its economic basis was weaker.

It does not yet seem quite clear how generally the eighteenth-century inflation had already eroded the revenues of the feudatories. In some fiefs, the real control over a large part of the land had been alienated by the feudatory through its concession on payment of a fixed and inalienable quit-rent (emphyteusis).[41] In the 1790s many baronial rights of taxation suffered expropriation by the Crown. However, elsewhere active feudatories succeeded in maintaining their position and income. Revenues derived directly from land (mainly in the form of tithes levied in kind, and therefore not subject to monetary depreciation), did not suffer the same reduction as other forms of feudal income.[42] The control of forests and pasture often yielded considerable profits, which rose with the increase in population and economic activity. Nor should one overlook the active role of some barons in the grain trade or even in other commercial enterprises.[43]

Ultimately, however, almost everything depended on the balance of power within the local community. Security of property was legally (and physically) far harder to establish than in the north. It was consequently impossible for the Neapolitan nobility to abandon privilege for property; without privilege, property itself became insecure. Unfortunately, very little detailed work has been done on the real effects of the abolition of feudalism by the French governments of 1806-15. But in some cases the feudal commission set up under Murat severely reduced the *terraggi* (feudal rents) levied by the feudatory, as well as expropriating other forms of revenue, and the income of some estates may have been reduced by as much as three quarters.[44] The decline of the old nobility and the rise of a class of new bourgeois proprietors, the *galantuomini*, seems to have been more rapid than in the North. The comparison suggests that such a replacement of personnel has very little to do with agricultural progress. Moreover, the reformers of the French period were only very partially successful in establishing a secure basis of legitimacy for private property. The history of the South gives many examples of the resistance of social realities to new legal norms. The sales of communal and Church land gave rise to endless litigation, which influenced local politics. The successful landowner was viewed with intense suspicion; there was a universal assumption, all too often justified, that he owed his position to political intimidation or legal chicanery.[45]

In Sicily, the old feudal nobility were better able to defend their position. Here the barons had been able to paralyse the action of the administration through parliament, and in the absence of French occupation they were able to dictate the terms of the abolition of feudalism themselves. Consequently, only monopolies, offices and rights of taxation were affected, and rights over land and agricultural produce were maintained almost intact. The loss suffered has been estimated at perhaps 10 to 15 per cent of total income, but this was largely compensated by the advantages of economic freedom: the emancipation of land from common rights, the abolition of feudal dues owed to the state, and above all freedom from price controls.[46]

Peasant society in the South also differed markedly in its salient features from the patterns typical of northern and central Italy. There was a sharp difference, for example, in the demographic behaviour of the two areas. Peasant families in most of the North and Centre (excluding wage labourers) shared the general European tendency towards late marriage. In the South this check on population expansion was lacking, except in a few privileged coastal areas. This was as much a consequence of proletarianisation as a cause; where the conditions for a stable peasant agriculture existed, marriages were delayed.[47] In any case, the South after 1750 knew no respite from the starkly Malthusian realities of an expanding population held in check only by pressure on the means of subsistence. After 1820, improved communications and the low prices brought about by the import of Russian wheat prevented the recurrence of a catastrophe such as the terrible famine of 1764; but this made long-term population pressure even more insupportable. Only from the 1880s on did mass emigration bring relief.

Population pressure was a potent cause of both ecological and social degeneration. In their desperate search for new lands to cultivate, the peasants invaded forests and extended arable at the expense of pasture. Deforestation and the cultivation of marginal land previously left for rough pasture produced dramatic erosion in the hills and flooding in the plains. Less spectacular, but serious, was the impoverishment of the land in some areas due to the cultivation of wheat and maize in rotation. Secondly, increased competition for scarce land drove up rents. This in turn made it more profitable for landlords to lease their lands to impoverished subsistence farmers rather than investing money in specialised crops or plantations.

The increasing impoverishment of the peasants in the later eighteenth century and the contrasting fortunes of a small number of bourgeois proprietors seem to have destroyed the anti-feudal alliance which existed earlier in the century. As the peasantry lost their economic independence they once again turned for protection and sustenance to the great landowners. On the other hand, their resentment of feudal exploitation was to some extent overlaid by newer grievances. The position of the rural bourgeoisie was not attained by more efficient farming, but by subletting and usury.

Within the peasant communities the main way in which the notables consolidated their landholdings was by the usurpation of communal property.[48] In 1799, thanks largely to the maladroit leadership of the Neapolitan Jacobins, the Parthenopean Republic was swept away by the reactionary revolt of the Santa Fede, and after the reconquest of Naples in 1806 the French had to fight a guerrilla war comparable in savagery to the Spanish. The red thread of violent peasant counter-revolution runs through Southern history from 1799 down to the massacre of Pisacane in 1857 and the 'great brigandage' after 1860. But the continuity should not be exaggerated. The reforms of Murat seem to have brought about a short-lived revival of the anti-feudal alliance between the provincial bourgeoisie and the peasantry. The liberal Carbonari revolution of 1820, though led by the new landowners and the professional classes, had strong peasant support. One of the critical features which made this possible is that the Carbonari in 1820, unlike later liberal movements, had many active supporters among the clergy, who formed something like 15 per cent of the active leadership of the movement.[49] To some extent, the alliance between radicals and the peasantry whose absence, according to Gramsci, determined the failure of the 1799 revolution and the Left in 1860, was actually a reality in 1820. It allowed the brief success of a liberal revolution, which was overthrown from outside by the intervention of the Austrian army.

The determinants of peasant political action in the kingdom of Naples in the nineteenth century are not easy to understand. The difficulty is not in understanding the peasants' grievances, but in seeing how they translated themselves into support for the Liberals or the Bourbons. Local traditions and loyalties were obviously important. In the Abruzzi in 1848 the peasants were reported to be singing 'the old Sanfedist hymn "Col tamburo e la grancassa, viva il re e la gente bassa"'.[50] In 1860, the Abruzzi was the first region in the kingdom of Naples where the peasants rose *against* Garibaldi.

Other regions showed less consistency. Calabria, the classic country of the brigands, was the mainspring of reaction in 1799, a centre of anti-Bourbon risings in 1848, overwhelmingly on Garibaldi's side in 1860, but much afflicted by brigandage in the next few years. Even to generalise about single provinces is rash; southern peasant communities were remarkably autarchic and their mutual jealousies were another source of conflicting political allegiances.

The solution of the enigma cannot be found in a simple model of class conflict. At times, whole peasant communities did rise against the landlords. At other times, landlords were able to raise private armies from their tenants and clients. So it is not easy to determine whether actions at a particular moment were determined by class antagonism or factional loyalty. Brigandage, sometimes interpreted as simply a form of social protest, would seem in reality to have been a more complicated phenomenon. It was not always reactionary in political terms. There were 'liberal brigands' as well as royalist brigands, though mainly during the period 1815-20. Social and political motives were intertwined with the purely criminal. The brigand chiefs, though in myth they were credited with the nobility and generosity of Robin Hood, were more likely to be savage and megalomaniac individualists. The skills needed for brigandage were most easily acquired by the shepherds, who were marginal outsiders in relation to the peasant community. The most famous brigand leader, Carmine Crocco, originally took to the hills after a 'crime of honour'. He then fought alternately for the Bourbons and the liberals, until in 1861, disappointed in his hopes for a pardon, he threw in his lot with Francis II. Certainly the brigands would not have been so formidable if they had not had widespread peasant sympathy. The law-breaker was a sympathetic figure in societies which had their own methods of resolving conflict which were at odds with the official system of law-enforcement.[51] At the outset of the 'great brigandage' of the 1860s there were mass peasant risings in the Basilicata. However, before concluding that the brigands were engaging in a kind of primitive class war, one should remember that they also received food and intelligence from pro-Bourbon landowners and their dependents. In a society riven by local faction, political divisions often cut across class divisions. One should be very cautious about generalisations which see peasants and the 'old order' united against the new, thrusting bourgeoisie. This might have been partially valid in 1799, but certainly not by the 1860s. In the Basilicata it was noted that the old proprietors, educated and with relatives in the free professions, tended to be liberal, while the first generation proprietors or 'new suits', were pro-Bourbon and helped the brigands.[52] Liberalism flourished best among those who had education and status as well as property.

Brigandage attracted the attention of Bakunin and other revolutionaries, but their attempts to turn peasant discontent into revolutionary channels, like the earlier one of Carlo Pisacane, were a total failure. These failures were the result of ignorance of local conditions, errors in timing or simple incompetence; they do not show that the southern peasants were an inherently conservative force. In southern Italy, unlike the North, peasant revolt was a recurrent and terrifying reality from the

1790s down to the 1860s. This was especially true in Sicily, where the government could not draw on traditions of loyalty to the dynasty, and where even priests often sympathised with rebels. In moments of crisis, when the authority of the state had temporarily been weakened, the southern peasant community was often capable of united action. In most cases, the essential objective was the recovery of the communal lands. On the other hand, in the intervals between revolutionary crises, southern villages presented the spectacle of what Gramsci called a 'great social disintegration'. The fragmentation and instability of landholdings meant that the same man might be labourer, sharecropper and proprietor all at once. This discouraged the emergence of modern forms of class solidarity.[53] Southern peasant society seen from the inside was fiercely individualistic, competitive and litigious. Vertical ties united patrons and clients in antagonistic factions. At the same time, patronage, though all-important, was a matter of conditional and shifting alliances rather than of the stable ties of dependence more characteristic of the *mezzadria* areas. The work of A. Blok on the *mafia* shows how even the most serious class-based movement in the South, that of the Sicilian *fasci*, was caught up in factionalism after the initial period of growth. Tensions between landlords and peasants were 'converted into a different form', as the contending factions 'built downward coalitions with segments of the ruling classes'.[54] The prickly Southern sense of personal honour encouraged disputes between equals, while there was nothing dishonourable in service to those of clearly superior status. 'Honourable men' were those with large numbers of clients.

Where the boundaries between landless labourers and owners of land were well-defined, and where there was an agricultural surplus worth fighting for, as in Aphulia, stronger class-based movements did develop. John Macdonald in an important article has shown that there were two kinds of regions in southern Italy, those with a high number of emigrants and those with a strong labour movement. The first were also regions with large numbers of small peasant proprietors and tenant farmers. It was the desperate tenants or smallholders, or their sons, in areas where subdivision of the land had reached the limits set by subsistence, rather than the landless labourers, who were the typical emigrants. More controversial is Macdonald's argument that the labour movement acted as a psychological substitute for the hopes of a 'promised land' overseas.[55] Macdonald's arguments are less clearly applicable to the North, where the importance of industry complicates matters, but there is a similar contrast between the Veneto, a region of high emigration, and Emilia, the region of greatest socialist strength. There has been little or no serious study of the effect of emigration on peasant communities in Italy. But some conclusions can be risked. Emigration, by taking the edge off population pressure, kept peasant discontent below the critical level. In some areas an actual shortage of labour developed and wages rose. The Basilicata, probably the most poverty-stricken of all the southern regions, and the epicentre of peasant revolt and brigandage in the 1860s, experienced such massive emigration that it became literally depopulated, and started to attract immigrants from other regions. Emigration had far-reaching effects on peasant culture. Many emigrants returned to their native villages; the 'Americans' became a part of the social landscape and a powerful solvent of tradition. The 'American' provided a new model for peasant aspirations. Thus emigration increased the tendencies making for differentiation and individualism within the peasant community at the expense of communal solidarity.

Factionalism and emigration weakened the Southern peasants' ability to sustain collective action over long periods of time. But one must not overlook the continued function of coercion in the social order of the *mezzogiorno*. Southern agriculture was not, clearly, a coercive system in the sense used by Barrington Moore to describe serfdom or plantation agriculture. It employed subtler methods of exploitation. Fundamentally, it rested on scarcity of land and scarcity of credit. One notorious mechanism of exploitation was the 'improvement lease'. The landowner would lease land for up to twelve years for a moderate rent, on condition that the peasant planted vines or olives. At the end, just when the new plantations were beginning to be profitable, he would take the land back. The same type of contract, with a shorter lease, was used for bringing uncultivated land under wheat. The condition of peasants who undertook this last kind of contract was described by one enquiry as being 'as sad' as that of the landless labourer. 'His subsistence and that of his family depends on chance': their ignorance of agricultural techniques contributed to the high rate of failure. Most peasants could only survive from one harvest to the next by borrowing grain from their landlord.[56]

The debt was calculated, though not actually paid, in money terms, and the landlord's profit was ensured by the difference between the high prices current at the time of the loan and the lower prices after the harvest, when repayment was due. In addition, many landlords charged interest, and some cheated the peasant by using different measures for the loan and for the repayment. Landlords tried to prevent their peasants from borrowing elsewhere, but in spite of this recourse to other money-lenders was common. Many usurers were themselves peasants; it was one of the few ways in which the richer of them could accumulate enough to acquire bourgeois status.[57] However, coercion, if not actually part and parcel of the system of exploitation, was necessary to control the periodic outbreaks to which the social and productive inadequacy of the system gave rise. Landlords maintained field guards, e.g. the notorious *campieri* of Sicily, to collect rents and prevent theft.[58] These were recruited from among those with a reputation for toughness, and often had, or acquired, criminal records. Much of the South was wild country. Even in normal times the Sicilian peasant would not go into the open country unarmed. The absence of law enforcement meant that the powers of coercion normally exercised by the state were instead largely left to private initiative. The mafia is the most notorious example, but a study of elections almost anywhere in the South reveals the reliance of local notables on strong-arm tactics. Violence should not be seen exclusively as a means of keeping the peasants down. The *mafia* and other forms of well-protected crime also offered, like usury, a chance for social advancement. How else but through the *mafia* could an illiterate Sicilian peasant become a large landowner? Such men were no doubt admired as well as feared.

Although the function of private violence remained important, and in Western Sicily, fundamental, unification meant that the landowners had a larger reserve of force to call upon in times of need. The inefficiency of the Bourbon state in repression was not the least of the reasons behind the growth of unitarian feeling among the propertied classes. In turn, the authoritarian features of the Italian state were greatly strengthened by fear of 'anarchy' in the *mezzogiorno*. Could the *partito d'azione* have prevented this outcome? Gramsci, as is well known, attributed the failure of the democratic left to present a real alternative to the hegemony of the right, to their lack of an 'organic government programme' which reflected the desires of the masses. This failure is contrasted by Gramsci with the success of the French Jacobins, and the explanation of the contrast is found to be that the former 'fought strenuously to ensure a tie between city and countryside', while the Italian left failed altogether to pose the agrarian problem.[59] It is important to note that Gramsci is, of course, not interested in retrospective moral criticism. He is well aware that the situation of the Italian left prevented them from behaving as the French revolutionaries had in 1789; his purpose is to employ the comparison to isolate the critical differences between the two political groups and the circumstances in which they acted. But this still leaves some problems open. In the first place, the alliance between urban revolutionaries and peasants in France was highly contingent and temporary, rather than 'organic', to use Gramsci's terminology, and its highpoint was before and not during the Jacobin tenure of power. Secondly, the coincidence between the urban and the peasant revolution in France was possible because both found a common enemy in 'feudalism'. But the French had abolished feudalism in Italy also, and the unique circumstances of the end of the feudal system could not be revived in 1860. This is not to deny that peasant grievances existed, or that there were 'residues' of feudalism, but to say that it was far harder than in pre-revolutionary France to find a single slogan or set of slogans which would have general relevance in different agrarian milieux. Still more important, peasant demands, in the South at least, aimed to reverse rather than to complete the freeing of private property from the encumbrances of the old order. The *mezzogiorno* in 1860 was both further advanced in its formal legal structures and more backward economically than France in 1789, and on both counts the situation was less favourable to revolution.

These objections, however, do not at all prove that agrarian revolution or reform was a non-issue. The objection advanced by R. Romeo, that it would have destroyed the legitimacy of the liberal state by striking at the inviolability of private property is not altogether convincing.[60] Certain forms of property were more menaced than others. Compared even with the French period, the procedure for the distribution of Church and demesne lands nationalised after 1860 was retrograde.[61] Peasant grievances were not centred around the issue of generic inequality of distribution, but around the feeling that they had been defrauded of their share in the partition of what formerly had been in one sense or another, *public* property. In consequence, a fairer distribution of Church and communal lands, and the recovery of the latter where they had been usurped by bourgeois landowners, would probably have been enough to win peasant support without a more general partition of the large estates. However, one should note again that the root of the peasants' distress lay in their inability to hold and cultivate the land profitably once they had got it. They were defrauded less often by careless or corrupt legislators than by moneylenders, who exploited their own lack of technique and resources.[62] No reform could possibly have 'solved' the southern question, and it is utopian to think that conditions in most of the South were ripe for the development of capitalist agriculture, or family farming for the market. But it is instead true that material and social conditions did not preclude the formation of a larger class of peasant proprietors in the fertile areas of the South, or a reform of the contractual relations between landlord and tenant. It was no revolutionary, in the usual sense of the term, but the enlightened Tuscan conservative Sidney Sonnino who wrote as follows in his 1876 report on the condition of the Sicilian peasants:

> What does it matter to the official economists that the goods of the Church go to augment large property . . . What does it matter if we renounce the only effective means of producing a social and economic revolution in one half of Italy, and to do that without political changes, drawing down the benedictions of thousands and thousands of families which are now a continual threat to civilization itself, and instead could become a sure source of support for the new order, and a force for the nation.[63]

Any simple-minded idea that agrarian reform in southern Italy of the 1860s and 1870s would have set in motion some miraculous process of national osmosis whereby peasants would have grown into happy patriots, whether republican or monarchist, ignores the inward-looking nature of peasant culture and the irrelevance of the nation to their concerns. But in the realm of myth and sentiment *initial* acts of justice or injustice during the foundation of a state may have an influence. In this sense both Mazzini's criticism of unification, that it was not founded on any kind of explicit 'original contract', and Gramsci's criticism of Mazzini, that by ignoring the countryside he emptied his 'social pact' of content for the majority, both appear relevant.

The evolution of the distribution of property after unification is difficult to gauge accurately. The census figures show an increase in the number of peasant proprietors between 1881 and 1901, followed by a decline between 1901 and 1911. But these figures are very probably a reflection more of the changing criteria of the census-takers than of real trends. The 1911 figures, however, at least make plain the extent and intractability of Italy's rural problems. Out of a total agricultural population of approximately 10 million, 5,100,000, or slightly more than half, were classified as labourers. Nor did the majority of these belong to the combative rural proletariat of the North. As many as 2.7 million out of the 5.1 million instead came from the *mezzogiorno*. Moreover, of the 650,000 classified as peasant proprietors, many were quasi-proletarians who could not survive on their small plots without working for wages.[64]

Enlightened conservatives saw the creation of a class of stable peasant proprietors as the necessary prerequisite for democracy. They sought to promote peasant proprietorship while also defending the sharecropping system in areas where it still functioned. This was unwisely seen as an alternative to industrialisation. Instead, industry and emigration alone made any solution possible. Otherwise, there was simply not enough land to go round.[65] The attempts at land reform in the late eighteenth century and early nineteenth century had failed because they had divided too little land among too many people with too few resources. The irony is that a major shift of land to the peasantry did occur, but too late for liberal democracy. Between 1911 and 1921 peasant proprietors increased from 18 per cent to 30 per cent of the agricultural population. Almost 2½ million hectares of land passed into the hands of 500,000 new owners.[66] Tenants benefited from the freezing of rents during the war and immediate post-war period, while in the latter years the prices of agricultural produce rose very rapidly. In parts of northern Italy, the landlords' inability to cope with the organised peasant movements led by the Socialists induced them to sell out. In these areas, where wage labour or sharecropping was still prevalent and where there was a strong labour movement, new peasant proprietors, once the old estates had been broken up, became an important source of fascist support. On the other hand, in regions like the uplands of the Veneto and northern Lombardy, where peasant proprietorship became the dominant form of agriculture, fascism found it hard to penetrate. In these areas, which had the highest rate of formation of new peasant property, Catholic organisations performed a vital function in organising and supporting the purchase of land by the peasants. Through co-operative and local banks they were able to provide the indispensable marketing and credit facilities. The priests served as intermediaries between the banks and the peasants, and their personal knowledge of their parishioners enabled them to make shrewd judgements about which should receive credit. Needless to say, control over credit in turn reinforced the social and political hold of the clergy. The co-operatives and *banche popolari* were also among the few institutions in which some peasants did take an active hand in management.[67]

In spite of the changes brought about by emigration in the south and industry in the north, it needed the upheaval of war to make a massive transfer of land possible. Even in the postwar period land reform by legislation was very limited in its effects. So one is left wondering if gradualism had any answer to the problem. Faced with the rise of agricultural trade unionism, many landlords after 1900 denounced the inadequacy of liberalism to deal with class conflict in the countryside, and began to advocate authoritarian and corporative controls. Agricultural strikes, as E. Malefakis has pointed out in the case of Spain, are both more destructive and less effective than industrial strikes, because of the seasonal fluctuations in employment and the perishable nature of agricultural produce.[68] Violence and the breakdown of the state's mediating function are much harder to avoid in agriculture than in industry. This was especially true in areas of high unemployment, where the use of blackleg labour could only be prevented by intimidation and boycott. These methods in turn provoked a counter-offensive by the employers' associations. Their use of violent methods during the 1908 general strike in Parma already prefigured agrarian fascism. Giolitti's conciliatory tactics had no ultimate answer to this problem, although his much-criticised financial concessions to the labourers' co-operatives did help to reduce the frequency of conflict.

The development of liberalism in Italy owed much to the activities of progressive landlords who wished to abolish restrictions which hindered production for the market. But their liberalism had limits which made it ultimately contradictory. They wanted to modernise the agrarian economy while preserving traditional patterns of social relations. In the South even the impulse towards economic modernisation was largely absent. Liberalism could work so long as rural Italy remained fragmented into a number of distinct publics, and so long as peasant participation in politics was slight and channelled through patronage networks. Reliance on these traditional mechanisms of control weakened the state and makes it impossible to regard the policy of the liberal state after 1870 as a coherent 'revolution from above'.

At the same time, both concern with the advance of socialism and new ideologies of national integration led to growing dissatisfaction on the right with the limited solutions of liberalism. War was seen as a possible answer. War, indeed, did achieve a kind of 'nationalisation' of the peasantry, but in a negative fashion. A politically awakened peasantry posed demands to the state that the latter could not or would not fulfil. The peasants made the greatest sacrifices (well over half the casualties), and they demanded that the state honour its promises of recompense. The kind of mass mobilisation for political and union action already achieved by the Socialists among the landless labourers now spread to large sectors of the peasantry in the strict sense, such as the *mezzadri* of Tuscany and Umbria. But there was still little coherence among the forces making for change. Neither peasant revolution nor rural socialism could provide a nationwide alternative. There was a fairly sharp demarcation line in 1919-20 between the regions of peasant land occupation to the south of Rome and the regions of agricultural strikes, mainly to the north. Communal action and trade union action were alternatives which revealed a different mentality, and the two never achieved a working alliance.[69] The party with the strongest support among all groups of the peasantry except the landless labourers was the Partito Popolare. The quarrel between Church and state had reinforced rather than diminished the peasant's disposition to see the priest as the indispensable mediator between him and the outside world. But at the same time the consequences of the Church-state dispute had delayed the emergence of an effective Catholic party which could have articulated the needs of those rural groups for whom the Socialists had scant appeal. Moreover, the ideological barriers between Catholicism and Socialism made any co-operation between the two major mass parties extremely difficult. The leadership of the Popolari was inexperienced and lacking in confidence, and they could neither replace the liberals nor accept a subordinate position. So, when traditional methods of control by landlords broke down, there was no political force capable of managing the crisis or of laying the foundations for effective democracy.

Notes

1. See Antonio Labriola, *Essays on the materialist conception of history* (New York, 1966), part 1, pp.66-7. This book was first written in 1895. 'A modern state built almost exclusively upon a peasant society in a country whose agriculture is in great part backward, is what creates this general sense of restlessness, of universal discontent'. I owe this reference to Dr Carlos Kohn.

2. For a good summary, see C.S. Maier, *Recasting Bourgeois Europe* (Princeton, 1975), pp.47-9, 305-22.

3. New York, 1966. See also J.M. Wiener, 'Social origins of dictatorship and democracy', *History and Theory*, 2 (1976), pp.146-76.

4. See E.J. Hobsbawm, review of Barrington Moore in *American Sociological Review*, vol.32, 5 (Oct. 1967), p. 822.

5. Barrington Moore, ibid., p.428 and *passim*.

6. K.R. Greenfield, *Economics and Liberalism in the Risorgimento* (Baltimore, 1965), pp.80, 263 and *passim*.

7. For Verri's ideas, see A. Anzilotti, 'Il tramonto dello stato cittadino', in *Movimenti e contrasti per l'unita italiana*, ed. A. Caracciolo (Milan, 1964), pp.8-11, 28-9; S. Cuccia, *La Lombardia alla fine dell'ancien régime* (Florence, 1971), pp.48-51.

8. C. Magni, *Il tramonto del feudo lombardo* (Milan, 1937), pp.245-335.

9. Cuccia, *La Lombardia*, p.24.

10. Ibid., pp.7, 54, 60.

11. See R. Ciasca, *L'origine del programma per 'l'opinione nazionale italiana' del 1847-48* (Milan, 1965).

12. *Riformatori italiani*, vol.3, *Riformatori lombardi, piemontesi e toscani*, ed. F. Venturi (Milan-Naples, 1958), pp.174-5.

13. G. Turi, *'Viva Maria!' La reazione alle riforme leopoldine (1790-1799)* (Florence, 1969); F. Catalano, 'Il problema delle affittanze nella seconda metà del settecento in un inchiesta piemontese del 1793', *Annali dell'istituto Feltrinelii* (1959), pp. 430-9. On the sale of Church lands in Tuscany and the attempt to

create a class of small proprietors, see M. Mirri, 'Proprietari e contadini toscani nelle riforme leopoldine', *Movimento operaio*, no.2 (March-April 1955) pp.205-15.

14. C. Pazzagli, *L'agricoltura toscana nella prima metà dell'ottocento. Tecniche produttive e rapporti mezzadrili* (Florence, 1973), pp.357-61.

15. Ibid., pp.340-2.

16. See A.V. Chaianov, *The Theory of the Peasant Economy* (Homewood, 1966), p.9; W. Kula, *Teoria economica del sistema feudale* (Turin, 1970), pp.207-8; R. Dumont, *Types of Rural Economy* (London, 1957), p.247.

17. C. Cattaneo in L. Einaudi (ed.) *Saggi di economia rurale* (Turin, 1939), p.208.

18. Pazzagli, *L'agricoltura toscana*, p.429.

19. D. Novacco (ed.), *L'inchiesta Jacini, Storia del parlamento italiano*, vol. XVII (Palermo, 1963), p. 196.

20. L. Gambi, 'Per una storia dell'abitazione rurale in Italia', *Rivista storica italiana* (1964) pp.450-1; Capponi estimated the cost of housing at from one half to one third of the total investment in a *podere*. Most landowners in the early nineteenth century would in any case have been unable to calculate the profits on investment with any degree of accuracy: modern cost accounting was almost unknown, and even double-entry book-keeping was exceptional. (Pazzagli, *L'agricoltura toscana*, p.377.)

21. Pazzagli, ibid., p.418.

22. *Carteggi di Bettino Ricasoli*, eds. M. Nobili and S. Camerani (Bologna, 1939), vol.3, p.312.

23. Pazzagli, *L'agricoltura toscana*, pp.235-49.

24. *Carteggi Ricasoli*, vol.4, pp.198-203.

25. A. Bellettini, *La popolazione delle campagne bolognesi alla metà del secolo XIX* (Bologna, 1971), Table 28, pp.150-1.

26. See the forthcoming article by C. Poni, 'The peasant family farm', in *Journal of Italian History*, 2 (1978).

27. E. Morpurgo (on the Veneto), in *Storia del parlamento italiano*, p.213.

28. L.C. Stivanello, *Proprietari e contadini nella provincia di Venezia* (Venice, 1873), p.88.

29. R. Romeo, *Cavour e il suo tempo* (Bari, 1969), vol.1, p.129 and chap.2 *passim*; pp.571-5.

30. E. Sereni, *Il capitalismo nelle campagne* (Turin, 1948), pp.302-3; G. Carocci, *Giolitti e l'età giolittiana* (Turin, 1961), pp.19-20.

31. C. Poni, *Gli aratri e l'economia nel Bolognese dal XVII al XIX secolo* (Bologna, 1963), pp.83-9, 102-6.

32. G. Biagioli, *Agrarian changes in 19th century Italy: the enterprise of a Tuscan landlord, Bettino Ricasoli* (Reading, 1970), pp.10-11.

33. G. Giorgetti, *Contadini e proprietari nell'Italia moderna* (Turin, 1974), pp.308-9, 421-2.

34. S. Silverman, 'Exploitation in rural central Italy: structure and ideology in stratification study', *Comparative Studies in Society and History* (1970) pp.334-7. She argues that the relationship between landlords and *mezzadri* in the 1950s was more exploitative than in the nineteenth century, even though the landlords took a smaller share of the surplus, because the services they performed declined. However, her conclusions do not seem applicable to the situation in Tuscany after 1880, when the landlords were demanding increased inputs of labour and capital from the peasant.

35. Giorgetti, *Contadini e proprietari nell'Italia moderna*, p. 295.

36. L. Messedaglia, *Il mais e la vita rurale italiana* (Piacenza, 1927), p.281.

37. *Storia del parlamento italiano*, pp.201-4.

38. L. Cafagna, 'La "rivoluzione agraria" in Lombardia', *Annali dell'Istituto Feltrinelli* (1959) pp.425-6.

39. See S. Lanaro, 'Nazionalismo e ideologia del blocco corporativo protezionista in Italia', *Ideologie*, 2 (1967) pp.36-93.

40. A. Massafra, 'La crise du baronnage napolitain', *Annales historiques de la revolution française* (1969) pp.218 ff.

41. R. Villari, *Mezzogiorno e contadini* (Bari, 1961), pp.37-9.

42. A. Lepre, *Feudi e masserie. Problemi della societa meridionale nel'600 e nel '700* (Naples, 1973), pp.77-80.

43. P. Macry, *Mercato e società nel regno di Napoli* (Naples, 1974), pp.338-40.

44. Villari, *Mezzogiorno e contadini*, pp.46, 184-8.

45. Ibid., p.47.

46. M. Aymard, 'L'abolition de la féodalité en Sicile', in *Annuario dell'Istituto di Storia Italiana per l'età moderna e contemporanea*, n.2 (1971) pp. 70-83.

47. G. Delille, *Croissance d'une société rurale: Montesarchio et la vallée Caudine aux XVII et XVIII siècles* (Naples, 1973), pp. 208-14.

48. The usurpation was not, however, confined to the bourgeoisie. The land hunger of the peasants drove them to encroach on the communal lands as well. Villari, *Mezzogiorno e contadini*, pp.40, 48.

49. R. Romeo, 'Momenti e problemi della Restaurazione nel Regno delle Due Sicilie', *Rivista storica italiana* (1955) p.417; A. Lepre, 'Classi, movimenti politici, e lotta di classe nel Mezzogiorno dalla fine del Settecento al 1860', *Studi storici*, n.16 (1975) pp.368-70.

50. Lepre, ibid., p.372.

51. E.J. Hobsbawm, *Primitive Rebels* (Manchester, 1959); A. Blok, 'The peasant and the brigand: social banditry reconsidered', *Comparative Studies in Society and History* (1972) pp.494-503, with reply by Hobsbawm, pp.503-5. See also J. Brögger, 'Conflict resolution and the role of the bandit in peasant society', *Anthropological Quarterly* (Oct. 1968) pp.228-39.

52. G. Aliberti, 'La vita quotidiana nella Basilicata dell'Ottocento', *Ricerche di storia sociale e religiosa*, n.7-8 (1975) pp.214 ff.

53. F. De Felice, *Agricoltura e capitalismo. Terra di Bari dal 1880 al 1914* (Bari, 1969), p.128.

54. A. Blok, *The Mafia of a Sicilian Village* (Oxford, 1974), p.122.

55. J. L. Macdonald, 'Agricultural organization, migration and labour militancy in rural Italy', *Economic History Review* (1963) pp.61-75.

56. Giorgetti, *Contadini e proprietari nell' Italia moderna*, pp.231-9; De Felice, *Agricoltura e capitalismo*, pp.35-43; *Storia del parlamento*, pp.324, 326.

57. L. Franchetti and S. Sonnino, *La Sicilia nel 1876*, vol.2, *I contadini* (Florence, 1877), pp.178-83; De Felice, *Agricoltura e capitalismo*, pp.75-95.

58. Franchetti and Sonnino, *I contadini*, p.35.

59. A. Gramsci, *Il Risorgimento* (Turin, 1949), p.73.

60. R. Romeo, *Risorgimento e capitalismo* (Bari, 1963), p. 36.

61. *Storia del parlamento*, pp.320-1.

62. Franchetti and Sonnino, *I contadini*, pp.188-9 for corruption in the administration of the charities which could have assisted the peasants. On the former role of the Church in providing credit to the peasants, see Villari, *Mezzogiorno e contadini*, pp.19-27.

63. Franchetti and Sonnino, *I contadini*, p.282; see also Gramsci's comments, *Il Risorgimento*, pp. 103-4: the Moderates were 'much bolder' than the left and did not hesitate to interfere with property rights in order to create 'a new class of large and medium proprietors tied to the new political situation'.

64. M. Bandini, *Cento anni di storia agraria in Italia* (Rome, 1963), pp.87-8.

65. For the fundamental nature of the problem of overpopulation, see G. Are, *Economia e politica nell'Italia liberale, 1890-1915* (Bologna, 1974), pp. 156-8.

66. Bandini, *Cento anni di storia agraria in Italia*, pp.165 ff.

67. See L. Gheza Fabbri, 'Crescita e natura delle casse rurali cattoliche', *Quaderni storici*, n.36 (Sept.-Dec. 1977) pp.789 ff. The first *casse rurali* were not founded by Catholics, but between 1892 and 1897 they became predominant. Thirty per cent of the total number of *casse rurali* in 1905 were in the Veneto.

68. E.E. Malefakis, *Agrarian Reform and the Peasant Revolution in Spain* (New Haven and London, 1970), pp.168-9.

69. On the traditional nature of the land occupations, see E.J. Hobsbawm, 'Peasant land occupations', *Past and Present*, n.62 (1974) p.130.

5 FROM SHARECROPPER TO PROLETARIAN: THE BACKGROUND TO FASCISM IN RURAL TUSCANY, 1880-1920

Frank M. Snowden

On the eve of the March on Rome, Tuscany was one of the fascist strongholds of Italy. Among the 16 Italian regions, only Emilia had more fascists or more *fasci*. In Italy one fascist in six was Tuscan.[1] And nowhere in the peninsula was the movement more violent, more organised or more intransigent. The Tuscans regarded themselves as the special guardians of the fascist revolutionary spirit.[2]

The purpose of this essay will be to examine the social background of this powerful Tuscan movement. Since fascism in the eight provinces of the region was primarily agrarian, our task will be to examine the fundamental institution of Tuscan rural society — the sharecropping system of *mezzadria*. It was the crisis of *mezzadria* and the emerging conflict between landlord and tenant that unleashed a civil war.

Classical Sharecropping

Landlord and Tenant

Under the traditional pattern of *mezzadria* the property of the landlord was divided into one or more estates. Each estate, or *fattoria*, was considered a single administrative unit and was subdivided into a series of peasant farms, called *poderi*.[3] The *fattoria* was the centre of administrative control, which was the exclusive prerogative of the proprietor; the *poderi* were the units of actual cultivation. The working of the land was governed by contract between the landlord and the peasant tenant (*mezzadro*) under the legal form of a partnership in a joint venture. Put most simply, the lord provided the land, and the *mezzadro* the labour, while the entire produce and the expenses of cultivation were divided equally. The proprietor's share of the crop was either consumed in whole or in part, or sold for profit; the peasant's share was his sole source of subsistence.

Here it is important to observe in some detail the workings of the system because a whole ideology of lordly inspiration concerning *mezzadria* has been propagated which renders Tuscan history incomprehensible. According to this 'official' view of the traditional Tuscan contract — a view which dominated the discussions of the Accademia dei Georgofili, the landlords' technical and agronomical society, and became the creed of propertied classes in the region — Tuscany in *mezzadria* had found the solution to the social question. In industry and in the northern countryside where wage labour prevailed, there was continual class conflict and constant danger to social order. Not so in Tuscany, where peasant and landlord were equal partners united by a common interest in the greatest productivity of the soil. The increase of either party was the benefit of both. Thus Pasquale Villari, exemplifying the 'official' doctrine, wrote,

The contract of *mezzadria*, as has been repeated a thousand times over, has here achieved its best form, and makes the peasant happy, honest, and at ease; it puts him in perfect harmony with the landlord, who has become his partner. This is the true solution to the social question; here socialism has not penetrated, and never will. If something similar could be done in industry, how many reasons for discontent, how many dangers could be avoided![4]

Much earlier, in 1847, another spokesman of the Tuscan landed aristocracy, Vincenzo Salvagnoli, declared:

The owner prefers the well-being and dignity of the tenant to the highest income; he cares not for a machine, but for the man; he desires not a servant but a comrade . . . In such a relation there is no desire on the one side to oppress, and no occasion for vengeance on the other. This benign economic relation has joined landlord and tenant together in a moral bond of civil harmony . . . These partners in agriculture would never stand as brother against brother in civil war.[5]

Moreover, the 'official' view continued, the tenant, beneficiary of such a salutary moral relation with his betters, could have no material ground for complaint. The standard of living of the Tuscan *mezzadro*, it was asserted, was the envy of the working classes of the world — honest, secure work; comfort; nourishment in abundance; and a model family life. Thus in 1920 the landlords' paper of the Mugello in Florence province reminded its readers that 'No class of workers in the world today has been able to achieve, or perhaps ever will be able to achieve, a standard of living equal to that which *mezzadria* provides the peasants.'[6]

A moment's reflection reveals the implausibility of such a vision. It was the landlord who held power in the form of the ownership of the means of production — the land, the peasant cottage, the seed, the fodder, the tools and machinery of cultivation, and the work animals — and in the form of the right of eviction; the *mezzadro* possessed only his own labour power and perhaps a few simple implements such as a hoe and rake, and the odd farm animal. It would have been surprising if the formal contractual equality of the 'partners' had negated the economic supremacy of the landlord. In fact, a number of secondary pacts supplementing the primary *mezzadria* relationship bear witness to the power of ownership. The specifics varied, but nearly everywhere the *mezzadro* was bound, beyond the surrender of half of the crop, to render special tributes and services to the lord of the estate. Typical additional duties were the obligations to work for a period of the year off the *podere* without compensation transporting the landlord's share of the harvest to market or digging ditches to improve the property; to provide the owner with established quantities of olive oil or wine, or a given number of fowls; to gather wood for the landlord's hearth; and to wash the landlord's linen. Moreover, the lord exercised the right to regulate the private life of his partner, superintending his dress and religious observance, forbidding him to marry without consent, to attend cafes and gaming rooms, and ordering him not to work off the estate. The sanction was eviction.

In addition, the provision that the tenant should assume 50 per cent of the expense of cultivation meant that his entitlement to half the product of his labour was but a legal fiction. The reason was that the peasant had no capital, so that he was compelled to receive advances of seed, fodder and fertiliser from the landlord's storehouse, to employ work animals from the owner's stables; and to use the equipment and tools of the proprietor's shed. The use of these items then figured at harvest time as so many deductions from the *mezzadro*'s due. The bookkeeping system of estimates (*stime*) by which the lord's capital was let allowed ample room for profit by the owner. The value of the advanced capital was reckoned at the start of the agricultural year at current market prices and then estimated again at the end when accounts were settled, any difference in price making a difference in the way the crop was apportioned. Here was an opportunity for speculation, and it seldom worked to the disadvantage of the proprietor as the market value of the landlord's capital was likely to be high in the off-season when it was advanced and low at harvest time when accounts were settled. Not unknown was the practice of advancing inferior grains against a return in full-value crops.[7] In any case, the fact that pacts were not written but based on informal agreement and local custom allowed ample scope for abuse by the powerful. In the quiet but unending struggle over the respective shares of the harvest, the economic power of the landlord decided the issue in his favour.

In addition to the silent conflict over the division of the product, there was another important opposition with regard to the actual size of the harvest. The landlord's claim was that there was no possibility of discord as both partners could only gain by the largest possible output, with the harmonious result that each worked spontaneously for the greatest good of the other. In fact, however, in the long run this formal symmetry of interest was overbalanced by the asymmetry of economic power. For the tenant, the stake was survival as he cultivated for subsistence; for the lord, it was a question of profit. The landlord, over a period of time, was able to exploit this difference of emphasis, together with his right to re-order his estate and its division into *poderi*, for his private advantage. The landlord, that is, stood to gain by increasing the intensity of cultivation by reducing the size of the *podere* to the minimum indispensable for the tenant family to subsist. From a smaller plot the requirement of survival was unchanged for the peasant, so that the landlord could obtain a greater exploitation of labour. Moreover, it was easily discovered that the possible minimum size of the *podere* was elusive: the labour the *mezzadro* could extract from himself and his family had a high upward elasticity. Thus there was a long-term tendency for the condition of the *mezzadro* to be reduced to a bare subsistence, obtained by ever greater toil within a family context in which limitations on hours, legal holidays and child labour legislation did not apply. Already in 1858, a student of Tuscan agriculture, P. Cuppari, observed,

> If the *podere* is too small, the landlord benefits at the expense of the sharecropper. Truly in such cases the peasant will be bound, by dint of industry and extraordinary labour, to seek to squeeze from his small *podere* a sustenance for his now excessive family . . . The gross product increases in this case as a result of the overwork of the peasant, who nonetheless gets no more than half of the product.
>
> From this is derived the tendency of the Tuscan landlords to draw ever more narrowly the boundaries of the *poderi* and to make investment in land rather than agricultural improvement. A limit to the trend continually to reduce the area of the *poderi* is provided only by the expense necessary to effect the division . . .[8]

If the tenant fell into arrears in his annual account with the estate, the landlord had a further instrument with which to extract a surplus or, as the Catholic theorist Giuseppe Toniolo termed it, a 'supplementary income'.[9] In such cases the *mezzadro* was able to settle accounts by working in the off-season for the landlord at disadvantageous wage rates well below those earned by day labourers. This was the phenomenon a recent study refers to as 'debt labour', by means of which the proprietor secured cheap labour year-round for the estate.[10] In bad years the landlord could partly offset the loss of revenue from his holdings by squeezing forced labour from the tenant through the debt mechanism.

It was the ability by various devices endlessly to intensify labour that was the magic economic secret of *mezzadria* which enabled it to survive into the modern world in the face of competition from more rationalised systems of agriculture.[11] Already in 1836 Marquis Capponi, one of the largest of Tuscan landlords, pointed accurately to unrelenting toil by the tenants as the vital economic underpinning of *mezzadria* – a toil that was as dear in human terms as it was cheap to the lords. 'Regarding man as an instrument of labour', wrote Capponi,

> our agriculture is costly in the extreme; but, under any other system, man would do less and cost more. The cultivator is always on the spot, always careful. His constant thought is, 'This field is my own' ... The amount of labour bestowed by the cultivator would prove too costly to the proprietor if obliged to pay for it; it would not answer his purpose.[12]

Moreover, contrary to the 'official' view of sharecropping life, recent studies of the *mezzadria* system have concluded that the remuneration of sharecroppers was not only low, but actually lower than that of any category of industrial worker.[13]

At the same time that the landlord compensated for low productivity by the overwork of the peasant family and by the low remuneration of its members, he further fortified himself against adversity by a minimum of outlay on welfare payments. The *mezzadro* received no pension, no sickness and disability compensation, and few attentions from costly charitable institutions. Thus, comparing the welfare conditions of *mezzadro* and worker, the socialists of Florence addressed the peasants in 1900 to point out the disadvantages of their position. Citing one example, the socialists explained:

> When a worker falls ill – since the labourers in the town have made themselves heard, and intend to be aided in their needs – he is received

free of charge by the hospitals, and the commune pays the bill with the money of everyone – that is, also with the money of you peasants who pay taxes. But if one of you peasants takes ill, he must bear his suffering and cause his family to suffer in toil. Or if the peasant wants to come to the hospital, perhaps for an operation, then he must meet the fee of 2.50 lire a day. It is as if you peasants were not impoverished labourers who need to be cared for by society . . . when, because of sickness, you cease to work and therefore to earn.[14]

For the peasant unable to work, the tenants themselves would provide, through the institution of the extended family – a solution at once thrifty and without prejudice to public order.

Of the benefit of their savings in welfare payments, the Georgofili were, of course, well aware. Carlo Massimiliano Mazzini discussed at length the legislation of 1883 and 1898 that provided accident, disability and old age compensation for workers in industry.[15] For Mazzini such benefits for industrial workers were a necessary means to combat social-ism[16] but he noted that 'this new burden that weighs on Italian industry is not light',[17] and he rejoiced that there was no need to extend welfare payments to the sharecroppers, who posed no subversive threat.[18]

Apart from its capacity to supply cheap labour, *mezzadria* seemed a highly vulnerable system, as a variety of factors produced a tendency towards backwardness and inflexibility in its production methods – a fact noted by nearly all students of this form of tenure. Speaking to the Georgofili in 1837, Cosimo Ridolfi seized the essential point when he noted that 'Neither is our land fertile, nor are we abundant in our use of fertilisers, and if production continues it is due solely to the great labour and diligence of cultivation which is obtainable only on estates held in *mezzadria*.'[19]

The organisation of *mezzadria* production for subsistence – a sort of miniature autarky of the *podere* – effectively precluded specialisation of cultivation and a rational division of labour.[20] The contract itself dis-couraged capital investment because half the return, at least in principle, went to the partner. In fact, *mezzadria* was best adapted to an environ-ment such as that of Tuscany where the facts of geology – a predomi-nance of hills and mountains and a thin rocky topsoil – made investment relatively unenticing and created very tangible difficulties for agricultural machinery. Moreover, the division of the estate into *poderi*, though it necessitated relatively small increments of on-going capital investment, required a very substantial initial outlay in peasant cottages, terraces, fences, trees, vineyards and irrigation systems. Much of this original investment was not readily convertible into the structures necessary for working the entire estate as a single agricultural unit. To transform the *fattoria* required of the landlord not only a new outlay of capital in a difficult physical environment, but also the abolition, at a stroke, of a substantial part of his inheritance of previous investment in the land.[20] *Mezzadria* was suited to the cultivation of crops which, like the Tuscan olive trees and vineyards, required close attention throughout the year. Thus *mezzadria* tended towards backward methods and slowness of change, for which the system compensated by its particular ability to secure diligent toil and to require of the propertied classes a low level of continuing investment and welfare expense.[21]

The Means of Social Control

Even if the idyllic picture of rural social relations described by men of property was belied by the reality of class opposition of interests, there was still good reason for concurring with the Georgofili in their evaluation of the political usefulness of *mezzadria* in preserving the appearance of social harmony. Our reasons, however, are not those advanced by the landowners. The idea of genuine class concord in the Tuscan countryside was contradicted by the underlying structure of opposing economic interests. It was mocked by the unbridgeable social distance between the partners and disproved by a whole history of class guerrilla warfare by the *mezzadri* in the form of petty theft, fraud and poaching. Even murder had a long subterranean history as the final recourse of desperate men.[22] Class harmony was further refuted by the landlords themselves, who did not trust so far in the community of interest between themselves and their tenants as to fail to provide their estates with the so-called *fattore* and his assistants (the *sottofattori* and guards), whose duties were those of policeman and judge. Their task was to enforce the landlords' exactions upon a less than enthusiastic tenantry.

The *fattore* was generally of humble rural origin – a *mezzadro* or household servant who, on the strength of years of reliable submission, had been promoted by stages as guard and *sottofattore* to the trusted position of chief overseer. The fact that the main qualification for the post was political reliability rather than expertise in agriculture is testimony to the nature of the office as the eye of the lord. A particularly clear statement is that of an anonymous Tuscan *fattore* who thus described the position for the socialist paper of Siena:

The *fattore* belongs to the category of men without class. He is the man who knows how to serve for little reward, who gains from the most abject servility a life without a future, if he is an honest man.

Nonetheless, this man without prospects . . . lends himself to all manner of shifty, evil, and sometimes brutal conduct towards the peasants.

Is there a trick to be played, a deed of violence to be done, a whim to be imposed? Call the *fattore*. Is there a peasant to be found for a dealing that will be happy and profitable for the landlord? Call the *fattore*. Is there a bargain to be struck with not overly scrupulous middlemen? Call the *fattore*.[23]

None the less, despite the evidence of a submerged current of antagonism, there is hardly a trace until after the First World War of genuine class warfare. There is no history in Tuscany (excluding Grosseto province, where *mezzadria* was not the rule) of large-scale brigandage or of sporadic *jacqueries* as in the South. Nor was there a record of peasant strikes or subversive organisations as in the North. It was this history of peasant docility that was dear to the Tuscan landed aristocracy.

An understanding of this docility and the developments which under-mined it is essential to an explanation of Tuscan fascism. Agrarian unrest and reaction in Tuscany were directly linked to the crisis of the *mezzadria* system. To explain fascism, we must begin by examining the conditions underlying the stability of Tuscan sharecropping and the influence which produced a major upheaval.

Although there was little reason to accept the ideology of the 'bond of love and gratitude'[24] between landlord and *mezzadro*, still the first factor accounting for the outburst of unrest was the serious decline in the relation between the partners. The landlord, despite the assertions of the Georgofili, was hardly inclined to desire a comrade in his tenant, or to value the well-being of the peasant above profit. None the less, there was, historically, a close personal link of a kind between the two classes in the countryside. The landlord, first of all, often resided on his property, played some part in the agricultural cycle, and interested himself in the affairs of the peasants. There was, of course, an antagonistic side in this involvement, as the owner sought to influence peasant life in the interest of the 'public quiet'. The other side of such involvement, however, was a tradition of lordly paternalism, that 'fragile bridge of community' across unresolvable contradictions of interest.[25] In time of sickness, the lord provided medicine and advice. In the event of a bad harvest, he mitigated hard times by extending credit or making a gift. On the occasion of the marriage of a tenant's daughter, the proprietor assisted in the provision of a dowry. In addition, he gave advice in the peasant's infrequent contacts with authority. It was the landlord who financed the few grand festivities of village life. The impulse to rebellion was thus blunted by the presence of the owner, by the conviction of his inevitability and usefulness, and perhaps by the memory of an act of largesse.[26]

In addition to the tie to the person of the landlord, the *mezzadro* was strongly bound to the land. In the first half of the nineteenth century Simonde de Sismondi, an attentive observer of the Tuscan countryside, stressed this point. 'The *mezzadro*', he wrote,

> lives on his *podere* as if it were his own inheritance. To it he gives his love . . . trusting in the future and feeling certain that after his death his fields will be kept and worked by his sons, and by the sons of his sons. Most *mezzadri* are born of fathers and grandfathers born on the *podere*.[27]

Even in the twentieth century, when security of tenure had been seriously undermined, Giuseppe Toniolo claimed that the hold of Tuscan *mezzadri* on the land was more secure than that of the owners, and Gino Sarrocchi, the Liberal deputy from Siena, announced in parliament that 'we have a large number of families who have been on the same *podere* for two hundred years'.[28]

In such statements, Sismondi, Toniolo and Sarrocchi, accepting the ideology of the Georgofili, made grossly insufficient allowance for eviction, the ultimate sanction and ever-present threat of lordly power. Recent studies suggest that, even in the mythical golden age of *mezzadria*, eviction was regularly used to guarantee obedience and to maintain productivity.[29] A tenant who did not perform to expectation had no future on the estate. Nevertheless, in comparison with other regions and with casual day labour, the Tuscan sharecropper did enjoy a relative security. Until the end of the agricultural year the *mezzadro* was safe, and on the annual day of reckoning a hardworking and deferential tenant could expect to have his contract renewed. Whatever his living standards, the *mezzadro* had at least a precarious niche in the social order.

Until the late nineteenth century, the *mezzadro* also felt a sense of independence. Objectively, of course, the landlord established the entire context within which the tenant laboured, providing tools and seed, building and maintaining the cottage, physically marking off the boundaries of the *podere*, determining the intensity of labour and the degree of remuneration, and linking the whole structure to the broader influences of the market. But the reality of lordly control was hidden from sight.

There was little need for fiats from above. The crops grown – chiefly wheat, corn, olives and grapes – were those that had been cultivated for centuries and the task confronting the peasant was directed by an ineluctable necessity. Since the tenant produced for his own sustenance with frequently no other source of income and since at the end of the year the contract was considered for renewal, application was ensured without the interference of the owner and his agents in day-to-day affairs. The *fattore* was a reminder of lordly power, but his supervision was distant and his interventions sporadic. He was traditionally book-keeper and policeman rather than manager or foreman. Thus the system of *mezzadria* acquired an appearance of impersonality as if the only obstacles to the peasant's enrichment were nature and the niggardliness of the Tuscan soil. If the *mezzadro* was discontented, against whom was he to revolt?

The sense of peasant independence was reinforced by the looseness of the economic relation of the *podere* to the *fattoria*. Traditionally, the direct dependence of the peasant farm on the lordly estate was strictly limited. In a backward agrarian system such as that which dominated central Italy, with soil-depleting crop rotations, scarce use of mechanical equipment or fertilisers, and a stunted development of animal husbandry, little capital was advanced by the estate and the tenant's recourse to the landlord's equipment was intermittent. The peasant family felt itself in large measure self-sufficient.

This feeling of self-reliance was underscored by the internal organisation of the extended *mezzadro* family. Since its task was self-sufficiency for as many as 20 members,[30] the patriarchal peasant family undertook a developed division of labour under the authority of the *capoccia*. The *capoccia* was the legal representative of the family in its dealings with the lord and with authority, and was its effective and authoritarian head. He determined the tasks to be performed in the fields, while his wife the *massaia* apportioned domestic industry – a major element in the sharecropping family economy – among the women of the household.

The family made all of its clothing from wool, hemp and cotton-waste. Thus Simonde de Sismondi, observing Tuscany before unification, wrote of his astonishment at the number of articles the peasants possessed – sheets, skirts, jerkins, trousers, skirts, dresses, and all in sufficient supply. It was the ability of the extended family to carry on such household production that lifted the *mezzadri* above the destitution of the wage labourers.[31] In a variety of ways, then, independence was reinforced while the attachment of the *mezzadro* to the existing order was secured by bonds of filial piety and family affection.[32]

More was involved, however, than ties of affection. In the patriarchal family an institution had been created that blunted the force of rising social protest, fostered division within the family rather than between the clan and the landlord, and decentralised the burden of estate management. This is more understandable if we recognise that both the share-cropping family and the institution of the *capocciato* were contractual and juridical rather than natural entities.[33] The peasant family (*famiglia colonica*), that is, was legally defined as all those who lived upon and cultivated the *podere*. Ties of blood relationship inevitably formed the nucleus of the peasant family, and often the natural family and the legal family were co-extensive. Frequently, however, the legal family was not united throughout by blood ties, but consisted of three or four family units living under the same roof. It was to this composite entity rather than to its individual members that the *podere* was entrusted. The 'family' was collectively responsible for all contractual obligations. Neither the death nor the flight of single members of the clan could deprive the lord of his due. In this way the legal fiction of the family served as an instrument of discipline over a large and scattered work force.

The interests of the proprietor were further guaranteed by the institution of the *capocciato*. Like the family itself, the internal hierarchy of the clan was a legal creation. The head of the family did not owe his position and influence simply to age and personal ascendancy. He was selected by the members of the family to represent them in their dealings with authority, but with the important proviso that the landlord could veto the choice of his tenants. Only a person acceptable to the owner and his agents could be invested as *capoccia*. That the landlord could thus intervene to determine the outcome of the selection process altered the nature of the office. The *capoccia* represented the owner as well as the tenants.

The legal powers of the office further distanced the head from the members of his family. The law stipulated that only the *capoccia* could reach juridical maturity: regardless of age, the other members of the family were locked in a permanent minority. Like children they could not quit the estate, marry, buy and sell land or establish savings accounts without his consent, whether or not there was a blood relationship. Only the *capoccia* could incur obligations in the market or conclude business with the landlord, and his decisions were binding on all. The head alone directed the division of labour within the family. Thus within the peasant household, a position of genuine privilege and control – a 'little tyranny' in the words of one landlord[34] – was created and sanctioned by law. As a result, the established order acquired a position of leverage and influence inside the family. The *capoccia* was aware not only of the divide which separated him from the owner but also of his own small pedestal of authority and domination. It is hardly surprising that in practice the *capocciato* became a force of moderation in the countryside, a buffer between lordly power and peasant discontent. Patriarchy institutionalised work-discipline in the home.

At the same time that latent opposition from below was thereby prevented from emerging as open conflict and from acquiring purpose and target, there was a virtual absence of horizontal links among the peasants themselves. As a result, the material premises for that sense of community indispensable to collective political action were missing. Marx pointed out that man cannot master his social relations before they have been created in fact. In classical Tuscan *mezzadria* the assertion of a social and class relation among the sharecroppers was an anachronism. In central Italy the famous and often misleading metaphor of the peasantry standing united like a sack of potatoes had a grim basis in fact. The isolation of the *mezzadro* family can hardly be overstated: the tenant lived as if he were the only peasant in Italy. Thus Sir John Bowring, reporting in 1836 to the British Parliament on the condition of agriculture in the Grand Duchy of Tuscany, noted:

> But there is a point of view which, it seems to me, has not excited sufficient attention: this is the universal *isolation* of the peasantry, which is a necessary consequence of the mezzeria system . . . Every peasant's family in Tuscany stands as it were alone: this is indeed a great gain for the public security; but it is a tranquility purchased at a terrible price — at the price of a stationary and backward civilization . . . I had occasion more than once to see four generations inhabiting the same cottage; but the last had not added a particle of knowledge to the ignorance of the first . . . In innumerable cases families have occupied the same farms for hundreds of years without adding a farthing to their wealth, or a fragment to their knowledge.[35]

This isolation was based, first of all, on the economic and physical structure of the *podere*. Physically, the Tuscan sharecropper did not live in villages from which he commuted to the fields as in the South, or from which he was recruited to work the land as was the case of the northern day labourers. Instead, he lived on the *podere* in the family cottage isolated even from the tenants of the same estate.[36]

Economically, the autarky of the tenant plot meant that the *mezzadro* was largely excluded from market relations. Similarly, the family was removed from class production relations. Historically, for example, there was little tradition of mutual assistance among the *mezzadri* or of the exchange of labour at harvest time.

The lack of contact among the peasants was not only a result of circumstance. It was actively furtherd by the landowners, who were well aware of the political benefits of isolating their tenants. Gatherings of all sorts were carefully discouraged as sources of vice and riotous behaviour. It was often within the contractual rights of the vigilant *fattore* to exercise the power of eviction, as one pact stated: 'in the event that a member of the family was in the habit of frequenting taverns, cafes, billiard rooms or other places of dissipation and vice.'[37] Even religious observance, in which the Church conveyed the very social message of class harmony and partnership that the landlords advocated and to which it added its own exhortations to patience and discipline, was meant to be reserved for festival days. The Tuscan *mezzadro*, in so far as it was in the power of the landlords, was not to have the opportunity to conceive of himself as part of a collective rather than as a toiling, self-reliant individualist.

The general social context of sharecropping life provided few countervailing influences. The state, even in the form of tax collector and military conscriptor, was a distant force impinging little on the peasant in the Grand Duchy. Education was rudimentary or non-existent, and communications poor. Emigration was not a feature of Tuscan society so that broad and possibly subversive influences were unlikely to arrive from peasants who had gone off to work in Turin, Milan or Switzerland. Altogether, the ignorance of the traditional *mezzadro* was complete. The information available to the Tuscan sharecropper in the mid-nineteenth century was confined to such events as the *fattore*, the landlord and the parish priest chose to relate.[38]

Commercial Changes and the New Mezzadria

Beginning with unification, however, and with increasing force from about 1880, a whole series of changes took place which radically altered social conditions in the Tuscan provinces, upsetting the entire mythology of partnership in *mezzadria* and creating the bases for civil war. At the most general level, these changes were associated with the development of capitalism as a world system and the way in which Tuscany belatedly became a part of the national and international market. A first major influence was Italian unity itself, which eliminated internal barriers to trade and thereby created the possibility of a regional division of labour in Italy. For the propertied classes, this integration of Tuscany into the world economic system implied the opportunity for increased profits from more intensive cultivation and the risk of declining returns from the traditional generalised subsistence agriculture. At the same time, unification under the auspices of the commercially advanced Piedmont entailed the use of the national state to further the development of Italian capital. In particular, the years after the Risorgimento witnessed the use of the state as an engine of primitive accumulation drawing capital from agriculture for investment in the industrial infrastructure of roads, railways and the merchant marine. The means employed were a regressive fiscal system which relied primarily on a variety of indirect taxes and direct taxes on agriculture which weighed most heavily on those least able to pay. Examples were the family tax, the land tax, the grist tax, the salt duties, the cattle tax. The burden of these fiscal measures fell most heavily on the agricultural provinces and, within them, on the peasantry.[39] By 1907 a leading representative of the Tuscan landed aristocracy, Francesco Guicciardini, estimated that in most Tuscan communes the tax burden levied by the local authorities alone reached 15 to 20 per cent of the total income from the land, with nearly the whole being borne by the peasantry. Moreover, Guicciardini continued, taxation, both local and national, was continually revised upwards so that 'the tax system for the sharecropper, is a genuine regime of oppression'.[40] Thus the development of Italian capitalism meant further impoverishment for the *mezzadri* and the creation of greater market outlets for the landlords, who thereby possessed a vastly increased incentive for investment. In the long run, these developments were subversive of the much praised 'public quiet'.

In the 1880s, moreover, the international market made its influence keenly felt in Tuscany with the large-scale arrival of grain from America. This trans-oceanic competition spelled a long-term decline in the price of wheat, and therefore a crisis of the *mezzadria* system, which was largely based on extensive wheat cultivation. This crisis was worsened at the end of the century by a tariff war with France, a major importer of two other leading products of Tuscan agriculture — wine and olive oil. With new market outlets to attract investment and declining prices there was a penalty for the continued reliance on the traditional crops and means of cultivation. From about 1880, therefore, there were major changes in the countryside.[41]

To understand these developments, however, one must keep in mind certain limitations which set outer boundaries to the new influences. One was the profound awareness of the Tuscan landholding class of the political benefits for men of property conferred by *mezzadria*. The Tuscan landlords had long theorised on the value of *mezzadria* as a solution to the social problem and on the privileged position of Tuscany in a strife-ridden peninsula. The contrast between the continuing calm of central Italy and the class antagonisms of the Po Valley only strengthened this consciousness. For political reasons there was an enduring opposition from the landlords to the Emilian idea of restructuring the countryside through the establishment of large commercial farms worked by wage labour.

What allowed the political preferences of the nobility to prevail was the fact that, as we have seen, other more narrowly economic considerations worked in the same direction. There was the obstacle to change of the investment already embodied in *mezzadria*, an obstacle which proved a serious impediment to the dismantling of the old structures. Then there were the facts of Tuscan soil and topography, which were not inducements to the introduction of mechanised equipment or the re-organisation of the estates as large-scale farms. Investment in Tuscany was attracted primarily in small increments.

In the period down to 1920 such investment occurred *within* the framework of *mezzadria*. The commercialisation of Tuscan agriculture followed a course radically different from the classical pattern of the Po Valley. Nevertheless, it did proceed rapidly from about 1880 with profound, if not immediately visible, political consequences. To appreciate these consequences, we must explore the differences that separated the new *mezzadria* from the traditional pattern.

The most obvious symbol of the new commercial trend was the introduction of such industrial crops as tobacco and sugar beet and of fodder for artificial pasture.[42] These crops were first planted in the fertile river valleys where physical conditions most nearly resembled the Po Valley. Already in the 1880s in the Chiana and Tiber Valleys of Arezzo and Siena provinces and in the lower Arno Valley of Pisa province, modern four-year rotations (corn – wheat – clover [broad beans or vetch] – wheat) with sophisticated irrigation techniques had begun to replace the traditional biennial alternation of wheat and corn, though these four-year rotations were still exceptions.[43] It was in 1881 that a Ministry of Agriculture report on Tuscany revealed the recent introduction of many of the changes associated with commercialised farming in the most fertile valleys where investment was first attracted. In these areas the plough, and especially the iron plough, was slowly replacing the hoe, and at Siena, public demonstrations had been made of a 'most powerful' plough drawn by several pairs of oxen capable of tilling the soil to a depth of 50 centimetres. Similarly the report noted the very first quadrennial rotations then being adopted on an experimental basis and the introduction of the first tobacco plants, as well as a more widespread use of animal fertilisers and the first tentative trials of chemical fertilising.[44]

With such tentative beginnings in the last quarter of the century, Tuscan agriculture rapidly absorbed the new methods of cultivation, at least in zones where soil, climate and topography favoured investment. By the post-war period, for instance, in the lower Arno Valley of Pisa province less than one third of the land under cultivation was sown with wheat.[45] A greater area was instead devoted to tobacco and sugar beet, and to artificial pasture for cattle. By 1922, progress having advanced beyond the iron plough, there were over 400 threshing machines in operation in Arezzo province alone.[46]

Thus in 1914, G. Gastone Bolla, summarising the changes which had occurred in Tuscan agriculture, wrote:

> No one can any longer deny that agriculture has become industry, and that agricultural production has become industrial production.
>
> This is proved by the fact that ... the art of cultivation, once empirical, has become scientific. It is proved by the use of fertilizers, machines, and electricity; by the breeding of animals and the selection of seeds; by the expansion of industrial crops and of the means of exchange and transport; by the existence of storehouses and places for the first refining of goods; and by the industries that are today tightly linked to and dependent on the primary agricultural enterprise.[47]

Clearly such major changes in the methods of production were associated with important changes as well in social relations. The landlord, involved ever more deeply in production for the market and spurred on by the imperatives of profit, tended to rationalise not only his methods of cultivation, but also his relations with his tenants. He gradually became an absentee figure relying on the management of his employee, the *fattore*. The bond between landlord and tenant became ever more impersonal, and the tradition of lordly paternalism atrophied from disuse. Leading landlords, from Guicciardini at the turn of the century to Pier Francesco Serragli in 1920, saw this devaluation of the traditional personal tie between landlord and tenant. Recognising its dangerous effects on rural labour relations, they called for a return of the owners to their estates and for a revival both of paternal protection of the peasants in time of need and of the traditional lordly interest in the details of production.[48] Already by Guicciardini's time, however, the personal bond between owner and *mezzadro* had frequently become a mere 'cash nexus'. The landlord's claims were no longer legitimised by a visibly useful role.[49] A suggestive illustration of the transformation in rural social relationships was the change in the tradition of paternal assistance in moments of hardship. In the new *mezzadria* the advances extended by the proprietors took on the character of loans bearing interest.

Guicciardini's appeal to the enlightened paternalism of the Tuscan aristocracy ran counter to the economic and social evolution of the region. It was, in effect, the swan song of a traditional relation fallen into abeyance. The next generation of landlords represented by Serragli combined a merely half-hearted appeal to the efficacy of paternalism as an antidote to subversion with a new and altogether more ominous call for an alternative policy of repression and retrenchment. By 1921 Serragli was a key figure in the organisation of squadrism.

As the link between tenant and proprietor deteriorated, the bond tying the *mezzadro* to the *podere* was seriously weakened. In the past, security had been a major factor in the stability of Tuscan rural society despite hardship, toil and a depressed standard of living. By contrast, insecurity was a marked feature of the new commercial system. The growing tax burden, of course, played an important role. The relation of city and countryside, now linked through the person of the tax collector, was not, however, the sole source of a slow expropriation of the *mezzadri*. The new agricultural methods involved ever increasing expenses for the peasant. Inherent in the sharecropping contract was the obligation of the peasant to divide not only the harvest but also the costs of cultivation. Historically, these costs had been comparatively small as agricultural methods in central Italy had been backward. The decision of the landlords to initiate more intensive farming for the market here marked a radical change. There was now a much greater outlay for seeds and plantings, for fertilisers and fodder, for tools and machinery. Taken together with the increased tax burden, the new expenses created a rapidly growing peasant indebtedness as the landowner became ever more a creditor rather than a partner. Guicciardini, for example, reported from his own estate of Cusona that of 31 *mezzadro* families, 7 had been in debt in 1895 for a total of 1,422 lire, whereas in 1911 the total debt had risen to 20,654.85 lire.[50] Guicciardini also indicated a major source of the worsening economic condition of the sharecroppers: the return to the tenant from the new crops was not sufficient to compensate for the growing costs of cultivation. Such was the logical result of a system in which expenses were equally divided between the partners, but the harvest − through a series of arrangements beneficial to property went in larger proportion to the owners. As costs increased, the tenant was caught in a 'scissors-crisis' between a fixed share (50 per cent) of increasing expenses and a substantially smaller proportion of the eventual return.[51]

Together with the increased expenses, conditions of living declined. Here precise indices are difficult to obtain, but there are several indications that all point in the same direction. One is the direct testimony of such major landlords as Guicciardini, who admitted the decline and analysed some of its causes.[52] Another is the appearance for the first time from the late nineteenth century of a sizeable incidence of the diseases of malnutrition, especially pellagra, and of the epidemic diseases of poor sanitation, such as cholera and hepatitis.[53] Descriptions of peasant living conditions in the new century portray a reality of overwork, misery and squalor for the Tuscan *mezzadro*. In the new *mezzadria*, Sismondi's comments on the abundance of clothes possessed by the peasants no longer applied. Even *l'Intrepido*, the fascist paper of Lucca, which had little political sympathy for the tenants, conducted an investigation in the summer of 1922 into the 'physical, hygienic, and sanitary conditions of the workers of the land' which disclosed a picture of living standards strongly at odds with the view of the Georgofili.[54] For the 'generality' of Tuscan sharecroppers, conditions were somewhat less than the envy of the working classes of the world.

L'Intrepido noted that about 300 days of the year were devoted to work, 248 in the fields and about 52 in and around the family cottage — repairing tools, selecting seed, tending hedges, mending clothes. The work day itself tended towards 14 hours, as a year-round average, with a high point in the autumn when the *mezzadri* even slept in the fields, and a low of 10 to 11 hours in the winter.[55] The diet was deficient in vitamins and protein. Its basis was ground meal prepared from wheat, corn or chestnuts, supplemented with potatoes, beans and vegetable soup garnished with pigs' fat. Meat and eggs were saved for feasts and wine was a luxury reserved for holidays and the harvest season.[56] Clothing was inadequate with a weekly change of underwear the rule and shoes a refinement saved for winter, for church and for trips to town. In the winter the tenants shivered in the cold.[57] Most striking of all was the description of peasant housing:

> The walls are not plastered outside, and they are blackened with smoke inside. The rooms are narrow, very low, and insufficient in number, so that it is impossible in the bedrooms to separate the sexes, and often even to separate the married couples from the others. There is no toilet. The floors are often formed of planks through whose cracks

there spreads throughout the house the pestilential stink of the squallid pigs sty underneath. The roofs are covered with broken tiles ... which admit the rain and sometimes the snow as well. The narrow windows often lack both frame and glass, and are closed only by wooden boards, so that in the winter even by day one must sit in the dark or brave the elements. The furniture is sparse and in disrepair. On the bed sometimes there is a mattress of wool or more frequently of fine chicken feathers, but very often this is missing altogether and what passes for a bed is a miserable mat of straw. In a word, everything bears the mark of poverty and hardship.[58]

Even the Mugello landlords' paper was capable of a far from sanguine account. It admitted that 'Many landlords have made the maintenance of the peasant dwelling their last concern, whether from the point of view of the structure of the building or of the appurtenances, not to mention the question of propriety and hygiene.'[59] More broadly, a leading Catholic paper noted that, '*Mezzadria* . . . in the last decade of the last century and the early years of this, has undergone a transformation wholly to the detriment of the peasant and to the advantage of the proprietor.'[60] Still another indication of growing hardship was the sudden beginning, from the turn of the century, of peasant emigration from the region – a phenomenon which until that time had been virtually non-existent.[61] The idea of peasant security had become a mockery.

So, too, the earlier independence of the peasant cultivator had become only a memory. We have already noted the long-term tendency for the landlord to reduce the size of the *poderi* in order to gain a greater intensity of labour. Now the increase in productivity associated with the new methods afforded the possibility of subsistence from a much smaller area. Hence the commercial revolution was accompanied by a drastic reduction in the average size of the *podere*. Furthermore, together with the smaller *podere* went a break-up of the extended patriarchal sharecropping family. Estimates of the size of the traditional family vary – as large as 20 to 30 members according to some authorities,[62] as small as 10 to 15 members according to others.[63] What is clear, however, is that the large families of 20 or more members which had once existed and which some authorities consider typical of traditional Tuscan *mezzadria* were wholly disappearing. The new average of seven members by 1930[64] marked a sharp fall, and still smaller families were common in the zones of most advanced commercial change.

The decline in size of the extended family accompanied a degeneration of the moral bonds among the family members. As increasing economic

pressures were exerted upon the clan, disputes over the internal division
of labour and of the crop became pronounced and bitter. Divisions began
to separate the generations as youths grew impatient of the traditional
authoritarian rule of the *capoccia* at a time when hardship was increasing,
and the prospects of an improved future seemed ever more remote.
Indeed, announcing the 'funeral of *mezzadria*', the Mugello landlord
A. Giovannini mourned:

> Between landlord and peasant, and among the members of the same
> household, harmony has been broken. Conflict dominates thought
> and attitude, gives rise to quarrels, and builds a wall of separation . . .
> The elders are unable to adapt to this state of war after having lived
> in relations of peace, so dear to the heart and conscience and also so
> useful to the furtherance of legitimate interests. The *massaie* as well,
> devoted and attached to disciplined tranquillity in the family, refuse
> to accept the arguments that inflame the young. The old patriarchal
> household traditions suffer and fall into disuse. Words are sometimes
> spoken that bite; and quarrels and disputes arise and are embittered
> by differing political beliefs and conflicting ideas, even in religion.[65]

In addition, the break-up of the peasant family worsened economic
insecurity by decreasing the possibility for a developed division of labour
within the family. As a result, the number of ancillary tasks performed
by the family declined, particularly domestic industry. This in turn
forced the *mezzadro* into greater reliance on market relations and thus
into greater indebtedness.[66] A downward spiral was begun in which
economic hardship and the declining family were at once cause and
effect of each other. The process was accentuated where specialisation
of cultivation was most advanced and industrial crops were grown.
Then, by definition, the traditional subsistence farming gave way to
extensive relations of exchange. The near autarky of the *podere* was at
an end.[67]

In any case, the independence of the *podere* had also been abolished
from another point of view — that of the relation of the peasant farm
to the estate management. Traditionally, this relation was one of day-
to-day independence of the *podere* and limited responsibilities for the
fattore. As the landlord invested more capital in agriculture, however,
the dealings of the *mezzadro* with the central estate underwent a marked
change. The concentration of the ownership of the means of production
in the hands of the proprietor made the sharecropper ever more similar,
in fact if not in legal form, to the rural proletarian of the North. The

independence of the tenant vanished as he grew increasingly reliant on the machines, the fertilisers and the technical knowledge of the landlord and increasingly subject to the supervision of the owner and his agents. Indeed, the changing functions of the *fattore* were among the most conspicuous features of the commercialisation of Tuscan agriculture. On the modernised *fattorie* he became the agent of rationalising directives from above and was made responsible for the technical direction of production. He overcame tenant reluctance to the introduction of the new crops, supervised the establishment of complex systems of rotation, selected seeds and attended to the use of fertilisers and machinery. The *fattore*, in a word, had become manager.[68]

Certainly the *fattori* saw themselves, in the changed circumstances, as a rising class of rural agricultural specialists with new claims to security, prestige and improved treatment from their employers. In the new century they founded an association of *fattori* to press their claims and a paper, *Il Fattore toscano*, to spread the glad tidings of the enhanced dignity of the landlords' agents.[69] The point is that a corollary of the increasingly managerial position of the *fattore* was the growing dependence of the *mezzadro*.[70]

The new position of the *mezzadro* was given clear expression in the worsening contractual terms to which he was subjected as commercialisation advanced. An important example is the contract in force at the turn of the century on the commercial estates of Count Giovanni Angelo Bastogi in the Chiana Valley of Siena province.[71] On Bastogi's holdings the new methods of cultivation gave rise to important innovations in the contract, all embodying onerous burdens for the tenant.

The influence of modernisation upon the contract is evident from the very titles of the clauses. Thus article 16 was entitled 'Threshing and the cost of machines', article 21 'Sulphuration of vines', article 24 'The turning over of the ground for corn', article 25 'Tobacco', article 26 'Sugar beet', and article 34 'Crop rotations and pasture'. In each case there were new obligations for the peasant, new occasions for oversight by the *fattore* and new fines to punish non-compliance.[72] The landlord, making heavy outlays of capital for crops requiring technical knowledge and application, was not content to rely on the judgement of the tenant. He intended to have his agent present to supervise every phase of the agricultural cycle. Thus the clause on tobacco was endlessly elastic in its single statement that, 'For the cultivation of tobacco the Peasant will prepare a part of the land . . . in the way indicated by the Landlords or their agents, and carry out such deep tillings as are ordered by the above mentioned, in accord with the applicable rules or special dispositions of the declining authority.'[73] The article on sugar beets was similar in spirit,[74] and the article on crop rotation stipulated that the lord and his agent would determine the area of each *podere* to be devoted to each crop and decide upon the method of cultivation.[75] The article on threshing outlined new expenses to accompany the introduction of commercial crops and machinery.[76]

In such provisions the former independence of the *podere* vanished. Bastogi recognises that the commercial crops had to be introduced against the stubborn resistance of the tenants.[77] At times he attributes this resistance to ignorance, superstition and fear of change. More substantial reasons, however, are easily inferred from the contract itself which provides for more work, increased expense and harsh discipline under the watchful eye of the *fattore*. Furthermore, Bastogi admits that the peasant growing commercial crops was subject to a much increased insecurity in accord with the vicissitudes of the market, and suggests that the *mezzadro*'s need to market his produce provided a less than scrupulous landlord with the opportunity to defraud the tenant of a portion of his share of the harvest.[78] Clearly all of this put a strain on the bond of partnership and love.

The declining position of the sharecroppers was further illustrated by the emergence in sizeable numbers from the end of the century of a variety of new sub-categories of semi-proletarianised *mezzadri* – *camporaioli*, *logaioli*, *vignaioli* and *mezzaioli*.[79] Like *mezzadri*, these new peasants worked on stable *poderi* where they divided the harvest in half with the landlord. There, however, the similarity with classical *mezzadria* ended. The new sharecroppers did not live on their plots, which were too small to provide accommodation. Instead, they commuted to the land from neighbouring villages or from labourers' barracks. Furthermore, they did not work in family units, but as single workers. Nor did the *camporaioli* grow enough for subsistence as their plots were not sufficiently large. Most, therefore, supplemented their income by working part-time as day labourers or as operatives in industry. Significantly, too, the longevity of tenure which had been a major factor in the stability of *mezzadria* no longer existed for the *camporaioli*.

The origin of the new contracts was simple: existing *poderi* were subdivided and given to tenants under radically different and less advantageous conditions. The *camporaioli* formed what was essentially a category of transition, a temporary halting place of peasants in the process of being reduced to the status of day labourers. The new semi-*mezzadri* first appeared in the commercially advanced valleys of central Tuscany where they cultivated specialised crops with machinery and tools they did not own but rented from the lord. They were a growing and, in some zones, already large work force. By 1930 they accounted for about 10 per cent of all the sharecroppers of the Chiana Valley in Arezzo province.[80]

In addition to the quasi-proletarians, more obvious products of the commercial pressures at work in the countryside were the stable nuclei of full-time wage labourers (*braccianti*) of the Chiana and Arno valleys. The *braccianti* marked the final stage in the reduction of *mezzadri* to the status of casual hands via the intermediate step of the *camporaiolato*. In key zones of the region there was formed that class of rootless proletarians against whom the Tuscan aristocracy had long warned as the chief carriers of the dreaded socialist contagion.

Together the *camporaioli* and *braccianti* were the clearest examples of a very general process of the proletarianisation of the sharecropping class: their living standards and security of tenure declined; they were gradually dispossessed of any meaningful control of the means of production and of the direction of their labour; they were pushed into broader relations with the market and their families broken up; and increasing numbers of them were finally driven from the land and forced to sell their labour power. What must be stressed is that what had occurred was not a series of separate and unrelated developments: the major changes taking place in the substance of *mezzadria* were the interlocking aspects of the single process of the commercialisation of Tuscan agriculture.

Not surprisingly, these developments had political effects which reduced the once pronounced differences between labour relations in central Italy and in the great zones of capitalistic agriculture in the North. The bonds which had linked the *mezzadro* to the social order — the ties to master, land and family — had been broken or seriously weakened, while the causes for discontent had been objectively multiplied through a growing burden of debt and taxation, through an increasing insecurity of tenure, and through worsening conditions of health and housing.

At the same time that the vertical ties of the *mezzadri* to the existing order were severed, a new network of horizontal class bonds was forged, providing the collective consciousness which was a major premiss of revolt. The traditional isolation of the *mezzadri* was overcome. In part this new communal spirit was the result of the greatly improved means of communication that linked the Tuscan countryside with impulses and influences from outside. In part it was the result of simple demographic increase. Then, too, there was the development of increasing market relations by the sharecroppers as their economic self-reliance was overthrown and they went to market as purchasers of goods and sellers of labour. Perhaps most important, the development of a collective consciousness was created by the peasants themselves. As the family declined in size, there arose during peak periods such as the threshing season a shortage of labour which began to be remedied by the mutual exchange of labour. In the zone of the Casentino (the upper Arno Valley in Arezzo province), for instance, it was reported by the post-war period that threshing was done almost entirely through the reciprocal exchange of labour among the *mezzadri*.[81] As a result, common action became possible as the peasants came to view their condition as a collective one.

Such a collective consciousness was given further powerful impetus by the First World War when conscription brought an army of peasant soldiers together in the trenches. Certainly the leaders of the mass struggle in the countryside stressed the importance of the war as an underlying cause of peasant militancy. *La Difesa*, the socialist paper of Florence, for instance, wrote,

It is the war that brought the peasant into contact with modern life. It pushed him into the factory side by side with the workers ... It placed him in the trenches along with the clerk who read him the papers and along with the professional men who explained the war. It transported him to the hospital ward, to the cities and towns, by train and by automobile. The peasant came to know first hand the humbug of the press, the honeyed promises, and the hatred for socialism. And he experienced the corruption of the sisters of charity.[82]

Finally, it should be added that with the advance of modernisation, the conservative influence of the Church in conditioning the political and social beliefs of the peasantry greatly waned. Ernesto Ragionieri, in a study of the commune of Sesto Fiorentino in the new bourgeois Italy, writes of the 'disintegration of parish life'.[83] Whereas the parish church had once been a focus for the few great occasions of peasant life, in Liberal Italy the multiplication of contacts and occasions of a commercial, political and lay character diminished the awe and importance of the church and created other rival repositories of attention, loyalty and hope – the town hall, the party, even the market place. By the propagation of a secular culture and ideology, united Italy weakened the esteem in which the clergy were held. At the same time, changes in the productive process associated with the capitalistic penetration of rural Tuscany evoked a non-religious response. In traditional *mezzadria*, the relation of the *podere* to broad economic forces and to the powers of the landlord had been partly hidden as the peasant felt that his struggle was largely one with himself and with the forces of nature – the soil, the rain and wind, the health of domestic animals and seed plants. In this setting, the power of intercession with divinity was of greater value than at a later time when the exactions of landlord and state and the vicissitudes of the market had both increased absolutely and become ever more apparent. The landlord was ever more visibly the source of orders and directives, and was clearly responsible for the introduction of new crops and methods that changed the face of the countryside. In all this the peasant came to know his position as the product of human agency; and his response was not religious but political. An important prop of the social order had been quietly removed.

Political Effects and Reaction

In view of the considerations outlined above, it is understandable that after several decades of intense commercial development, the 'public quiet' was finally and dramatically broken by the *mezzadri*.[84] The post-war explosion had been heralded by two earlier events of 1902 and 1906 which had been insufficiently appreciated at the time, but marked the end of an era in Tuscan history. In 1902 the first strike of *mezzadri* ever to occur in the region took place, and it occurred precisely in the area where commercial changes had first been introduced and had gone furthest – the Chiana Valley communes of Chiusi, Chianciano and Montepulciano. In the same year the socialists noted that 'even in our Tuscany the peasants are beginning to understand the necessity of organisation', and reported the establishment of the first peasant League.[85] The first agitation in 1902 was then followed in 1906 by further strikes of sharecroppers in some of the most advanced zones of Florence and Arezzo provinces.[86]

After the dress rehearsals of 1902 and 1906, the post-war burst of political militancy among the *mezzadri* should have caused little surprise. In fact, however, the 'official' view of *mezzadria* as guarantor of social stability had so dominated discussion of the social question that neither right nor left of the political spectrum was prepared to confront the new situation. Even the socialist party shared with the landowners the view of the impermeability of *mezzadria* to socialist influence. The revolutionary paper *La Difesa*, for instance, greeted the sudden emergence of vast rural agitation with unconcealed astonishment. Commenting on the post-war development of political militancy among the *mezzadri*, the Florentine paper exclaimed: 'Anyone who has followed the phases of the agrarian struggle in Tuscany . . . can only be amazed by the mental transformation of our peasants. Who could ever have foreseen it?'[87] In a similar vein the socialist paper of Siena wrote of the sharecroppers whom 'no one would ever have believed capable of a demonstration of strength, determination and solidarity'.[88] And the Empoli socialists remarked that 'It seems like a dream'.[89]

In fact, however, the movement, which began in the spring of 1919 as a series of largely spontaneous local strikes throughout the commercially advanced areas of central Tuscany, demonstrated considerable 'strength, determination and solidarity'. The impulse to a radical reordering of rural social relations came from below. Indeed the essential demands put forward in a hundred different localities were a response to broad pressures which were similar throughout the region and remained unaltered throughout the post-war struggles. Although the movement was rapidly channelled and led by the two rival parties of the rural Tuscan left – the socialist PSI and the Catholic PPI, what was notable was that the parties adopted a range of demands for contractual reform that they found in large measure already formulated. Their tasks were to unify and generalise the struggle that had aleady begun, to provide it with continuity and organisational framework, to broaden it to include wider political objectives and class allies, and to articulate its aims more fully. For this the demands advanced in 1919 formed the basis.

The demands of the striking sharecroppers fell roughly into three categories.[90] The first category attempted to fix the division of the harvest between landlord and tenant more nearly in accord with the theoretical proportion of 50/50. For this purpose the *mezzadri* called for the abolition of all special levies and *corvée* labour, the establishment of written rather than oral contracts, and the institution of arbitration boards to settle disputes. They also sought to reform debt labour by asking that all work performed off the *podere* be remunerated at the current market rates for wage labour. These demands did not affect the substance of the traditional contract, but were intended to protect the tenant from the arbitrary exercise of unequal power. Though unwelcome, such claims were considered negotiable by most landlords.[91] Indeed, the reforming advocates of enlightened paternalism, led by P.F. Serragli, actually pressed for prompt concessions on these issues in the hope of assuaging tenant discontent without altering the underlying distribution of power. An astute proprietor, it was reasoned, could maintain his position despite a few new constraints.

The second category of demands was more contentious, as the *mezzadri* sought to reduce the financial burden which had fallen upon them as a result of modernisation. The strikers insisted that the landlord alone assume the expense of providing chemical fertilisers, threshing machines and maintenance facilities. They also demanded that the owner meet the cost of planting the new commercial crops up to the moment when they became productive, and that he provide insurance and veterinary care for livestock. At the same time the sharecroppers tentatively raised the question of taxation, proposing that the proprietor assume full payment of the cattle tax. And to ensure the permanence of the redistribution of wealth, the tenants demanded union recognition.

These second demands were considered unacceptable by the land-lords and were met by intransigent opposition. One immediate reason was that such measures were put forward at a time when Italian farmers were in no mood to be generous. Agricultural production had declined as a result of the war. Worse still, in the inflationary 'monetary revolution' that began during the war and continued into the post-war years, agri-cultural prices lagged behind the general price level. In the circumstances, concessions were not to be made lightly.[92]

It may be objected that the same consideration applies to the demands of the first category. The difference, which explains the employers' attitude, is that the first demands affected profits in the short term, whereas demands in the second category threatened to undermine profitability as such. The provisions that the peasant meet his share of the expenses of cultivation and taxation and provide for his own welfare were essential underpinnings of the whole *mezzadria* system. To have removed these features would have compromised the ability of the landlords to modernise agriculture without destroying *mezzadria*. The margins for reformist concessions were narrow. *Mezzadria* had survived into an era of world competition by its capacity to exact a high level of exploitation of labour. To reform the contract threatened the whole arrangement. As Serragli said, *mezzadria* could no longer function if the peasant appeared no longer 'as a partner concerned for the common good, but acted like a day labourer who thinks of the amount of his own remuneration and who therefore argues, debates, and protests'.[93] At stake was the whole direction of capitalist development in Tuscany.

Most important of all in the post-war conflict, however, was a third group of demands that sought to institute direct tenant control over the workplace, and were clearly revolutionary. One was that eviction be made illegal except for the provisions of the Civil Code. Since eviction was the ultimate sanction which ensured compliance with the exactions of the system, this demand was fundamentally subversive. If the tenant gained full security of tenure, the power vested in ownership would dissolve. Again Serragli protested in the name of the aristocracy. Eviction, he argued, was 'the sole means of restoring discipline among the share-cropping masses'.[94] Secondly, the strikers called for equal rights for tenants in the direction of the estates. In some areas — most notably Siena, the famous 'red province' — farm councils of the *mezzadri* (*consigli di fattoria*) were established as the instruments for the exercise of this right.[95] With unforeseen speed and clarity the issue was drawn between the partners. As the socialist paper *La Difesa* of Florence wrote,

These [i.e. eviction and equality of right between landlord and peasant in the direction of the estates] are the two questions that are the centre of the peasant battle, and it is here that the landlords have committed themselves to the staunchest resistance. In fact, this attitude is to be understood if we remember that through victories on these questions of a moral and legal order, the peasants hope to achieve the abolition of *mezzadria*, which is the most typical form of the ancient domination of the bosses.[96]

Once begun in 1919, the strike movement, initially involving a series of local disputes, became increasingly powerful and widespread. By the autumn of 1919 and spring of 1920, a succession of massive province-wide agitations had won major concessions from the landlords' organisations. And in the summer of 1920 the tenants gained their greatest victory. The great socialist strike of 1920 revealed a peasant solidarity throughout the region that was wholly without precedent. Even by Emilian standards the agitation was impressive as 500,000 sharecroppers (72,000 families) out of the total of 710,800 Tuscan *mezzadri* took part.[97] Under the threat of losing the entire wheat crop, the Agrarian Association capitulated in the third week of July, signing the famous 'Red Pact' that granted the *mezzadri* in all of Tuscany security of tenure and a voice in the direction of the estates, together with virtually all the other improvements demanded.[98] The property rights of the Tuscan landlords had been seriously compromised. The new contract decreed a revolution in rural social relations. To have accepted the Red Pact as final, the landlords would have needed to resign themselves to the demise of the old social order. Instead, they regarded defeat as only provisional and used the time gained by concessions to organise a counter-offensive to destroy the threat of rural socialism once and for all.

The need felt by the Tuscan aristocracy to organise its own self-defence was underscored by what it regarded as the patent failure of the government to defend the rights of property. Beyond police measures to protect the 'right to work', the government had done little to reassure the landlords. Indeed, the fall of the Liberal majority in Parliament and the crumbling of the Liberal parties in the provinces indicated that the state was no longer able to defend property, while the failure of the government to intervene during the occupation of the factories in the autumn raised doubts about government resolve. Of particular effect on the growing disillusionment of landowners with the state was the attempt by the Liberal ministry to outrun peasant discontent by introducing a series of reforms into rural labour relations. By a succession of decree laws the state began in 1919 to operate a welfare programme for the benefit of agricultural workers, including *mezzadri*. The chief features of the programme were compulsory accident, old age and disability insurance, all involving major contributions from the proprietors. Accident insurance for the tenants was to be financed entirely by the landlords through a tax surcharge of 3 per cent of taxable wealth.[99] The premiums for the old age and disability schemes were to be divided between the employer and the insured. The cost to the landlord was L24 per year for each adult male sharecropper, L18 for women and L12 for minors.[100]

These provisions, taking effect at a time of agricultural crisis, raised a storm of outrage from the proprietors. Every meeting of the Agrarian Association (AAT) until the March on Rome raised the issue and condemned the intiative of the government.[101] The view of the Tuscan landlords was that they were being crushed between the unions and the state. According to the AAT, the government was attempting to gain popularity by bartering away the profitability of Tuscan agriculture. The position of the Association was uncompromising. Welfare payments for *mezzadri* were an intolerable burden and 'an absurdity'. As G. Chiostri, secretary of the AAT, explained: 'The *mezzadro* has no need for insurance against disability and old age. For him, the solidarity binding the various members of our peasant families is the best form of provision.'[102] From the start, the landlords' conversion to reaction was an attempt to destroy not only the threat of bolshevism but also the belated rural reformism of the Liberal state.

In any event, whatever its intentions, the Liberal state seemed to the farmers to be on the verge of being overwhelmed. Already after the elections of 1919 the leading national newspaper representing agrarian interests, *Il Resto del Carlino* of Bologna, had written with evident gloom that the results

appeared to be the political liquidation of the Liberal bourgeoisie that . . . has governed Italy.

The defeat, which is the defeat not just of the government, but of the Liberal and secular state, the crisis of a regime, and the end of a historical era, are all apparent.[103]

With such a feeling of crisis already in 1919, one can easily imagine the mood of the landlords after the major defeats in the strikes of 1920. An indication of their attitude was provided in August when a national agrarian congress took place at Rimini among representatives of the agrarian associations of the Veneto, Emilia-Romagna, Tuscany, the Marches and Umbria. The mood of the congress, as described by the correspondent of *Il Resto del Carlino*, was one of defiance towards the government and of determination to resort to self-help.[104] Among the most militant, Marchi, the representative of the Tuscan Agrarian Association, said:

> If the farmers of Italy cannot find in themselves the strength to face the dangers that threaten them, we are wasting our time in discussion. We must realise that by now the state has no authority to help us and that only the farmers themselves can rectify the present situation.[105]

The gloomiest reflections of the landlords were more than confirmed by the autumn local and provincial government elections of 1920 when the PSI (Socialist Party) won 2,162 of Italy's 8,059 communes (it had held only 300 in 1914) and 25 of the 69 provinces.[106] In Tuscany, six of the eight Tuscan provincial councils (Lucca and Massa-Carrara being the exceptions) had socialist majorities, as did 149 of the 290 communes, while of the remaining communes the PPI (Popular Party) had secured 52. The most alarming results of all, from the standpoint of the ruling classes, came from Siena province, where of 36 communes, the PSI won 30 as well as 32 of 40 seats on the provincial council.[107]

The local elections not only confirmed fears of the continuing socialist advance but also – and this was crucial – they overturned the traditional local control of the ruling classes. The landlords now saw a vital element in their domination overthrown and themselves ousted from local bodies they had come to regard nearly as much their own as the land. Whole networks of influence, patronage and clientele relations were suddenly jeopardised. Further, with control of local political power, the bargaining power of the union movement was greatly multiplied. Above all, the landlords now found themselves the objects of an unwonted use of the powers of local taxation. A whole series of levies was placed upon men of wealth. From the landholding viewpoint, the most menacing development was the decision of the new socialist-controlled communes to impose a new expropriatory surcharge upon the land. After a year of socialist local government in vast areas of Italy, Arrigo Serpieri, the friend of property, calculated in November 1921 that in 1920 the three old income taxes yielded a total of 900 million lire of which only 128 million were produced by taxes on land, to which local surcharges added a further tax burden of 323 million. By contrast, in 1921, the burden alone of local surtaxes on land was over 802 million lire.[108] To cite a Tuscan example of the new burden on property, the provincial council of Florence province in April 1921 voted a massive increase in the land surtax, bringing it from a total of L9,949,930 in 1920 to L25,400,000.[109]

In this climate of revolutionary crisis, it is understandable that the fascist movement made its first appearance in rural Tuscany as the instrument of lordly retrenchment. The commercialisation of agriculture in Tuscany had proceeded in such a fashion as to destroy the mechanisms of social control built into the structure of traditional *mezzadria*, but without providing the alternative instruments of a mature industrial capitalism. Fascism filled the gap. It was a repressive and violent means of containing the class tensions of the modernisation of the countryside.

Notes

1. Statistics on the number of *fasci* and fascists in every province in 1921-2 are provided by Renzo De Felice, *Mussolini il fascista*, vol.I (Turin, 1966), pp.8-11.

2. Curzio Malaparte, for instance described Florence as the 'proudest, purest, and most upright fascist province'. 'Tutti debbono obbedire', *Battaglie fasciste* (27 December 1924). The leading role of Tuscan fascism was a recurrent theme of the paper.

3. According to the 1921 census, the population of Tuscany was 2,789,879. The principal categories of the agricultural population were:

peasant proprietors	289,311
leaseholders	27,326
sharecroppers	710,793
day labourers	357,024

Ministero dell'Economia Nazionale, *Risultati sommari del censimento della popolazione eseguito al 1 dicembre 1921* (Rome, 1925). In 1930 there were about 4,100 *fattorie* in Tuscany of an average size of just over 200 hectares. Ministero per la Costituente, *Rapporto della commissione economica: Agricoltura*, I, p.213; and Angelo Camparini and Mario Bandini, *Rapporti fra proprietà impresa e mano d'opera nell'agricoltura italiana: Toscana* (Rome, 1930).

4. Quoted in Ernesto Ragionieri, 'La questione delle leghe e i primi scioperi dei mezzadri in Toscana', *Movimento operaio*, VII (1955) p.454.

5. Quoted in Carlo Pazzagli, *L'agricoltura toscana nella prima metà dell' 800* (Florence, 1973), p.429.

6. A. Giovannini, 'I funerali della mezzeria', *Il Messaggero del Mugello* (28 March 1920). For other classic statements of the 'official' view of *mezzadria*, see Sidney Sonnino, 'La mezzeria in Toscana', in Leopoldo Franchetti, *Condizioni economiche ed amministrative delle province napoletane* (Florence, 1875); Giuseppe Toniolo, *Trattato di economia sociale* (Florence, 1915-21), vol.II, *La produzione*, pp.237-41; and the interview with Marquis Capponi in John Bowring, *Report on the Statistics of Tuscany, Lucca, the Pontifical and the Lombardo-Venetian States* (London, 1837) in *British Parliamentary Papers, 1839*, vol.XVI (165) p.43.

7. On the landowners' use of *stime*, cf. Reginaldo Cianferoni, 'I contadini e l'agricoltura in Toscana sotto il fascismo', in Unione Regionale delle Province Toscane, *La Toscana nell'Italia unita, 1861-1945* (Florence, 1962), pp.390-1n; and Giorgio Giorgetti, 'Agricoltura e sviluppo capitalistico nella Toscana del '700', *Studi storici*, IX (1968) p.749.

8. Cianferoni, ibid., p.387. Cf. also Luciano Radi, *I mezzadri: le lotte contadine dell'Italia centrale* (Rome, 1962), p.88.

9. Radi, ibid., p.239.

10. Frank McArdle, *Altopascio: A Study in Tuscan Rural Society, 1587-1784* (Cambridge, 1978), chap.3.

11. On peasant overwork, cf. Pazzagli, *L'agricoltura toscana*; Carlo Scarperi, 'Il mezzadro si ribella', *La Difesa* (24 July 1920); and 'Il problema agrario', *l'Intrepido* (28 May 1922).

12. Quoted in Bowring, *Report on the Statistics of Tuscany*, pp.42-3.

13. Mario Tofani, 'I mezzadri dell'Italia centrale', in Ministero per la Costituente, *Rapporto*, II, p.476; and Giorgetti, 'Agricoltura e sviluppo'.

14. 'Ai contadini', *La Difesa* 31 May 1900.

15. *L'Assicurazione e la legislazione sociale* (Florence, 1898).

16. Ibid., pp.3-4.

17. Ibid., p.11.

18. Ibid. Mazzini returned to the theme in *Assistenza, previdenza ed assicurazioni sociali* (Florence, 1912).

19. Quoted in Giorgio Mori, *La Valdelsa dal 1848 al 1900: sviluppo economico, movimenti sociali e lotta politica* (Milan, 1957), p.25.

20. For Capponi's view of 'the erroneous self-sufficing principle' of *mezzadria*, cf. Bowring, *Report on the Statistics of Tuscany*, p.42.

21. On *mezzadria* as an obstacle to the rationalisation of agricultural production, cf. J.C.L. Simonde de Sismondi, *Tableau de l'agricolture toscane* (Geneva, 1801), pp.207-19; Giorgetti, 'Agricoltura e sviluppo'; and Mario Mirri, 'Mercato regionale e internazionale e mercato nazionale capitalistico come condizione dell'evoluzione interna della mezzadria in Toscana', in Istituto Antonio Gramsci, *Agricoltura e sviluppo del capitalismo* (Rome, 1970), pp.393-428.

22. The frequency of theft by *mezzadri* is conveyed by such Tuscan proverbs as: 'Tra mal d'occhio e l'acqua cotta, il padrone non gliene tocca' and 'Cento scrivani non guardano un fattore e cento fattori non guardano un contadino'. Quoted in Giuseppe Giusti, *Raccolta di proverbi toscani* (Florence, 1913), pp. 18 and 8. On the prevalence of crime in the Tuscan countryside, cf. McArdle, *Altopascio*, chap.9.

23. 'La figura morale e giuridica degli agenti rurali', *Bandiera rossa-Martinella*, 6 January 1921. The position of the *fattore* is discussed by G.A. Bastogi, *Una scritta colonica* (Florence, 1903), pp.40-52.

24. Quoted in Pazzagli, *L'agricoltura toscana*, p.410.

25. The accounts of the landlord Ferdinando Vai for his *fattoria* of Mulinaccio in Florence province are eloquent with regard to the importance of paternal aid. Archivio di Stato di Prato, Archivio Vai Rurale, Filza 421 (Mulinaccio: conti

colonici dal 1 giugno 1912 al 31 maggio 1913). On the role of paternalism in *mezzadria*, cf. Sydel F. Silverman, 'Patronage and Community-Nation Relationships in Central Italy', *Ethnology* IV (1965) pp.172-90; and *Three Bells of Civilization: The Life of an Italian Hill Town* (New York and London, 1975), pp.87 ff.

26. On the direct involvement of landowners with their estates, cf. Camparini and Bandini, *Rapporti fra proprietà impresa*, p.20.

27. 'Della condizione degli agricoltori in Toscana', *Biblioteca dell' economista*, serie 2, vol.II (Turin, 1860) p.549.

28. *Atti del parlamento italiano*, Camera dei Deputati, Legislatura XXV, Sessione 1919-1920, Discussioni, VII, p.6576.

29. McArdle, *Altopascio*, pp.157-9.

30. On the size of the sharecropping family, see below, p. 154.

31. Simonde de Sismondi, 'Della condizione degli agricoltori in Toscana', *Tableau de l'agricolture toscane*, pp. 551-2.

32. Giorgetti, 'Agricoltura e sviluppo', pp.749-50.

33. On the tenant family and the *capocciato*, cf. Mario C. Ferrigni, *Il capoccia nella mezzeria toscana: appunti di diritto civile* (Florence, 1901); Bastogi, *Una scritta colonica*, pp.52-9; and Raffaele Cognetti De Martiis, 'La famiglia colonica e la consuetudine', *Rivista di diritto agrario*, XI (1932) p.199.

34. Ferrigni, *Il capoccia*, p.26.

35. Ibid., p.41.

36. On peasant isolation, cf. 'Ai contadini', *La Difesa*, 12 May 1901.

37. Quoted in Pazzagli, *L'agricoltura toscana*, pp.414-15. For similar provisions, cf. Bastogi, *Una scritta colonica*, p.137.

38. Mori, *La Valdelsa*, p.17.

39. On the Italian fiscal system as a means of primitive accumulation, cf. Rosario Romeo, *Breve storia della grande industria in Italia* (Rocca San Casciano, 1972), chap.2. For the specific measures employed, see the sections on finance in Epicarmo Corbino, *Annali dell'economia italiana*, 4 vols (Città di Castello, 1931-8).

40. *Le recenti agitazioni agrarie e i doveri della proprietà* (Rome, 1907), pp.39-40.

41. The role of trans-oceanic competition and tariff war in the crisis of *mezzadria* is discussed by Giorgio Mori, 'La mezzadria in Toscana alla fine del xix secolo', *Movimento operaio*, VII (1955) and Mirri, 'Mercato regionale'.

42. For the introduction of tobacco in the Chiana Valley, cf. Ciro Marchi, 'La coltivazione del tabacco in Valdichiana', in Accademia R. Economico-agraria dei Georgofili, *Atti*, quinta serie, vol.V, disp.3a (1908) pp.283-360. The importance of sugar beet is stressed in 'La coltivazione delle barbabietole', *Giovinezza* (19 March 1922). For discussion of the crop systems in each zone of Tuscany, cf. Camparini and Bandini, *Rapporti frà proprietà impresa*. Also useful is Vittorio Peglion, *Le nostre piante industriali: canapa, lino, bietola da zucchero, tobacco, ecc.* (Bologna, 1919).

43. Giunta per la Inchiesta Agraria, *Atti*, vol.III, fasc.1: *La Toscana agricola: Relazione sulle condizioni dell'agricoltura e degli agricoltori nella IX circoscrizione* (Rome, 1881), p.276.

44. *La Toscana agricola*, pp.271-8; and Ministero d'Agricoltura, Industria e Commercio, *Notizie intorno alle condizioni dell'agricoltura negli anni 1878-1879* (Rome, 1881).

45. Istituto Nazionale di Economia Agraria, *Inchiesta sulla piccola proprietà coltivatrice formatasi nel dopoguerra*, 15 vol. (Rome, 1938). Cf. volume by M. Bandini, *La Toscana*, p.86.

46. Telegram of deputy prefect Cassini to Ministero dell' Interno, Dir. Gen. della P.S., 12 July 1922, Archivio Centrale dello Stato, PS (1922), b.45, fasc. Arezzo, sottofasc. 'agitazione agraria', n.731. Cf. also Mori, *La Valdelsa*, pp.69-70.

47. 'Applicabilità del contratto d'impiego ai fattori', *Il Fattore toscano* (7 May 1914).

48. Cf. Francesco Guicciardini, *Le recenti agitazioni agrarie e i doveri della prodrietà* (Florence, 1907); Piero Francesco Serragli, 'Le agitazioni dei contadini e l'avvenire della mezzeria', reprinted in *La mezzadria negli scritti dei Georgofili*, vol.II (Bologna, 1935), esp. pp.186-90; and Vittorio Racah, 'La mezzadria e i doveri del proprietario', *Il Fattore toscano* (15 February 1913).

49. Emilio Sereni, *La questione agraria nella rinascita nazionale italiana* (Rome, 1946), pp.192-3.

50. Guicciardini, *Le recenti agitazioni agrarie*; Mori, *La Valdelsa*, pp. 244-5.

51. Ministero per la Costituente, *Rapporto*, I, p.218. On the new burden of expenses, cf. also Giovanni Perini, 'La mezzadria in Toscana e la revisione del patto colonico', *Il Messaggero del Mugello* (22 June 1919); and Guicciardini, *Le recenti agitazioni agrarie*, p.31. The role of commercial change in increasing peasant expense emerges clearly from the accounts of the Mulinaccio estate of 35 *poderi* belonging to the Vai family in Florence province. For the year 1912-13 more than half of the total tenant expenses for cultivation were for chemicals for the ensulphuration of vines. Archivio di Stato di Prato, Archivio Vai Rurale, Filza 421 (Mulinaccio: conti colonici dal 1 giugno 1912 al 31 maggio 1913).

52. See above, pp. 152-3.

53. An official medical report of 1884 on the health of *mezzadri* in the Elsa Valley is quoted in Mori, *La Valdelsa*, pp.198-9.

54. See the weekly articles signed 'L.M.', 'Il problema agrario: condizioni fisiche, igieniche e sanitarie dei lavoratori della terra', *l'Intrepido* (4 June 1922-6 August 1922).

55. 'L.M.', 'Il problema agrario', *l'Intrepido* (9 July 1922 and 16 July 1922).

56. On the diet of *mezzadri*, cf. ibid. (25 June 1922).

57. Ibid. (2 July 1922).

58. Ibid. (18 June 1922).

59. Francesco Nicolai, 'La Fratellanza Colonica Toscana', *Il Messaggero toscano* (2 March 1920).

60. Giulio Alvi, 'I proprietari terrieri al bivio', *Il Messagero toscano* (2 March 1920).

61. From Tuscany in 1876-7 297 people emigrated for every 100,000 inhabitants, as compared with 1,330 per 100,000 in 1913-14. Commissariato Generale dell'Emigrazione, *Annuario statistico della emigrazione italiana dal 1876 al 1925* (Rome, 1926), p.10. The Georgofili themselves noted that the chief causes of emigration from Tuscany were the increasing burdens of taxation and indebtedness. Conte Donato Sanminiatelli, 'Sulla emigrazione rurale, specialmente della Toscana', Accademia R. Economico-agraria dei Georgofili, *Atti*, quinta serie, vol.IX, disp.1a (1912) pp.217-19.

62. Osservatorio d'Economia Agraria per la Toscana, *L'Economia agraria della Toscana* (Rome, 1939), pp.85 and 85n.

63. W.K. Hancock, *Ricasoli and the Risorgimento in Tuscany* (London, 1926), pp.12-14. Capponi simply suggests a range in size from 6 to 8 members at one extreme to 20 to 25 members at the other. Bowring, *Report on the Statistics of Tuscany*, p.41.

64. Osservatorio d'Economia Agraria per la Toscana, *L'Economia agraria*, p.85. The census of 1921 indicated an average of 7.6 per family. Ministero dell'Economia Nazionale, *Risultati sommari*.

65. 'I funerali della mezzeria', *Il Messaggero toscano* (28 March 1920).

66. On the importance of household industry in the sharecropping economy, cf. Simonde de Sismondi, 'Della condizione degli agricoltori in Toscana', pp.551-2.

67. Tofani points out some of the long-established links with the market. 'La

mezzadria nell'Italia centrale', in Ministero per la Costituente, *Rapporto*, II, p.480.

68. On the changing relations between *fattoria* and *podere*, cf. Giorgetti, 'Agricoltura e sviluppo', p.757; and Mirri, 'Mercato regionale', pp.398-9.

69. On the new role of the *fattori*, see 'Impressioni di agricoltura toscana', *Il Fattore toscano*, (24 November 1912); 'I tre casi', *Il Fattore toscano* (22 May 1913); 'Esame di coscienza', *Il Fattore toscano* (7 April 1914); 'Applicabilità del contratto d'impiego ai fattori', *Il Fattore toscano* (7 May 1914); and 'Chi siamo e cosa vogliamo', *Il Fattore toscano* (22 May 1914).

70. The proletarianisation of *mezzadri* is discussed by Sereni, *La questione agraria*, pp.190-5 and *Il capitalismo nelle campagne 1860-1900* (Turin, 1948). Cf. also Radi, *I mezzadri*, pp.327 ff.

71. Bastogi, *Una scritta colonica*, pp.71-149.

72. Ibid., pp.107 ff.

73. Ibid., p.115.

74. Ibid.

75. Ibid., p.124.

76. Ibid., p.107.

77. Ibid., pp.116-18.

78. Ibid., pp.116-18.

79. On the *camporaioli*, see Ministero per la Costituente, *Rapporto*, I, pp.261-3; Camparini and Bandini, *Rapporti fra proprietà impresa*, pp.18-20; Mario Tofani, 'Piccole imprese di contadini compartecipanti in Toscana', *Rivista di economia agraria*, VI (1931) pp.299-341; and Mori, *La Valdelsa*, pp.71-2.

80. Camparini and Bandini, *Rapporti fra proprietà impresa*, p.19.

81. Ibid., p.12.

82. Carlo Scarpini, 'Il mezzadro si ribella', *La Difesa* (24 July 1920).

83. *Un comune socialista: Sesto Fiorentino* (Rome, 1953), pp.177-86.

84. In 1920, Arrigo Serpieri reported, a greater percentage (27.84 per cent) of the agricultural population of Tuscany struck than in any other region. *La guerra e le classi rurali italiane* (Bari, 1930).

85. 'Le leghe dei contadini in Toscana', *La Difesa* (12 January 1902).

86. On the first strikes, see Guicciardini, *op. cit*; Radi, *I mezzadri*, pp.102-9; and Lando Magini, *Gli scioperi dei mezzadri nel circondario di Montepulciano* (Siena, 1902).

87. Carlo Scarpini, 'Il mezzadro si ribella', *La Difesa* (24 July 1920).

88. 'Movimento febbrile', *Bandiera rossa – Martinella* (8 November 1919).

89. *Vita nuova* (19 October 1919).

90. For enumeration of the peasant demands, cf. 'La riforma del patto colonico', *La Nazione* (3 October 1919).

91. For the reaction of landowners to the peasant demands, cf. Serragli, 'Le agitazioni dei contadini', pp.156-67.

92. The economic position of the landlords is discussed in Serpieri, *La guerra*. A list of major agricultural prices for the period 1915-1921 is provided in Ministero per la Costituente, *Rapporto*, I, tabella 13, pp.518-19.

93. Quoted in Carlo Rotelli, 'Lotte contadine nel Mugello, 1919-1922', *Il movimento di liberazione in Italia*, XXIV, no.107 (1972) pp.39-64.

94. *Il Nuovo giornale* (1 November 1921).

95. Recognition of *consigli di fattoria* was among the demands that the Siena Chamber of Labour advanced in the strike of 1920. Telegram of prefect Emilio D'Eufemia to Ministero dell'Interno, Dir. Gen. della P.S., 27 June 1920, ACS, PS (1920), b.60, fasc. Siena, sottofasc. 'agitazione agraria', n.677.

96. 'La gigantesca battaglia dei coloni toscani', *La Difesa* (15 July 1920).

97. See above, n.96.

98. The text of the new regional pact signed on 6 August 1920 is in *La Nazione* (8 August 1920).

99. 'Riassunto delle disposizioni principali per l'assicurazione dei coloni contro gli infortuni del lavoro', *Bollettino mensile della Associazione Agraria di Prato* (8 April 1921).

100. 'Norme per l'assicurazione obbligatoria per invalidità e vecchiaia dei coloni, personale di fattoria, ecc.', *Bollettino della Associazione Agraria di Prato* (8 April 1921).

101. The concern of the Agrarian Association throughout this period can be traced in the *Bollettino dell'Associazione Agraria Toscana* and the *Bollettino della Associazione Agraria di Prato*.

102. 'In tema di assicurazioni sociali', *Bollettino dell'Associazione Agraria Toscana* (1 October 1922).

103. 'La rivincita dello Stato', *Il Resto del carlino* (20 November 1919).

104. 'Il Convegno agrario di Rimini', *Il Resto del carlino* (31 August 1920).

105. Ibid.

106. 'I risultati delle elezioni amministrative', *Il Resto del carlino* (26 November 1920).

107. *Bandiera rossa – Martinella* (31 October 1920).

108. Arrigo Serpieri, 'Le sperequazioni tributarie', *Il Resto del carlino* (20 November 1921).

109. 'La sovrimposta sui terreni', *La Nazione* (14 April 1921). The importance attached by the landlords to the new taxes is suggested by 'L'assemblea dei proprietari terrieri contro l'aumento delle imposte fondiarie degli E.L.', *La Nazione* (24 June 1921) and 'Il convegno nazionale agrario per la questione dei tributi locali', *Il Resto del carlino* (25 September 1921).

6 AGRARIANS AND INDUSTRIALISTS: THE EVOLUTION OF AN ALLIANCE IN THE PO DELTA, 1896-1914

Anthony L. Cardoza

Historians and political theorists have long recognised the central role played by an agrarian-industrial bloc in the economic and political development of Italy. Beginning with Gaetano Salvemini and Antonio Gramsci, students of Italian history have attributed the political weaknesses of the Liberal state and the deformations in the economy after 1861 to an alliance between northern entrepreneurs and semi-feudal landowners of the South. The bloc found expression in the systems of political transformism and economic protectionism that corrupted parliamentary life and distorted industrial development. Many historians have argued that this alliance reached its fullest development during the fascist regime, which, to gain the support of southern landowners, sacrificed economic growth to ensure social stability.[1]

The agrarian-industrial bloc in Italy, however, should not be reduced simply to an alliance between northern capitalists and semi-feudal southern landowners. Such an emphasis obscures the equally significant inter-penetration of industrial and commercial agrarian interests in northern Italy that began at the end of the nineteenth century. The formation and evolution of this northern capitalist bloc was strikingly evident in the Po Delta which, along with the Piedmontese rice areas, became the most advanced agricultural zone of Italy in the period prior to the First World War. Situated in the south-eastern part of the Po Valley, the Delta throughout much of the nineteenth century had been a largely undeveloped frontier region with vast expanses of sparsely populated swamp and marsh land. During the last three decades of the century, private and publicly financed land reclamation projects brought about an agronomic revolution that drastically altered the physical and social face of the zone. With few of the restrictions imposed by traditional structures and customs, entrepreneurial interests were able to build up on the newly reclaimed lands a capitalist system of production, characterised by large commercial farms that employed masses of day labourers and specialised in the cultivation of rice and industrial crops. Unlike most other regions on the peninsula, in the Po Delta the absence of the Church, a strong class of old aristocratic landowners, and a stable population of peasant cultivators gave social relations a distinctive form; a raw and unmediated class struggle prevailed in which the protagonists were capitalist farmers and landless day labourers, who developed the strongest rural union movement in all of Europe. In the post-war era, this struggle underlay the crisis that would make the Po Delta the 'cradle' of Italian fascism. Emerging from the provinces of the Delta as a preventive counter-revolution against the socialist unions, agrarian fascism transformed Mussolini's marginal extremist organisation into a major political force on the national level.[2]

The convergences of agrarian and industrial interests in the Po Delta must be located within the general development of Italian capitalism.

The Po Delta

Po Delta: Agriculture and Industry

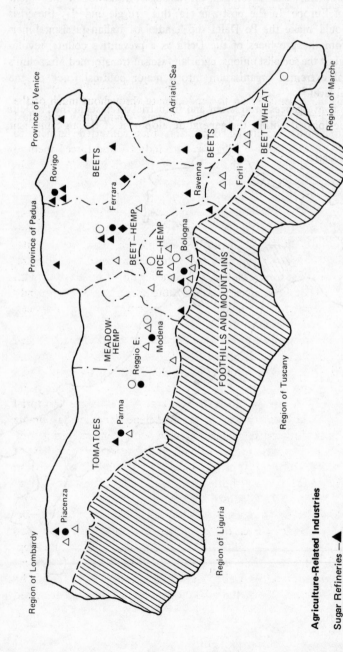

Agriculture-Related Industries

Sugar Refineries — ◀

Hemp Processing — ◆

Chemical Fertilisers — ○

Agric. Machinery — △

Sources: Credito Italiano, *Societa italiane per azioni: Notizie statistiche, 1914; Archivio Centrale dello Stato*, Ministero delle Armi e Munizioni, Busta 2, Fascicolo 20, 'Elenco delle ditte del Veneto ed Emilia specializzate nella fabricazione di macchine agricole', 12 March 1917;

This alliance, far from being a sign of economic backwardness, reflected a new and decisive expansion of industrial capitalism into the countryside. Indeed, the inter-penetration of northern Italian economic groups closely paralleled developments in other European nations during the industrial revolution's 'second wind'. The latter half of the nineteenth century saw the growing subordination of agriculture to the industrial world's demands for foodstuffs and raw materials as well as to the imperatives of technological innovations in the fields of communications and transport. By the 1880s concentration, cartels and marketing agreements began to predominate throughout much of the European and American economies. Overseas competition unleashed an international agricultural depression that converted farmers to protectionist 'iron and rye' alliances with industry and forced them to cut costs, while increasing the productivity of their lands. As a result, commercial farmers turned to mechanisation, introduced chemical fertilisers and started to produce for the expanding food processing sector.[3] A similar pattern of changes emerged in the Po Delta between 1896 and 1914. Government policies, the lure of profits and pressures from organised labour all favoured economic collaboration and integration of commercial agrarian and industrial interests. Rural entrepreneurs organised consortia and established intimate connections with chemical and machine concerns, while more specialised growers' syndicates became inextricably linked to the burgeoning agricultural processing and refining sectors.

Although in many respects developments in the Delta conformed to general capitalist trends of the period, deep structural problems and distortions of the Italian economy gave the alliance between northern industrialists and commercial farms a unique blend of instability and aggressiveness. A narrow domestic market, the excessive territorial concentration of industry and an extreme dependence on favourable world economic conditions made Italian entrepreneurs highly vulnerable to international recessions and tended to sharpen conflicts of interest within the bloc. At a time when most European and American farmers faced a mounting shortage of hired hands because of the insatiable demand of new industries and urban occupations for labour, agrarians of the Delta confronted a radically different situation. Delayed and uneven growth in the industrial sector slowed the absorption of surplus workers in agriculture, accentuating the 'artificial over-population' in the countryside that greatly intensified labour discontent and militancy in the Po Delta.[4] The same problems reinforced the authoritarian character of the alliance. Economic weakness increased the vulnerability of both industrialists and agrarians to pressures from organised labour, linking the interests of the two groups in a way that had few parallels elsewhere in Europe. In response to recurring recessions and labour unrest, a united front of employer associations gradually took the offensive against the trade union movement and the Socialist Party; ultimately it attacked the political compromises and social reforms of the Liberal Prime Minister, Giovanni Giolitti. The network of relations and interests that resulted from economic interpenetration had rather special consequences in the Italian setting, estranging the capitalist entrepreneurs from the old liberal political class and drawing them toward new authoritarian solutions to the problems of production, labour relations and interest representation on the eve of the First World War.

The Premisses for Agrarian and Industrial Collaboration

The premisses for collaboration between agrarian and industrial groups lay in the extraordinary growth of the Italian economy between 1896 and 1914. In a highly favourable international economic climate, the state, capable entrepreneurs and new commercial banks helped stimulate the greatest relative economic progress of any major European nation during this period. Manufacturing production more than doubled, the annual rate of growth reached record highs, and capital investments in plant and equipment rose by 114 per cent in the first decade of the century. The older textile manufacturers completed their conquest of the domestic market and enlarged their export activities; steel, hydro-electric and automotive industries were born.[5]

The economic expansion of these years was characterised by a mutually reinforcing relationship between industry and agriculture. The growth of the new industries sparked a general reawakening of the Italian economy that greatly encouraged expansion in the agricultural sector. The rising standard of living, the growth of cities and improved transportation all stimulated demand for farm products. At the same time that agricultural prices rose by 50 per cent, interest rates fell and the burdens of debt and taxation declined.[6] Production of wheat, Italy's most important crop, rose more than 60 per cent while dramatic progress was made in the cultivation of commercial crops.[7] In turn, increased agricultural production helped to balance foreign accounts and to avoid more serious tensions in the price system.

The chief protagonists of the agricultural expansion were the large commercial farms of the Po Valley. With only 13 per cent of the nation's farm land, this plain accounted for nearly a third of the total national agricultural production by 1910. While wheat yields in the rest of Italy remained relatively low and stationary, growers in the provinces of Emilia steadily increased their average output per hectare. By the outbreak of the First World War, wheat productivity in the leading provinces of the North stood well above the national average.[8] The Po Valley also monopolised the development of highly profitable industrial crops. The region of Emilia accounted for over half the hemp and a quarter of the tomatoes grown in the entire country in 1911. The same year, Emilia and the neighbouring provinces of the Veneto produced over 80 per cent of the total production of sugar beets.[9]

The exceptional advances of agriculture in the Po Valley were favoured by a variety of social and political agents. Already in the 1890s, a group of agrarian entrepreneurs in the northern plain were prepared to take advantage of the new opportunities for profit that arose after 1896. Unlike the older absentee landowners, these men were essentially 'agricultural industrialists' concerned with maximising profits by increasing production and lowering costs.[10] The imperatives of commercial competition predisposed them toward more efficient methods of cultivation, mechanisation, fertilisers and crop specialisation and by the late 1890s they had begun to build the large and modern farms that would enable them to reap huge profits in the favourable economic climate of the new century.[11]

The policies adopted by the Italian state greatly aided the designs of these entrepreneurs. Farmers capitalised on the responsiveness of the government to pressures from agrarian interests during the severe agricultural depression of the 1880s. In 1887 an improvised northern lobby succeeded in winning the first agricultural tariffs, which protected cereal crops and sugar beets rather than such prevalently southern products as olive oil, wines and citrus fruits. Duties on imported wheat quadrupled, and rice and oats received comparable protection.[12] The extremely high duty on sugar provided an important stimulus for the cultivation of sugar beets, which had previously been a marginal and unprofitable crop. The tariff virtually excluded foreign competition and, together with certain international agreements in 1902, gave growers and refiners a virtual monopoly of the domestic market.[13] The commercial farmers of the Po Valley emerged as the chief beneficiaries of the new protective regime. Far more than the southern agriculturalists, they gained from the grain duties a substantially higher level of profits. For them alone, the tariff provided a powerful incentive to elevate their production through new capital investments and the employment of more modern systems of cultivation. Their enterprising mentality, their superior organisation and their greater resources enabled them to raise the monetary value of their product well above the level achieved prior to the crisis of the 1880s.[14] Similarly, sugar protection benefited almost exclusively producers of the Po Delta who alone had the soil, climate, capital and technical expertise required to grow the crop.[15] In taking advantage of these circumstances, northern agrarians were naturally drawn into new and more intimate relations with suppliers of chemical fertilisers and farm machinery as well as with agricultural processing firms.

The Italian state also encouraged collaboration between commercial farmers and industrial interests in other less dramatic ways. Property taxes fell steadily from the mid-1880s until 1910, freeing capital for investments and improvements on the farms of the Po Valley.[16] During the same period, the budget of the Ministry of Agriculture nearly tripled, allowing the government to ease agricultural credit terms and establish experimental stations, schools of agriculture and travelling chairs of agriculture, the *cattedre ambulanti*. After the founding of the first one in Rovigo in 1886, the *cattedre* spread throughout the Po Valley where they provided a wide range of services for enterprising farmers: laboratories to evaluate soils, seeds and fertilisers; experimental fields to determine the most productive factors for local conditions; numerous public conferences and private consultations.[17]

An additional impetus for the convergence of agrarian and industrial interests came from the pressure of an aggressive rural labour movement. During the 1880s the mass of landless day labourers or *braccianti*, who had been drawn to the northern plains by the employment opportunities on the large estates and land reclamation projects, began to organise local leagues. Under the special working and living conditions of the plain, these labourers evolved into rural proletarians with many of the characteristics of industrial workers.[18] Beginning in 1885, the peasant leagues set in motion a wave of strikes and labour agitations in the Po Delta that had no counterpart in any other European country. Despite periodic setbacks and defeats, the leagues gradually gained strength and displayed an increasing capacity to exact concessions from agricultural employers.[19] In response to the strikes and rising labour costs, growers moved to raise productivity and reduce their demand for hired hands through mechanisation, the increased use of chemical fertilisers and a shift to less labour-intensive crops. The relationship between labour unrest and farm investments was clearly understood by the large farmers themselves. As one leading agrarian spokesman affirmed in 1902, 'two years of strikes have been more valuable than twenty years of technical propaganda . . . for the spread of agricultural machinery'.[20]

By encouraging mechanisation, chemical fertilisation and crop innovations, government policies and labour pressures helped produce a new and more intimate relationship between capitalist farmers and certain sectors of Italian industry. Indeed, the exceptional growth of agriculture in the Po Valley after 1896 both reflected and stimulated the interpenetration of the two sectors. However, other factors determined the precise form of this inter-penetration. The disastrous drop in agricultural prices during the 1880s had convinced major northern growers of the inadequacy of the free market in dictating their relations with industrial suppliers and buyers. The experience of a 'scissors' crisis between agricultural and manufacture prices in that decade had pushed enterprising agrarians to unite as a means of ensuring 'fair and equitable' prices and a more 'valid and secure defence' against speculative commercial interests and large industrial firms.[21] Likewise, industrialists, after intermittent recessions in the 1870s and 1880s, began to see the advantages of formalising their dealings with agrarians in order to expand and regulate their markets in the countryside. Thus collaboration found its clearest expression, both locally and on the regional level, in a group of new institutions that served to stabilise and systematise agrarian-industrial relations.

Agrarian Consortia and Industrial Suppliers

The first and always the most important organisational link between agrarian businessmen and machine and chemical manufacturers were the agrarian consortia, which began to make their appearance in the Po Valley during the late 1880s. Organised as commercial intermediaries by groups of prominent landowners and leaseholders, the consortia offered growers a range of benefits on a co-operative basis. By establishing direct contacts with manufacturers and making bulk purchases, the consortia could provide their members with industrial supplies and equipment at reduced prices. Moreover, their technical experts could check the quality of supplies to protect growers from frauds and could give them valuable counsel on the types of machines and fertilisers best suited to local conditions.[22] After 1892 the activities of these local consortia were buttressed by a national organisation, the Italian Federation of Agrarian Consortia or *Federconsorzi*, which assumed as its main functions the promotion of new consortia and the acquisition of chemical fertilisers. Gradually, the *Federconsorzi* broadened its field of activity to include the purchase of machines and seed, the leasing of machinery and tools, the collective sale of members' produce, and the encouragement of rational methods of cultivation.[23]

The formation of consortia on the provincial level marked the convergence of agrarian and banking interests. In order to assure growers the credit required to expand their purchases of industrial supplies, the consortia needed to establish a privileged relationship with the rural banks. In a zone like the Po Delta, these banks, which were often dominated by prominent local landowners, recognised 'how their own prosperity [was] intimately tied to the progress of agriculture'.[24] Often the rural banks directly took part in the creation of consortia. The founders of one of the earliest consortia in Parma included five board members of the local *Cassa di Risparmio*, which completely financed the new organisation during the first year. Likewise, in the province of Bologna a group of banks headed by the *Cassa di Risparmio* and the *Banca Popolare*, together with some of the 'most noted and influential agriculturalists', founded the Bolognese Agrarian Consortium in 1901. As in Parma, the Bolognese banks became shareholders in the consortium and financed its initial operations.[25]

The rural banks provided the consortia with essential credit assistance. In Piacenza and Cremona, the *Banca Popolare* gave the consortia special accounts to facilitate purchases by participating growers. The consortia of Bologna and Parma arranged similar credit terms with the *Cassa di Risparmio*, enabling agrarians to buy seed, fertilisers, and machines prior to the growing season and to pay for them after the sale of their crops. Nor did banks limit their activity to ordinary credit assistance. In Parma, for instance, the *Cassa di Risparmio* gave the consortium highly favourable mortgage and loan arrangements for the construction of a vast central warehouse in 1900.[26] Such co-operation between banks and the consortia proved beneficial for both parties. The growers in the consortia were quick to avail themselves of the advantageous credit terms and greatly increased their purchases of fertilisers and machines. For the banks, involvement in the consortia led to a tremendous and profitable expansion of their activities.[27]

Despite their power to buy industrial products at lower prices, the consortia also offered definite advantages to designated industrial interests. The vastly expanded demand for industrial goods, the simplification of commercial operations and the enhanced market stability offered by the *Federconsorzi* all served to attract the interest of industrial suppliers. During the first decade of the century, when chemical and machine industries had not yet attained a high degree of concentration, collaboration with the *Federconsorzi* appeared as the best alternative to ruinous competition among producers. In fact, industrial spokesmen recognised that the consortia potentially represented a 'defence against the risks of competition' and the foundation for a new market system in which 'prices and conditions' could be discussed and accorded 'between . . . two general federations'.[28] Moreover, the *Federconsorzi* served as a research and design *cum* publicity department for chemical and machine manufacturers. Beginning in the late 1890s, the Federation published and distributed a stream of pamphlets, promoting and illustrating the rational use of nitrate and phosphates as well as agricultural machines; the provincial consortia reinforced this service on the local level in their monthly bulletins. At the same time, the technical office of the *Federconsorzi* carried out extensive research on the construction and modification of plows, reapers and tractors which it placed at the disposal of manufacturers.[29]

Chemical fertilisers were the first products to be extensively marketed through the consortia; as such, they clearly illustrated both the benefits and difficulties of collaboration. The consortia initiated their activity in this area because fertilisers were a product in high demand among growers that was easily marketable, since it did not require substantial capital investments. For the Italian chemical industry, with its shortage of experienced scientists and technicians, the market for fertilisers was a natural area of expansion prior to the First World War.[30] As a result, contact between the consortia and manufacturers developed rapidly after 1900. For the purchases of phosphates, which were largely produced in northern Italy, the *Federconsorzi* provided its provincial affiliates with a model contract that they used to establish specific agreements with individual firms. Beginning in 1903, the *Federconsorzi* also assumed responsibility for purchases of imported fertilisers through the creation of special import companies that arranged agreements with foreign producers for supplies that the Federation eventually distributed to the various consortia.[31]

In quantitative terms, such arrangements appeared to provide definite benefits to both commercial farmers and chemical firms. Between 1895 and 1910, total sales of phosphates by the *Federconsorzi* rose from 36,621 quintals per year to nearly 900,000. By 1910 the Federation could claim control of 40 to 50 per cent of the national market for chemical fertilisers and even high percentages in the northern plain.[32] During the same period, the Italian chemical industry had its greatest area of expansion in the production of fertilisers for agriculture. Output of fertilisers jumped sixfold in the fourteen years after 1895. In 1905 the industry also began to extend its activity beyond phosphates to the production of nitrogenous fertilisers and by 1913 provided one-third of the country's consumption of this product. Significantly, growing production was accompanied by technological innovation and mechanisation of the industry.[33]

Despite this overall growth of production and commercial activity, relations between the consortia and fertiliser manufacturers were far from smooth and untroubled. The problems of over-production, price instability and speculation shaped and conditioned collaboration, provoking frequent tensions and conflicts between consumers and producers throughout the first decade of the century. Already in 1900 over-production in the chemical sector unleashed a fierce competition that drove fertiliser prices down to, and sometimes below, costs. In response to this disastrous situation, virtually all the manufacturers joined together in 1901 to form a marketing cartel, the *Società Generale per la vendita del perfosfato minerale*. Operating out of Milan, the cartel regulated production and set prices according to the average cost of production. As a result of these agreements, fertiliser prices rose to an acceptable level, but the efforts of certain firms to undercut the *Federconsorzi* by offering more advantageous terms to independent growers provoked no small discontent in the consortia.[34]

After a period of relative stability, a new crisis of over-production hit the chemical sector in 1907 at the same time that the Italian economy as a whole began to feel the effects of the international financial slump. This crisis rekindled tensions and conflicts between the consortia and producers. For their part, spokesmen of the consortia claimed that consumers of phosphates were having to pay for the excessively high dividends that the chemical companies paid to their stockholders. In particular, they expressed alarm at the sharp price fluctuations for phosphates and related stock market speculation that threatened the *Federconsorzi* with serious financial losses.[35] Yet initially the difficulties of the chemical industry proved advantageous to agrarian interests; over-production in the domestic market and the exploitation of new phosphate deposits in Africa and America lowered prices, enabling the *Federconsorzi* to win a new type of contract that protected its members from the prevailing price instability.[36] However, as a consequence of the crisis, important structural changes took place in the chemical sector and collaboration began to shift increasingly from the local consortia to the national level. Competition in the chemical industry quickly led to a growing concentration within the sector and by 1913 two firms controlled two-thirds of domestic production of phosphates. Such concentration greatly facilitated the revival of a marketing cartel that came to control nine-tenths of national production, which gave it an enormous advantage with respect to local markets. The reorganisation of the chemical industry demanded greater centralisation of power in the hands of the *Federconsorzi*, which was forced to renegotiate a general contract directly with the cartel in the last years before the war.[37]

The polemics and disputes between the consortia and chemical manufacturers in the decades prior to 1914 have led propagandists of the *Federconsorzi* and subsequent historians to emphasise the fundamentally conflicting character of relations between the two interests. Indeed, they have tended to portray the consortia and the manufacturers as sharply distinct and opposing forces, engaged in a relentless war of position.[38] This emphasis not only inflates the significance of the disputes, but also obscures the increasing integration of agrarian and industrial groups during the period. As early as 1897, the consortia and influential agrarian groups had become directly involved in the production of chemical fertilisers. In 1899 the *Federconsorzi* provided the capital for the founding of a chemical firm, the *Fabbriche Riunite degli Agricoltori Italiani* in Milan, while a number of provincial consortia set up factories for the production of phosphates, on their own initiative, in Brescia, Mantua and Melegnano.[39] The influential role of the consortia in the sector became evident during the recession of 1900. Far from opposing the formation of a chemical cartel, agrarian leaders praised its as the 'path of salvation' and the most rational response to 'commercial exigencies'. The Riunite Company immediately joined the cartel and Enea Cavalieri, the company's president and one of the founders of the *Federconsorzi*, actually served on its board of directors.[40]

Agrarians expanded their activity in the chemical sector in the years between 1906 and 1908 in an effort to stabilise prices on the fertiliser market. In a brief span of time, the consortia of Piacenza, Cremona, Parma, Montebelluna and Reggio Emilia set up co-operative factories, while prominent agrarian businessmen moved into important positions within local chemical firms.[41] The *Federconsorzi* actively encouraged such initiatives, becoming in 1908 a stockholder in an Italian-Belgian mining company in order to supply the factories with phosphate minerals. Within two years the consortia controlled thirteen factories capable of producing roughly 13 per cent of the yearly national output.[42] Although the factories were designed to offset the dominance of the large firms, they necessarily entailed a new level of agrarian-industrial integration in the production and marketing of chemical fertilisers that began to modify traditional sectoral divisions between agriculture and industry.

The marketing of agricultural machines also gave rise to collaboration between the consortia and manufacturing groups, but commercial operations did not attain the same levels as those for fertilisers because of the small size of the Italian industry and the limited capital of the consortia. These circumstances, however, favoured a far more pronounced convergence of interest between the two groups, with few of the tensions and contrasts that marked the fertiliser market in the prewar period. While the high costs of imported machines pushed the consortia to encourage the growth of a domestic industry, manufacturers needed the consortia to help create a market and to refine and specialise their equipment. As a result, the consortia and the machine industry began an intimate and mutually rewarding relationship that would continue in the decades after the war.

Although imports of machines rose steadily after 1897, the real surge in demand did not come until after the great strike wave of 1901. To meet part of this new demand, the provincial consortia established direct contacts with local firms for the acquisition of relatively unsophisticated farm machinery. In a region such as Emilia where industry had traditionally been tied to the agricultural sector, collaboration between the consortia and manufacturers encountered few obstacles.[43] The leading industrialists of Bologna, for instance, were integrated into the provincial elite so that the consortium merely provided an institutional channel for arrangements between them and the large agrarian buyers of the province, who steadily increased their purchases of machines in the first decade of the century.[44] Through similar agreements in other neighbouring provinces, small and middle-sized firms, producing such machines, developed; by the war seven firms in Bologna and nineteen in the region of Emilia specialised in the manufacture of ploughs, motors, pumps and harvesting machines.[45]

The marketing of larger and more complex machines required the direct intervention of the *Federconsorzi* which proposed to organise collective purchases of machines directly from the major suppliers. Propagandists of the Federation claimed that such bulk purchases would bypass speculative middlemen and reduce the administrative and transport costs to a minimum. In the fall of 1902 a separate joint-stock company was set up to deal directly with producers and to arrange the purchases. The insufficiency of the domestic industry forced the *Federconsorzi* and its commercial company to seek agreements with American and German firms. The Federation's large acquisitions as well as its promotional activities assured it a privileged relationship with foreign producers since, as the consortia boasted, they understood that 'in a country like Italy, where knowledge of machines is still backward, it is in their interest to support the agrarian organisations'.[46] The *Federconsorzi*'s statistics appeared to support the claim; in 1905 the Federation's sales of agricultural machines represented a third of total imports.[47] At the same time, the consortia established a close working relationship with the few important domestic manufacturers. From its inception the agrarians' commercial company enjoyed the financial support and direct participation of leading industrial figures, while throughout the pre-war period the technical office of the *Federconsorzi* collaborated with Italian firms in the modification of machine models and in the promotion of Italian-made machines.[48]

Thus by 1914 the agrarian consortia had become the most important agent in accelerating the interpenetration of commercial agriculture, rural banks and industry. Through its initiatives the *Federconsorzi* had encouraged the new needs and relationships in the Po Delta that had increasingly tied the fortunes of capitalist farmers to those of their industrial suppliers. In this respect, it had a key role in a more general process which witnessed the gradual subordination of agricultural enterprise to the interests of finance and industrial capital.[49] The development of relations between the consortia and chemical and machine manufacturers also reveals major long-term trends. Recurrent recessions and cut-throat competition in the first decade of the century resulted in major structural changes in both industrial and agricultural organisation. As manufacturing concentrated in the hands of a few large firms, effective power and decision-making shifted from the local consortia to the *Federconsorzi*.

These trends continued after 1914. In 1918 the *Federconsorzi* became the exclusive representative of FIAT for the sale of tractors; the following year it assumed a similar function for the *Società Italiana Ernesto Breda*, the largest manufacturer of threshing machines in Italy. Mutually rewarding collaboration continued into the 1920s. By 1928 domestic machine firms controlled 78 per cent of the national market and the *Federconsorzi* marketed 85 per cent of the domestically produced machines sold in Italy. In the monopolistic conditions of the 1930s, a few giant corporations, such as FIAT and Montecatini, and the *Federconsorzi* became the chief arbiters of agricultural activity in the Po Valley.[50]

Commercial Farmers and the Agricultural Processing Industry

A second and politically more important area of agrarian-industrial inter-penetration involved the growers and processors of industrial crops such as hemp, tomatoes, and sugar beets. Relations between growers and processors were more interdependent than those between the consortia and industrial suppliers, since the factories depended on the growers for raw materials and the growers found their chief market in the processing factories. The greater specialisation of the growers of these crops gave them a much clearer sense of common interests and objectives than could possibly exist among the diverse groups of farmers in the consortia. As a result, they tended to require a different form of organisation; cartels or syndicates of growers for specific crops, rather than general farmers' consortia, handled negotiations with the appropriate industrial trusts or large corporations. Such organisation, however, did not develop spontaneously. On the contrary, it developed primarily in response to problems of free competition, over-production, price instability and the conflicts that they created between producers and suppliers.

Hemp was one of the first and most important industrial crops in the Po Delta. As early as the sixteenth century, the plains of Bologna, Ferrara, Modena, Ravenna and Forli had been a great centre of hemp cultivation. During the nineteenth century, production rose steadily until the 1880s, when competition from a variety of other textiles provoked a slump in the hemp market.[51] Growers reduced the cultivation to the best suited lands so that quality and productivity rose, and by the opening years of the twentieth century they had achieved a new level of stability and prosperity.[52]

An Italian hemp-processing industry to absorb domestic production developed only gradually, however. The first processing factories had been founded during the 1840s in Emilia, but as late as 1876 growers exported 75 per cent of their harvests. The dominance of the English, French and German textile industries discouraged Italian initiatives in this area throughout the second half of the century. Only with the general expansion of the economy after 1896 did the Italian hemp industry begin to develop. In the north a small number of entrepreneurs founded the first large companies, stimulating a general modernisation in the sector.[53]

A far more dynamic development took place in the cultivation and processing of tomatoes and sugar beets during the first decade of the century. Increased foreign demand, combined with certain technological innovations, sparked the rapid growth of an industry for the production of tomato concentrate and the spread of tomato cultivation in Emilia after 1900. In Parma, where this new agricultural-industrial undertaking was centred, the first modern factories were built in 1902. Within a decade the number of factories grew from 3 to 44; exportation of tomato preserves increased from 48,000 quintals to over 400,000. The tremendous demand created by the processing industry and the high profits it assured led growers to extend their cultivation of tomatoes, which rapidly became the most important crop in the high plain of Parma.[54]

Advances in tomato processing paled in comparison to the tremendous growth of the sugar-refining industry. Before 1880 the industry was virtually non-existent in Italy, while a mere 250 hectares in the entire country were under cultivation with sugar beets. Refiners received their first great stimulus from the government in the midst of the agricultural depression in the form of indirect subsidies and a tariff, which assured them control of the internal market.[55] Exploiting these favourable conditions, a few entrepreneurs began to experiment with beet cultivation in the Po Delta. The crop soon found a favourable reception among the large commercial growers. In provinces such as Ferrara, where the Bank of Turin and the major land reclamation companies had invested vast sums of capital, sugar beets offered the fullest return. In other provinces, growers were drawn to the cultivation of the crop by the fall in hemp and wheat prices during the 1890s.[56] The success of the initial experiments sparked an explosive expansion at the turn of the century. In just two years from 1898 to 1900, 28 refineries were founded in the Po Delta and annual sugar production rose from 59,000 quintals to nearly 600,000, while acreage devoted to the cultivation of sugar beets increased tenfold.[57] After the international Brussels Agreement of 1902, which gave Italian refineries a monopoly of the domestic market, industrial and agricultural production grew at a steady but less dramatic pace until shortly before the First World War. By 1913-14 17 plants in Emilia and 39 in the nation as a whole produced nearly 3 million quintals of sugar per year and the area under the crop was over 200,000 acres.[58]

Although agrarian-industrial inter-penetration within the sugar sector was evident from the outset,[59] relations between hemp and sugar beet growers and industrial processors only gradually assumed an organised and systematic form, chiefly in response to the problems created by chaotic expansion and over-production. As in the chemical industry, concentration increasingly prevailed in hemp and sugar processing and cartels were formed to regulate production and markets. Growers reacted to these developments by seeking to form their own piecemeal cartels in order to control supply and protect their bargaining position. While the extent and success of these organisations varied enormously from province to province and from sector to sector, they did provide the foundations for later growth and consolidation.

The hemp industry, after a period of rising prices and expansion in the first years of the century, encountered serious problems of over-production in 1907 and 1908 as a consequence of the American finan-cial crisis and declining demand in England.[60] The lively competition that had characterised the industry prior to 1907 gave way to general agreements among the major northern firms, who had formed a cartel for the purchasing of raw hemp and the marketing of their finished products by 1913. One firm, the *Linificio e Canapificio Nazionale*, emerged as the dominant force within the cartel. By the end of the war it had absorbed the other major companies and become the largest Italian textile corporation.[61]

Hemp growers responded to the recession and the concentration in the processing sector by attempting to form their own local cartels. With the first indications of an impending recession in the autumn of 1907, a group of prominent landowners in Bologna organised a provin-cial syndicate of hemp growers to negotiate the collective sale of their crops, establish storage facilities for surpluses and arrange credit assist-ance. As conceived by its sponsors, the syndicate was to regulate pro-duction, counter-balance potential coalitions of buyers and keep prices at a remunerative level.[62] Amid the full-blown recession of 1908, growers in Ferrara and Modena founded their own provincial syndi-cates and agrarian leaders began to put forward proposals for a much wider coalition of syndicates to control the supply of hemp on the market.[63]

The aspirations of the hemp syndicates far outstripped their actual accomplishments. Organisers encountered enormous difficulties in trying to unite the large number of highly varied farm units involved.[64] Moreover, the revival of the market in the fall of 1909 removed the immediate impetus for the syndicates which quickly lapsed into in-activity. On the eve of the First World War the growers lacked any organised representation in their dealings with the processing firms. None the less, these early efforts clearly foreshadowed later develop-ments. Fascist syndicates of producers in the 1920s and cartels between producers and manufacturers of textile fibres in the 1930s would embody many of the ideas and objectives articulated by the major hemp farmers in the pre-war era.[65]

Concentration, cartels and organised collaboration developed far more fully in the sugar beet industry before the First World War. From its founding, the refining sector was dominated by a few large companies who quickly expanded their influence over the smaller firms in the first decades of the century.[66] Alarmed by the disorderly and speculative expansion of the industry, the major firms formed their own cartel in 1904, the *Unione Zuccheri*. The cartel was designed to regulate production, distribute the work equally among the factories and standardise contractual relations with the growers.[67] The concentrated might of the sugar cartel in the local markets forced agrarians to begin organising. As early as 1900 sugar beet growers held their first national congress in order to establish uniform criteria in their dealings with the refiners and to prepare the ground for eventual organisations of their own.[68] In contrast to the hemp growers, sugar beet farmers were a relatively small and highly capitalised group that could more easily be integrated into a marketing organisation. Consequently, after the founding of the *Unione Zuccheri*, the first growers' syndicates soon arose in the provinces of Rovigo, Adria and Ferrara to control the cultivation of the crop and to represent the farmers in negotiations with the trust and independent firms. The decisive impetus for the consolidation and spread of these syndicates came from the recession of 1908. Faced with large surpluses of unsold sugar from the previous year, refiners reacted by cutting their purchases of sugar beets after years of steadily rising demand. Amid accusations that the refiners were attempting to unload their losses on the growers, new syndicates were organised in other provinces of the Po Delta and agrarian interests mobilised against the sugar trust. From 1908 relations between growers and refiners gradually took on a more organised form, with annual and multi-year contracts to resolve the difficult issues of quality controls and prices. The provincial syndicates, in turn, provided the foundations for the National Federation of Sugar Beet Growers, which would begin operations in 1917.[69]

Despite recurring conflicts over marketing arrangements, growers and refiners of sugar beets found ample opportunity for co-operation on two main issues prior to the war: on resistance to the demands of the unions and in defence of protectionism. The pressing need for collaboration against organised labour became evident in the winter of 1908-9 when agricultural labourers and refinery workers in Bologna co-ordinated a series of strikes and boycotts on the beet farms and in the refineries. With their reciprocal interests damaged by a common enemy, agrarian and industrial groups forgot their recent differences and began to seek a unified strategy of defence. This search culminated in a joint agreement in the spring of 1909, which agrarian leaders characterised as 'the first strand of what will become a tighter network of economic relations between agricultural and industrial producers'. The Agrarian Federation of Bologna, the growers' syndicate and the *Unione Zuccheri* committed themselves to work together for a 'victorious resistance' against the unions and to create a mutual insurance fund against strike damages. The pooling of resources and the co-ordination of anti-strike initiatives proved highly effective; by the autumn of 1909 the employer coalition had broken the strikes and boycotts. More importantly, the victory of the growers and refiners in Bologna set an example for other provinces where agrarian and industrial interests were beset by labour unrest.[70]

The sugar trust and the growers were equally united in their defence of high protective tariffs. Duties on sugar, which were four times the wholesale price of the imported product, had drawn the frequent protests of free traders during the first decade of the century.[71] In order to reduce sugar prices for popular consumption and to placate its free trade critics, the government proposed a substantial reduction of the tariff in the fall of 1909. The plan aroused the immediate opposition of the *Unione Zuccheri* which brought all its influence to bear against any reduction of the existing rates. The refiners found solid allies in the growers' syndicates. In mid-November 1909, the leading agrarian journal of the Po Delta strongly attacked the proposed tariff, charging that it would mean 'the immediate bankruptcy of all the Italian sugar refineries' and a 'nearly lethal blow' to the flourishing cultivation of sugar beets.[72] Later the same month at the second National Agrarian Congress, spokesmen for the beet farmers denounced the plan as a threat to agricultural progress and succeeded in winning delegate support for the campaign of the refiners. Confronted by this alliance of agrarians and industrialists, the government dropped the proposed reduction and the sugar industry continued to enjoy its privileged position for the remainder of the pre-war era.[73]

Such improvised alliances evolved into more systematic collaboration in the last years before 1914 when agrarian and sugar-refining interests shared control of *Il Resto del Carlino*, the most important daily paper in the Po Delta. Founded in 1885, the Bolognese daily had maintained a pro-union stance until the fall of 1909 when a group of agrarian businessmen headed by Enrico Pini and Emilio Maraini purchased it.[74] Under the new owners, the paper drastically changed its political orientation, becoming a vocal supporter of the agricultural employers against the peasant leagues. After the paper ran into difficulties in 1913, Maraini served as the intermediary in paving the way for financial participation by a consortium of prominent sugar refiners, who purchased 50 per cent of the stock in the paper. In recognition of this convergence of interests, two new directors were appointed to manage the daily: Lino Carrara, an aggressive agrarian lobbyist, and Filippo Naldi, front man for the sugar refiners. In short order *Il Resto del Carlino* became the most authoritative defender of sectoral privileges in the heartland of the sugar industry and one of the most important expressions of agrarian-industrial collaboration in pre-war Italy.[75]

The anti-union and protectionist alliance of sugar beet growers and refiners underscored the importance of economic interdependence in providing the conditions for a broader political bloc of agrarian and industrial interests in the years before 1914. From 1900 labour militancy and trade and tariff issues helped to create new interest configurations that transcended the confines of narrow local and sectoral concerns, spurring the organisation and collaboration of agrarian and industrial pressure groups. The recession of 1908 and the subsequent slowdown in the Italian economy reinforced these trends. Faced with sluggish markets and falling profits, both commercial farmers and manufacturers increasingly felt the need to reduce labour costs and resist more effectively the political and social demands of the socialist trade unions. In this context, the agrarian-industrial bloc of the Po Valley began to assume a more organised and active role in the political life of the country.

Against Unionism: Agrarian-industrial Interest Group Politics

The labour movement, one of the key factors in stimulating economic inter-penetration in the decades after 1896, also sparked significant changes in the behaviour of agrarian and industrial interests at the political level. The growing power of organised labour on the municipal level and in Rome forced agrarians and industrialists to develop a new role for themselves in the Italian political system. In order to counteract the mass organisations of the Socialist Party, entrepreneurs had to construct their own organisations for systematic intervention in labour conflicts and in the political decision-making process. In this respect, northern economic interests followed the lead of their German counterparts, who by the 1890s had already formed potent lobbies.[76] Initially, the governments of Giolitti encouraged these organised interest groups as essential ingredients in the creation of a new social equilibrium and era of mutual accomodation. Giolitti's expectations, however, were frustrated by structural problems in the economy that tended to intensify working-class radicalism and to make employers particularly tenacious in their defence of traditional privileges and pre-rogatives. The growth of agrarian and industrial interest groups increased social and political polarisation in the Po Valley in the last years before the First World War.

Prior to 1900 entrepreneurs of the Po Valley had few incentives for developing independent, organised interest groups. Throughout the second half of the nineteenth century, the mediation of provincial notables adequately represented their interests, while the various government coalitions had proven highly responsive to their demands for repression of strikes and trade union activity. Only in the late 1890s did such informal interest representation begin to break down under the stress of changing social and political conditions. In the fields and factories of the Po Valley, employers came to face more organised strikes and disciplined labour organisations that could no longer be ignored or dealt with exclusively by police action. At the same time, the appointment of Giovanni Giolitti as Minister of the Interior in 1901 resulted in a decisive shift in government policy on labour-management disputes. Intent on broadening his base of support on the left, Giolitti refused to back the employers indiscriminately in all conflicts with workers, insisting instead on a policy of government neutrality in peaceful, non-political strikes.[77]

Agrarian and industrial interests initially reacted to these developments by forming local associations of resistance where labour militancy was most pronounced. Between 1898 and 1902 steel, machine and ship manufacturers in Genoa, Milan and Monza set up organisations to combat strikes and influence municipal politics.[78] The spring and summer of 1901 saw similar developments in strike-torn rural areas of the Po Valley where agrarian associations arose to oppose the peasant leagues. During the first years of the century, the vision of these organisations seldom extended beyond municipal or provincial borders. In the countryside the engrained individualism of the landowners, conflicts between landowners and leaseholders, and the distrust of the small farmers frustrated the first attempts to build a wider regional organisation of agrarians.[79] As a rule, the local agrarian associations led an ephemeral existence, functioning only during strikes and then disbanding once the immediate danger had passed. Similarly, the early industrial associations contented themselves with local successes, without formulating any broader programmes of political and economic intervention.[80]

This organisational situation changed drastically in the years after 1906. Economic recession and renewed pressure from the labour unions combined to forge a new interest-group and class consciousness among agrarian and industrial employers that transcended provincial borders, while a younger generation of entrepreneurs came to the forefront who rejected the political mediation of old liberal leaders and reorganised the associations on a broader and more systematic basis. In the second half of 1907, the Italian economy began to feel the effects of credit stringency that spread from the United States to Europe. Especially hard hit were the mixed credit banks in Italy that had committed most of their deposits in loans to industries and in stock adventures. One of the largest credit banks nearly collapsed and the remaining financial institutions reacted with strong measures to restrict credit.[81] Industrial recession accompanied the financial crisis. The deflationary policy of the banks, along with rising prices for raw material and excess production, proved particularly damaging for the automobile, cotton, steel, shipbuilding and sugar-refining industries.[82] With their close ties to some of these industrial sectors, commercial farmers of the Po Delta were also hit by the recession. The Agrarian Consortium of Bologna, for instance, had had to halt its ambitious programme of expansion in 1908, its board of directors reported, because of the plight of 'industries closely linked with [its] business operations'. At the same time, over-production in the textile and sugar industries led to a drop in demand for hemp and sugar beets with its inevitable consequences for growers.[83]

Precisely when agrarian and industrial entrepreneurs saw both their profits and their margins of accommodation with organised labour reduced by the economic slump, they confronted a new wave of demands from a resurgent trade union movement. After the lull following the general strike of 1904, strikes and labour violence reached new highs in the years after 1906. Apart from the strictly economic strikes, industrialists in major cities of the north also had to contend with a number of political general strikes called to protest police violence in 1906 and 1907.[84] Simultaneously, the farm workers' leagues succeeded in founding a stable national organisation, the *Federterra*. In response to chronic unemployment in the Po Valley, which had negated many of the gains won on issues of wages and work hours, the *Federterra* adopted a strategy designed to gain control of hiring in the countryside. Following guidelines set by the national federation, the local leagues demanded their own employment offices to ensure equal distribution of available work and to regulate migrational currents of the day labourers. Despite their seemingly innocuous functions, the offices threatened to give the leagues the means for unprecedented intervention in areas of farm management previously the exclusive domain of the employers.[85] In key provinces of the Po Delta, agrarian interests faced an even more immediate threat from the leagues controlled by revolutionary syndicalists who organised a series of exceptionally bitter and violent agricultural general strikes in 1907 and 1908.[86]

Beginning in 1906, the militancy of agrarians and industrialists was channeled into new organisational initiatives by a new generation of entrepreneurs. These younger entrepreneurs were openly dissatisfied with the traditional methods of interest representation and they stressed the need for the independent and direct political involvement of the economic elites. For them the local liberal clubs and provincial notables, who had perennially served as the political mediators of the upper classes, were anachronisms in an era of mass politics and organised pressure groups. As one Bolognese agrarian organiser expressed it, they offered programmes 'so vague and generic that they no longer signify anything, only a history by now gloriously exhausted [and] not a programme for future conquests'. Such entrepreneurs insisted that commercial farmers and manufacturers had to unite on their own to protect 'the legitimate interests of capital and business enterprise in all legislation, in all the political action of the government'.[87]

With the strikes and economic difficulties of 1906-8, employers in both agriculture and industry discovered a range of common needs and interests which drew them to proposals for organised representation and collective action. After strikes in a number of cotton firms in 1906, leading industrial spokesmen founded the Industrial League of Turin. Representing the major chemical, electrical, automobile and textile firms of the city, the League quickly forged a rigidly disciplined employer front that used black lists and lock-outs and even had the power to fine employers who broke ranks.[88] The success of the League in combating strikes and curbing worker demands inspired wider and more ambitious initiatives in the following years. In the spring of 1908, representatives of 450 firms joined together in the Piedmontese Industrial Federation to protect their 'collective interests' and to champion 'the right to work'. From Turin, organisations of employer resistance spread to other manufacturing centres of northern Italy, culminating in the summer of 1910 in the founding of the Italian Confederation of Industry (CII).[89]

Developments in the agricultural sector paralleled those in industry. In the wake of the bitter syndicalist strikes in the spring of 1907, agrarian associations from various zones of the Po Valley met in Parma to establish the *Federazione Interprovinciale Agrari (Interprovinciale)*.[90] Under the guidance of militant young agrarian leaders like Lino Carrara of Parma and Giovanni Enrico Sturani of Bologna, the *Interprovinciale* set out to co-ordinate the activities of the provincial organisations and to unify anti-union resistance on a broad territorial basis. Dropping the rhetoric of class co-operation cherished by the older landowners, the *Interprovinciale* adopted as its central task the intransigent opposition to the demands of the socialist leagues. To combat organised labour more effectively, it tightened discipline within the associations, making agrarian employers sign promissory notes to ensure loyalty during strikes and boycotts. Mobile squads of 'free labourers' were organised to break strikes, 'interprovincial corps of volunteers' to defend against the coercion of the leagues. The *Interprovinciale* also created the *Mutua Scioperi*, an insurance company with the exclusive task of compensating agrarian employers for damages due to strikes, boycotts and lock-outs. Carrara eloquently expressed the orientation of the new federation a few months prior to the second great syndicalist strike in Parma in January 1908: 'Hit by boycotts, we will respond with the lock-out; we will answer violence with violence. The working class may be strong, but the employer class is equally strong.'[91] Following the victory of the Agrarian Association of Parma that year, the *Interprovinciale* entered into a phase of rapid growth and consolidation. Much like the Industrial League of Turin, it also provided the impetus for a national organisation, the National Agrarian Confederation (CNA), which was founded in the summer of 1910.[92]

From their inception, both agrarian and industrial organisations advocated intersectoral collaboration to combat labour agitation and to advance common political and economic policies in Rome. Men like Gino Olivetti and Luigi Bonnefon Craponne of the Industrial League were well aware of the benefits that had resulted from agrarian-industrial co-operation in Germany, and they saw the natural convergence of interests with agrarian groups of the Po Valley, who also faced a powerful and aggressive labour movement. Consequently, they looked with favour on collaboration in matters of social legislation and labour relations.[93] For its part, less than a year after its founding, the *Interprovinciale* called for the unification of 'the entire employer class in the various branches of economic activity' into a single '*fascio*' in order to protect its general interests more effectively.[94]

With the creation of the CII and the CNA in 1910, active co-operation began to develop, both nationally and on the local level. During the summer of that year, the CII came to the aid of the *Interprovinciale* in a protracted dispute with the leagues of Ravenna over ownership and control of the threshing machines. In a letter of protest to the Italian Senate, the secretary of the industrial confederation strongly defended the stand of the agrarian employers and denounced the league demands as threats to the entire industrial class, since their general implementation would lead to the 'total subversion of the established order in our companies'.[95] Such support did not go unnoticed by agrarian spokesmen. After its victory in the dispute, the official organ of the *Interprovinciale* rejoiced that in the agrarians' 'great battle in defence of industrial liberty' they could now count on the 'strong phalanx of the Italian industrial bourgeoisie'.[96]

The same year the two employer organisations began to intervene jointly in the corridors of power in Rome on issues of social policy. At first, agrarian and industrial representatives focused their lobbying activity on the reform of the *Consiglio Superiore del Lavoro*. Founded in 1902, the *Consiglio* provided a seat for the discussion of social and labour legislation; its opinions on important economic questions were influential and it reflected the impulse for social reforms. Lobbyists of the two employer confederations, claiming to express 'the complete agreement between the employer classes, industrial and agrarian', promoted a sweeping restructuring of the *Consiglio* that would ensure an effective role for the 'real capitalist Italy' and curtail the excessive influence of the socialist labour organisations.[97] They demanded that the agrarian and industrial associations, rather than the Minister of Agriculture, Commerce and Industry, select the employer representatives. These representatives, being 'particularly competent and free from any parliamentary concerns', could prepare the legislation that best responded to 'the real needs of the population'. To combat the influence of the socialists, the lobbyists insisted on the inclusion of representatives of the catholic, republican and liberal unions on the *Consiglio*. The benefits for agrarians and industrialists were evident. Not only would the change give them a direct role in the formulation of social policy, but it would also reinforce divisions within the trade union movement.[98]

Outside of Rome, the two employer confederations pursued a number of joint initiatives. In April 1911, Olivetti of the CII participated in the third National Agrarian Congress to demonstrate, in his words, 'the solidarity that unites all those who, in different areas of activity, contribute to the production and development of national wealth at a time when every principle of liberty and justice is threatened with subversion'.[99] In the autumn of 1911, the CII and the CNA co-sponsored the first International Congress of Industrial and Agricultural Organisations in Turin. Although the congress did not adopt Olivetti's plan for an Employer International, it did pave the way for more systematic colla-boration the following year when the two confederations co-founded a monthly journal, *L'Italia Industriale ed Agraria*, which helped deter-mine a unified policy on issues of mutual concern. Co-operation evol-ved within the Chamber of Deputies as well. Parliamentary supporters of the two confederations – organised respectively in the Agrarian Central Committee and the Industrial Parliamentary Group – coll-aborated closely to resolve potential conflicts of interest and to build a common front on issues of social legislation, labour policies, trade and tariffs.[100]

On the provincial level, agrarian and industrial employers launched joint offensives against the labour organisations. In many provinces of the Po Delta, co-operation had developed informally within the framework of the agrarian associations.[101] After 1911, however, a more highly articulated and organised employer bloc arose, as agrarian and industrial associations shifted from a defensive to an offensive strategy. No longer content with blocking new labour demands, they now sought to withdraw concessions won by the unions in previous con-tracts. Especially with the recession of 1913, employers moved to reduce labour costs, adopting an intransigent stance not only against the revolutionary syndicalists but even against the reformist unions.[102]

In the province of Bologna, collaboration found its clearest expres-sion in the alliance of the Bolognese Agrarian Association (AAB) and the Federation of Building Contractors (*Edile*). In the spring and summer of 1912, the organised agrarians actively supported the *Edile* in a series of struggles against the construction unions. In mid-April for instance, when the contractors called a lock-out against bricklayers in various communes, the AAB instructed its members 'not to employ bricklayers that refuse to work for the federated contractors'. The president of the AAB proclaimed that their support was 'inspired by the principle that agricultural and industrial property owners have common aims and defence needs'.[103] When bricklayers' and transport workers' unions ordered a boycott against non-union labourers in 1913, the two allies quickly took up the challenge. Beginning in mid-February, the secretaries of the *Edile* and the AAB accompanied squads of armed 'volunteers for the freedom of labour' who protected the boycotted workers and brought in strike-breakers. Within a week the boycott collapsed and the unions voted to return to work.[104] A similar form of co-operation emerged in Parma in 1912. Not confronted by any serious labour agitation in the countryside, the provincial agrarian association devoted itself almost exclusively to supporting industrial firms boycotted by the socialist unions.[105] Conversely, the following year the agrarians of Ferrara received invaluable aid from local industrial and banking firms in their victorious resistance to the employment offices of the leagues.[106]

Developments in Bologna, Parma and Ferrara exemplified the general counter-offensive that the agrarian and industrial employers mounted in 1913 throughout the Po Valley. In sharp contrast to the ideologically and factionally divided trade unions, the employer associations displayed an unprecedented unity and militancy. As the economist Riccardo Bachi reported, 'employer unionism' had displayed an exceptional vitality, engaging in 'great struggles . . . in order to triumph on issues of principle, without defections, with a method and spirit analogous to that of the labour organisations'.[107] Utilising lock-outs and free labourers and imposing a rigid discipline on individual employers, the associations handed the unions a string of defeats from Turin to Reggio Emilia. As a result, employers were able to transfer the burdens of the recession on to the unions and the workers.[108] But more importantly, the counter-offensive of 1912-13 revealed the agrarian and industrial groups' intensified hostility to even moderate reformist trade unions, as well as their determination to drastically restrict the role of organised labour in social and economic bargaining. In an era when other European nations were beginning to develop the new institutional arrangements and distributions of power that would create a conservative consensus in the 1920s,[109] the economically vulnerable northern Italian elites pursued policies that only intensified social conflict.

The Agrarian-industrial Bloc: Between Transformism and Nationalism

The growing militancy of the agrarian and industrial associations in their dealings with organised labour profoundly altered relations between economic interests and the leading liberal political groups. While in pre-war Germany there was a growing affiliation of political parties with economic interest groups, in Italy the absence of any modern bourgeois party and the continued dominance of a few parliamentary managers led to a widening breach between the associations of employers and the liberal political elite.[110] This breach found its most concrete expression in the clash between the associations and the govern- of Giovanni Giolitti. In the years after 1901, Giolitti had sought to broaden support for the Liberal state by assimilating the working class into Italian politics. The success of such an endeavour depended not only on the moderation of the socialist movement, but also on the willingness of employers to co-operate with trade unions and make concessions to the workers. Although for the most part employers had been willing to go along with Giolitti's programme during the period of dynamic growth in the first years of the century, the economic and financial crisis of 1907-8 led to a change in their attitude. Faced with mounting costs and reduced profits, entrepreneurs became increasingly hostile to the prime minister's social policies, his tolerance of strikes and his treatment of labour's demands as legitimate interest-group grievances.

Both the *Interprovinciale* and the industrial confederation articulated this hostility, attacking Giolitti's policy of government neutrality in labour-management disputes. In 1908, in the first issue of the *Bollettino Federale Agrario*, agrarian leaders denounced the government's approach to strikes as the 'grossest partisanship'. In their view, the non-intervention of the state protected 'the right not to produce, the right to strike', but not 'the right to produce, the right to work, which requires intervention for the removal of those obstacles to free and legitimate activity'. Not surprisingly, the *Interprovinciale* strenuously opposed all proposals for compulsory arbitration and called upon the associations to confront the authorities in moments of conflict with a clear choice: 'either you intervene or we will defend the liberty of our workers.'[111] The same themes characterised the propaganda of the industrial associations, which repeatedly charged that Giolitti's policies benefited only unions at the expense of the economic prerogatives and rights of entrepreneurs. Under the tutelage of Giolitti, they claimed, the right to strike had become an obligation: 'Almost daily, we must report acts of violence by strikers . . . while the authorities look on impassively' — a situation which they saw as a menace to individual liberty and to the nation's productive base.[112] The agrarian and industrial interest groups were equally united in their opposition to the prime minister's social programmes, which imposed 'major sacrifices without corresponding benefits because their burdens fall for the most part on the employer class and because their underlying principles ignore the most fundamental realities'.[113]

With the employers' counter-offensive against the unions in 1912 and 1913, verbal attacks led to direct confrontation with government authorities, both in the countryside and in industrial centres. During one labour dispute in the summer of 1912 in Bologna, the fiery agrarian leader, Alberto Donini accused the local prefect of intentionally ignoring the criminal character of the unrest in order not to 'compromise a political programme that for many years has been characterised by concessions and surrenders'.[114] The prefect informed Giolitti that he could no longer maintain 'cordial relations' with agrarian leaders who 'offend representatives of the government'.[115] Immediately thereafter, Donini stormed out of a meeting with the prefect, declaring: 'I will not allow myself to be imposed upon by prefects or even by Giolitti.' In his report on the incident, the prefect emphasised Donini's intentionally provocative attitude, seeing it as part of a strategy 'to provoke the rupture which the Bolognese Agrarian Association considers useful to its policy of reaction and hostility to the directives of the government'.[116]

In the spring of 1913, a far more serious confrontation took place in Turin. The Industrial League called a lock-out in all the steel and automobile plants to try to crush the unions. Alarmed by the industrialists' intransigence, Giolitti moved against what he considered their 'excesses'. The prefect of Turin forced the president of the Industrial League to resign and threatened to deny police protection to the factories and to withhold government contracts from firms involved in the dispute. While Giolitti succeeded in ending the lock-out, he did so at the price of further alienating an already embittered and hostile industrial lobby.[117]

The clash between Giolitti and the employer associations reflected the more general problem of political representation for economic interest groups in a parliamentary system that lacked clearly defined, cohesive and ideologically consistent parties. The development of organised interest groups had weakened, if not broken, the traditional links between entrepreneurs and influential local liberal politicians. The loose network of municipal and provincial political associations that comprised the Liberal Party could not provide the type of organised representation and coherent national programmes that the broad new agrarian and industrial interest groups demanded. The effectiveness of the Socialist Party, the only really organised political party, in advancing its interests underscored the insufficiencies of the liberal political class in the eyes of agrarian and industrial lobbyists. One agrarian spokesman observed in 1910 that while the employer associations had no 'authoritative representatives in the chamber who could interpret their ideas and interests', the socialist trade unions had their own 'deputies who carried on an activity completely co-ordinated with their interests'.[118]

Giolitti's mediating skill had helped preserve the amorphous liberal movement, but it did not resolve the problems of lobbying and influence that concerned agrarian and industrial spokesmen, whose views on the Italian parliamentary system as a whole were shaped by their growing awareness of the inadequacy of the politics of personal prestige. The discontent of their associations was evident in their relentless attacks on parliamentary transformism and ministerial coalitions, based on personal ambitions and shallow electoral concerns. In their propaganda, the associations stressed the enormous gulf between the 'legal' country and the productive classes and strongly criticised the methods of political recruitment of the old parties of order. The Industrial League of Turin, for instance, denounced in 1911 the 'wide and deep separation between the people who produce and pay and the fraction that governs, drawn for the most part from among the provincial lawyers, professors, and state functionaries'.[119] Both agrarian and industrial spokesmen frequently lamented that production was being sacrificed because of the political personnel's economic incompetence and because of the excessive influence of parliamentary factions. The Agrarian Central Committee and the Industrial Parliamentary Group were designed precisely to bypass the old political groupings and to insert 'the productive elements of the nation' into the political arena.[120]

The growing anti-parliamentarianism of key economic interests in the Po Valley drew them toward the new authoritarian proposals for economic development and labour discipline launched by the Italian Nationalist Association in the last years before the war.[121] A clear affinity of ideas and language existed between young agrarian leaders like Lino Carrara and the early nationalist intellectuals: Giuseppe Prezzolini and Giovanni Papini. Despite some differences, both groups shared a strong hostility toward the socialist movement, Giolittian reformism and the old liberal leadership with its 'platitudes of '48 and '59'.[122] Moreover, both rejected the politics of compromise and concession, advocating instead a 'bourgeois resurgence' spearheaded by a dynamic and combative new economic elite.[123] In the aftermath of the recession of 1908, there was also a clear convergence of ideas between entrepreneurial groups and leading nationalist economists like Enrico Barone. With his proposals for producers' syndicates to supplant cutthroat competition, rationalise production and resist union demands, Barone found a highly receptive audience among prominent industrial and agrarian interests who were actively forming cartels, marketing syndicates, lobbying groups and leagues of resistance.[124]

Enthusiasm for the Nationalist Association became steadily more evident in employer circles after 1912. When Enrico Corradini, a leading spokesman for the movement, came to speak in Bologna, the organ of the sugar refiners and agrarians, *Il Resto del Carlino* gave special attention to the speech and extolled the virtues of the 'new and solid forces' of the Nationalist Associations that were 'decisively entering Italian political life'.[125] In the spring of 1914, the National Agrarian Confederation strongly endorsed the Nationalist economic programme which, it asserted, 'truly seems a copy of the programme for which . . . the Italian agrarian associations have fought for many years'.[126] The same year Gino Olivetti of the Italian Confederation of Industry envisioned an alliance between the Nationalists and the 'producer classes' for the expansion of Italian markets abroad and the containment of the socialist movement, while major industrial associations began a strident campaign for economic nationalism or the so-called 'national product'.[127]

With the founding of the Nationalist Association in 1910, influential figures from the agrarian and industrial world became directly involved in the organisation. In Bologna the provincial Nationalist Group was founded in 1911 by two high officials of the Bolognese Agrarian Association and some of the largest landowners in the province.[128] Two years later, Dante Ferraris, president of the Industrial League of Turin and vice-president of FIAT, joined with certain of the most important sugar refiners and arms manufacturers to finance the Nationalist daily, *L'Idea Nazionale*. In addition, Ferraris became an active member of the Nationalist Group of Turin and by the summer of 1914 served as the chief interlocutor between the Nationalists and the major industrial consortia.[129] This convergence of northern economic oligarchies with the Nationalist Association revealed a crucial shift in political behaviour and objectives on the part of the most aggressive groups of the agrarian-industrial bloc. As the historian Valerio Castronovo has noted, on the eve of the First World War the Nationalist Association was rapidly emerging as the new 'party of opinion' of the productive bourgeoisie, with an ideology and programme that clearly marked it as a forerunner of the totalitarian state of the 1920s and 1930s.[130]

Conclusion

Both in its achievements and in its shortcomings, the pre-war agrarian-industrial bloc in the Po Valley foreshadowed significant long-term trends in Italian capitalism. The trend toward increasing industrial concentration and inter-penetration of manufacturing, financial and agrarian interests in the fascist era was already becoming evident in the years immediately after 1900. The pre-war formation of industrial cartels, the growth of the agrarian consortia and the establishment of local agreements between commercial farmers and their industrial suppliers laid the foundations for the post-war national contracts between the *Federconsorzi* and the industrial monopolies. The early efforts of sugar beet and hemp growers to form syndicates and to standardise their relations with refiners and processors prefigured the great agrarian-industrial cartels of the inter-war period that would regulate production and set market quotas. The sugar-beet lobby, in particular, had emerged by 1909 as the influential interest group which in the 1920s would guarantee a privileged position for both growers and refiners. This lobby was the most advanced expression of an informal system of interest representation and economic bargaining that had developed between major agrarian and industrial groups by 1914, a system that fascism would subsequently institutionalise in the corporative state.

While many of these trends were present in all industrial countries, in Italy the alliance between agrarians and industrialists assumed a distinctively authoritarian form. Economic inter-penetration helped create a new area of consensus between the two groups in their shared concern with an aggressive and steadily advancing labour movement both in the countryside and in the industrial centres of the North. The agrarian and industrial organisations that were founded after 1906 sought to surmount sectoral conflicts of interest and construct a united front by pursuing policies to exclude organised labour from any effective social bargaining and to transfer the burdens of crises on to the workers and consumers in the form of reduced wages, increased unemployment and high prices. Designed to protect the large producers and ensure acceptable profits, this strategy foreshadowed the policies that the fascist regime would adopt during the great depression. At the same time, the growth of organised interest groups created serious friction between important elements of the productive bourgeoisie and Italy's liberal political elite. Mounting dissatisfaction with their traditional political mediators – along with the need to resist working-class radicalism – predisposed agrarian and industrial interests toward more authoritarian movements: nationalism before 1914, fascism in the post-war era.

The continuities between these pre-war and post-war developments, however, should not be over-simplified. The convergence of northern agrarian and industrial groups with the fascist movement after 1920 stemmed not only from their growing concentration and power, but also from their weaknesses and shortcomings. Despite the victories in the counter-offensive of 1912-13, the employer associations did not represent a cohesive and hegemonic bloc on the eve of the First World War. The unity of employers in the campaign against the unions and Giolitti masked, but could not resolve, important contrasts and conflicts of interest among the various economic groups that comprised the bloc. The issues of taxation, credit and terms of exchange generated tensions between commercial farmers and manufacturers that became particularly acute in periods of economic recession and often prevented united action. Moreover, growing inter-penetration led to new conflicts that cut across simple sectoral divisions between agriculture and industry. The protectionist interests of the sugar lobby, for instance, clashed with the export-oriented coalitions that linked hemp and rice growers to their respective processing sectors.

A more serious problem was the lack of political unity within the bloc. Certain prominent agrarian and industrial personalities such as Enrico Pini of Bologna and Giovanni Agnelli remained close to Giolitti and his methods of political mediation right up until 1914.[131] Nor was there any effective consensus among the anti-Giolittian forces. While many influential financial, industrial and agrarian groups rallied to the Nationalist Association, others remained tied to the old moderate right headed by Antonio Salandra and Sidney Sonnino.[132] Later in the immediate post-war period, such political differences — exacerbated by war-time developments — would help to divide and paralyse the parties of order.

Despite their growing economic power, the more aggressive entrepreneurs were faced with a political dilemma. While rejecting the tutelage of the old parties of order, they were unable to find a replacement for them. As economic lobbies representing well-defined interests, the agrarian and industrial organisations could scarcely assume the role of a new political elite capable of winning a broad base of consensus among the other classes in Italian society. Indeed, they encountered serious difficulties in formulating a political programme that went beyond the partisan defence of special interests and entrepreneurial prerogatives. Far from cultivating a neutral image, agrarian and industrial leaders tended to exalt resistance and coercion, giving priority to immediate economic concerns at the expense of long-range needs for social peace and political stability. Their narrow corporative vision of class relations left little room for the mass political and social appeals essential to the creation of any new conservative consensus within a democratic parliamentary system. This limited vision helps explain why the Nationalist Association remained an elitist movement without adequate parliamentary representation or substantial mass support until its merger with the Fascist Party in 1923. During the strikes and tumults of the post-war years, the inability of agrarian and industrial interest groups to develop their own viable political alternative to the antiquated liberal clubs would influence their attitudes toward Mussolini's movement.

Thus, developments in the Po Valley prior to 1914 suggest that the convergence of northern economic oligarchies with fascism needs to be viewed on two levels. On one level, there was a clear convergence between the objectives of these groups and the policies of the fascist regime, which reinforced and accentuated trends toward concentration, inter-penetration and cartellisation. On another level, the decline of the old liberal elite, which was accelerated by the formation of new economic interest groups, left a political gap that was filled by the fascist movement.

Notes

1. For Gramsci's views on the agrarian-industrial bloc, see *Selections from the Prison Notebooks* (New York, 1971), pp. 55-113. On the importance attributed to this bloc in the development of Liberal Italy, see among others Giuliano Procacci, *History of the Italian People* (London, 1970), pp. 344-9; Christopher Seton-Watson, *Italy from Liberalism to Fascism* (London, 1967), pp. 82-4; Emilio Sereni, *Il capitalismo nelle campagne* (Turin, 1947); Idomeneo Barbadoro, *Storia del sindacalismo italiano*, vol. I, *La Federterra* (Florence, 1974), p. xlvi. For the role of the bloc under fascism, E. Sereni, 'La politica agraria del regime fascista' in *Fascismo e antifascismo (1918-1936). Lezioni e testimonianze*, vol. I (Milan, 1972), pp. 298-304.

2. In strictly geographical terms, the Po Delta extends southward from the Adige River through the provinces of Rovigo and Ferrara to the plains sections of Bologna, Ravenna and Forlì. For the internal purposes of this essay, the term Po Delta will be broadened to include the provinces of Parma, Modena and Piacenza. In the later sections of the essay, the discussion will extend to the entire Po Valley in order to deal more fully with agrarian-industrial interest-group politics. On the transformation of the zone in the late nineteenth century and its social consequences, see E. Sereni, *Il capitalismo*, pp. 188-9, 263-6, 300-10 and I. Barbadoro, *La Federterra*, pp. 37-56. For developments in the Piedmontese rice areas in the same period, see Valerio Castronovo, 'Agricoltura e capitale finanziario e industriale: la risaia' in *L'economia italiana dal periodo giolittiano alla crisi del 1929* (Turin, 1971). Renzo De Felice, *Mussolini il fascista. La conquista del potere 1921-1925* (Turin, 1966), pp. 3-20 underscores the central role of the Po Delta in the growth of fascism.

3. On the general economic trends of the period, see E.J. Hobsbawm, *The Age of Capitalism 1848-1875* (London, 1975), pp. 173-92 and Carlton J.H. Hayes, *A Generation of Materialism 1871-1900* (New York, 1941), pp. 98-102. Karl Kautsky, *La questione agraria* (Milan, 1971), pp. 292-328 provides an analysis of the tendencies towards agrarian-industrial interpenetration.

4. For a concise summary of the problems in the Italian economy, see Luciano Cafagna, 'Italy 1830-1914' in *The Fontana Economic History of Europe*. vol. IV, part I (London, 1973), pp. 279-328. On the concept of artificial over-

population, see E. Sereni, *Il capitalismo*, pp. 345-69.

5. On the industrial expansion of this period, see Alexander Gerschenkron, *Economic Backwardness in Historical Perspective* (Cambridge, Mass., 1962); Rosario Romeo, *Breve storia della grande industria in Italia* (Bologna, 1963).

6. C. Seton-Watson, *Italy from Liberalism*, p. 288; Giuseppe Orlando, 'Progressi e difficoltà dell'agricoltura' in *Lo sviluppo economico in Italia*, vol. III, *Studi di settore e documentazione di base* (Milan, 1969), p. 22.

7. For statistics on growing wheat production and rising productivity, see Giorgio Porisini, 'Produzione e produttività del frumento in Italia durante l'età giolittiana', *Quaderni Storici*, n. 14 (1970) pp. 510-11. For sugar beet production, see Luigi Perdisa, *La bietola da zucchero nella economia italiana* (Rome, 1938), p. 16. G. Orlando, 'Progressi e difficoltà', p. 43 offers additional statistics on agricultural expansion.

8. In contrast to the national average of 10.5 quintals per hectare, the major wheat-growing provinces of the North – Rovigo, Ferrara, Cremona, Milan, Padua and Bologna – averaged over 17.5 quintals in the last years before the war. For the regional variations in wheat productivity, see G. Porisini, 'Produzione e produttività', pp. 516-18. On the overall dominance of northern agriculture, see G. Valenti, 'L'Italia agricola dal 1861 al 1911' in *Cinquanta anni di storia italiana*, (Milan, 1911), p. 91.

9. E. Sereni, 'Note per una storia del paesaggio agrario emiliano' in *Le campagne emiliane nell'epoca moderna* (Milan, 1957), pp. 44-5; *Annuario statistico italiano, 1911*, pp. 102-3.

10. Tomaso Crispolti, 'Della partecipazione del lavoro al prodotto della terra', *Annali della Società Agraria Bolognese*, vol. XXXIV (Bologna, 1894), pp. 137-8.

11. On these agrarian entrepreneurs, see E. Sereni, *Il Capitalismo*; Agostino Bignardi, *Construttori di terra* (Bologna, 1958); Alessandro Roveri, *Dal sindacalismo rivoluzionario al fascismo. Capitalismo agrario e socialismo nel Ferrarese (1870-1920)* (Florence, 1972); G. Porisini, 'Aspetti e problemi dell'agricoltura ravennate dal 1883 al 1922' in *Nullo Baldini nella storia della cooperazione* (Milan, 1966); Luigi Zerbini, *Illustrazione delle principali aziende agrarie del Bolognese* (Bologna, 1913).

12. The wheat duty, which had remained at 1.4 lire during the previous seventeen years, was increased to 5 lire in 1888 and to 7.51 six years later. See Mario Bandini, 'Consequenze e problemi della politica doganale per l'agricoltura italiana' in Ministero per la Costituente, *Rapporto della Commissione Economica*, vol. I, *Agricoltura* (Rome, 1946), p. 393; Luigi Preti, *Le lotte agrarie nella valle padana* (Turin, 1955), pp. 106-10; Giampiero Carocci, *Agostino Depretis e la politica interna dal 1876 al 1887* (Turin, 1956), pp. 415-60; G. Orlando, 'Progressi e difficoltà, p. 28.

13. L. Perdisa, *La bietola da zucchero*, pp. 18-23.

14. V. Castronovo, *Storia d'Italia*, vol. IV, book I (Turin, 1975), pp. 140-1; G. Porisini, 'Produzione e produttività', pp. 513-15; G. Valenti, 'L'Italia agricola', p. 133.

15. See L. Perdisa, *La bietola da zucchero*, pp. 10-16; C.J. Robertson, 'The Italian Beet-Sugar Industry', *Economic Geography*, vol. XIV (Jan. 1938) pp. 1-13; *L'Italia Agricola* (Apr. 1927) pp. 206-10.

16. Property taxes, which had been over 125 million lire in the mid-1880s, fell to 106 million by 1900 and to 84 million in 1910. See G. Orlando, 'Progressi e difficoltà', p. 29.

17. On the operations of the travelling chairs of agriculture, see for example *Annali dell'Ufficio Provinciale per l'Agricoltura ed Atti del Comizio Agrario di Bologna*, IX (1901-2), p. 17 and XV (1908), p. 10.

18. For the formation of this rural proletariat and its leagues, see E. Sereni, *Il capitalismo*, pp. 340-3; Giuseppe Medici and G, Orlando, *Agricoltura e dis-*

occupazione, vol. I, *I braccianti della bassa pianura padana* (Bologna, 1952), p. 74; Idomeneo Barbadoro, *Storia del sindacalismo italiano dalla nascita al fascismo*, vol. I, *La Federterra* (Florence, 1973), pp. 3-57; Renato Zangheri, *Lotte agrarie in Italia. La Federazione Nazionale dei Lavoratori della Terra, 1901-1926* (Milan, 1960), pp. I-XXXIV; Thomas R. Sykes, 'Capitalist Agriculture in Italy: The Mobilization of Day Laborers in the Po Valley, 1901-1915' (typescript).

19. While in the 1880s only 20 per cent of the strikes had a favourable outcome for the labourers, in the first decade of the new century 61 per cent of the strikes ended favourably. See G. Orlando, 'Progressi e difficoltà', p. 34; Giuliano Procacci, 'Geografia e struttura del movimento contadino' in *Lotta di classe in Italia agli inizi del secolo XX* (Rome, 1970), pp. 82-130.

20. Società degli Agricoltori Italiani, *I recenti scioperi agrari in Italia e i loro effetti economici* (Rome, 1902), p. 16.

21. *Bollettino Mensile del Consorzio Agrario Bolognese*, II, n. 11 (1902) p. 230.

22. *Federconsorzi ed i consorzi agrari. Note informative* (Rome, 1947), pp. 5, 12; *Federconsorzi: Sessant'anni di vita al servizio dell'agricoltura italiana 1892-1952* (Rome, 1952), p. 46; C. Pareschi, 'La cooperazione agraria in Emilia', *L'Italia Agricola* (Apr. 1928), p. 186; *Boll. Consorzio Bolognese*, n. 11 (1902), pp. 253-4.

23. *Federconsorzi. Note informative*, p. 6; *Giornale di Agricoltura* (July 10 1977), p. 9.

24. *Boll. Consorzio Bolognese*, II, n. 11 (1902) p. 257. In the province of Bologna, the director of the Banca Popolare, Vincenzo Sani, was one of the most important local landowners; the agrarian entrepreneur, Augusto Peli, served on the board of directors of both the Consortium and the Cassa di Risparmio. On the activities of Sani, see *L'Agricoltura Bolognese*, V, n. 3 (March 1911) pp. 55-8; for Peli, *La Cassa di Risparmio in Bologna nei suoi primi cento anni* (Bologna, 1937), pp. 163, 269.

25. Antonio Bizzozero, *Diciotto anni di cooperazione agraria 1893-1910. Consorzio Agrario Cooperativo Parmense* (Parma, 1911), pp. xxiv-xxvi; 'Relazione dell'amministrazione per l'esercizio 1901', *Boll. Consorzio Bolognese*, II, n. 1 (1902) pp. 7-8.

26. On the Banca Poplare and the consortia, see A. Bizzozero, *Diciotto anni*, p. XLII-XLVI and p. 97; *Primo Consorzio Agrario Cooperativo di Piacenza. Cenni storici e dati statistici* (Piacenza, 1925), p. 14. For the Cassa di Risparmio and the Consortia of Bologna and Parma, see *Boll. Consorzio Bolognese*, III, n. 3 (1903) pp. 51-3 and Bizzozero, p. 97.

27. For the expanding activity of the consortia and rural banks in this period, see A. Bizzozero, *Diciotto anni*, p. XIX and statistical tables; *Boll. Consorzio Bolognese* (December 1916); *Primo Consorzio Piacenza*, pp. 32-4; *La Cassa di Risparmio Bologna*, pp. 381-403; G. Porisini, 'Aspetti agricoltura ravennate', pp. 271-2.

28. See letter of chemical manufacturer to president of the Federconsorzi cited in Angelo Ventura, 'La Federconsorzi dall'età liberale al fascismo' in *Quaderni Storici*, n. 36 (December 1977) p. 691.

29. On the promotional and research activities of the Federconsorzi, see Giuseppe Ravasini, 'L'attività culturale della Federazione italiana dei Consorzi agrari' in *L'Italia Agricola* (March 1932) pp. 225-33; *Federconsorzi: Sessant'anni*, p. 55.

30. For a general discussion of the Italian chemical industry before 1914, see L. Cafagna, 'Italy 1830-1914', pp. 316-17.

31. A. Ventura, 'La Federconsorzi', pp. 692-4; *Federconsorzi: Note informative*, p. 12.

32. A. Ventura, 'La Federconsorzi', pp. 696-7 and p. 735.
33. Giovanni Morselli, *Le industrie chimiche italiane* (Milan, 1911), pp. 33-4;
R. Romeo, *Storia grande industria*, p. 67; L. Cafagna, 'Italy 1830-1914', p. 316.
34. A. Bizzozero, *Diciotto anni*, p. 117, 135-7.
35. Ibid., p. 234, 256-7. Sharp price fluctuations put the consortia in the position of having to sell fertilisers at prices above the market because of pre-existing contracts and delays in delivery.
36. Ibid., p. 271; A. Ventura, 'La Federconsorzi', p. 694.
37. The two major chemical firms were the Unione italiana concimi and the Società colla e concimi. The first of these had emerged by 1911 as the largest supplier in the Po Valley with its 26 factories (five in Emilia alone). For developments in the chemical industry and the Federconsorzi, see G. Morselli, *Industrie chimiche*, pp. 33, 125; A. Ventura, 'La Federconsorzi', pp. 694-5.
38. For the most recent presentation of this view, see A. Ventura, 'La Federconsorzi', pp. 691-700.
39. *Federconsorzi: Sessant'anni*, pp. 55-6; A. Bizzozero, *Diciotto anni*, pp. liv-lv.
40. A. Bizzozero, *Diciotto anni*, p. 117, 135-7. For the role of Cavalieri in the *Federconsorzi*, see *Federconsorzi: Sessant'anni*, p. 46.
41. On the co-operative factories, see A. Bizzozero, *Diciotto anni*, lv; *Primo Consorzio Piacenza*, pp. 14-16; Credito Italiano, *Società italiane per azioni. Notizie statistiche, 1914*, vol. I, p. 806; C. Pareschi, 'La cooperazione agraria', p. 186. In Bologna one of the most influential landowners in the province, Enrico Pini, became the president of the Società Bolognese per l'industria dei concimi e prodotti chimici after 1907. The company evolved into one of the most important producers for the local and regional market.
42. *Federconsorzi: Sessant'anni*, p. 56; A. Ventura, 'La Federconsorzi', p. 695.
43. Luigi Perdisa, *Monografia economico agraria dell'Emilia* (Faenza, 1937), pp. 57-62; A. Calzoni, 'L'evoluzione dell'industria bolognese', *La Mercanzia*, XXXIII, n. 6 (1968) pp. 521-34.
44. Frank De Morsier, for example, owned the second largest machine firm in Bologna and was a prominent figure in both local liberal political circles and provincial agrarian organisations. As a result, he was able to establish close ties with the Bolognese Consortium, which awarded his firm a direct commission for the construction of certain specialised farm machines as early as 1904. See *Boll. Consorzio Bolognese* (1904) Supp. 2, p. 53. On increasing sales of machines, see ibid., XI (1911) n. 2, pp. 7-16 that contains a list of all buyers of certain machines during the previous three years, a list that includes the names of the major leaseholders and landowners in the province.
45. See *Archivio Centrale dello Stato*, Ministero delle Armi e Munizioni, Busta 2, Fascicolo 20, 'Elenco delle ditte del Veneto ed Emilia specializzate nella fabbricazione di macchine agricole', 12 March 1917.
46. See 'Dei mezzi atti a diffondere l'uso della macchina agricola in Italia', *Boll. Consorzio Bolognese*, II, n. 11 (1902) p. 256.
47. *Federconsorzi: Sessant'anni*, p. 68; A. Ventura, 'La Federconsorzi', pp. 703-5.
48. For industrial participation in the commercial company, see A. Ventura, 'La Federconsorzi', p. 701.
49. For a discussion of this process as it unfolded in the Piedmontese rice areas, see V. Castronovo, 'Agricoltura e capitale financzario e industriale'.
50. The growth of Italy's agricultural machine industry in the 1920s is particularly striking, considering that prior to the First World War it represented a mere 10 per cent of the sales in the country. On developments in the 1930s, see Paul Corner, 'Rapporti tra agricoltura e industria durante il fascismo', *Problemi del socialismo*, XIV (1972) pp. 740-1.

51. Consiglio Provinciale dell'Economia Corporativa, *La provincia di Bologna nell'anno Decimo. Monografia statistica-economica* (Bologna, 1932), p. 632. On the history of hemp cultivation in the region, see G. Procacci, *History of the Italian People*, p. 183; Roberto Roversi, *Canapa ed autarchia* (Rome, 1939), pp. 11-13; Vittorio Peglion, *Piante industriali: Produzione, commercio, regime doganale* (Rome, 1917).

52. Giovanni Proni, *La canapicoltura italiana nell'economia corporativa* (Rome, 1938), p. 40; V. Peglion, *Piante industriali*, p. 29.

53. The leading firms were the Linificio e Canapificio Nazionale, the Manifatture Italiane Riunite and the Ditta Ing. Clateo Castelini e C. See Ernesto Sessa, *Della canapa e del lino in Italia* (Milan, 1930), pp. 53-4; G. Proni, *La canapicoltura*, pp. 54-5.

54. Attilio Todeschini, *Il pomodoro in Emilia. Importanza economica della coltivazione* (Rome, 1938), pp. 3-34; Pr. Giulio Gennari, *Le provincie di Parma, Reggio Emilia e Modena nella struttura generale della loro economia agraria e nei rapporti fra datori di lavoro e lavoratori* (Parma, 1921), p. 2; Gaetano Briganti, 'Le colture intensive specializzate', *L'Italia agricola e il suo avvenire* (Rome, 1919), pp. 190-1.

55. L. Perdisa, *La bietola da zucchero*, pp. 10-13; C.J. Robertson, 'The Italian Beet-sugar Industry', p. 12.

56. A. Roveri, *Dal sindacalismo*, p. 139; C.J. Robertson, 'The Italian Beet-sugar Industry', pp. 7-9.

57. L. Perdisa, *La bietola da zucchero*, pp. 14-16; Luigi Zerbini, 'Le bietole da zucchero', *L'Italia Agricola* (April 1927) p. 208; A. Roveri, *Dal sindacalismo*, pp. 139-40; 'Bieticoltura ravennate', *L'Italia Agricola* (December 1927) p. 788; C.J. Robertson, 'The Italian Beet-sugar Industry', p. 12.

58. V. Peglion, *Le piante industriali*, p. 92; L. Perdisa, *La bietola da zucchero*, p. 16.

59. The founder of the earliest experimental fields and refineries in Bologna, Emilio Maraini, was also the president and managing director of the most important sugar company in the country. Count Luigi Golinelli, a large landowner, founded one of the first plants in Ferrara, initially to process the produce from his own estate. The president of the Bonora Refinery of Ferrara, Antonio Bonora was the leaseholder of one of the largest and most modern commercial farms in Bologna. The agricultural investment company, La Codigoro, which had substantial holdings in Ferrara, was also one of the principal stockholders in a major Genoese refining company. On the activities of Maraini and Gulinelli, see L. Perdisa, *La bietola da zucchero*. pp. 13-15 and L. Zerbini, 'Le bietole da zucchero', p. 207; for Bonora, see *L'Agricoltura Bolognese* (15 Oct. 1921); for La Codigoro, A. Roveri, *Dal sindacalismo*. pp. 139-40.

60. For the causes of the recession, see the *Bollettino Federale Agrario* (15 Oct. 1908).

61. On the growing concentration within the sector, see E. Sessa, *Della canapa*, pp. 54-5; *ACS*, Min. Arm. e Mun., B. 189, Verbali of the Comitato regione della Mobilizazione industriale, Bologna 15 and 22 Sept. 1917.

62. See 'I produttori di canapa si muovono', *Boll. Consorzio Bolognese*, n. 8-10 (1907) pp. 98-102.

63. *Bollettino Federale Agrario* (15 Oct. 1908).

64. See L. Perdisa, *Monografia economico agraria*, p. 230.

65. For the problems of the hemp syndicates, see the *Boll. Federale Agrario* (1 Jan. 1910) and V. Peglion, *Le piante industriali*, p. 53. On the developments under the fascist regime, see G. Proni, *La canapicoltura italiana*, p. 275.

66. For the major corporations of the sugar refining industry, see Credito Italiano, *Società Italiane 1914*, pp. 1012-30. On the expansion of the Società Eridania, in particular, see A. Roveri, *Dal sindacalismo*, p. 140.

67. L. Perdisa, *La bietola da zucchero*, pp. 251-2.

68. See 'Atti del primo Congresso nazionale dei Bieticultori' reprinted in *Rassegna Economica del Polesine* (November 1951), pp. 43-4.

69. On the slump of 1908 and the agrarian mobilisation, see *Boll. Federale Agrario* (15 Oct., 1 Dec. and 15 Dec. 1908 and 1 Mar. 1910). For the formation of the growers' syndicates, see L. Perdisa, *La bietola da zucchero*, pp. 252-3; V. Peglion, *Le nostre piante industriali* (Bologna, no date), p. 101; Julo Fornaciari, 'La Federazione nazionale bieticultori', *L'Italia agricola* (March 1932) pp. 235-6; *Boll. Consorzio Bolognese*, V. (1905) n. 10-11, p. 202. The initial activities of the national federation in the last year of the war are discussed in Riccardo Bacchi, *L'Italia economica nel 1919* (Rome, 1920), pp. 271-2.

70. For the growth of this anti-union coalition, see *Boll. Federale Agrario* (15 Jan., 15 Mar. and 1 Sept. 1909).

71. C. Seton-Watson, *Italy from Liberalism*, p. 289; R. Romeo, *Breve storia*, pp. 67-8. On the agrarian groups hostile to sugar protection, see Ignazio Zampieri, 'Nell'industria dello zucchero', *Boll. Consorzio Bolognese*, IX, (1909) n. 12, pp. 184-6.

72. *Boll. Federale Agrario* (15 Nov. 1909).

73. See Confederazione Nazionale Agraria, *Atti del II Congresso Agrario* (Bologna, 1911), pp. 150-1; C. Seton-Watson, *Italy from Liberalism*, p. 289.

74. Nazario Sauro Onofri, *I giornali bolognesi nel ventennio fascista* (Bologna, 1972), p. 90.

75. V. Castronovo, *La stampa italiana dall'Unità al fascismo* (Bari, 1973), pp. 213-15 and by the same author, 'Il potere economico e fascismo' in *Fascismo e società italiana* (Turin, 1973), pp. 58-9.

76. For developments in Germany, see Hans-Jürgen Puhle, 'Parlament, Parteien und Interessenverbände 1890-1914' in Michael Stürmer (ed.), *Das kaiserliche Deutschland* (Düsseldorf, 1970), pp. 340-77.

77. On Giolitti's strategy and policies, see Giampiero Carocci, *Giolitti e l'età giolittiana* (Turin, 1961), chaps. I and II.

78. Guido Baglioni, *L'ideologia della borghesia industriale nell'Italia liberale* (Turin, 1974), pp. 490-1.

79. On the early efforts to form a regional agrarian organisation, see two publications of the Confederazione Nazionale Agraria, *L'organizzazione agraria in Italia, Sviluppo, ordinamento, azione* (Bologna, 1911), pp. 5-9 and *Annuario Agrario 1913-14* (Bologna, 1914), pp. 10-11.

80. In these years, such improvised organisations appeared to achieve their objectives. By 1904 the number of provincial federations of day labourers, for example, had dropped from 22 to 13, while membership in the first national federation, the *Federterra*, fell from 227,791 to 45,000 between 1901 and 1904. G. Procacci, *La lotta di classe in Italia*, pp. 301-4. For the limits of the early industrial associations, see G. Baglioni, *Borghesia industriale*, p. 491.

81. Franco Bonelli, *La crisis del 1907. Una tappa dello sviluppo industriale in Italia* (Turin, 1971), pp. 8-11; Mario Maragi, *I cinquecento anni del Monte di Pietà* (Bologna, 1972), p. 226.

82. For a summary of the industrial recession, see G. Carocci, *Storia d'Italia dall'Unità ad oggi* (Milan, 1975), pp. 175-81.

83. On the financial difficulties of the Consortium, see the annual report of the board of directors in *Boll. Consorzio Bolognese*, X (1910) n.1, pp. 6-7. For the problems of the hemp and sugar beet growers, see *Boll. Federale Agrario* (15 Oct. 1908).

84. For strike statistics, see Maurice Neufeld, *Italy: School for Awakening Countries* (Ithaca, 1961), pp. 346-7, 547.

85. See E. Dugoni and N. Mazzoni, 'Gli uffici di collocamento. La loro utilità

norme, moduli, istruzioni per l'impianto e funzionamento degli uffici' in R. Zangheri, *Lotte agrarie in Italia* (Ravenna, 1910), pp. 219-27; I. Barbadoro, *La Federterra*, pp. 210-11.

86. On the strike in Ferrara, see A. Roveri, *Dal sindacalismo*, pp. 189-208; for the strikes in Parma, see Biagio Riguzzi, *Sindacalismo e riformismo nel Parmense* (Bari, 1931) and Thomas R. Sykes, 'Revolutionary Syndicalism in the Italian Labour Movement: The Agrarian Strikes of 1907-08 in the Province of Parma', *International Review of Social History*, XXI (1976) part 2, pp. 189-91.

87. See the article by the agrarian spokesman G.E. Sturani in *Il Resto del Carlino* (26 May 1910).

88. G. Baglioni, *Borghesia industriale*, p p. 489, 501-3. The most influential founders were Giovanni Agnelli, Luigi Bonnefon Craponne and Gino Olivetti.

89. On the successes of the League, see ibid., p. 505. For the spread of the industrial organisations, see Mario Abrate, *La lotta sindacale nella industrializzazione in Italia, 1906-1926* (Turin 1966), pp. 52-4.

90. For the founding of the *Interprovinciale*, see *Bollettino dell'Associazione Agraria Parmense*, VI, n. 10-13 (9 Nov. 1907).

91. Ibid., Vii, n. 1 (2 Jan. 1908). The various policies of the *Interprovinciale* are elaborated in Confed. Naz. Agraria, *Atti del II Congresso Agrario, Bologna, 28-29 Novembre 1909* (Bologna, 1911), pp. 111-17; G.E. Sturani, *La Mutua-Scioperi. Sue basi economiche e suo ordinamento* (Bologna, 1909).

92. See *Boll. Federale Agrario* (15 June 1910) and L. Preti, *Le lotte agrarie nella valle padana*, p. 221.

93. G. Baglioni, *Borghesia industriale*, pp. 542-4.

94. *Boll. Federale Agrario* (15 Sept. 1908).

95. CII, 'La questione delle macchine' cited in Silvio Fronzoni, 'Dalle consociazioni agrarie della Provincia di Bologna alla Confederazione Nazionale Agraria' (senior thesis, University of Bologna, 1973), pp. 244-5.

96. *Boll. Federale Agrario* (1 April 1911).

97. CII and CNA, *Per la riforma del Consiglio Superiore del Lavoro* (Turin, 1910), pp. 1-2.

98. Ibid., pp. 2-15; G. Baglioni, *Borghesia industriale*, pp. 540-1.

99. *Boll. Federale Agrario* (1 April 1911).

100. See CNA, *L'organizzazione in Italia*, pp. 82-3; V. Castronovo, *Storia d'Italia*, p. 199; G. Baglioni, *Borghesia industriale*, p. 544.

101. This informal co-operation was often the result of the close economic relations among local manufacturers, merchants and landowners. Frank De Morsier, the Bolognese machine manufacturer, was managing director of the Interprovinciale and the prominent insurance representative Giuseppe Franchi sat on the central committee of the Bolognese Agrarian Association. CNA, *Annuario Agrario 1913-14*, pp. 31-42.

102. Riccardo Bachi, *L'Italia economica nel 1913* (Turin, 1914), pp. 249-50; G. Carocci, *Storia d'Italia*, p. 206.

103. *Il Resto del Carlino* (20 April 1912); *Archivio di Stato di Bologna*, Cat. 6, Fasc. 2, Mayor of Imola to Prefect (15 April 1912).

104. See *Il Resto del Carlino* (11 and 14 Feb. 1913).

105. CNA, *Annuario Agrario 1913-14*, p. 49.

106. A. Roveri, *Dal sindacalismo*, pp. 271-80.

107. R. Bachi, *L'Italia economica 1913*, pp. 249-50.

108. Ibid., p. 178; G. Carocci, *Storia d'Italia*, pp. 206-7.

109. See Charles S. Maier, *Recasting Bourgeois Europe: Stabilization in France, Germany, and Italy in the Decade after World Word I* (Princeton, 1975), pp. 9-11.

110. On the pre-war situation in Germany, see ibid., p. 11.

111. *Boll. Federale Agrario* (1-15 Aug., 1 Dec. 1908).

112. CII, *Conflitti del lavoro e Legislazione sociale*, p. 7 cited in G. Baglioni, *Borghesia industriale*, p. 537.

113. *Boll. Federale Agrario* (15 Sept. 1911).

114. See the leaflet of the Associazione Agraria Bolognese, 'La vertenza Zerbini' in *ASB*, C6 F2, 1912.

115. *ASB*, C6 F2, Prefect to Giolitti, 21 June 1912.

116. *ASB*, C6 F2 Prefect to Giolitti, 23 June 1912.

117. M. Abrate, *La lotta sindacale*, p. 101; G. Baglioni, *Borghesia industriale*, p. 547; V. Castronovo, *Giovanni Agnelli* (Turin, 1971), pp. 41-6. For a sample of the industrialists' views on Giolitti, see the article of Bonnefon Craponne in *L'Italia Industriale e Agraria*, III, n. 2 (1913).

118. *Boll. Federale Agrario* (1 May 1910).

119. *Bollettino della Lega Industriale di Torino*, V. (6 June 1911), cited in G. Baglioni, *Borghesia industriale*, p. 536n.

120. See note 100.

121. For information on Italian nationalism and the Nationalist Association in particular, see Franco Gaeta, *Nazionalismo italiano* (Naples, 1965).

122. Giovanni Papini, 'A Nationalist Programme' in Adrian Lyttleton (ed.), *Italian Fascisms from Pareto to Gentile* (New York, 1975), p. 100.

123. For the striking similarities between the ideas of the Nationalist intellectuals and the agrarian militants, see ibid.; F. Gaeta, *Nazionalismo italiano*, p. 77, 184n; Nicola Tranfaglia, *Dallo stato liberale al regime fascista* (Milan, 1973), pp. 100-1; the speeches of Carrara printed in CNA, *Atti del II Congresso* and in *Il Resto del Carlino* (25 April 1909 and 7 June 1910).

124. On Barone, see Richard Webster, *Industrial Imperialism in Italy, 1908-1915* (Berkeley, 1975), p. 373.

125. *Il Resto del Carlino* (13 March 1913).

126. *L'Italia Industriale e Agraria* (April-May 1914).

127. Gino Olivetti, 'I nazionalisti e la borghesia lavoratrice' in ibid.; M. Abrate, *La lotta sindacale*, p. 55.

128. *Il Resto del Carlino* (29 May 1911).

129. V. Castronovo, *La stampa italiana dall'Unità al fascismo* (Bari, 1973), pp. 210-11 and *Agnelli*, pp. 54-5.

130. V. Castronovo, 'Il potere economico e fascismo', pp. 53-5.

131. On the political views of Pini, see *ASB*, C5 F1, Prefect to Ministry of Interior, 20 March 1913; for those of Agnelli, see V. Castronovo, *Agnelli*, p. 56.

132. See for example, the article of Frank De Morsier, 'Il ministero Salandra ed una politica nazionale', *Italia Industriale e Agraria* (April-May 1914).

7 FROM LIBERALISM TO CORPORATISM: THE PROVINCE OF BRESCIA DURING THE FIRST WORLD WAR

Alice A. Kelikian

Historians of modern Italy have only recently begun to examine the qualitative change in the behaviour of the industrial community that was prompted by the experience of the First World War. Although the war-time organisation of capital and labour foreshadowed dominant features of Mussolini's corporate state, scholars of the fascist economy have largely focused their attentions on the post-war period, thus belying the war mobilisation's decisive impulse towards the authoritarian developments of the following decade.[1] Similarly, those studies concerned with the inadequacies of revolutionary trade unionism during the *biennio rosso* tend to neglect the distortions precipitated by the First World War in the traditions of the working class.[2] This essay is an attempt to describe the awkward transition from the anarchic liberalism of small-scale producers to a new corporatism, marshalled under the aegis of the war authorities, in the province of Brescia. While the north-east Lombard area should not be regarded as typical of any other manufacturing centre in a country as varied and fragmented as Italy, its economic growing pains do illustrate the predicament of industrialisation on the peninsula.

Brescia is a region of great physical contrasts. Hemmed in by the Alps to the north and by the Iseo and Garda lakes on either side, arid mountains and fertile slopes occupy almost 70 per cent of the total landscape. These upland districts, rich in deposits of high quality iron ore as well as in potential sources of hydro-electric power, seemed marked by nature for industrial development in the latter half of the last century. South of the provincial capital lay the broad wheat plains of the *bassa bresciana*. There, with the exception of some cotton shops and silk mills, agriculture was to remain the predominant economic activity.[3]

Already in the mid-nineteenth century, the iron forges of the Valcamonica compared favourably with other mining centres in Lombardy and Piedmont. The arms manufacturers of the Val Trompia were renowned throughout Europe and enjoyed an international market, while half the foundries on the peninsula were concentrated in the backwoods province. Yet the forces of industrialisation took their time to disrupt the urban-rural balance of the local community. Although the vigorous progress of the metal-working firms coincided with the collapse of viticulture and mulberry cultivation during the years preceding national unification, the industrial spurt was selective and short-lived – lasting little over twelve years. The old metal trades were expanded, not transformed, and by 1882 the iron masters near Breno, who had boasted nine blast furnaces in 1854, could afford to run only three.[4]

The slump of the late 1880s hit the north Italian metal shops with particular severity as the vast majority of Lombard firms specialised in finished steel: like engineering they were damaged by the protective tariffs benefiting the big producers and shipbuilders. The high cost of primary materials especially hurt the arms dealers, dependent on exports, though it was not just the recession, triggered by the tariff war, crisis in agriculture and credit-inspired inflation, that destroyed the prospects of nascent industry in the province. The entrepreneurs of Brescia had a bad reputation. It was the belief of Sandrini, a member of the Jacini commission, that poor commercial spirit, limited outlook and timid capital were much to blame for the capricious nature of industrial development in the zone.[5] Apart from veritable innovators like Beretta, Gregorini and Glisenti, the bulk of manufacturers were strictly small-time. Some owners preferred to operate on the brink of marginality, though most companies seemed unable to compete with the larger outfits near Milan; improved transport facilities meant local customers could now go elsewhere. Giuseppe Zanardelli, the patron of Brescian liberalism, expressed contempt for the 'antediluvian methods' used by the firms. The ironworks in the highlands were archaic, the mines primitive at best. A number of miners were only seven or eight years old, 'embodiments of impotence and illness'.[6] All came from peasant stock and returned to the farm late in the day to labour on smallholdings, but this double life does not appear to have bothered the management much. In fact, the rural recruit was favoured by the prudent employer, who viewed the moonlighter's ties to the land and to the family as an assurance against occupational solidarity in the factory.[7]

Brescia was never a princedom so it had no real aristocracy. Arms production instead came to represent ennoblement for the aspiring bourgeois *di provincia*. The armaments business could not be considered as just another conservative family enterprise: it was the most respectable trade in the area. Zanardelli wrote that the firm in Gardone resembled 'a sort of feudal estate'.[8] There was nothing flashy about the owners, who were not employers but rather 'gentlemen'. Cultivating good familial relations with their workers, these entrepreneurs paid the highest hourly wages in the province. Although the Val Trompia notables were less grasping than other industrialists in iron and steel, they would hardly pass as enlightened on questions of management and organisation. One arms manufacturer, attempting to defend the artisan base of his operations, gave the simple formula of hard work and perseverance to spur productivity. A prominent lawyer from the town complained that 'the *padroni* . . . ignore the investment of capital and the division of labour'.[9] Massimo Bonardi, also a barrister, had to agree with his associate: the famed workshops of Brescia looked more like sitting-rooms, 'with the inhabitants waiting around the house for various chores to do'.[10] Indeed the magnate Pietro Beretta, noted for his modernity, installed his fifteen-year-old son Giuseppe on the shop floor and the boy had to work his way up to the top. Family principle and team spirit ranked even above profit. When Antonio, another son, left to join Garibaldi at Bezzecca, the young redshirt took a group of artisans to fight alongside him. With liberation, after all, the demand for firearms would surely be reduced and fewer workers therefore needed.[11]

While Antonio Beretta's timing was off, the predicted slackening did come to pass, forcing all but the most advanced firms of the Val Trompia into temporary inactivity. The decline in the production of raw silk was even more dramatic, and silkgrowers of the area never managed to recapture the initiative. Yet the crisis that almost obliterated the industry from local economic life also transformed it by encouraging concentration. As investors from Milan and Bergamo stepped in and bought out the Brescians, the cocoons were transferred from the province to Piedmont and the Veneto. Large, mechanised factories replaced the old mills, and by 1890 the number of *filande* had been reduced to 68 – a seventh of the 1876 figure – while units of production increased almost fivefold. Over 6,000 workers were engaged in the trade.[12]

The cotton industry was slow to take root in Brescia, but by 1890 real progress could be seen: some 1,175 workers found employment in the sector, which claimed 44,180 spindles and 477 looms. This achievement did not reflect the merits of home-grown entrepreneurship since both impulse and capital came from outside. The first cotton manufacturing factory was opened in 1837 by a Swiss financier who, starting out with more than 1,500 spindles, quadrupled the number in 10 years. Next a Milanese merchant set up a steam-powered shop in 1859, and three foreign companies entered the contest in the 1870s to build no less than eight large factories.[13] Woollen textiles were also introduced to the region by a firm based in Switzerland. Founded in 1890, the Lanificio di Gavardo operated nearly 14,000 spindles five years later and 25,000 by the turn of the century. The company's expansion was phenomenal, and finally the Brescians tried to emulate it. Two local enterprises were established in the late 1890s with adequate capital, yet the imitations quickly faltered. Italy's great wool crisis of 1900 almost eliminated the new concerns, though the Lanificio not only survived but also bought one of them out. By the end of the sector's recession in 1904, the company controlled over 32,000 spindles.[14]

Despite this expansive atmosphere, in 1890 industry engaged about 23,000 workers — less than 5 per cent of the provincial population. Moreover, the textile factories and metal shops were not concentrated near the town but isolated on the periphery, localising the impact of change. Domestic village labour managed to persist. According to official reports, 3,600 handlooms in home use could still be counted, and the divide between cultivator, artisan and worker continued to be woolly well into the twentieth century. Brescia was basically a rural community, and its industrial revolution — like that of Italy as a whole — had yet to come.[15]

In 1900 textiles still represented the modern sector of the provincial economy, as ill-developed heavy industry was slow to recover from a period of crisis and regression which ended in 1896. Meeting its 1890 level of productivity, silk had made a fast come-back by 1903. Cotton boomed; in step with the Lombard trend, the branch trebled its output over the same 13-year period. The development of 'white coal', itself a testimony to industrialisation, mushroomed after the recession. Between 1900 and 1911, the production of hydro-electric energy in the province multiplied more than sixfold.[16]

Only the metallurgical sector seemed still-born. The iron and steel firms took their time to convalesce, and the number of metal-workers employed during 1903 was merely 2,755, 40 per cent below the 1890 total.[17] Yet by clearing out the multitude of charcoal-burning enterprises buried in the highland districts, the contracting market set the stage for the expansion of modern, large-scale production. Finally during the years 1903-10, Brescian 'little steel' broke out of its artisan shell.[18]

The engineering and steel industries cannot be dismissed as congenitally retarded. Among the traditional family businessmen, there were indeed a few adventurers. In 1890 Attilio Franchi, a second-generation entrepreneur, hoped to install a modern rolling mill near the town centre but with no financial backing he had to settle for a modest blast furnace. After the Banca Commerciale finally came through with some long-term credit, Franchi was able to introduce the latest technology and by 1900 he had earned his mill. The industrialist's line of finished pig iron products gradually expanded until 1905, when the nationalisation of the railways and the consequent extension of the network brought life to the steel-working concerns. Setting a pattern that would later prove ominous for the sector, the government became his major customer in 1906.[19]

Another local firm, the Officine Meccaniche Tubi Togni, made a fortune on land reclamation and on the harnessing of Alpine rivers for electricity. Giulio Togni came from the *aristocrazia fontanara* of the province: his father, a famous artisan, specialised in the construction of decorative fountains. Young Togni continued the family business, taking it one step further. In 1884 he set up a plant for the manufacture of tubes and aqueducts, used in the building of hydro-electric power stations. By 1905 he had moved on to seamless tubes as well as railway axles, and when the firm went public in 1906 Togni began to dabble in rare alloys.[20]

The world financial crisis of 1907, however, punctured Brescia's industrial renaissance. The depression hit the fragile Italian economy especially hard, and silk — which received the most debilitating blow — was first to succumb.[21] By 1911 the number of spindles in the sector had been whittled to almost a third of the 1904 figure of 76,000; after the First World War the total added up to a mere 20,000.[22] Cotton was slow to heal since new foreign competition doubled the effect of the 1907 drop in export prices, while provincial iron and steel underwent withdrawal symptoms after rail fever. Togni's government orders trickled, but private aqueduct work provided some relief.[23] For those like Franchi and the steelman Tempini, who depended exclusively on high state expenditure, operations came to an abrupt halt. The single motor-car company in the zone suffered the heaviest capital losses and the Bianchi lorry manufacturers, in business only two years before the slump, went bankrupt. The logical conclusion of all this uneven, feeble growth might have been rationalisation and concentration. But by shouldering the burden of over-expansion, the state averted industrial retrenchment in the province. Franchi, Togni, Tempini and numerous others continued to exercise both ownership and control of their family enterprises, which were salvaged by military contracts for arms production in 1910.[24]

The fickle behaviour of local industry left its mark on the provincial labour movement. Although the Confederation of Labour (CGL) branch in the area derived its support from the proletarian elite of metalworkers, it by no means represented the majority of operatives in the category: in 1914 the Brescia metallurgical federation enrolled only 16 per cent of those engaged in heavy industry.[25] Labour militancy did increase in the province after 1912, but the CGL and the town Camera del Lavoro were not partners to it.[26] The announcement of wage reductions and lay-offs in cotton and silk ignited agitation by female workers, organised

by the Catholics. Other strikes broke out in the steel shops scattered
throughout the uplands, though the participants were grouped in independent communal leagues. FIOM had called three 'regional' strikes in
1914 and 1915, all of which ended favourably for the rank and file, yet
they affected metalworkers employed by only two companies.[27]

The geographical dispersion of the industrial proletariat and an
unfavourable economic conjuncture do much to explain the CGL's
difficulty in mobilising the provincial working class in disciplined strike
action. Only a fraction of the factories and workshops were located
within the town limits: all the textile concerns and most of the steelworks still hid among the valleys and slopes, where the price of water
power and labour remained low. Furthermore, the moderation and
gradual reform preached by the cautious union leaders could only satisfy
the ranks given full employment and high wages. Yet far from improving
the besetting problem of unemployment, the years 1913-14 deepened
the protracted recession.[28] In September 1914 the Zust automobile firm
dismissed two-thirds of its 300-member work force, while the largest
steel company threatened to dismiss all 790 employees.[29] Pay scales in
cotton and wool textiles underwent further reductions, but most workers
kept their jobs. In the silk branch, however, both wages and positions
on the shop floor fell drastically. The infant chemical and cement concerns alone managed to hold their own. Subject to these ups and downs
of industrial development, the reformist labour militants could hardly
promise to better the material conditions of the working class.[30]

The First World War and the massive mobilisation that accompanied
it did much to enliven the sluggish tempo of local enterprise. The wide
distribution of government contracts to metallurgical and engineering
firms throughout the north shortened the time-lag between Italy and the
rest of Europe; high operating costs, low investment and insufficient competition were not unique to Brescia for, apart from notable exceptions
like Milan and Turin, the story seemed the same in other manufacturing
zones. General Dallolio, the mastermind of the mobilisation programme,
labelled the Italian steel sector as 'fictitious' and, hoping to cure this
fundamental weakness of the national economy, he sought to insert
heavy industry into a new capitalist order which would be regulated by
the state 'to improve and accelerate production'.[31]

It is difficult to exaggerate the impact of the war mobilisation on the
social and economic structures of Brescia. All 17 steel and machine
factories worked exclusively for the armed forces ministries by 1916.
Many of the smaller workshops specialising in the manufacture of arms
received subcontracts from the state arsenal in Gardone Val Trompia,

while three firms in the Val Sabbia did piece-work for FIAT. The autarky of provincial community began to fade away.[32]

The class most noticeably changed by the momentum of the economic effort was the proletariat. In 1910 only 6 of the zone's 52 iron and steel shops employed more than 100 labourers each.[33] Then the industrial population divided almost equally between workshops and factories, and only during the mobilisation did the predominance of the latter become firmly established. The number of those engaged in the metal-working trades swelled almost overnight from 8,059 in 1915 to 20,534 by the second half of 1916.[34] Creating a new category of semi-skilled workers whose interests were quite different from those of the traditional artisan organisation in the sector, this rapid growth continued until mid-1917.[35]

Not only did the industrial mobilisation give immediate relief to chronic unemployment, but the CGL gained accreditation as the legitimate representative of organised labour. Not surprisingly, membership soared in the CGL-affiliated unions, yet the provincial labour leaders became more moderate and less avid in their economic demands. They intended to maintain the privileged position that participation in the regional committees of arbitration had won them.[36] The federation's active role in mediating disputes between workers and employers in the war industries was quite distant from the socialist party's passive neutralism on the intervention question. The promotion of such diametrically-opposed policies on the same rank and file could not but provoke serious divisions within the local labour movement, capping internal dissension.[37]

Officially, discord within the Italian labour movement found resolution by merely separating politics from the unions. The moderate CGL would devote itself exclusively to economic action while the maximalist PSI remained concerned with strictly political issues. Reasonably successful at the national level, the temporary truce permitted both groups to enjoy a considerable degree of autonomy and to advocate conflicting lines on the war question. In Brescia, though, it failed miserably and the socialist party slid languidly into torpor. As FIOM's following increased fivefold during the first two years of war, PSI membership continued to shrink through 1918.[38] The primacy of the CGL (which was more interesting in finding jobs than in pursuing socialism) over the provincial party and the local chamber of labour showed how little the anti-militarist cause weighed in balance against the arguments for collaboration with the war machine.[39]

The attitude of the rank and file on the war issue resounded the weakness and ambivalence that tore the organisational fabric of the working class. The neutrality of the Brescia workers during May 1915 was indubitably as genuine as it had been unanimous. They resented the harsh, military rules of discipline enforced in the war industries, all equipped with little jails on the shop floor, but naturally preferred unpleasant factory conditions to the front. During the first 20 months of the mobilisation, their mood remained one of resignation. Full employment and spiralling pay scales until 1917 do much to explain this apparent indifference.[40]

The FIOM leaders should not be accused of having sold out to the state. The few partial strikes that did break out during the first year of war were in fact organised by Edgardo Falchero, an indefatigable trade unionist. Intent on using his position as workers' delegate to extract concessions from industry with the assistance of the state, he had no qualms about participating on the Lombard committee of arbitration. On 25 November 1915, Falchero staged a walk-out of nearly 800 metalworkers from an engineering factory, but the rank and file voted to resume production after one day of agitation.[41] Falchero's position among the working masses was insecure and often contested in the province; the employers' resistance to his ambitious campaign for a uniform scale of wages in heavy industry found its complement in the indiscipline of union members, who repudiated his leadership after 1916. Suffering from the effects of the economic downturn and instability in employment, the FIOM ranks lost confidence in activists like Falchero, installed by the national federation.[42] Instead, the workers resorted to liberal absenteeism, a practice especially popular among women, as a means by which to express their grievances. When unity was achieved within the local union movement, it frequently entailed rejecting the guidance of the central organisation. Already in January 1917 the metallurgical league of the Val Trompia had independent recourse to the mixed commission in Milan after an indemnity scheme authored by FIOM had been shelved. Later in the year a workers' delegation from a large armaments combine presented its own set of demands to the arbitration committee, bypassing the national federation. So while all this local action strengthened the union's following in single factories and individual communes, it also weakened the credibility of the FIOM leadership, which could not control the conduct of its member leagues.[43]

The freedom enjoyed by the rebellious Brescians did not last very long. The reduced strength of the national federation coincided with severe shortages in steel supplies and hydro-electric energy; employers were able to exploit the profound disarray of organised labour by turning their difficulty to good advantage and enforcing regular, unpaid furloughs.[44] Claiming it lacked sufficient primary materials to maintain full production, the Metallurgica Bresciana company effectively cut down the work week from six days to five without indemnifying its 9,000 employees.[45] Not only did such petty tactics increase the mutual hostility between workers and the management, but they also exacerbated tensions within the labour movement itself. The obligatory abstentions affected the proletariat's most expendable elements first — the new class of floating peasant-workers that had come off the land and into the factories only three years before. The high salaries and overtime hours of the metallurgical league's staunchest supporters — qualified metalworkers — aroused the suspicions of the semi-skilled operatives, who felt the union had made a deal with industry and the state at their expense. The great disparities in wage scales and terms of employment did little to detract from the league's image of partiality, and some recent recruits began to disown the agreements negotiated by the local leadership.[46] A cursory examination of earnings in heavy industry is revealing. During the spring of 1918 the average daily wage for a semi-skilled labourer in artillery was about 9 lire.[47] Most metalworkers at the MIDA steel combine made 12 to 15 lire, while some were paid as much as 40.[48] Although the going rate at the Metallurgica Bresciana plant was 10 lire a day for women, a number of specialists got 90 to 98 lire and a few foremen took home 120 lire.[49]

Uniform but less favourable conditions of work in other sectors often produced a sense of occupational solidarity or class consciousness. As employees of the state, railwaymen were not vulnerable to the divisive tactics of individual owners. Speculation and profiteering accompanied the great influx of prosperous metalworkers to the zone so that by 1917 the cost of living in Brescia had climbed to 15 per cent above the Milan figure.[50] While salaries in heavy industry kept in step with the inflated prices, the real wages of railway workers plunged below the 1914 level and all members of the trade felt the effects of the drop almost equally.[51] This common lament both stimulated and sustained militancy during the war.

Although the railwaymen were organised in a unified and combative union — compelled only by war-time political considerations to moderation — they remained economically and socially isolated from the rest of the working class and represented but a fraction of it. More important numerically were those engaged in the province's 28 textile factories. These labourers seemed better off than the railway workers since daily take-home pay averaged 1.80 lire, yet the terms of employment in light industry were most precarious.[52] Oppressed by frequent crises of the international clothing market and by war-time shortages in supplies, textiles provided little security to the unskilled worker. During 1918 real wages plummeted to 58 per cent of the 1914 standard, and the numbers on the payroll dropped from 11,065 at the outbreak of war to 8,401.[53] While the move of trained female labour to more lucrative jobs in the factories under government contract initially offset the decline of traditional industries, womanpower also fell first victim to unemployment once arms production started to fall away. A vicious cycle had been created. Because the attractive pay offered by the metal, machine and chemical companies drew experienced hands from those cotton and wool concerns which managed to stay in business during the war, textile manufacturers could only rely on casual workers, who tended to be local farm girls.[54] The constantly changing work force in the sector would have presented the most enterprising union with a formidable task. Perhaps aware of the odds against organising them, the CGL made no attempt to mobilise the new, marginal members of the industrial population. The socialist textile federation occupied a small room in the town chamber of labour and enrolled a minority of operatives in the wool industry, which had been outfitting Italian soldiers. The independent leagues founded by the Catholics before the war disappeared after intervention, so the textile ranks were left to their own devices. They remained detached from the industrial proletariat and agriculture stayed their primary interest. Women still put in evening hours on private plots; absenteeism developed into a real problem during the summer months, forcing some mills to close shop during the seasonal flood back to the fields.[55]

The grievances of unorganised workers in the manufacturing industries were voiced through old, individualist channels of rural wrath. Popular disorders broke out with greater frequency in the provincial hinterland, but they proved easier to control and to dilute. Urban unrest, however, was a much more delicate affair. The privations engendered by the onset of demobilisation gave rise to an explosion of petty violence and crime in the town. Pitched brawls between factory workers and discharged soldiers occurred almost nightly in 1918. Though some observers believed that disruptive *imboscati* should be despatched to the front, most bourgeois spokesmen recognised that labour's co-operation with the state was vital to the success of the war effort. But while the mass repression of the working class risked counter-productive results, leading trade unionists could certainly be isolated and disarmed. Many industrialists approved of such pre-emptive assaults on the ascendancy of radical enthusiasm. At a time when labour relations were beginning to unsettle, those who banked on order and hierarchy on the shop floor hoped to dissuade any workers with subversive aspirations. The FIOM delegate Falchero appeared the obvious candidate for the role as victim since he, according to members of the business community, continued to abuse his position on the mixed government commission by taking political liberties which jeopardised employer independence in management functions.[56] Unwilling to accept the presence of unions in his concerns, the iron master Franchi appealed for a little help from his friends. After Falchero had toured the Val Trompia one day, the military authorities prohibited him from re-entering the town limits at the request of the old-style entrepreneur.[57] When the FIOM official later complained about the severe measures adopted by Franchi to restore deference in his work force, the employer retaliated by convincing Bacchetti, prefect of the province, to petition the ministry of the interior for Falchero's removal from the zone.[58]

This was no way to pursue collective bargaining, especially since Falchero's notoriety in Milan circles gave him too much clout. The prefect also tried to transfer Baudino, secretary of the local metallurgical league, from Brescia to the Adriatic. Again it was Franchi who encouraged Bacchetti to banish the metalworker, though the prefect revoked the recommendation within weeks. The idea of combat was apparently too awful to contemplate, so Baudino became more practical in outlook. Abandoning his old vigour, the reformist agreed 'to struggle in a more conciliatory and persuasive manner'.[59]

The prefect's policy of neutralising prominent militants might have been viable during the first years of war, when the economic interests of the working class seemed to converge with those of industry, but by 1918 the end was near and the quick profits over. The reduced demand for labour, which started to touch all categories in heavy industry, reflected the slip in government spending; skilled metalworkers were becoming restive too. The industrialists also showed new signs of anxiety. Feeling the after-effects of the boom economy, they petulantly assumed a more obdurate posture.[60]

The specific issue that sparked a period of revolutionary agitation during the spring and summer of 1918 was the refusal of Franchi's new manager at the Metallurgica Bresciana combine to discuss wage increases with the workers' factory commission. Hand-picked by the industrialist, who had recently acquired controlling interest in the company, the engineer Jarach intended to reduce costs while increasing productivity.[61] The technician meant to get the most out of his employees by instilling discipline and pushing them to the limit. The factory jail swelled during his first month at the plant; by Jarach's ninth week at the job, offenders had to queue for days to serve their time. He was authoritarian and un-compromising, but the rigorous programme did produce the desired effect. The workers, of course, expected pay bonuses for their extra labours, yet rather than grant new concessions the management preferred to retract previous ones.[62]

Eager for the protection of public authority in trade disputes and for co-ordination with the state in economic decisions, dated liberal stalwarts like Franchi would not respect the other side of the corporatist coin — centralised bargaining with organised labour. Not only was the company reluctant to come to terms with the union movement, but the old pater-nalism had now disappeared. The belligerent tone of the management left a strike as the workers' only resort. On 10 May 1918 nearly half of the company employees initiated a walk-out, and within a few hours Jarach was ready to talk with their elected officials. The engineer and the factory commission reached a temporary agreement, unfavourable to the mass of unskilled labour. The men picked up their tools, but the women refused to return to work until indemnity for obligatory absten-tion was guaranteed by the firm. When the police tried to coerce the agitators back behind the factory gates, they met violent resistance. Tensions were aggravated when Jarach, hoping to circumvent FIOM's intervention, called a lock-out. Finally, the prefect ordered the arrest of strike leaders, dampening further unrest.[63]

Franchi continued his battle against trade unionism, though the line of attack changed. Instead of pestering militants with national connec-tions, the industrialist concentrated on eliminating grass-roots activists. Bacchetti dutifully translated Franchi's instructions into action, and the local metallurgical league was slowly purged of potential leaders. Soldiers attending public meetings of FIOM were often transferred from the province, while civilian members of the government-sponsored factory commissions would lose their jobs soon after their election to agencies. The industrialist first charged the employees with some disciplinary violation, which would be confirmed by the *carabinieri* in a detailed report under separate cover. Against the collusion of industry with the lower levels of state authority, the unions had no defence.[64]

FIOM's usual recourse to the war office in Rome failed to protect three activists from getting the sack. One Brescian unionist went to the capital to meet with the Under-Secretary Nava, who assured the moderate Squarci that Franchi would be censured by the ministry of arms and munitions, but when the militant returned home he received notice of

his impending departure from the zone.[65] Chastened by the cantanker-
ous employer, local organisers became cagey. Throughout September
1918 Falchero urged strike, but the Brescia league would foil the delegate's *comizi di piazza* by holding rival meetings. As Falchero moved further
to the left, the provincials showed more caution; internecine bickering
increased in face of employer intimidation.[66]

Franchi's antiquated policy of containing the advance of organised
labour was imitated by other firms as a speedy way to cut costs. Both
the MIDA and the Tettoni steelworks tightened pressures during the
summer of 1918: militants were sacked, collective agreements ignored,
real wages reduced through the exaggerated use of unpaid furloughs.[67]
That same year the Acciaieria Danieli bypassed the government's mixed
commission in Milan altogether.[68] Although unsuccessful wage claims
and ineffective work stoppages reinforced the political self-confidence
of industry, they also sanctioned its organisational complacency. Able
to cope with working-class unrest on their own terms, employers of the
province did not feel obliged to look to association. Moreover, the
assistance offered by both the civilian and military guardians of order in
defending the interests of capital allowed the provincial captains of
industry to remain loosely grouped. Perhaps unified in immediate tactics,
the owners had yet to formulate common, long-term strategies.

During the autumn of 1918 the industrialists pugnaciously pressed
their advantage. Falchero and his FIOM crew were powerless to check
the negotiation of secret agreements between workers and individual
employers. The national federations shrank as a result, since few disputes
now reached the regional committee of arbitration. No longer in a position to prevent the progressive drop of real wages, Falchero turned his
attention to the problems of demobilisation.[69] Meetings were held to
discuss insurance programmes and redundancy pay, but those who
attended would face arrest and before long the unionist had no audience.
The Milan socialist Filippo Turati petitioned the government in protest
against the violations of justice, yet the prime minister's personal assur-
ances to him did little to halt the offensive against organised labour.[70]

Internal divisions widened as the strength of trade unionism declined.
Conflict persisted on the stale issue of collaboration, and the heated
war-time debate over the CGL's participation in collective bargaining
during the industrial mobilisation found its post-war match in the
commissionissima battle. The dispute that revived tensions between the
national socialist leadership and the labour federation stemmed from
the reformist Rigola's decision to partake in another government commission, which sought to ease the transition to peace-time conditions.

The unionist's intention to work with the prime minister's initiative met with the opposition of the PSI, which later forbade all members to assist the official party. Rather than accept the party's subordination of economic action to political issues, Rigola resigned as secretary of the CGL. From July through September 1918, the Socialist Party was split from its trade union base.[71]

The national conflict later had serious repercussions for the local labour movement. Because of his position as FIOM arbiter in Lombardy, the maximalists in Brescia portrayed Falchero as a traitor to his own class. Hardened by the experience of the war mobilisation, Falchero had little enthusiasm for co-operating with the new state agency but his reluctance to advance the supremacy of the party led him to support participation. Though Falchero's popularity had largely declined, the new secretary of the provincial metallurgists was a mediocrity and commanded an even smaller following than his FIOM rival.[72] The head of the railway union had the makings of a real leader, but his extremist rhetoric began to disturb some metalworkers. These three men, who sought to represent the masses but never really did, fought out the decisive action. In September Falchero acquiesced to the pressures of the other two, leaving the province 'for fear of contamination'.[73]

Although their conflicts resulted from a favoured economic and political position, the local industrialists also fell to fighting with each other as a result of the mobilisation. The war boom brought about a prosperity that exposed the rickety foundations of provincial industry. Entrepreneurs who faced near bankruptcy before intervention found opportunity and privilege miraculously bestowed from above; profit suddenly became freed from the staid market forces of supply and demand. The state let owners escape rationalisation for it made domestic competition superfluous and eliminated the imports of German finished steel products, which used to haunt the Lombard firms.[74] Furthermore, government credit policy promoted expansion at minimal short-term risk to the private company. Franchi, for example, acquired control of the Mannesmann steelworks at Dalmine without ever having to increase the capital stock, thanks to the Banca Commerciale. Later he absorbed the Gregorini plant of Lovere and the Metallurgica Bresciana combine by breaking peace-time credit barriers.[75]

In their clumsy, haphazard attempts to expand and diversify within the Brescia-Bergamo area, the ironmasters began to step on each other's toes. The greatest subterranean dispute among businessmen in industry concerned state concessions to local operators for the development of water power plants under the Bonomi decree of 1916.[76] The major constraint on the production of combat equipment, which had already caused manufacturing output to double in the zone, was fuel. The Idro lake promised to be the richest source of hydro-electric energy around, so Franchi, Togni and the Società Elettrica Bresciana all entered the contest for the right to harness it.[77] Franchi, counting on his Commerciale connections to win him the bid, lost the bank's favour to Togni, another COMIT customer with FIAT links to boot. The controversy between the three contenders reached its climax in 1917, when the electrical company proceeded to the offensive. The main supplier of 'white coal' in north-east Lombardy, an old Commerciale affiliate though now part of the Edison group, began to initiate cuts in kilowatt-hours. Approved by the Milan mobilisation board, whose member Carlo Esterle happened to be director of Edison, the reductions in current principally affected the Franchi and Togni firms. Thus Franchi fell victim to the political favouritism and bureaucratic partiality that had consecrated his provincial dominion, while Togni possessed enough acumen to see the way the wind was blowing. The steelman aligned with the Società Elettrica Bresciana, and the joint corporate venture resulted in the birth of the Società Lago d'Idro.[78] Frittered current flow continued to limit the productive capacity of the Franchi enterprises, and by October 1918 the industrialist's tab at the Banca Commerciale had passed the 80 million lire mark. He tried, however, to trade on his injured position by bullying organised labour. In addition to using supply shortages as a pretext to lay off workers without indemnity, he threatened to dismiss two-thirds of the Metallurgica Bresciana staff unless the government came through with special subsidies and long-term credit.[79]

Munitions orders declined, but Franchi was reluctant to tool down. Even with the restoration of unlimited electricity allowances, the magnate would have trouble finding a peace-time market for the firm's products. Hoping that inflation would cancel out his debts, Franchi unwisely continued to buy out smaller steel and machine shops to keep up with the demands of his sole client – the state. No attempts were made to tame disorderly expansion until the spring of 1918, when he tried to reduce costs while increasing, not redressing, productivity. As the end of the mobilisation closed in, he could not escape the shadow of insufficient, speculative over-expansion.

Blinded by myopic individualism, Franchi responded to waning returns by tightening the screws on his work force.[80] Already in 1917 Franchi had become a notorious exploiter of female and child labour as a ready source of cheap, untrained help. The turnover of casual positions was highest in his factories, and over 41 per cent of the workers at one plant were female — 16 per cent above the national war-time average, which included some light industry. Franchi instituted new methods of payment to maintain the widest wage gap between skilled and unskilled categories in the province.[81]

Franchi, whose shop stewards were the best paid in the province, did not consider the inflated salaries granted to a minority of qualified metalworkers as concessions to the labour movement: he fought the growth of unionism by trying to divide the loyalties of the rank and file. Rather, the industrialist believed the other employers guilty of appeasement in recognising the socialist trade organisation as the legitimate representative of the work force and accepting collective agreements. The Idro affair bred another conflict of mentalities in the local business community. On one hand Togni was open to the penetration of 'outside' capital into the area, whereas Franchi preferred to fight the trust. Though Franchi had long opposed the marked concentration of the great industrial giants, transparent self-interest reinforced his old-fashioned liberalism. Jealous of the hydro-electric power plant, he felt cheated; corporate monopoly strategy had been advanced at his expense. A number of family enterprises, notably the arms manufacturers of the Val Trompia and the Val Sabbia, belonged to the Franchi faction.

As the traditional spokesmen of protectionist heavy industry, the Brescia nationalists instead promoted the electrical group's cause.[82] Their champion was Filippo Carli, secretary of the chamber of commerce. He argued that the government had already behaved with gross partiality as far as local steelmen were concerned; small, conservative companies should not have received hefty war contracts in the first place. To surrender control of Italy's hydro-electric resources to the clutches of provincial entrepreneurs would seal the fate of the national economy.[83] Concentration and bureaucratisation of production had to be made concomitants of state intervention. Carli's defence of the electrical firm was also motivated by his close ties to Giacinto Motta of the Edison complex. The Società Elettrica Bresciana, for its part, did not hesitate to embrace the Nationalist newspaper *Idea Nazionale*. The company had done well by the war and logically supported the continuation of high state expenditure and protection; the increase in its capital assets accounted for 14 per cent of the fresh investment in Brescia during the first eighteen months of combat.[84] For the engineer Ferrata, head of the Officine Riunite steelworks, prolongation of government collaboration was the key to the maintenance of factory discipline since the mobilisation system 'had adapted the scientific principles of Taylor to the Latin spirit and pride'.[85]

The rift between the nationalist camp and the old liberals generated great friction. Franchi's acrid attacks became regular events at the Camera di Commercio meetings until 1919, when he stopped attending them. Togni would usually be accused of selfishly promoting the invasion of local entrepreneurial autonomy, Carli denounced for trying to regiment employers. Franchi and Redaelli, another impresario in the nineteenth-century mould, both became patrons of Mussolini's *Popolo d'Italia*, which then seemed to take up the small producer's cause.[86]

Hostility was heightened by professional rivalry. For all his money and influence, the self-made Franchi could never rise to the stature of Togni, the authoritative leader of the provincial industrial establishment. His colleague's foresight reinforced Franchi's resentment, for Togni was among the few Brescian manufacturers to anticipate demobilisation when he balanced operations early in 1917. Co-ordinating factory dismissals with military discharges, he eased the transition to peace-time normality and managed to avoid the difficulties with labour that so plagued Franchi. All uniformed workers were transferred to the artillery plant, where lay-offs would occur.[87] Not only did all civilian employees continue to work with the firm on the production of seamless tubes, but Togni was also able to promise returning conscripts their former positions. Since the lucrative contract he had extracted from his Edison friends for the construction of water mains would require 500 more people on the assembly line, Togni could afford to be magnanimous with labour. Instead of ignoring the presence of trade unions, the modern employer promoted their growth 'in the interests of class collaboration'. Proposing to save his workers from the hands of 'miserly employers who speculate on the hunger of others', he opened a company co-operative.[88] In refusing to admit the newly-formed Catholic metalworkers' union on the Lombard mixed commission, the industrialist revealed his later inclination towards corporatism. Unlike Franchi and the majority of local employers who welcomed the entrance of a more moderate contender on the side of labour, Togni would only recognise the 'organised' representative of the metalworkers – FIOM.[89]

Instead of stubbornly resisting change, Togni followed the fashion. Although the firm's profits reached record levels in 1918, when the holding's capital doubled too, he sold out to the ILVA steel trust one year later.[90] Togni's resignation to post-competitive industrial concentration was, however, the exception. Franchi's position and outlook can be seen as more symptomatic of the general malaise afflicting north Italian steel concerns. While it was assumed that local companies had hoarded vast reserves by operating under monopoly conditions, the actual gains of the smaller manufacturers were in fact slight. Industrialists such as Franchi, Pietro Pasotti and Radaelli could compete for munitions orders only by undercutting the big outfits. Franchi, whose very survival depended on government contracting, offered to produce what Terni-Vickers Armstrong supplied, but at two-thirds their price. The Naples arsenal accepted Franchi's bid even though his plant was not equipped to meet the navy's specifications.[91] Some of Franchi's pig iron had to be processed by Ansaldo, which exacted immediate payment, to meet the requirements of his fussy client. The government, though, took months and often years to disburse, so that by November 1918 the armed forces ministries had run up an account of nearly 100 million lire.[92]

Reinforcing the marginality of non-trust firms, the economic mobilisation created an artificial market for provincial iron and steel. The situation was quite different in light industry. The principal effect of the war was to accelerate the transformation of textile manufacturing under way since the late nineteenth century. Only the most vigorous companies could recover from the succession of slumps that beset their international markets and withstand new foreign competition. The decline of hand weaving and silk spinning coincided with the concentration of larger, mechanised factories capable of expanding their units of production. Vittorio Olcese, for example, came from Milan in 1896 to manage the Feltrinelli cotton mill at Cogno.[93] During 1906 the mechanical engineer, backed by a Catholic financier, broke with his employers to set himself up in business. Starting with 120,000 spindles, he made good use of the hydro-electric resources of the Oglio river. Olcese's wartime military orders brought more credit opportunities and allowed him to absorb six smaller firms while forming larger units. By 1919 he had bought out the Feltrinelli brothers to operate a total of 234,000 spindles.[94] Similarly, in 1907 Emilio Antonioli founded the Lanificio di Manerbio, financed by two woollen manufacturers from Roubaix, and the company's capital stock grew from two to three million lire between 1912 and 1915, during which period units of production doubled. Antonioli cashed in on the war, clothing the Italian army, but his boom was based on sound expansion so it did not stop once the mobilisation ended. In 1919 he acquired full ownership of the company as the number of spindles under his control increased by 60 per cent.[95]

The textile manufacturers, less interested in association than employers in iron and steel, were more prone to individualism. It was the war which forced them to look to organisation. Light industry carried little weight in the mobilisation system; the ministry of arms and munitions assured the metallurgical and machine firms of a skilled labour force, making it difficult for the textile companies to maintain trained or regular workers.[96] Not only did the high wages paid in the metal trades sap light industry of experienced help, but with the price of *mano d'opera* up, wage reductions became almost impossible to effect. Though the textile manufacturers preferred to come to terms with labour independently of employer associations or trade unions, the war had rendered their conciliatory paternalism obsolete. The high mobility of labour established in the sector during the European conflict precluded any influence an employer once had over his operatives, especially since many were radicalised as a result of the war experience. Unable to exert an institutional leverage against self-assertive heavy industry, the textile notables could achieve nothing better than ineffective alliances limited to small, local issues. Giorgio Mylius, president of the Associazione Cotoniera Italiana, recognised the need to co-ordinate cotton interests. He tried to form a provincial pressure group in 1917 but found his colleagues poor recruits. While they seemed to favour an end to intervention and war-time controls on exports, their impatience and defensive mentality were not conducive to the development of long-term goals or collective action. When the area manufacturers responded to the 1918 crisis of the clothing market with habitual indiscipline, the Brescia cotton lobby collapsed.[97]

Farmers looked more aggressively to organisation. Provincial agriculture, the nationalist Ferrata complained, remained a backwater of landed property and conservative capital; he believed the state needed to take a tougher line with the lethargic Brescians and 'coerce' rural employers to mechanise their farming techniques.[98] The nationalist's static image of life in the countryside, however, is somewhat misleading for underneath the apparent stagnation and sloth real struggles smouldered. Power eluded the backward-looking landowners, and the initiative passed to the capitalist leaseholders, who numerically were in the minority. The proprietors nostalgically whined about their hungry peasants, 'who once were contented with half the crops but now erroneously think they are entitled to the security of contracts',[99] while tenant farmers instead took collective action. Although the provincial leaseholders lagged behind their impetuous neighbours in Mantua and Cremona, they did exert considerable local influence: nine basin mayors were tenant farmers. The issue of taxation on war profits prompted these self-made men to form their own association and, under the leadership of Tommaso Nember, the *grandi affittuari* concerned themselves with labour relations as well.[100] Nember's group favoured an agricultural mobilisation of labour which would provide government protection to employers and regiment workers in the interests of rural modernisation.[101] Despite the pressures of agrarian spokesmen throughout the Po Valley, state intervention in farm management was not forthcoming at the national level. But in the Brescia plains, leaseholders mustered all their connections in local politics to succeed where their Emilian associates had failed. During the spring of 1917 the prefect finally authorised a seasonal migration of sorts when hundreds of soldiers, paid at the going rate for casual workers, were despatched to the fields. At the height of the labour shortage in wool, the ability to drain male hands from textiles showed a new collective sophistication unmatched by other employer groups.[102]

Almost imperceptibly, the countryside had changed. The quiet life was over, the old indifference gone. The organisational coherence of the leaseholders testified to a growing public sensitivity. Aware of their marginal position in the provincial order of things, the prosperous farmers sought to assume a political importance in the municipal scene despite their small numbers. The rising rural bourgeois were not simply agrarians but active entrepreneurs. Giovanni Battista Bianchi, mayor of Maderno, did not confine himself to farming: he had purse strings in four small cotton factories of the Veneto.[103] Emanuele Bertazzoli, founder of the Consorzio Agrario di Bagnolo Mella, toyed with speculative land reclamation projects in Cremona and helped establish two local chemical concerns. Carlo Gorio, who like Nember was tied to the Credito Agrario Bresciano in which the Banca Commerciale also had a stake, even ventured into national politics. Before forming the Consorzio Co-operativo at Orzinuovi, the senator had been involved in silk production.[104]

As the war drew to a close, notables in both the basin and the town looked confidently to the future. The last three decades, Filippo Carli felt, had reinvigorated the upper classes by giving them a national consciousness and some sense of purpose. The nationalist believed the bourgeoisie was in a position to be disinterested as a result of intervention and advocated workers' participation in profits to make up for past employer 'infantilism'. For the liberals had been something of a tease with the masses: 'we thought the proletariat could be seduced with political liberties while the workers really wanted economic freedom.'[105] The post-war emphasis should be on class collaboration; labour would get non-voting shares in the firm while capital maintained control.

Other members of the chamber of commerce were not so easily persuaded to adopt such a conciliatory approach. The influence of industry perhaps widened after intervention, but the government had served as a buttress. Spoiled by state mediation during the mobilisation, many employers now seemed afraid to go it alone. They counted on continued protection from Rome to make Carli's social paternalism superfluous:

> we want these workers truly to understand that real, lasting con-
> quests cannot be obtained through ill-advised labour action or by
> violent, immature demonstrations; therefore, we propose that
> obligatory arbitration be established and that all work stoppages
> be outlawed.[106]

With demobilised soldiers returning home and local workers freed from military restrictions in the shops, the initial optimism of more business-men began to fade. The Camera del Lavoro suddenly boasted over 10,000 adherents; after a two month slump, the provincial PSI increased its pre-war numbers fivefold.[107] Moreover, popular discontent, especially acute in the countryside, stimulated non-socialist militancy and the CGL, which had operated under monopoly conditions during the mobilisation, soon had competition. The numerical possibilities of the Catholic union move-ment made the town's liberal guardians jumpy. The war changed the terms of social conflict in Italy, and the province of Brescia slowly syn-chronised with the rest of the peninsula. Forced to look beyond parochial boundaries, conscripts returned from the trenches embittered. The mobilisation of labour had been a corollary of the war economy, so those exempt from serving on the front could not preserve their isolation either. But while the harsh, insecure conditions of work radicalised a large part of the provincial labour force, the divergent interests of its members deferred the development of a well-organised trade union movement. Though collaboration with the economic effort caused membership in the unions to swell, it also laid bare the working-class community's weakest sinew – the territorial division of reformist and revolutionary strike action. The structural provincialism of proletarian politics remained intact during the war, which did no more than incor-porate doctrinal disputes into the organisational stuff of Italian socialism.

The war had equally equivocal consequences for the world of industry. The momentum of the mobilisation provoked the rapid but precarious expansion of provincial iron and steel; state support allowed the problems of industrial rationalisation and employer association to be eluded, though the more prescient leaders saw the need for both. Ultimately what seemed to present opportunity for small competitive business doomed local entrepreneurial autonomy: by ushering in concentration, the war mobilisation disturbed Brescia's economic seclusion.[108] As the state assumed an activist role in advance of cartellisation and the resolu-tion of social discord, public and private domains began to overlap.

Notes

1. One exception to this trend is A. Caracciolo, 'La crescita e la trasformazione della grande industria durante la prima guerra mondiale', in G. Fuà, *Lo sviluppo economico in Italia*, vol. III (Milan, 1969).

2. M. Clark does shed light on factory conditions in Turin during the First World War, see *Antonio Gramsci and the Revolution that Failed* (New Haven, 1977).

3. B. Benedini, *Terra e agricoltori nel circondario di Brescia* (Brescia, 1881).

4. A. Sapori, *Attività manufatturiera in Lombardia dal 1600 al 1914* (Milan, 1959), pp. 164-6; A. De Maddalena, 'L'economia bresciana nei secoli XIX e XX', in *Storia di Brescia*, vol. IV (Brescia, 1963), pp. 559-62.

5. *Atti della Giunta per l'Inchiesta agraria e sulle conditizioni della classe agricola*, vol. VI, fasc. 2 (Rome, 1882), p. 295.

6. G. Zanardelli, *Notizie naturali, industriali ed artistiche della provincia di Brescia* (Brescia, 1904), p. 90.

7. G. Robecchi, *L'industria del ferro in Italia e l'officina Glisenti a Carcina* (Milan, 1868), pp. 8-9.

8. G. Zanardelli, *Notizie naturali*, pp. 107-9; see also A. Giarratana, *L'industria bresciana ed i suoi negli ultimi 50 anni* (Brescia, 1957), pp. 66-7.

9. Quoted in O. Cavallieri, *Il movimento operaio e contadino nel Bresciano (1878-1903)* (Rome, 1972), p. 65; see also U. Vaglia, *L'arte del ferro in Valle Sabbia e la famiglia Glisenti* (Brescia, 1959), pp. 5-15.

10. Quoted in Camera di Commercio e Industria di Brescia, *L'economia bresciana. (Struttura economica della provincia di Brescia)*, vol. IIa (Brescia, 1927), p. 41.

11. A. Giarratana, *L'industria bresciana*, p. 67; M. Cominazzi, *Cenni sulla fabbrica d'armi di Gardone di Valtrompia* (Brescia, 1861), pp. 2-13; G. Luscia, 'Sulla proposta formazione di una Società Anonima Bresciana per l'industria del ferro in Valtrompia', in *Commentari dell'Ateneo di Brescia* (1865-1867) pp. 69-72.

12. A. De Maddalena, 'L'economia bresciana', p. 561; Camera di Commercio e Industria di Brescia, *L'economia bresciana*, vol. IIa, p. 125; B. Benedini, 'Sulle industrie e sui commerci bresciani', in *Commentari dell'Ateneo di Brescia* (1882), pp. 180-2.

13. F. Ghidotti, *Palazzolo 1890. Notizie sull'agricoltura, l'industria e il commercio e sulle condizioni fisiche, morali, intellettuali, economiche della popolazione* (Palazzolo sull'Oglio, 1969), pp. 16-18; A. Giarratana, 'L'industria nei secoli XIX e XX', in *Storia di Brescia*, vol. IV (Brescia, 1963), pp. 1018-19; T. Spini, *Niggeler e Kupfer S.p.A. Filatura e tessitura di cotone (1876-1963)*; G. Luzzatto, *Storia economica dell'età moderna e contemporanea*, vol. II (Padua, 1948), pp. 399-400.

14. Camera di Commercio e Industria di Brescia, *L'economia bresciana*, vol. IIa, pp. 121-8; for similar patterns of development in the Veneto see S. Lanaro, *Società e ideologie nel Veneto rurale (1866-1898)* (Rome, 1976), pp. 49-57.

15. D. Brentana. *La vita di un comune montano* (Brescia, 1934); A. Fossati, *Lavoro e produzione in Italia dalla metà del secolo XVIII alla seconda guerra mondiale* (Turin, 1951), p. 170; C. Seton-Watson, *Italy from Liberalism to Fascism: 1870-1925* (London, 1967), pp. 78-81; A. Gerschenkron, *Economic Backwardness in Historical Perspective* (Cambridge, Mass., 1962), pp. 74-9.

16. De Maddalena 'L'economia bresciana', pp. 570-5; Camera di Commercio e Industria di Brescia, *Statistica Industriale al 30 Gennaio 1911. Industrie Varie* (Brescia, 1911), pp. 5-6.

17. Camera di Commercio, *Statistica Industriale*; U. Vaglia, *L'arte del ferro*, pp. 15-16.

18. Camera di Commercio e Industria di Brescia, *Statistica Industriale al 30 Giugno 1910. Industrie Mineralurgiche, Metallurgiche e Meccaniche* (Brescia, 1910), pp. 15-28.

19. R. Webster, *Industrial Imperialism in Italy 1908-1915* (Berkeley, 1975), pp. 87-8; A. Giarratana, *L'industria bresciana*, pp. 48-9.

20. Giarratana, *L'industria bresciana*, pp. 51-2; *Le officine metallurgiche Togni in Brescia* (Milan, 1912).

21. Camera di Commercio ed Arti della Provincia di Brescia, *Sul progetto di un Consorzio per al tutela degli interessi serici* (Brescia, 1908), pp. 3-4

22. Camera di Commercio e Industria di Brescia, *L'economia bresciana*, vol. IIa, p. 126; see also R. Romeo, *Breve storia della grande industria in Italia* (Rocca San Casciano, 1961), pp. 68-70.

23. *Tubi Togni. Condotte forzate 1903-1923* (Milan, 1926), pp. 2-5.

24. R. Webster, *Industrial Imperialism in Italy*, p. 88; Camera di Commercio e Industria di Brescia, *Constituzioni, Modificazioni, Scioglimenti di Società* (Brescia, 1911).

25. Archivio Centrale dello Stato (ACS), Min. Interno, Direzione Generale di Pubblica Sicurezza (DGRPS), Serie G1, Associazioni, b. 8, fasc. Camera del Lavoro, for Federazione Italiana Operai Metallurgici (FIOM) membership see 'Elenco delle Organizzazioni', May 1914.

26. A. Pepe, *Storia della CGdL dalla guerra di Libia all'intervento 1911-1915* (Bari, 1971); in 1912 Brescia reported the lowest percentage (33.8) of strike participants in all of Lombardy, p. 350.

27. *La Provincia di Brescia* (16, 21 and 23 September 1914); *Avanti!* (16 and 20 March 1915).

28. ACS, Presidenza del Consiglio, Prima Guerra Mondiale, fasc. 17.2, Brescia, sfasc. 1, 8 August and 20 September 1914, sfasc. 4, 2 October 1914.

29. Ibid., sfasc. 6, Società Lombarde Ligure, 4, 9 and 29 September 1914.

30. *La Provincia di Brescia* (5 and 8 July 1914).

31. Camera dei Deputati, *Atti Parlamentari del Regno d'Italia*, Legislatura XXVI (1921-1923), documento XXI, vol. II (Rome, 1923), pp. 108-9; the Comitato Centrale di Mobilitazione Industriale (CCMI), founded during the summer of 1915 under Dallolio's direction, administered the distribution of war contracts and primary materials to industry. Although those employed in the firms granted 'auxiliary' status were exempt from active service, they had to observe army disciplinary regulations. Regional committees of arbitration were set up to mediate disputes between workers and employers, and the CGL sat as labour's sole representative on these mixed commissions. L. Einaudi, *La condotta economica e gli effetti sociali della guerra italiana* (Bari and New Haven, 1933), pp. 99-111.

32. Archivio di Stato di Brescia (ASB), Fondo Camera di Commercio, R. Arsenale, Contratti di Guerra, b. 11-21, April-September 1915; ACS, Min. Armi e Munizioni, CCMI, b. 2, fasc. Brescia, sfasc. 6 (catalogue, n.d.).

33. Camera di Commercio e Industria di Brescia *Statistica Industriale al 30 Giugno 1910*, pp. 15-22.

34. F. Carli, *Problemi e possibilità del dopo-guerra nella provincia di Brescia. II: Inchiesta sui salari nel 1915 e 1916* (Brescia, 1917), pp. 14-15.

35. Camera di Commercio e Industria di Brescia, *L'economia bresciana*, vol. IIb, p. 76.

36. ACS, Mostra della Rivoluzione Fascista (MRF), b. 81, fasc. Confederazione Lavoro, 24 September 1915 and 29 May 1916.

37. Ibid., 12 August 1915.

38. *Almanacco Socialista Italiano* (Milan, 1921), pp. 480-1.

39. ACS, Min. Interno, DGRPS, Serie G1, Associazioni, b. 8, fasc. Camera del Lavoro, 4 and 26 July 1917.

40. Real wages in industry, 1915-26:

Brescia all sectors		Brescia heavy industry	Italy all sectors
1914	100,000	100,000	100,000
1915	103,69	99,71	93,73
1916	134,63	125,08	85,25
1917	135,87	114,73	73,28
1918	108,96	88,66	64,79
1919	94,62	83,66	93,41
1920	114,37	100,27	114,75
1921	125,65	109,91	127,39
1922	129,92	107,79	123,98
1923	132,82	121,95	116,40
1924	126,60	122,52	112,96
1925	126,16	121,67	112,15
1926	124,37	114,30	111,82

Source: Camera di Commercio e Industria di Brescia, *L'economia bresciana*, vol. IIb, pp. 50-126, and A. Fossati, *Lavoro XVIII*, p. 634.

41. ACS, Min. Interno, Casellario Politico Centrale, fasc. 1932, E. Falchero, 26 November 1915.

42. ACS, Min. Armi e Munizioni, CCMI, b. 232, Comando di Brescia, 19 February 1917.

43. Ibid., b. 215, Unione Professionale Triumplina, 7 January 1917.

44. Ibid., Comando di Brescia, 24 September 1917.

45. Ibid., b. 222, Comitato Lombardo, 16 April 1918.

46. Ibid., b. 215, Comando di Brescia, 1 February 1918; see also ACS, MRF, b. 14, fasc. Comitato Regionale Lombardo, 13 September and 11 October 1918.

47. Camera di Commercio e Industria di Brescia, *L'economia bresciana*, vol. IIb, p. 96; F. Carli, *Problemi e possibilità*, appendix.

48. ACS, Min. Armi e Munizioni, CCMI, b. 222, verbale, 21 May 1918.

49. Ibid., b. 216, 16 April 1918; Camera di Commercio e Industria di Brescia, *Variazioni nel costo della vita e nei salari a Brescia prima, durante e dopo la guerra* (Brescia, 1920), Table II.

50. ACS, Min. Armi e Munizioni, CCMI, b. 133, fasc. 1, 'Caroviveri', September 1917.

51. ACS, Min. Interno, DGRPS, Serie G1, Associazioni, b. 8, fasc. sindacato ferrovieri, 22 July 1914; Camera di Commercio e Industria di Brescia, *L'economia bresciana*, vol. IIb, p. 123.

52. Ibid., p. 97.

53. F. Carli, *Problemi e possibilità*, pp. 18-20.

54. ACS, Min. Armi e Munizioni, CCMI, b. 70, fasc. mano d'opera feminile, Comando di Brescia, 13 June 1918.

55. Ibid., b. 232, verbale, 21 July 1917.

56. Ibid., b. 171, fasc. 43, verbale, 1 April 1918.

57. Ibid., 5 May 1918.

58. Ibid., 20 June and 6 July 1918.

59. Ibid., 15 May 1918.

60. Abrate, *La lotta sindacale nella industrializzazione in Italia 1906-1926* (Turin, 1967), pp. 176-81.

61. ACS, Min. Armi e Munizioni, CCMI, b. 171, fasc. 43, verbale, 1 and 2 April 1918.

62. Ibid., 10 May 1918.

63. Ibid., 11 May 1918; b. 71, fasc. 78, Metallurgica Bresciana, 10 and 11 May 1918.

64. ACS, Presidenza del Consiglio, Prima Guerra Mondiale, fasc. 19.25, F. Turati, 12 December 1918.

65. ACS, Min. Armi e Munizioni, CCMI, b. 215, verbale, 5 July 1918.

66. Ibid., Federazione Nazionale Metallurgica, 13 August 1918.

67. Ibid., b. 71, fasc. 78, Comitato Lombardo, 23 July 1918.

68. Ibid., b. 215, verbale, 12 June 1918.

69. Ibid., b. 171, fasc. 43, Comando di Brescia, 8 September 1918.

70. ACS, Presidenza del Consiglio, Prima Guerra Mondiale, fasc. 19.25, F. Turati, 13 December 1918.

71. ACS, MRF, b. 81, fasc. Confederazione Lavoro, riunione del consiglio direttivo, 16 July 1918; R. Bachi, *L'Italia economica nel 1918* (Città del Castello, 1919), p. 309.

72. ACS, MRF, b. 14, fasc. Comitato Regionale Lombardo, 11 October 1918.

73. Ibid., 13 September 1918.

74. R. Bachi, *L'Italia economica nel 1916* (Citta del Castello, 1917), pp. 212-15; S. Golzio, *L'industria dei metalli in Italia* (Turin, 1942), p. 55; A. Fossati, *Lavoro XVIII*, p. 471.

75. A. Fossati, *Lavoro XVIII*, p. 522; G. Scagnetti, *La siderurgia in Italia* (Rome, 1923), pp. 281-2; R. Webster, *Industrial Imperialism*, pp. 88-9.

76. G. Mori, 'Le guerre parallele. L'industria elettrica in Italia nel periodo della grande guerra (1914-1919)', *Studi Storici*, XIV (1973) pp. 319-35; L. Einaudi, *La condotta economica*, pp. 157-9.

77. A. Giarratana, *L'industria bresciana*, p. 53; E. Barni, *Per una politica della acque* (Brescia, 1917), pp. 14-16.

78. Credito Italiano, *Società Italiane per Azioni. Notizie Statistiche 1922* (Rome, 1923), p. 1166; see also *Le società idroelettriche e la recente legislazione* (Brescia, 1917), pp. 14-16.

79. ACS, Presidenza del Consiglio, 1918, fasc. 3.986, Prefect of Bergamo, 13 November 1918; Franchi did, however, receive smaller hydro-electric concessions, see G. Scagnetti, *La siderurgia in Italia*, p. 339.

80. ACS, Min. Armi e Munizioni, CCMI, b. 71, fasc. 78, Operai: Ditta Franchi, 17 March 1918.

81. Ibid., b. 70, fasc. mano d'opera feminile, 13 June 1918; b. 232, Comando di Brescia, 12 January 1917 and 13 April 1918.

82. A. Lyttelton, *The Seizure of Power, Fascism in Italy 1919-1929* (London, 1973), pp. 206-7.

83. *Idea Nazionale*, 10 December 1916; D. Civilta, *Il problema idroelettrico in Italia e l'attività delle Imprese Elettriche* (Rome, 1922).

84. F. Carli, *Problemi e possibilità del dopo-guerra nella provincia di Brescia. III: Inchiesta sul capitale e sulla tecnica* (Brescia, 1917), p. 7.

85. M. Ferrata, *La mobilitazione industriale e il dopo-guerra* (Brescia, 1917), p. 7.

86. R. De Felice, *Mussolini il rivoluzionario, 1883-1920* (Turin, 1965), pp. 467-8.

87. *La Provincia di Brescia* (23 January 1919).

88. ACS, Min. Armi e Munizioni, CCMI, b. 223, verbale, 5 September 1918.

89. *La Provincia di Brescia* (27 December 1918).

90. Credito Italiano, *Società Italiane per Azioni. Notizie Statistiche 1920* (Rome, 1921), p. 777; R. Bachi, *L'Italia economica nel 1919* (Città del Castello, 1920), p. 181.

91. Camera dei Deputati, *Atti Parlamentari*, p. 47.

92. ACS, Presidenza del Consiglio, 1918, fasc. 3.986, Prefect of Bergamo, 29 October 1918.

93. *Il Cotonificio Vittorio Olcese nelle sue origini, nelle sue vicende, e nella sua attività* (Milan, 1939), pp. 3-10.

94. Camera di Commercio e Industria di Brescia, *L'Industria Tessile al 1 Gennaio 1923* (Brescia, 1923), pp. 50-5.

95. A. Giarratana, *L'industria bresciana*, pp. 92-3.

96. ACS, Min. Armi e Munizioni, CCMI, decreti di ausiliarità, b. 2, fasc. Brescia, sfasc. 6, cc. 13, 10 September 1915.

97. *La Provincia di Brescia* (15 February 1919).

98. M. Ferrata, *La Mobilitazione*, pp. 6-7.

99. *La Provincia di Brescia* (24 August 1918).

100. Ibid., (11 April and 2 September 1916).

101. Ibid., 14 January 1917; see also F. Piva, 'Mobilitazione agraria e tendenze all'associazionismo padronale durante la grande guerra', *Quaderni Storici*, XII (1977) pp. 808-35.

102. *La Provincia di Brescia* (21 March 1917).

103. See G. Bianchi, *Per l'agricoltura e per i contadini nel 'dopo guerra'* (Brescia, 1919), pp. 13-14, 20-1.

104. A. Giarratana, 'L'industria nei secoli XIX e XX', pp. 1135-7; ASB, Gabinetto della Prefettura, b. 28, fasc. 21, Bertazzoli (n.d. but April 1917); ACS, Presidenza del Consiglio, Prime Guerra Mondiale, fasc. 17.2, sfasc. 2, Camera di Commercio, 7 August 1914.

105. F. Carli, *La partecipazione degli operai alle imprese* (Brescia, 1918), pp. 4-5, 18.

106. M. Ferrata, *La Mobilitazione*, p. 11.

107. *Avanti!* (8 April 1919); *Almanacco Socialista Italiano*, p. 481.

108. Camera di Commercio e Industria di Brescia, *Intorno al problema del cambio* (Brescia, 1917), pp. 10-14.

8 FASCIST AGRARIAN POLICY AND THE ITALIAN ECONOMY IN THE INTER-WAR YEARS

Paul Corner

Fascism as economic stagnation

The structure and workings of the Italian economy under fascism attracted considerable interest among scholars — both Italian and non-Italian — during the course of the 1930s. Sereni, Grifone, Rosenstock-Franck, Welk, Schmidt, Einzig, Guerin — these and others published studies either during or immediately after the fall of the regime.[1] Surprisingly, this interest did not continue in the years after the war. Until very recently historians have tended to direct their attention to the origins of fascism and to the early development of the regime, to its organisation and structure, and to the foreign policy of Mussolini and his ultimate entanglement with Hitler. Economic historians, on the other hand, have been far more interested in discussing the process of industrialisation in Italy prior to the First World War or in identifying and weighing the relative importance of the various factors which produced the economic miracle of the late 1950s and early 1960s. In general, there has been a tendency to neglect the 1930s in Italy, to move from the formation of the regime to the problems of the reconstruction after the Second World War, and, as a consequence, the Italian economy under fascism has been largely ignored. At most, the formation of state holding companies (IMI and IRI) has merited comment as representing interesting forerunners of economic institutions which would become generalised after the war.[2]

The failure to follow up the debate has several explanations. In part it undoubtedly reflects the feeling that the real novelty of fascism lay in its political rather than economic expression. To some extent it may also be attributed to the fact that, whereas the origins of fascism and the post-war reconstruction are issues which lend themselves directly to present-day political debate in Italy, the fascist economy has appeared to be very much less relevant. But more important perhaps — and clearly underlying both points made above — is the feeling, openly expressed in many works, that there is little or nothing of significance to be said, that the corporative state was never a reality, and that fascist pretensions to have an original approach to the problems of managing the economy produced far more rhetoric than real achievement. Some writers have even suggested that the fascists were not really interested in economics; that economic development as a national goal was something much too weak and degrading for Mussolini. Here the emphasis is placed on the political aims of fascism, the economy clearly relegated to second place where it is mentioned at all. In other authors, there appears what is in many ways an extension of this view. Fascism is seen as provoking *necessarily* a period of economic stagnation because of an intrinsic conflict between the social priorities of fascism and the changes inevitably brought about by economic development. Absence of economic growth is considered the price paid for the maintenance of social stability and of certain positions of privilege within Italian society. It is argued that a halt to economic development was precisely the condition for the survival of those privileges; it was only without economic growth that the social pressures accompanying that growth could be avoided. Social conservatism impeded the 'normal' evolution of the productive forces of Italian capitalism, therefore, and simply 'crystallised' the economy as it was at the advent of fascism.[3] Fascism is defined as 'a fundamental economic stagnation on the basis of a compromise to conserve a social order at a backward level'.[4]

It is not difficult to understand why this view prevailed throughout the 1950s and 1960s and still has its supporters today. The economic development of Italy since the Second World War has served to provide a vivid contrast with the preceding period, undoubtedly far less dramatic in terms of economic progress. And, for differing political motives, it has been convenient for the principal anti-fascist parties to stress the different scale of economic development achieved under a liberal, democratic regime as opposed to a fascist dictatorship, and, indeed, to attribute that development in part to the different political context in which it has been achieved. The Christian Democrats have had a very obvious interest in encouraging comparison between the economic miracle, achieved under their auspices, and the years of apparent stagnation under fascism. The Italian Communist Party has also tended to make the same comparison. For long attached to the interpretation of fascism promulgated at the seventh congress of the International in 1935, the Communists have stressed that fascism was the political expression of a restricted clique of monopoly capitalists, financiers and landowners — all of whom, in order to preserve their positions, distorted the 'normal' pattern of economic development and impeded the growth of the 'progressive' forces of Italian capitalism and the formation of a strong progressive bourgeoisie, with whom the Communists hoped to form an alliance. The economic progress of the post-war years was welcomed, therefore, in as far as it freed these progressive forces apparently frustrated by fascist stagnation and opened the way to the alliance strategy. That fascism was both socially reactionary *and* economically regressive became a fundamental tenet of this strategy.[5]

Nor, of course, is it difficult to find elements within fascism which would appear to justify this interpretation. There were, for example, strong currents of 'anti-capitalism' among the early fascists; many of them took a considerable time to realise that, after crippling the socialist movement, they could not simply turn round and begin to dictate terms to the landowners and industrialists who had encouraged their anti-socialist campaign.[6] Suggestions of 'anti-capitalism' remained throughout the regime and were sufficiently strong at times to worry a few of the leading industrialists.[7] Certainly the first fascist government, if it clearly rejected anti-capitalism, had no real economic policy beyond that of reducing as far as possible the intervention of the state in economic matters. In its 'Manchesterian' phase, fascism stressed the importance of political will rather than economic manoeuvring in overcoming the economic difficulties which faced Italy. And, if this phase soon passed, and fascism was forced to intervene more and more in the running of the economy, the regime was always eager to present itself as being substantially different from other Western capitalist countries and concerned to pursue different goals. In this respect, Mussolini's attacks on the evils of 'supercapitalism' seemed to demonstrate a rejection of the traditional economic values of the capitalist West and an intention to replace those values with something radically different.

But the approach which has stressed the economically regressive and 'stagnationist' character of fascism has always drawn greatest support from the emphasis placed by the regime on agriculture. It is the championing of the agricultural sector which appears most anachronistic in a country already well advanced in the process of industrialisation. The battle for wheat, the land reclamation programmes, the laws against movement from the rural areas, above all the great propaganda slogan of ruralisation – all appeared to conflict with the logic of the further development of an industrial economy. Moreover, the terms on which ruralisation was justified went far beyond a straightforward desire to strengthen the secondary sector for the overall good of the economy. Mussolini, a vociferous exponent of the theme of ruralisation ('we must ruralise Italy, even if it needs millions and takes half a century')[8] argued that the one way in which Italy could avoid the evils of supercapitalism lay through a 'return to the land' of those who had recently left rural areas for the towns. In this manner, the sterility of industrial society – considered to lie at the root of the 'crisis of modern civilisation' – could be avoided and the supposedly healthy qualities of a rural society maintained. But the intention was not to renounce the struggle with other nations; rather it was suggested that through the expression of superior moral values characteristic of a predominantly rural society Italy would in the end show herself superior to other Western nations so clearly in crisis. Thus moral and ideological consider-ations clearly outweighed more mundane economic calculations; indeed, it seemed implicit in the glorification of rural society that it was only by restraining the growth of industry that the alleged stability of that society could be maintained.[9]

Many practical expressions of fascist agrarian policy have seemed to confirm that this was what the regime aimed to achieve. The reintro-duction of a high level of grain protection in 1925 is seen as reinforcing those agricultural figures synonymous with backwardness and pre-capitalist relations of production – the Southern *latifondisti*. These, it is argued, were able to survive well into the twentieth century because of the preferential tariff treatment accorded them, but at the cost of retarding the progress of the Italian economy. Whereas a radical change in the structure of southern agriculture would, in the long run, have been beneficial for all areas of the economy, increasing the overall value of agricultural production and serving to enlarge the size of the internal market through a better distribution of national income, fascism chose instead to protect the *latifondisti* and conserve the social and econo-mic structure of the South. It is precisely because of what is considered to be the renewed weight of the backward southern landowners within the political alliance which fascism represented that Sereni feels able to speak of 'the transformation of Italian society in an agrarian direction' during the fascist period.[10]

Policies concerned with the relations of production in agriculture appear similarly anachronistic. The defence and development of a class of small peasant proprietors (*la piccola proprietà coltivatrice*) and the efforts to reduce the number of landless wage labourers by offering them sharecropping contracts (the policy of *sbracciantizzazione*) appeared to run against the general trend of capitalist development in agriculture. The defence of the small proprietor appeared to conflict with the more obviously modern policies of rationalisation and mech-anisation of holdings on the basis of large-scale production and the reduction of unit costs. Its justification was couched in moral and social rather than economic terms; the small proprietor was seen as an important element of social stability, strongly independent and individualist, and a sturdy defender of the family on whom he relied for so much of his labour. Equally the policy of *sbracciantizzazione* appeared to conflict with the interests of many of the capitalist farms of the North which relied on the desperate conditions of over-population in th countryside to guarantee them low-cost labour. With the defeat of the socialist organisations, it might have been expected that farmers would once again rely on the free-for-all of the labour market to ensure low-cost labour. Instead they persisted in putting forward the policy of *sbracciantizzazione* through sharecropping contracts, at least in appearances moving away from pure capitalist relations of production through a straightforward wage relationship and towards those pre-capitalist forms of production they had done so much to destroy during the previous 50 years. Again the rationale behind this policy was expressed in terms of social stability rather than economic benefit, suggesting that where farmers were forced to choose between continued rapid capitalist development and social stability, they chose the latter.

A Reappraisal

The evidence for the 'stagnationist', 'anti-economic' interpretation of fascism may seem irrefutable; yet recently this view has been subjected to criticism. A closer examination of the structure and financing of Italian industry under fascism has led to a radical reappraisal of the development of the Italian economy during the 1920s and 1930s. Attention is drawn to the considerable industrial expansion which took place between 1922 and 1929, to the way in which Italy weathered the international crisis, and to the rapid recovery of industrial production after 1934. Moreover it has been pointed out that a simple quantitative assessment of industrial production neglects many of the important *qualitative* changes which took place in the structure and methods of finance of Italian industry. Here the reference is to the progress made by several of the more 'modern' industries — notably the chemical and electrical industries — within the industrial structure, to the strengthening and concentration of the basic heavy industries of iron and steel, to the growth of the engineering industry, and — most important — to the decisive intervention of the state in the direction and financing of industry through the creation of IMI and IRI. These changes, it is suggested, were of importance not only during the 1930s when protectionist policies and economic sanctions virtually isolated the Italian economy from the economies of other nations, but also in the period after 1945 when Italy moved towards the 'economic miracle'.[11]

As is clear, this reassessment of the economy under fascism has tended to stress changes in, or relating to, the industrial sector. How, then, does agriculture fit in to the picture? Is it possible to make a similar reassessment for the sector which, as has been seen above, has for long been considered the bastion of those conservative and economically regressive forces which constituted the real victors under fascism? Broadly, there are two issues in question here. Did fascist agrarian policies, as put into practice within the agricultural sector, really harm the interests of capitalist agriculture and promote those of *rentier* landlords and backward *latifondisti*? And, secondly, is it realistic to interpret the emphasis given to ruralisation and 'rurality' in fascist propaganda as an indication that the agricultural sector was becoming relatively more important as fascism turned away from economic policies which aimed at the formation of an industrial economy? We will seek to answer these questions in the following pages.

The Application and Impact of the Agrarian Policies of Fascism

Fascism achieved its first major successes at least in part because of the agrarian policies it put forward. In many northern provinces, the important innovations promised in the structure of landholding and the relations of production produced a wave of sympathy for the fascist cause. The original agrarian policy presented in the first months of 1921 held out hopes that a social pacification of the countryside could be achieved on the basis of the slogan 'the land to he who works it and makes it flourish' and urged a greater degree of collaboration between employer and employed. Exploiting expectations raised by war-time promises made by Italian governments to the troops, the policy had some initial success among those who hoped to own a piece of land of their own. Yet the impetus of the first months was soon lost; in practice the fascist agrarian programme was modified and watered down after March 1921.[12] Agrarians became aware very rapidly of the problem of reconciling the continued existence of large-scale agricultural concerns with many aspects of the policy proposed by the fascists and acrimonious debates developed during 1921 between those who had accepted the agrarian programme in good faith and those who wished to back down on many of the pledges made. As a consequence, while the movement continued to advocate publicly both the extension of the class of small proprietors and a reduction in the number of landless labourers through 'association', 'participation' and 'class collaboration', it was to this second aspect of the programme that most emphasis was given. In many northern provinces where socialist policies had aimed at the proletarianisation of all the intermediate groups of leaseholders and sharecroppers, the fascists began a concerted effort to reinforce these categories. As the socialists rightly saw, the unity they had sought to create among the rural classes was being systematically undermined by a policy directed to precisely the opposite end.[13] Where that form of limited sharecropping which most affected the landless workers (*compartecipazione*[14]) had been abandoned under the pressure of the socialist leagues, it was immediately restored. Where the socialists had succeeded in abolishing the category of fixed contract labourers (*obbligati*), fresh contracts were signed and former *obbligati* restored to their positions. And where landowners had been prevented from signing or renewing contracts with *mezzadri*, they immediately made new agreements. Relatively little land changed hands as a result of the fascist land programme. Far from that division of holdings which the first fascist agrarian programme had encouraged many people to expect, the early years of fascism saw a gradual strengthening of the intermediate categories in agriculture – sharecroppers and small leaseholders – and a fresh increase in the number of fixed contract labourers and other dependent labourers.

Subsequent years served to confirm this pattern. Official statistics, unreliable as they certainly are, none the less suggest the trend which underlies the changes in the relations of production during these years. The census reports show that a measure of *sbracciantizzazione* was undoubtedly realised. The percentage of landless workers in agriculture (*lavoratori*) fell between 1921 and 1936 from approximately 44 per cent of the total population active in agriculture to 28 per cent; the number of officially classified landless day labourers (*braccianti* or *lavoratori a giornata*) fell even more rapidly – from 39 per cent to 19 per cent. A closer look at the statistics shows how this had been realised, however. There was no overall increase in the number of proprietors; the categories which expand are those of leaseholders, occupying in the main very small units (from 7 per cent in 1921 to 18 per cent in 1936), and the independent sharecroppers or *coloni parziari* (from 15 per cent to 19 per cent).[15] The dramatic fall in the number of landless day labourers reflected the tendency in certain provinces to expand the categories of fixed contract labourers and *compartecipanti*. In the province of Ferrara, for example, where the socialists had succeeded in organising some 70,000 *braccianti* in 1920 and had used this strength to prohibit the employment of both fixed labourers and *compartecipanti*, the census of 1936 shows some 43,000 *compartecipanti*, while the fixed labourers total 5,722. A similar pattern is suggested by the census

figures for the neighbouring province of Rovigo — 28,153 *comparteci-*
panti, 4,148 fixed labourers and only 27,733 officially recognised day
labourers.[16] Such figures evidently permitted the fascists to vaunt a
massive reduction in the number of *braccianti* employed in agriculture
while at the same time saying nothing about the real conditions under
which the majority of the landless labourers were employed.

The reorganisation of the agricultural labour force evidently served
more than simple propaganda purposes, however. The obvious interpretation to be put on these changes — and that conventionally forwarded
— is that of social pacification, understood in the sense of breaking the
back of organised labour and reinforcing socially stable forms of cultivation of which sharecropping was the most favoured. It is suggested
that fascism sought, through the division of the rural labour force and
the restoration of certain forms of sharecropping, to move away from
the simple wage relationship in agriculture in an attempt to protect
landowners and farmers from the perils accompanying pure capitalist
relations of production.

Unquestionably, the first fascist agrarian programme was intended
to offer incentives to workers to desert the socialist movement. Yet the
same policies of *sbracciantizzazione* and reinforcement of the intermediate groups in agriculture continued to be followed with considerable energy in later years, particularly during the crisis years of 1927-33.
It becomes necessary to ask why the fascists remained so attached to
these policies in times in which, quite obviously, after the monumental
collapse of rural socialism in 1921-2, they had the means to maintain
social stability without resorting to major restructuring of the relations
of production in agriculture. It is also necessary to ask why it was
precisely the most advanced areas of agricultural capitalism — Emilia,
Lombardy, the lower Veneto — which seemed most enthusiastic promo-
ters of a policy apparently so much in conflict with the furtherance of
their capitalist interests.

Reasons for such behaviour can be found in an examination of the
choices which landowners and large capitalist farmers faced during
moments of economic crisis. Broadly speaking, the choices were, on the
one hand, a reduction of unit costs by streamlining production and
becoming more efficient — a solution which clearly required heavy
investments in mechanisation — or, on the other, a direct reduction of
investment capital at risk through a reduction of the costs bearing on
the capitalist farmer — this in the hope that the crisis could be seen
through without too great losses. This second solution involved, typically, leasing land which had previously been worked by the proprietor

and relying on rents rather than profits for income (a solution difficult
to realise at a time of falling prices when leasing becomes less attractive), or attempting to reduce the costs borne by the proprietor through
a reduction of the wages of the day labourers, through a change in the
type of cultivation (labour-intensive crops could be substituted for
those which required only a minimum amount of attention), or through
the return to some form of sharecropping in order that a certain
proportion of the costs of production (and therefore of the risk involved) should be shouldered by the sharecropper.[17] This last solution
of the extension of sharecropping was particularly attractive because it
not only reduced the landowner's costs but also linked the income of
the worker to the prices of the agricultural products. At a time of
falling prices this meant, of course, that at least a part of the weight
of the crisis was carried by the sharecropper, who, as a simple day
labourer, might have received some protection from the crisis by
previously contracted daily wage rates.

The changes in the relations of production which occurred during
the years 1927-33 seem to correspond fairly exactly with the second
solution outlined above. After 1925, with the end of the inflationary
boom and the beginnings of the decline in agricultural prices,[18] private
investment in agriculture shows a marked fall. Even the heavy public
spending in agriculture was not backed up by those private investments necessary for a full exploitation of the public investment.
Responsible in part for this fall in investment was the undoubtedly
high cost of mechanisation, which meant a change in the scale of
agricultural costs for many farmers, and which could be faced by only
a relatively limited number of farmers at a time of falling prices when
the incentives to investment were low. But the failure to meet the
crisis through an increase in mechanisation meant that the alternative
policy — that of a reduction of the costs bearing on the farmer — had
to be followed. It seems likely therefore, that the changes in the relations of production witnessed by fascism permitted a reduction in the
costs borne by the proprietor or farmer; the emphasis on *compartecipazione*, particularly in areas of capitalist agriculture, and the extension of other forms of sharecropping suggest a growing tendency during
these years for landowners to reduce their dependence on the market,
relying where possible on the low cost returns of sharecropping, or on
rents, for their income.

The figures provided by Tassinari for income in agriculture support
this interpretation.[19] While the comparative incomes of employer and
employee remain fairly stable in zones where the system of cultivation

is dominated by small leaseholding or by sharecropping, those capitalist zones which remained dependent on day labourers show much greater variations — greater profits in good years but greater losses in bad. The response represented by a return to sharecropping offered most, therefore, to those zones where pure wage relationships between agrarian landowner and worker threatened to produce the greatest losses. By exploiting the relative flexibility of the modern farm and increasing the amount of land worked through sharecropping or on a short-term lease, the capitalist agrarian could defend himself from the crisis by passing some of the costs and some of the risks to workers who were still compelled to produce their rents or provide a certain proportion of the capital for a sharecropping contract.[20]

The way in which agrarians' income was protected is suggested by the generally worsening conditions experienced by sharecroppers and day labourers. Sharecroppers undoubtedly saw a hardening of the terms on which they farmed. The employer's contribution to the working capital was often reduced, while the share of the product allocated to him was increased.[21] The limited sharecropping contract of *compartecipazione al prodotto*, like the employment of fixed labourers (*obbligati*), permitted a far greater exploitation of labour. This was acknowledged unwittingly even by fascist writers. Pagani, for example, speaks of the 'higher level of work which *compartecipazione* permits' and adds that 'if one were to use day labourers there are many small jobs which the employer would not have done because they would not be economically justified'.[22] Such comments are indicative of the fact that the payment in kind envisaged in many of these forms of cultivation permitted a remuneration of labour at a level below that established by the fascist unions for the labourer paid by the day.[23]

Although figures relating to the payment of day labourers are not reliable, there seems little doubt that wages fell considerably. Sereni's figures for real wages are based on 1928, by which time large reductions had already been carried out. Even so, they show that in the period 1928-38 salaries never rose above the 1928 level, while in the last three years of the period the fall from that level accelerates rapidly (1928 = 100, 1938 = 72).[24] A confirmation of this decline is found in the general decline in consumption of many foods during the 1930s. There is a marked fall in the average consumption of proteins, fats and carbohydrates.[25] The usual consumption of the typical agricultural labourer was, of course, far below the national average. For him the irony of the situation was that he was usually expected to work longer hours for a reduced return.

It is difficult, therefore, to avoid the conclusions of many of the anti-fascists of the time. The relations of production established under fascism were intended to permit the maximum exploitation of labour in relation to cost. The weight of the crises of these years was supported by those intermediate categories of sharecroppers and small lease-holders, while the agrarians managed to guarantee for themselves a certain security of return. Fascism witnessed, therefore, a substantial redistribution of income within the agricultural sector. Labourers, *compartecipanti, mezzadri* — all of whom had improved their positions under the socialist movement — saw their share of the total product fall back to pre-war levels. Landowners and large leaseholders — particu-larly the agrarian entrepreneurs of the North — gained ground, enjoying the freedom of manoeuvre of a regime which permitted them to main-tain a certain level of profitability in unfavourable circumstances.[26]

The much publicised development of smallholding during fascism might appear to contradict these conclusions.[27] Here, however, it is essential to consider both the extent of the development and the role of the small landholder within the agricultural sphere. As is well known, the years following the First World War saw a rapid expansion of the class of small peasant proprietors in both North and South. War-time legislation favourable to peasants, political pressures on the larger landowners and — with the exception of 1920-1 — consistently rising agricultural prices — all combined to make the acquisition of property both possible and attractive. Prior to 1926 in fact, it seems that there was something of a rush for land, the purchasers being convinced that rising prices would soon permit them to pay off the debts incur-red in making the purchase.[28] Many new proprietors, particularly in the South, benefited from the strong demand in the first half of the decade for the high value specialist crops — oil, citrus fruits, wine, tomatoes — almost entirely destined for export given the weakness of the home market.[29] In championing the small peasant proprietors during the early years of the regime, the fascists were, therefore, doing little more than attempting to elevate to the level of policy a trend already very clearly defined.

The steady growth of this class of small proprietors was halted abruptly, however, in 1926-7 when the fall in agricultural prices and the revaluation of the lira caught many heavily indebted small proprietors without adequate reserves, forcing them to retrocede their lands and return to sharecropping contracts on almost any terms. Calculations about subsequent developments are made difficult by the diverse criteria adopted by successive censuses. The 1931 census shows an increase in the percentage of small proprietors with respect to the total agricultural population (from 33 per cent in 1921 to 36 per cent in 1931), although it appears that the fascists, in their eagerness to justify their claims to be the defenders of the small proprietors, counted even those with no more than a patch of garden as smallholders.[30] Any expansion of the class after 1930 probably occurred through the colonisation of reclaimed lands (although only to a limited extent, as will be seen below), and through the pulverisation of certain medium sized units squeezed by economic crisis and unfavourable legislation. Thus, in the inquests on the agricultural structure of Italy carried out after the Second World War, it is shown that some 54 per cent of the proprietors in agriculture occupied less than 4.1 per cent of the total cultivable surface.[31] This suggests very strongly that the tendency to pulverisation and the growth of a class of small peasant proprietors was in no way antagonistic to the further concentration of large holdings;[32] rather, concentration and pulverisation were simultaneous and parallel movements, carried out at the expense of the medium sized unit. Certainly there is nothing to suggest that the emphasis placed by fascism on the small proprietor in any way damaged the territorial integrity of the larger holdings in the hands of the principal proprietors and capitalist farmers.[33]

Nor was an increase in the number of small proprietors harmful to the economic interests of the agrarians with large holdings.[34] As was inevitable, the land taken by the smallholder was usually the poorer land and the expense and labour involved in improving the quality of the plot was placed firmly on his shoulders. Moreover, through the *consorzi*,[35] the larger owners could dominate the access to the market of the small proprietor. This was true both for the purchase of the principal products used in agriculture, in which the *consorzio* might hold a monopoly, and for the sale of produce. The fascist policy of building up stocks of foodstuffs (*ammassi*) by regulating the market permitted the powerful agrarians to control fairly precisely the price paid to the small producer. Often, in the name of protecting the peasant farmer, prices were fixed in relation to his costs, thus presenting handsome profits to the more efficient larger units. In addition, the inability of the peasant to survive while waiting for the sale of his produce through the *ammassi* (which often required him to wait several months for payment) forced him to take short-term advances on the crop. These were provided — at interest — by the better placed members of the *consorzio* or by the banks. As the economic pressure on the peasant became greater as a result of these circumstances, he would be forced to take up work outside his own plot, often as a seasonal labourer. Thus the large agrarian had at his disposition a reserve of labourers who, because of the possession of some land, would often work for less than those who had none. And, as if these advantages were not sufficient, there was the additional advantage of social stability. Only in a really extreme case would the small proprietor identify his interests with those below him in the agricultural hierarchy; opposition to fascism was rarely translated into a desire for proletarianisation. The social divisions so useful to fascism could thus be maintained. Where they were not, the land, often improved at the cost of considerable sacrifice to the small proprietor and his family, simply passed to the bank or to the large proprietor.

The fate of many of these new small proprietors is indicative of the tendency of fascism to bolster the position of the large farmers at the expense of the small. Other aspects of the regime confirm this impression. For example, the small producer was consistently more highly taxed than was the large.[36] Even when, during the 1930s, the taxman began to address himself increasingly to the larger proprietors and capitalist agrarians – particularly with the *imposta straordinaria immobiliare* and the *prestito sulla proprietà immobiliare* – the criteria which determined the taxable value of an estate were such as to permit the really large proprietors to escape payment on the basis of any realistic assessment.[37] Conversely, when it came to the provision of agrarian credit – an extremely important aspect of farming – it was only the larger farmers who were able to make their weight felt with the banks and secure favourable terms.

A consideration of the battle for wheat and the projects for land reclamation presents very much the same picture. Clearly there were other, non-agricultural, reasons for the implementation of these policies, as will be seen below; but, as they were put into practice, they were of most benefit to those already occupying positions of strength in agriculture. Agricultural protectionism was of most benefit to those who produced most for the home market – the efficient capitalist farms of the Po Valley. The small producer, either only partially involved in the market or growing specialised products for export, felt no benefit; indeed the high price of bread resulting from protectionism further restricted the internal demand for specialised products. Equally the emphasis placed on wheat – not a labour-intensive crop – was welcome to those agrarians who were seeking, in the years of the crisis, to reduce costs of production through a reduction of labour costs. Grain protection gave them an artificially high price for a crop which was

well suited to their purposes in other respects as well. And the fact that
profits could be made on a basic food crop of fairly rigid demand provided a cushion against the rapid fall in the prices of other products.
Given the compression of salaries and consumption of many products,
the battle for wheat helped to changed the structure of production at a
time when the structure of demand was also changing. In Emilia, for
example, the region of capitalist agriculture *par excellence*, there is a
clear inverse correlation between the area sown to industrial crops
(hemp, sugar beet), the prices of which fell rapidly during the crisis,
and the area sown to grain (wheat, maize) in the period 1927-33.
Protectionism clearly permitted grain to be used as a substitution crop
during the period in which the preferred crops of the capitalist farms
remained unprofitable. In fact, prices paid for food crops were consistently higher than those paid for industrial crops during the period
1927-33. Once the crisis began to pass, in 1933-4, the structure of production reverted very rapidly to what it had been in the boom years of
1925-6. Smallholders, whether peasant or capitalist, were much less able
to benefit from this kind of manoeuvre; crop substitution was simply
not possible for those producing specialist crops such as wine, fruit or
olive oil.[38]

A similar pattern of advantage can be seen in the programmes for
land reclamation. A glance at the figures for investment in agriculture
in these years reveals that a high percentage was government investment, assigned to works of land reclamation or land improvement.[39]
Equally noticeable, however, is the immense gap between work pro-
grammed and begun and work completed. It was calculated in 1946
that some 58 per cent of reclamation work begun had been completed,
while of irrigation projects begun only 32 per cent had been finished.
Of these improved lands only 16 per cent had been genuinely transformed according to the original proposals, which foresaw the division
of improved land among independent peasants.[40] The disparity
between ministerial aims and their realisation is clear. Much of the
money allocated to the programmes was evidently used, under pressure
of the crisis, for essentially unproductive public works; much was paid
to landowners who never moved a finger to justify the receipt of such
subsidies.[41] More serious, however, was the fundamental difference of
interest between government and proprietors. While many landowners
welcomed improvements at the state's expense and relished the prospect of increased rents as a result of the improvements, the proposal
for the final subdivision of the improved land had little attraction for
them. It promised to be expensive at the outset (the final stages of the

transformation were the responsibility of the individual landowner) and, more important, subdivision threatened to limit very greatly the freedom of the landowner in taking full advantage of the improvements. Thus the final private investment necessary in order to realise the original idea of the reclamation programmes was rarely forthcoming. Instead the land was often leased as it stood, and the final improvements made by the tenant, or else worked at *compartecipazione*. Public works programmes, manoeuvred in this way, served only to reinforce the positions of those already dominant.

But if agrarian policy in general favoured the large proprietors and the large capitalist entrepreneur against the small man, within the dominant group some gained more than others. One of the interpretations outlined in the introduction above was that the *latifondista* of the South achieved renewed weight under fascism; in fact, it seems likely that the opposite was the case. Not that fascist policies were not of benefit to the South. Unquestionably the battle for wheat and agricultural protectionism provided a defensive wall behind which the more backward and less efficient estates could survive in a way which would not have been possible in conditions of open competition. A high grain price helped, of course, to keep rents high in the South and guarantee the income of the *latifondista*. Equally, the reclamation programmes did not ignore the South. But a closer analysis of comparative benefit suggests that the South lost ground with respect to the North. The advantages to capitalist agrarians of the North of agricultural protectionism and the battle for wheat have already been mentioned; greater efficiency and flexibility meant that policies which in the South permitted the maintenance of the *status quo* could be translated in the North into positive advance. Similarly a breakdown by destination of the funds allocated for land reclamation reveals that the lion's share went to the centre and the North; the South saw very much less of the money or of the benefits which, directly or indirectly, followed its use.[42] This in itself is a very clear indication of which groups had greater political weight within the fascist political alliance.

This hypothesis is confirmed by an analysis of the value of agricultural production for the four principal types of agriculture in Italy. This shows that the capitalist areas of the Po Valley saw a marked increase in their percentage of the total value precisely during the years of fascism.[43] That this was achieved in large part through exploitation of the agrarian policies of fascism is beyond doubt. To continue to insist, therefore, on the elements of apparent backwardness in Italian agriculture under fascism and on the figure of the *latifondista*, and to pass over the considerable progress made by capitalist agriculture, would seem to be misleading. In all probability, the *latifondista* of the South emerged from fascism in a position relatively weaker with respect to the capitalist area of the North than he had been at the beginning of the regime.[44] Production statistics suggest that the distance between capitalist and non-capitalist agriculture increased under fascism; the economic dualism which had been a feature of the development of the agricultural sector from well before fascism (and which was in large measure also a geographical division) became more pronounced.[45] It seems unrealistic, therefore, to continue to argue that fascism was the regime of the backward elements in agriculture or that the maintenance of social stability — clearly very important to the regime — was not, in the short term at least, perfectly compatible with the continued development of the capitalist area in agriculture.

Fascist Agrarian Policy in the Context of Italian Economic Development

Such a conclusion might give the idea that fascism was the regime of the landed proprietors and large tenant farmers of the North — a not unreasonable hypothesis given the prominence of these figures in stimulating and financing the first fascist operations against the socialists in 1920-1. That these groups gained from the development of their limited class reaction into a political regime is unquestionable. But is this in itself sufficient to justify the claim that fascism saw 'the transformation of Italian society in an agrarian direction'? Did the emphasis given to themes of ruralisation really mean that fascist economic policy tended to favour the agricultural rather than the industrial sector, and, by implication, that fascism retarded economic growth by favouring the sector normally subordinate to industry in a developed capitalist economy?

To answer these questions it is necessary to put agrarian policy in the wider context of the economic problems facing the regime. To a very considerable extent these problems originated in economic choices made in the phase of industrialisation preceding fascism — choices which conditioned very strongly the path which fascism would follow. This requires further explanation.

From the first, Italian industry had been confronted by two major problems — the shortage of indigenous capital and the weakness of the internal market.[46] In part, the two were connected; capital accumulation realised through the maintenance of low wage levels compressed consumption and damaged internal demand. As a consequence Italian industry had developed in a strongly dualistic manner; on the one hand there were the heavy industries, particularly iron and steel, which produced exclusively for the home market and which relied on government contracts for a large part of their sales; on the other there were the lighter industries — of which textiles was the strongest — which, because of the weakness of the home demand, exported a large part of their production. The textile industry, for example, provided 53 per cent of all Italian exports in 1913. Exports of finished products were never sufficient, however, to pay for imports of raw materials and food-stuffs. Prior to the First World War Italy experienced great difficulty with her balance of payments and was forced to rely heavily on introits from tourism and on remittances from Italian emigrants in order to pay her debts abroad. Following the war, which saw a great expansion of heavy industry in Italy, there were great hopes that the constant check to expansion of the economy — the problem of the balance of payments — could be overcome by achieving a higher level of exports in markets newly opened to Italian penetration by the collapse of Austria-Hungary and the defeat of Germany. In fact, for a few years after the war the Italian economy saw a very rapid expansion of exports — largely textiles and specialised agricultural products — to markets in Western and central Europe.

It was an expansion which could not be expected to last indefinitely, however, and which in point of fact was never adequate to remedy the problem of the balance of payments. It was based in part on the rapidly depreciating value of the lira and on a temporary receptivity of foreign markets to Italian produce following the war. In addition, the growth of the textile industry provoked expensive imports of machinery required to replace outdated equipment. Tourism failed to revive after the war, and remittances fell seriously during the 1920s. Even that market for Italian produce which emigrants had provided declined under the impact of competitively priced local substitutes. Most important, Italian agriculture proved unable to provide for the needs of the country. Grain imports, which had run high since the end of the war, constituted some 40 per cent of the balance of payments deficit by 1925 and contributed to making the balance of payments problem particularly chronic.[47]

Failure to resolve this problem over the period 1922-5 had serious consequences. Confidence in the lira weakened and the currency continued to decline in value. This provoked inflation within the country which led in turn to a speculative boom and to a flight of capital, both of which detracted resources from saving or from long-term investment in industry. By early 1925 the government was forced to intervene to avoid a total collapse of the financial market. As is already well documented, it is from this point that the need for the stabilisation of the lira became obvious.[48] Further depreciation of the currency threatened not only the political basis of the regime, through an erosion of the savings of the petit bourgeoisie, but also jeopardised the long-term interests of Italian industry. The restructuring of Italian industry clearly required after the war in order to bring the production of industry more into line with the changing international demand could only be realised with heavy investment; financial instability threatened two possible sources of capital — savings and foreign loans acquired through the international capital market. Stabilisation required, therefore, that the balance of payments deficit should be drastically reduced through a considerable reduction of imports, both by increased protectionism and a reduction of consumer demand; at the same time it was hoped that a clear restoration of political stability within the country would, when combined with the declared intention to stabilise, encourage foreign investment within Italy. The very heavy revaluation of the lira in 1927 ('Quota 90') reflects these considerations. While it had a disastrous effect on Italian exports, both industrial and agricultural, it undoubtedly opened the way to American loans to Italian industry and encouraged saving and investment from private sources within Italy.[49] Heavy industry, producing for the home market and dependent on cheap imported raw materials, was the principal beneficiary.

But revaluation — while it offered a solution to certain problems — created many others. The decision to sacrifice the export industries was justified in certain quarters at the time by the argument that those industries, despite their importance for the balance of payments, were essentially 'weak' — that is, either offering a product for which world demand was falling (as in the case of textiles) or commodities for which demand was extremely elastic (as in the case of the specialised products of agriculture) and therefore subject to major fluctuations. In these circumstances it was felt that the long-term interests of the economy lay in strengthening the more modern industries (metal, mechanical and chemical) which represented areas where world demand was growing.[50] A consequence of this kind of reasoning was — at least implicitly — the policy of autarky; the sacrifice of exports, which necessitated the limitation as far as possible of imports, made import substitution the only practical alternative. Here, however, the massive internal crisis provoked by the deflationary effects of revaluation threatened to curtail home demand precisely at the time when the home market had become of supreme importance to industry. Because of this the self-financing of industry through sales became difficult and the banks became the principal source of investment capital. The world crisis of 1929, which closed the door on further American investment in Italy, made the problem more acute, and it is not surprising to find industry turning increasingly to the state for capital during the early 1930s. The attempt to resolve the problem of shortage of capital through stabilisation and the access to foreign capital which that would provide had failed, therefore, but the attempt had served to reinforce the predominance of heavy industries over light and had substantially reduced Italy's trading links with the international economy. As a consequence, the old problems – capital and market – were bound to re-assert themselves with fresh intensity; but with the difference that industry was clearly forced to rely on indigenous capital and on the home market.

Fascist agrarian policies appear to have been one aspect of an overall strategy designed to meet the difficulties facing the Italian economy from 1925 onwards. As a hypothesis it may be suggested that the primary concern behind these policies was the need to guarantee funds for the restructuring and further development of certain branches of Italian industry. The gains made by the capitalist farmers and the large landed proprietors were fully consistent with the logic of this strategy; they were encouraged by the regime in anticipation of a sizeable transfer of resources from the agricultural to the industrial sector. The protection afforded to agriculture, the defence of the profits of the capitalist agrarians and of the rents of the landed proprietors – these were pre-conditions of that transfer. It was essentially a policy of strengthening the strong; only those likely to buy the products of heavy industry, or to save, or to invest in industrial concerns merited the protection of the regime since it was only these who possessed resources that might be transferred – willingly or unwillingly, and by direct and indirect mechanisms – towards non-agricultural activities. The alternative policy – a fundamental redistribution of income within Italy in the hope of stimulating consumer demand and permitting capital accumulation to industry through the market – presented too many difficulties.[51] Stimulation of demand through a mildly inflationary policy, while acceptable to many industries, threatened the political basis of the fascist regime by eroding the savings of the petit bourgeoisie. Moreover, the industrial structure of Italy, traditionally weighted totwards heavy industries rather than those producing consumer goods, was hardly adapted to meet a general increase in consumer demand. The danger was that, as in the period prior to 1925, an increase in home demand for consumer products would be satisfied through imports and therefore of little advantage to the principal Italian industries, while at the same time further increasing the balance of payments deficit. In addition, it has to be remembered that in the agricultural sector, a large proportion of the population lived at subsistence level; a modest increase in income for such people was unlikely to be translated into a demand for the products of industries which fascism was most concerned to protect. At most it was likely to provoke an increased demand for foodstuffs – an area where Italy was already in great difficulty and eager to minimise imports.

The deflationary policy pursued by fascism in the interests of currency stabilisation excluded any general increase in consumer demand, therefore, and made necessary a different method of capital accumulation towards industry. Within this different strategy the interests of agriculture were clearly subordinated to those of industry. This is seen almost from the first move in the process of stabilisation. The battle for wheat, proclaimed in terms which emphasised national independence from foreign suppliers, was in reality a policy designed to reduce a disastrous balance of payments deficit through the substitution of Italian for foreign grain. This was done – as has been seen – primarily because of the damaging consequences of that deficit for Italian industry and in the hope that, through stabilisation, American banks would see their way to granting loans to industry. Ironically, independence in grain production was part of a general policy by which heavy industry would become more dependent on foreign capital. Similarly the fate of the producers of specialised agricultural products was clearly linked to the interests of industry. Sacrificed by the high level of revaluation, which made their produce more expensive in export markets, the small proprietors involved in this kind of production appear to have survived only through a deliberate policy of dumping on foreign markets.[52] While the producer obviously suffered in these circumstances, the foreign exchange obtained through dumping helped to balance a foreign account in which the principal item was raw materials for industry.

The two examples given here suggest strongly that the interests of industry were those which prevailed. Agrarian policies appear to have been formulated in such a way that, while satisfying many of the agrarian reformers concerned to increase efficiency and maximise production, they also came to the help of industry in the areas of greatest difficulty – those of capital and market. With regard to capital the channels by which funds flowed towards industry are fairly well known. Broadly speaking, it is possible to distinguish between direct investment in industry on the part of farmers and landowners and a variety of indirect channels by which industry benefited from wealth created in agriculture. As yet, relatively little is known about direct investment in industry by agrarians. Certainly prior to the First World War capitalist farmers and landowners of many northern regions had shown considerable interest in funding chemical, mechanical and pro-cessing industries connected with agriculture.[53] Whether this continued after the war remains to be seen. It is possible that the tendency during the inter-war years for whole areas of production to be dominated by a relatively few concerns limited the possibilities for the kind of fairly restricted regional initiative of pre-war years. Instead agrarians may have distributed their investments through the stock market towards the growing number of limited companies. There is a certain amount of evidence to support this hypothesis; the simple disproportion between the increase under fascism of the social capital of the limited companies and the increase in national income points to a reallocation of resources in favour of the companies. It must also be noted that, at the end of the Second World War, 70 per cent of the social capital of the limited companies was held by industry.[54] Sereni, in pointing to the increased presence of the landed aristocracy on the councils of many of the companies, lends credence to the theory that this rapid develop-ment of the limited companies was achieved, at least in part, through the investment of money derived from agriculture.[55] The extent of this direct investment is still to be ascertained, however. Whether the stock market, undoubtedly flourishing in certain periods under fascism, succeeded in attracting the investments of a stratum of landowners and farmers below the landed aristocracy is as yet uncertain. It is probable that in some cases direct investment was extremely attractive. Given the uncertainties which faced agriculture in these years, the prospect of a high return on capital from – for example – investment in the sugar industry must have been as enticing to the beet growers of Emilia and the Veneto during the fascist regime as it had been in the years before the war. Whether, from an interest in transformation industries and industries clearly linked to agriculture, agrarians moved to an interest in totally different industries is another matter.

Probably far more important than direct investment were those less direct processes which channelled funds towards industry. Of these, savings occupied a major role. Particularly important after 1929 when the possibilities of obtaining foreign capital for investment in Italian industry disappeared, savings were encouraged by the revaluation of the lira and the policy of deflation and were sustained both during and after the crisis by the intervention of the state and its assumption, in effect, of the role of banker. Public loans and sale of government bonds — particular features of the late 1920s and the 1930s — provided a source of capital which could be redistributed according to the designs of the regime. It is not possible at this stage to determine precisely what proportion of this saving came from agriculture. Obviously a sizeable quantity of private saving could be expected to come from the urban middle and lower middle classes. Yet certain points should not be overlooked. First among these is the fact that, if fascism saw the point at which industry overtook agriculture as the sector producing the largest proportion of the national product, for much of the period it was still the agricultural sector which predominated.[56] And, while no general figure for profitability in agriculture is available, the fact that less than 5 per cent of total investment for the period was employed in agriculture (public spending included) suggests that agrarians were re-investing only a small proportion of their profits in agriculture.[57] Where the surplus went is uncertain. It may simply have been 'treasurised' and thus lost to sight. It is more reasonable to suppose, however, that a considerable proportion found its way into savings. Figures suggest that much went to the *Casse di Risparmio* (rural savings banks) and particularly to the *Casse Postali* which traditionally attracted the savings of many in the agricultural sector, if not the really big capitalist entrepreneurs. The increase in the deposits held by these last institutions after 1928 is notable, moving from 10,000 million lire in 1928 to 33,000 millions in 1939.[58] The rise in the first years of this period probably reflects the success with which government deflationary policy encouraged private saving. The continued rise after 1934, when inflationary tendencies again became manifest, is no less indicative of public reaction to government policy, however. Almost the entire increase in deposits in these years was accounted for by the sale of government guaranteed *buoni fruttiferi* (investment bonds) — a fact which reveals the crucial role played by the state in restoring public confidence in saving after the banking crises of the early 1930s. The importance of this can be appreciated simply by considering the substantial contributions made by the *Casse di Risparmio* to the financing of IMI and IRI, to the subscriptions to national loans, and the prompt support always given by the *Casse* to the repeated issues of Treasury bonds.[59] The much publicised 'defence of saving' concealed in all probability a massive movement of funds towards the industrial sector.

The central position of the banks, particularly the provincial *Casse di Risparmio* which were much consolidated and concentrated under fascism, in effecting this transfer is clear. Not only were they responsible for collecting savings accumulating in rural areas, but the subsequent reinvestment of these funds outside the agricultural sphere gave very considerable influence to the banks.[60] It is possible that it was through the banks that the real integration of agrarian and industrial interests occurred. The board of the local banks, composed in large measure of landowners and, in the North, capitalist agrarians, were able to distribute funds over a far wider area than had been the case before the First World War when the *Casse* had had a much more modest function. Indeed, the large number of landowners on the boards of industry may reflect above all the influence which certain landowners had within the banks and the access which they had to important sources of capital for industry.[61]

The subtraction of resources from agriculture, realised through the banks and with the collaboration of many prominent landowners, was, none the less, the subject of great resentment among many others involved with agriculture. This – indicative of the division of interest within the sector between those convinced that agriculture could still protect itself from subordination to the industrial sector and those already with interests outside that sector – is itself clear proof that a considerable transfer of resources was taking place. Alberto De' Stefani, former finance minister, voiced this resentment very explicitly in 1928 when speaking on behalf of the *Associazione nazionale dei consorzi di bonifica*:

As long as only 10 per cent of the deposits administered by the banks are employed in investments in agriculture or land, we shall remain isolated and our ideas of technical improvement unrealised. Yet 50 per cent – half of all deposits administered by the banks – comes from Italian farmers. The difference . . . constitutes a body of wealth earned by farmers which the banks fail to redistribute among the farmers themselves. Eight tenths of deposits and savings coming from these people is taken up by public loans and goes to strengthen industry and the cities. Even the state, in exercising its financial powers has learned strongly in the direction of an industrial and urban policy.[62]

If so many of the policies pursued by fascism were of benefit to agrarians, it is apparent that in the important fields of credit and banking agricultural interests were subordinated to the logic of the development of an industrial economy.

Agrarians might also have pointed to the part played by taxation in draining wealth from agriculture. Calculations made in 1930 showed that a good 25 per cent of national income was collected immediately by the state in taxes.[63] Much of this came through indirect taxes, a fact which suggests that the agricultural population — still over 50 per cent of the active population of Italy — bore a considerable share of the weight of taxation. Direct taxes on agricultural incomes, even if evaded by the really large proprietors, undoubtedly increased the extent to which agriculture contributed to the revenue of the state.

But the factor which was most telling in making clear the changed relationship between agricultural and industrial sectors was the control exercised over the market by a relatively few industrial concerns. One major objective of fascist agrarian policies had been the utilisation of the large market within agriculture for the products of industry. Protectionism, with its corollary of import substitution, permitted Italian industries to increase their share of such markets, even when the overall volume of demand was not increasing. In certain areas, fascism also attempted to increase demand; the heavy public spending which purported to defend agriculture had as not its least important aspect the creation of a fresh internal market. Projects for land reclamation, for example, were clearly intended to stimulate internal demand at a time when other markets were either closed or closing. The enthusiastic response of Montecatini and other industries to the announcement of the land reclamation programmes needs little explanation; the demand for chemical fertilisers, irrigation plants, agricultural machinery and other equipment could be expected to rise and the industries affected reacted accordingly. Considering the forces involved, it is not difficult to understand why so little of the reclaimed land was ever fully transformed as envisaged by the original reclamation projects. Industrial concerns were unlikely to be served by an expansion in the number of small peasant-operated units. While the large farmer could be convinced of the convenience of technical improvements, the small proprietor or sharecropper, often heavily in debt, was unlikely to find either the money or the use for expensive fertilisers or machinery.

For the industries concerned, the creation of a market in agriculture was of particular importance because of the terms on which they traded with that market. The tendency to concentration and cartellisation in industry evident after 1927 — itself a clear indication of the limits of the home market and the desire among producers to reduce competition

— meant that markets opened up by protectionism and public spending were dominated by a relatively few industries. Agriculture had little protection against this dominance. The *Federconsorzi*, co-operative organisations which had attempted to counter the strength of industry by a policy of bulk buying on behalf of a large number of agrarians, were slowly outmanoeuvred under fascism by economic and political interests far stronger than those represented by the *Federconsorzi*. Their position as a counterforce to the weight of certain industrial monopolies was rapidly undermined and they ceased to have any real effect on the prices of the industrial products needed by agriculture.[64] The chemical concern Montecatini succeeded for example in reaching an agreement with the *Federconsorzi* which gave it total control of entire sections of the chemical fertiliser market, thus ensuring not only sales but also the advantages of monopoly prices. Agriculture, not well organised as a sector and still largely competitive in structure, could offer little resistance to this domination. Indeed, its position was further worsened by the monopoly enjoyed, even at a regional level only, by those industries which bought agricultural products. It is only necessary to cite the examples of sugar beet and hemp, both commodities whose production and price were largely dictated by the related industries of transformation, to appreciate the significance of this monopoly. In effect, the vast majority of the producers were isolated from the open market both as buyers and sellers and could only suffer as a consequence.[65]

The result of this situation is seen in the development during fascism of the scissors movement — the relative decline in the value of agricultural products in respect of industrial products. The point at which agriculture lost its relative advantage came in 1929, according to Sereni, and in following years the position was never reversed.[66] In large measure the movement reflected the different structures of the two sectors, the one still at the stage of competition, the other already monopolistic. This difference was crucial for many industries since it permitted those profits which only monopoly could provide. The favourable terms of trade enjoyed by industry meant, in fact, that certain key industries were able to reduce their dependence on the availability of external capital and possibly proceed to the stage of self-financing by the later 1930s.

The continuation of this disadvantageous position could not but have an adverse effect on the balances of many of the weaker farms. If some were reduced to virtual subsistence farming, others were forced to borrow, mortgage and ultimately to sell. The figures given by Sereni for the expropriation of properties for failure to pay taxes, often very small sums, are especially eloquent in this respect and demonstrate as few other statistics can how little fascism was really the regime of the small property holder.[67] Apart from the larger proprietors, the principal beneficiaries of these difficult conditions were the banks. Recourse to the banks by those unable to find resources elsewhere meant that an ever larger proportion of rents and income deriving from land was diverted directly to the banks, either as repayments on loans or simply as interest on debts contracted. The attempt of farmers to establish through the *Federconsorzi* an autonomous financial institute to aid landowners and farmers in difficulty and free them from the pressures of the traditional banks proved a total failure, and they continued to be dependent on those banks.[68] The extent of this dependence is shown by Sereni's calculations that the value of mortgages with the banks rose under fascism from some 326 million lire in 1922 to around 15,000 million in 1938, and that between 600 million and 800 million lire was required to service these debts each year.[69] Again this represented finance available to other sectors of the economy.

Such figures indicate clearly the extent to which the agricultural sector was subordinated during fascism to the interests of other areas of the economy. But the severity with which this subordination was experienced within that sector varied very greatly. While labourers, sharecroppers and small proprietors all suffered because of the drastic compression of wages and consumption, the increased taxation, the poor credit facilities and the unfavourable terms of trade, the same is not necessarily true of the large proprietors and tenant farmers. Not only were they able to shift the load of the crisis on to their dependent workers, but the opportunities open to them to spread their interests and participate in developments outside the sector – banking, insurance, industry, building – may well have provided a cushion against the full effects of subordination. Until more information is available, the extent of the integration of agricultural and non-agricultural interests during this period will remain uncertain. But it seems reasonable to suggest, with Sereni, that many agrarians were well integrated and were, therefore, party to and beneficiaries of the general economic conditions from which so many others suffered. Subordination there was – a substantial redistribution of wealth between the two major sectors of the economy – but it is probable that many of the principal figures in agriculture were careful to see that the redistribution of resources was accompanied by a similar redistribution of their interests.

Other aspects of agrarian policy, less directly related to the issue of capital accumulation, fit in well with the above hypothesis. The laws against urbanisation, for instance, far from reflecting a refusal of capitalist and industrial values, merely sought to deal with the problem of employment in a period of economic crisis. Industrial development of the type favoured by fascism from 1925 onwards could not but create difficulties with regard to employment. Heavy industry — capital-intensive rather than labour-intensive — drained resources away from those industries which might, in other circumstances, have permitted a rapid growth in the industrial labour force. As the report presented to the *Costituente* documents, the capacity of industry to absorb fresh labour was extremely low during the second decade of the regime — and this at a time when emigration from Italy was virtually blocked.[70] To some extent, the increase in party and state bureaucracy compensated for this trend; but the problem remained. Keeping people working on the land was one solution, even if it meant that they were under-employed. From the point of view of both subsistence and public order, rural under-employment was far preferable to urban unemployment.

Similarly the rhetoric of ruralisation was part of an operation which compelled people to continue living in the sector where consumption was lowest but which provided them at the same time with a 'myth' to compensate them for that fact. But it is important not to under-estimate the suggestivity of a propaganda based on rural values for urban populations, many of very recent formation and with strong links with the countryside. The difficult conditions of an urban working class, caught in an international economic crisis, made the ideology of ruralisation an attractive, if bogus, panacea for urban discontent.

The Limits of the 'Stagnationist' Interpretation

The analysis presented here of the role of the agricultural sector and the function of agrarian policy suggests that those interpretations which have tended to stress the backward aspects of the Italian economy under fascism owe more to political convenience than historical accuracy. Agriculture, far from becoming the bastion of pre-capitalist forces and the dominant sector within the economy, appears rather to have performed an essential function in respect of the principal economic changes of these years. By providing finance for industry through a multitude of channels, by offering a market, and by providing a reservoir for labour, the agricultural sector helped to make possible those qualitative changes of both industrial and financial structures which constitute the main features of the interpretation which rejects theories of economic stagnation and immobility.

There are two principal weaknesses of those interpretations which stress 'feudal residues', pre-capitalist relations of production, or other archaic aspects of fascism. First, they tend to neglect the extent to which fascism both protected the capitalist farms already in existence and encouraged the further entry of finance capitalism into the countryside. Obviously the relations of production favoured by fascism did permit the survival beyond their time of antiquated forms in agriculture; yet this cannot alter the fact that – for capitalist agriculture – those relations were a means of defence against crisis rather than an effort to turn the clock back. There are simply no signs that capitalist agriculture emerged from fascism either structurally or economically weakened – quite the contrary. Many of the provisions of the regime encouraged, either directly or indirectly, the movement of property towards the larger farms. Equally important was the penetration of finance capitalism into the countryside. Limited companies in agriculture, enormous investments on the part of the state, the increasing pressure exerted by the banks – all these were features which were bound sooner or later to have their effect on the methods and motivations of farming. As with the Po Valley 50 years earlier, injections of capital into agriculture exerted an influence over an area far larger than that immediately involved in transition. If other criteria of the regime tended to limit the potential of this entry of finance capitalism, it was none the less part of a process which was not to be reversed.

The second weakness of these interpretations is essentially an error of perspective; they tend to proceed from an examination of fascism in agriculture and an excessive emphasis on the archaic aspects of the regime in the countryside to general judgements about fascism which bear all the hallmarks of a distorted sectorial study. The dangers of forming general judgements on the basis of developments in the agricultural sector alone should be obvious from what has been said above. These dangers are seen most clearly perhaps in respect of the relations of production favoured by fascism, an area where it might seem most difficult to counter accusations of stagnation. Apart from the consideration that beneath the juridical forms of independence or semi-independence permitted by fascism there was often an effective proletarianisation, it must also be recognised that these relations of production were imposed not in order to obstruct the progress of capitalist development but precisely to aid it. Given the circumstances of the 1920s and 1930s together with the particular weaknesses of Italian industrial development, the policies pursued in the countryside assume a function within the logic of the further development of this industry. And in this respect, the integration of capitalist interests in agriculture and industry during this period is of special importance since it suggests that the developments which took place were not the work of a mono-polistic clique – somehow parasitic and extraneous to the 'true' process of capitalist development – but of that same capitalist class which had existed before fascism and which was in large measure to exist after it. In effect, capitalism adapted itself in these years to utilise many of the pre-capitalist elements still present in the countryside. To move from the identification of these pre-capitalist elements to the view that fascism was itself pre-capitalist and opposed to the further development of Italian capitalism is to mistake the means for the ends.

Such a judgement says nothing, of course, about the *success* of the fascists in furthering industrial development. Rejection of theories which lean heavily on ideas of stagnation, or monopoly capitalism directed by plutocratic and parasitic cliques does not necessarily imply that fascist management of the economy was perfect. In fact, it is not difficult to identify many apparent weaknesses in the Italian economy during the regime. Critics of fascist policy have noted the persistence of serious regional imbalances, the distortion of the agricultural sector as a consequence of the return to protectionism in grain, the removal of all stimuli for entrepreneurial spirit in industry through the savage compression of home consumer demand and the reduction of foreign trading contacts. As a consequence, it can be argued, innovation in industrial techniques was discouraged and productivity remained much lower than in the comparable industries of Italy's trading competitors. Whereas in other countries the return to protectionism during the inter-war years permitted an increase in efficiency through a restructuring of industry, in Italy the closed economy of fascism simply defended established positions and established profits and thus protected in-efficiency.

Many of these points are undoubtedly correct. Productivity did remain low, and Italian agriculture did lose much of its livestock pro-duction as a result of the privileged position given to grain. But what is less clear is the extent to which such observations constitute criticisms of fascism. Many appear to be based on the contrast between what is variously described as a healthy, rational, progressive or even demo-cratic capitalism and the capitalism of fascism, and are clearly strongly influenced either by the continuing legacy of the definitions of fascism devised during the regime by the Communist movement, and in particu-lar by that definition current after the VII Congress by which fascism represented only a small part of the capitalist classes, or by a desire to read back in time the lessons and experience of the Italian boom of the post-war years. They demonstrate on occasions the great danger when employing ideas of misdirected economic policies or failed opportunities of doing so on the basis of an abstract model of development which fails to take full account of the historical situation of Italy in the inter-war years.

Two examples will serve to make this point better. It is certainly true that the introduction of a high level of grain protection as a prelude to the battle for wheat helped to reinforce the position of the landed proprietors of the South and served to distort agricultural production by severely damaging livestock production and discouraging investment in specialised crops. What is much less clear is what other course of action could have been adopted *in the short term* in order to meet the balance of payments deficit, with all that that implied for the stability of the currency and, ultimately, for the future of Italian industry. A major reduction of imports of raw materials and machinery for industry (the other principal component of imports) would have produced an even more profound effect on the economy.

Similarly the much more complex question of the alleged failure of fascism to expand home demand to a greater degree after 1926 begs a large number of questions. While it appears self-evident that a less repressive social policy and higher wages would have had a beneficial effect on industry through the expansion of the home market, it must also be recognised that an increase in real wages might have had an adverse effect on exports, very dependent in this period on low-cost production in order to maintain high volume. And this in turn might have forced a reduction of imports of raw materials and machinery on which industry depended in order to realise that restructuring and technological modernisation which was required to meet both home and international demand on competitive terms.

With both these examples the fundamental problems — the inefficiency of Italian agriculture and the constraints to the growth of industry represented by the balance of payments — were related much more to the characteristics of Italian economic development prior to fascism that to the choices of fascism. The obvious long-term solution was a major restructuring of both agricultural and industrial sectors; but, once again, it is not readily apparent precisely how Italy was to deal with her very pressing problems in the short term, particularly in relation to the balance of payments, in order to be able to proceed to the long-term solution.

However, these more general points on the alternative economic policies open to the regime go beyond the scope of this paper. In reality,
too little is known about many of the major problems for it to be
possible to make any concluding remarks about the successes or failures
of fascist economic policies. For example, the extent to which fascism
was conditioned in its economic choices by a pattern of capitalist
accumulation already well established is still uncertain. Similarly, the
impact on Italy, clearly in a subordinate position within Western capitalism, of the difficult international economic conditions of the inter-
war years is still largely undefined. Much detailed research is needed on
these and many other issues, and, in the process, many commonly held
views may well be revised. It may be suggested, for example, that
Gramsci's concept of the 'historic bloc', so useful as an analytical tool
for the period before the First World War, is partially misleading when
applied to the fascist period because of the undue stress it has encouraged some writers to place on the backward features of the regime
to the neglect of some of the more dynamic elements. Similarly much
of the free-trading *liberismo* underlying anti-fascist writing may have to
be revised. But such revision will not affect the political judgement to
be passed on fascism. The essential point of this examination of fascist
agrarian policies has been to reassert the relationship between fascism
and capitalist development in Italy. The politically and socially reactionary nature of the regime should not be taken to mean that it was
also *necessarily* economically regressive, as appears to have been the
position of many commentators of the time. Indeed, to make such an
equation risks obscuring the very close links between fascism and the
process of capitalist industrialisation in Italy. It can easily lead to the
conclusion that fascism was in some way extraneous to the 'true'
course of development of Italian capitalism, rather than an expression
of the many stresses and tensions which that same capitalist development had provoked within Italian society.

Notes

1. See E. Sereni, *La questione agraria nella rinascita nazionale italiana* (Rome,
1946); P. Grifone, *Il capitale finanziario in Italia* (Rome, 1945); L. Rosenstock-
Franck, *L'economie corporative fasciste en doctrine e en fait* (Paris, 1934);
W.G. Welk, *Fascist Economic Policy* (Cambridge, 1938); C.T. Schmidt, *The
Plough and the Sword; Land, Labour, and Property in Fascist Italy* (New York,
1938); P. Einzig, *The Economic Foundations of Fascism* (London, 1933); D.
Guerin, *Fascisme e grand capital* (Paris, 1936).

2. For example, M.V. Posner and S.J. Woolf, *Italian Public Enterprise* (London,
1967).

3. See F. Grassini, 'Alcune linee della politica industriale fascista' in *Fascismo e Antifascismo. Lezioni e testimonianze* (Milan, 1962), pp. 286-90. For many statements in the same sense, see E. Sereni, 'La politica agraria del regime fascista', in the same anthology, *passim*.

4. V. Foa, 'Le strutture economiche e la politica economica del regime fascista', in the anthology cited in note 3, p. 283.

5. Emilio Sereni argues that, in as far as it is the expression of monopoly capitalism, fascism is the principal obstacle to any further economic development: 'It is clear . . . how capitalism, in its present monopolistic phase, has for some time past been transformed into the fundamental obstacle to the development of productive forces in Italian agriculture, as in the overall economy of the country.' He insists that the defeat of fascism will leave the way open for a 'free and healthy development of the productive forces' of Italy. See Sereni, *La questione agraria*, pp. 210 and 207. The references are to the reprint, Turin 1975. For further information on the changes in the Communist analysis of fascism see G. Sapelli, *L'analisi economica dei comunisti italiani durante il fascismo* (Milan, 1978). Sapelli illustrates well the extent to which many Communist theoreticians, even in the 1920s, were convinced that accumulation and profit were virtually irreconcilable with fascist policies of protectionism and restriction of the home market. This caused them to underrate the extent to which the Italian economy was capable of development, to insist exclusively on the negative aspects of fascist economic policy without seeing its strengths, and – ultimately – to adopt a substantially free-trading position in opposition to the protectionism of fascism. The reasons for this approach are, of course, readily apparent in the political situation of the time. None the less, many of the positions taken up at this time have been excessively influential in subsequent interpretations of the economy under fascism.

6. For examples of fascist anti-capitalism, see A. Lyttelton, *The Seizure of Power* (London, 1973), pp. 65-7; P. Corner, *Fascism in Ferrara* (London, 1974), pp. 193-200. For general comments on fascist anti-capitalism, see Barrington Moore Jr., *The Social Origins of Dictatorship and Democracy: Lord and Peasant in the Making of the Modern World* (London, 1967), p. 448.

7. R. De Felice, *Mussolini il duce: gli anni nel consenso, 1929-36* (Turin, 1974), pp. 169-74.

8. B. Mussolini, *Opera omnia*, 22, p. 360, Ascension Day speech, 26 May 1927.

9. On ruralisation see R. De Felice, *Mussolini il duce*, pp. 147-57. The levels to which propaganda on ruralisation had arrived are well illustrated by a comment of Ugo Spirito in 1930. Spirito wrote that ruralisation 'now runs the risk of becoming an end in itself, an absolute, concealing the fact that the ideal of every modern society must be that of a throughgoing industrialisation and that industry and progress and industry and civilisation are terms of equal weight . . . An agricultural country is today an anachronism.' Quoted in De Felice, ibid., p. 152.

10. Sereni, 'La politica agraria del fascismo', p. 300.

11. The best example of this reappraisal is to be found in E. Fano Damascelli, 'La restaurazione antifascista liberista; ristagno e sviluppo economico durante il fascismo', in *Il Movimento di Liberazione in Italia*, June-September 1971, pp. 47-99. See also N. Poulantzas, *Fascisme e dictature* (Paris, 1970), for interesting but often confusing comments on the same lines.

12. For a more detailed treatment of the agrarian programme of early fascism, see Corner, *Fascism in Ferrara*, chap. 7, *passim*.

13. *Mezzadri* in particular, and other sharecroppers to a lesser extent, were traditionally 'two-faced' – resenting the domination of the landowner and there-

fore inclined to be favourably disposed to movements which put the landowner under pressure, but at the same time very much aware of the superior status of the sharecropper with respect to the landless labourer and therefore antagonistic to policies of proletarianisation of the intermediate groups. This tension was inevitably increased in areas where the *mezzadro* felt his relatively superior position very strongly, as in Emilia where pressure from landless labourers was strong; where there were few landless labourers and the *mezzadro* felt less threatened by pressures from below him, as in Tuscany, the *mezzadro* felt much freer to direct his attention exclusively against the landowner. In these areas it was correspondingly more difficult for the fascists to exploit divisions within the various groups employed in agriculture.

14. *Compartecipazione* was a system of sharecropping with several variations according to region. Broadly speaking, it involved a yearly contract for one or more crops. Labourers were provided with materials and seed and allocated a piece of land in which to cultivate that seed. The crop would be divided between the labourers (*compartecipanti*) and the owner according to a previously agreed quota. In practice, the owner would often advance money to the labourer at the beginning of the season and then expect repayment in kind, i.e. a greater share of the crop at harvest time. For these reasons, it was a low-cost system, well suited to crops which required a great deal of attention. See G. Giorgetti, *Contadini e proprietari nell'Italia moderna* (Turin, 1974), pp. 460-1.

15. O. Vitali, *La popolazione attiva in agricoltura attraverso i censimenti italiani* (Rome, 1968), Table 4, p. 204.

16. *VIII Censimento generale della poplazione*, 1936, vol. iv, *Professioni*, Table 6.

17. Note the significant title of K.D. Dmitrev, *How to Assure an Income from Land Without Investing Capital* (Moscow, 1897), which was a tract on the advantages of the sharecropping system. Cited in the anthology, *Agricoltura e sviluppo del capitalismo* (Rome, 1970), p. 100.

18. The following figures give some idea of the decline in agricultural prices. On a base of 100 for 1925, the price index of maize in 1931 was 46, of rice 43, of hemp 24, of wool 23 and of lemons 18. These figures are given in G. Tassinari, *Le vicende del reddito dell'agricoltura dal 1925 and 1932* (Rome, 1935), p. 322.

19. Ibid., chap. 16, *passim*.

20. On the advantages for the landowner of the various forms of sharecropping see Giorgetti, *Contadini e proprietari*, pp. 459 ff. On the issue of risk sharing, with which Georgetti also deals, see J.S. Cohen, 'Rapporti agricoltura – industria e svillupo agricolo' in *L'economia italiana nel Periodo fascista*, eds P. Ciocca and G. Toniolo (Bologna, 1976), p. 386.

21. For the kind of changes effected in the province of Bologna, see A. Marabini, 'La mezzadria in Italia' in *Lo stato operaio* (1936), pp. 218-28.

22. A. Pagani, *I braccianti della valle padana* (Piacenza, 1932), p. 86. Similar conclusions about the function of *compartecipazione* can be drawn from an article by G. Gennari, where he suggests that the system permits 'the adoption of particularly labour-intensive crops, something which is not always practicable when he [the employer] is forced to use only workers paid by the day'; see 'Presente situazione contrattuale dei rapporti di mezzadria, colonia parziaria, e compartecipazione' in *Rivista di economia agraria*, 2, 1949. The same points are made by Giorgetti, *Contadini e proprietari*, pp. 453 ff.

23. A. Marabini, 'La politica fascista della sbracciantizzazione' in *Lo stato operaio* (1935), pp. 429-36.

24. Sereni, *La questione agraria*, p. 307.

25. Istituto centrale di statistica, *Sommario di statistiche storiche dell'Italia 1961-1965* (Rome, 1968), Table 106, p. 138.

26. Sereni attempts an estimate of this redistribution, calculating that between 1924 and 1937-8 labour's share of the total income deriving from agriculture fell from 65 per cent to 54 per cent. Rents rose from 20 per cent to 21 per cent of that total, while profits rose from 15 per cent to 25 per cent. Sereni, *La questione agraria*, p. 301.

27. For the sake of clarity it is as well to emphasise the difference between stable, long-established small proprietors, who benefited from fascism in many ways, and those small proprietors who had only acquired land during the years following the First World War. The reference here is clearly to the second type.

28. See G. Lorenzoni, *Inchiesta sulla piccola proprietà contadina coltivatrice formatasi nel dopoguerra. Relazione finale: l'ascesa del contadino italiano nel dopoguerra* (Rome, 1938), pp. 254 ff.

29. A. Cadeddu, S. Lepre, F. Socrate, 'Ristagno e svilluppo nell'agricoltura italiana, 1918-1939' in *Quaderni storici*, 29-30 (May-December 1975) pp. 397 ff.

30. A conclusion confirmed by G. Muzzioli in 'Le campagne modenese durante il fascismo. Sette anni di crisi 1927-33', in *Studi storici* 4 (1974) pp. 908-49.

31. Istituto nazionale di economia agraria, *La distribuzione della proprietà fondiaria in Italia* (Rome, 1948).

32. A. Serpieri, *La struttura sociale dell'agricoltura italiana* (Rome, 1947), *passim*.

33. K. Kautsky, *La questione agraria* (Milan, 1971), pp. 190 ff.

34. On the question of the utility of the small proprietor to the large, see K. Kautsky, ibid., pp. 190 ff, and V.I. Lenin, *The Development of Capitalism in Russia* (Moscow, 1960), pp. 148 ff and 267 ff.

35. The *consorzi* were co-operative organisations intended to aid the individual farmer in both buying and selling. On the changing function of the *consorzi* see A. Ventura, 'La Federconsorzi dall'età liberale al fascismo: ascesa e capitolazione della borghesia agraria' in *Quaderni storici*, 35 (December 1977) pp. 683-733.

36. The tax on agrarian incomes, established in 1924, was 10 per cent on lower incomes, but only 5 per cent on the incomes of the larger proprietors. A *mezzadro* paid two thirds of the taxes on the income deriving from the farm, while the proprietor (who received half, or even more, of the income) paid only one third. A. Marabini, 'La mezzadria in Italia'.

37. E. Sereni, 'La vita italiana. L'aristocrazia terriera' in *Lo stato operaio* (1939) pp. 210-11.

38. For a more detailed treatment of the progress of capitalist agriculture during fascism, see P. Corner, 'Considerazioni sull'agricoltura capitalistica durante il fascismo' in *Quaderni storici*, 29-30 (May-December 1975) pp. 519-29.

39. O. Vitali, *La popolazione attiva*, graph 1, p. 33.

40. Ministero per la Costituente, *Rapporto della commissione economica presentato all'Assemblea della Costituente*, part 1, *Agricoltura*, pp. 372 ff.

41. The example of a proprietor of Codigoro (Ferrara) who received 800 million lire in state subsidies and did nothing with it is given by Sereni in 'La politica agraria', p. 302.

42. For these figures see *Annuario statistico dell'agricoltura italiana 1939-42, V, Bonifica e trasformazioni fondiarie*.

43. Corner, 'Considerazioni', Table 1, p. 520.

44. Fano Damascelli, 'La restaurazione antifascista liberista', p. 87.

45. Corner, 'Considerazioni', pp. 528-9.

46. This account of Italian industrial development is based on many sources, among which are: P. Grifone, *Il capitale finanziario*; R. Romeo, *Breve storia della grande industria in Italia* (Rocca San Casciano, 1961); and, in particular, for the period before the war, Giovanna Procacci, 'Caratteri dello sviluppo economico in Italia dalla fine del secolo alla prima guerra mondiale', in *Archivio*

sardo del movimento operaio e contadino, 4-5 (December 1975) pp. 81 ff.

47. On the problems facing Italy during this period, and in particular in the key years of 1925-6, see: G. Tattara and G. Toniolo, 'L'industria manifatturiera: cicli, politiche e mutamenti di struttura (1921-37)' in Ciocca and Toniolo, *L'economia italiana*, pp. 103 ff; G. Toniolo, 'Ricerche recenti e problemi aperti sull'economia italiana durante la grande crisi', and, by the same author, 'Crisi economica e smobilizzo pubblico delle banche miste', both in *Industria e banca nella grande crisi 1929-34*, ed. G. Toniolo (Milan, 1978), pp. 18 ff. and 284 ff. respectively; F. Guarneri, *Battaglie economiche tra le due grandi guerre* (Milan, 1953). Also to be noted are the acute comments of Gramsci on the Italian economic situation in 'A study of the Italian situation', now in English in *A. Gramsci, Selections from political writings 1921-26*, ed. Q. Hoare (London, 1978), pp. 400 ff.

48. On stabilisation see F. Guarneri, *Battaglie economiche*, pp. 150 ff; R. Sarti, 'Mussolini and the Italian industrial leadership in the battle of the lira 1925-27' in *Past and Present*, 47 (1970) pp. 97-102; G. Falco and M. Storaci, 'Fluttuazioni monetarie alla fine degli anni venti; Belgio, Francia, e Italia' in *Studi storici*, 1 (1975) pp. 57-101.

49. See G.G. Migone, 'La stabilizzazione della lira; la finanza americana e Mussolini', in *Rivista di storia contemporanea*, 2 (1973) pp. 43-130.

50. This was the view of S. Spinelli quoted in M. Paradisi, 'Il commercio estero e la struttura industriale' in Ciocca and Toniolo, *L'economia italiana*, pp. 271 ff. The particular reference is on pp. 283-4.

51. See the comments of Gramsci on Fordism, in which he notes that in countries industrially backward the mass of the workers and peasants are not seen as a market; instead such countries look for markets overseas, usually in countries even more backward, and rely on protectionism and low salaries at home in order to permit exploitation of foreign markets through dumping; A. Gramsci, *Quaderni del carcere* (Turin, 1975), 11, p. 799.

52. Fano Damascelli, 'Problemi e vicende dell'agricoltura', pp. 482-4, and Cadeddu, Lepre, Socrate, 'Ristagno e sviluppo', pp. 505 ff.

53. See the article by Anthony Cardoza in this volume.

54. Costituente, *Industria*, vol. 1, pp. 306 ff.

55. Sereni, *La questione agraria*, pp. 90-6. His conclusions are confirmed for Tuscany in the period following the First World War in the article of G. Mori, 'Per una storia dell'industria della regione', in *La Toscana nel regime fascista 1922-1939* (Florence, 1971), (Atti del Convegno di studi promosso dall'Unione regionale delle province toscane *et al.*, May 1969), pp. 170-1.

56. Istituto centrale di statistica, *Sommario*, Table 110, p. 143.

57. P. Ercolani, 'Documentazione statistica di base' in *Lo sviluppo economico in Italia*, ed G. Fua (Milan, 1969), vol. 3, pp. 440-1.

58. Istituto centrale di statistica, *Sommario*, Table 84, p. 106.

59. Grifone, *Il capitale finanziario*, pp. 78-147 *passim*.

60. See the comments of Gramsci for the importance of the link between landowners and banks: 'The landowners are not just arbiters of the situation in the countryside; indeed, this precisely serves them for other purposes, which are less well known, but far more important from the point of view of their class interests. It is a fact that the landowners today own the banks. To own the banks means, in a word, to hold in one's hands also the destiny of industry.' From 'The agrarian struggle in Italy' in *Selections from political writings, 1921-26*, p. 66.

61. See Sereni, 'La vita italiana', where he claims that 161 seats on the boards of the Casse di Risparmio were occupied by landed aristocracy.

62. Ventura, 'La Federconsorzi', pp. 710-11.

63. Grifone, *Il capitale finanziario*, p. 81 (of the Turin 1971 edition). He quotes from Mortara's *Prospettive* for 1930.

64. Ventura, 'La Federconsorzi', pp. 711 ff.
65. E. Sereni, 'Capitale finanziario e agricoltura in Italia' in the volume by the same author, *Capitalismo e mercato nazionale in Italia* (Rome, 1966), pp. 287-364.
66. Ibid., p. 319. Similar conclusions can be drawn from the table reproduced in M. Scotton, 'Il prezzo delle macchine agricole' in *Rivista di economia agraria* (1949) 1, p. 53.
67. Sereni, *La questione agraria*, p. 123.
68. Ventura, 'La Federconsorzi', pp. 719-20.
69. Sereni, *La questione agraria*, pp. 138-9.
70. Costituente, *Industria*, vol. 1. p. 264. On the issue of internal migration during fascism, and, in particular, on the ambivalent position of many industrialists who continued to want an influx of labour to the towns, see A. Treves, *Le migrazioni interne nell'Italia fascista. Politica e realtà demografica* (Turin, 1976).

NOTES ON CONTRIBUTORS

Anthony L. Cardoza is an assistant Professor of History at Loyola University of Chicago. He received his doctorate from Princeton University where he also taught as an instructor. A Fellow of the American Academy in Rome, he is currently revising for publication a book-length study of agrarian elites and the origins of Italian fascism.

Paul Corner studied at St John's College, Cambridge, and Balliol College, Oxford. He was a researcher at the Fondazione Luigi Einaudi in Turin between 1970 and 1971 and held a Junior Research Fellowship at St Antony's College, Oxford, from 1971 to 1972. Dr Corner is the author of *Fascism in Ferrara 1915-1925* (London, 1974) and has published articles and reviews in a number of journals. He is currently Reader in Italian history at the Graduate Centre for Italian Studies in the University of Reading.

John A. Davis received his first degree at Magdalen College, Oxford and took his postgraduate studies at St Antony's College, Oxford and the Italian Institute for Historical Studies, Naples. Since 1972 he has taught modern European history at Warwick University and has published a book and articles in Italy on the nineteenth-century origins of the problem of the South. At present he is working on southern Italy and the Napoleonic empire and preparing a book on nineteenth-century Italian social history.

Paul Ginsborg received his first degree and DPhil at Cambridge. From 1971 to 1977 he was a lecturer in history at the University of York, and since then he has been living in Italy, where he is at present teaching modern history at the University of Turin. He is the author of *Daniele Marin and the Venetian Revolution of 1848-9*, published by Cambridge University Press in 1979. From January 1980 he is taking up a lectureship in politics at the University of Cambridge.

Alice Kelikian was educated at Princeton and took her postgraduate studies at St Antony's College, Oxford. She held fellowships at the Einaudi Foundation, Turin (1974-6) and at the Italian Institute for Historical Studies, Naples (1976-7). She has been a Lecturer in modern

275

European history at the University of California, Riverside since 1978 and received her DPhil from Oxford in 1978.

Adrian Littelton is Professor of History at the Johns Hopkins University, Bologna Center. Formerly Professor of modern history, University of Reading, Fellow of St Antony's College, Oxford, 1968-75, he is the author of *The Seizure of Power: Fascism in Italy 1919-1926* (London, 1973).

Frank M. Snowden received his BA in government from Harvard University in 1968 and a BPhil and DPhil in politics from Oxford. He was Assistant Professor of History at Yale University from 1975 to 1978 and is at present a lecturer in history at the Royal Holloway College, University of London. An article 'On the Social Origins of Agrarian Fascism in Italy' was published in the *European Journal of Sociology* in 1972 and a book entitled *Le origini del fascismo in Toscana* is forthcoming with Einaudi.

INDEX

Action Party 47, 50, 51, 52-3, 56, 57, 59, 61
Agrarian Association (AAT) 164
agrarian bourgeoisie 69-71
Agrarian Central Committee 201
agrarian consortia 179-86; over production 182
agrarian developments 186-91; *see also* unionism
agrarian industrial bloc 172, 198-202; conclusions 202-5
agrarian policies *see* fascism
agrarian reform 108
agrarian revolution 128
Anderson, Perry 13, 30 n6, 39, 40 46, 63 nn19, 22, 65 n63

Barrington Moore, Jr., 105, 119, 126, 270 n6
Bolognese Agrarian Association (AAB) 197, 200
bourgeois democracy, definition 34, 35
bourgeois revolution 36-8; classic 37; concept 31, 32, 33; definition 36-7; era 43; Italian 42-5; typology 38-42
brigandage 123-4

Christian Democrats 240
collaboration, agrarian and industrial 176-9
Communist Party 25
Communist Party, Italian (PCI) 43, 45, 67, 240
Confederation of Labour (CGL) 217-19, 222, 225, 226
Consiglio 196
consorzio 250
cotton industry 215-16
Croce, Benedetto 13, 18, 45, 46, 48

de'Medici 82-3, 90, 93; strategy 87, 96-7
Dobb, Maurice 42, 63 n24

economic development *see* fascism, agrarian policies

eighteenth century reform 107
emigration 124, 130
Engels 36, 63 n18

FIOM 218-20, 223, 224, 225, 229
'failed revolution' 17
fascism 20-3, 28-9, 203; agrarian policies 244-54, and economic development 254-65, and industry 256-7; deflationary policy 258; economic stagnation 239-43; reappraisal 243-4; resistance 114; stagnationist interpretation 265-9, weaknesses 266-7
Federation of Building Contractors *(Edile)* 197
Federconsorzi 204, 263-4; *see also* agrarian consortia
French occupation 77-9

Gentiloni Pact 19
Giolitti, Giovanni 18-19, 23, 43, 131, 176, 191, 192, 198-9, 200-1, 204
Gramsci, Antonio 11-30, 29 n1, 31-61, 62 n9, 100 n2, 127, 205 n1, 269, 273 nn51, 60; analysis 12-13, 16 67-8; city countryside analogy 88; conclusions 20-1

industrial developments 214-33
industrialisation 119-20
Industrial Parliamentary Group 201
industry, in Brescia 213-19
Italian Confederation of Industry (CII) 194, 195-6, 197

Jacobinism 53-7, 127

Lenin, V.I. 36, 38, 41, 62 n12
liberalism 104-5, 131
liberal movement, origins 106
Liberal Party 200
Liberals 25, 164
Liberals, southern 94-7, 99

maize diet 118

277